T0323686

CREATING CORPORATE SUSTAINABILITY

This compelling volume considers three significant modern develop-ments: the ever-changing role of women in society; a significant and growing dissatisfaction with current dominant understandings of corpor-ate governance, corporate law and corporate theory; and the increasing concern to establish sustainable business models globally. A range of female scholars from across the globe and from different disciplines interconnect these ideas in this unique collection of new and thought-provoking essays. Readers are led through a carefully planned enquiry focussing initially on female activism and the corporation, secondly on liberal attempts to include women in business leadership and, finally, on critiquing the modern focus on women as a 'fix' for ethical and unsustain-able business practises which currently dominates the corporate world. This collection presents a fresh perspective on what changes are needed to create the sustainable corporation and the potential role of women as influencers or as agents for these changes.

BEATE SJÅFJELL is a professor in the Faculty of Law, at the University of Oslo.

IRENE LYNCH FANNON is a professor in the School of Law at University College Cork.

CREATING CORPORATE SUSTAINABILITY

Gender as an Agent for Change

Edited by

BEATE SJÅFJELL
University of Oslo

IRENE LYNCH FANNON
University College Cork

CAMBRIDGE
UNIVERSITY PRESS

CAMBRIDGE
UNIVERSITY PRESS

University Printing House, Cambridge CB2 8BS, United Kingdom

One Liberty Plaza, 20th Floor, New York, NY 10006, USA

477 Williamstown Road, Port Melbourne, VIC 3207, Australia

314–321, 3rd Floor, Plot 3, Splendor Forum, Jasola District Centre, New Delhi – 110025, India

79 Anson Road, #06–04/06, Singapore 079906

Cambridge University Press is part of the University of Cambridge.

It furthers the University's mission by disseminating knowledge in the pursuit of education, learning, and research at the highest international levels of excellence.

www.cambridge.org
Information on this title: www.cambridge.org/9781108427111
DOI: 10.1017/9781316998472

© Cambridge University Press 2018

First published 2018

Printed in the United Kingdom by Clays, St Ives plc

A catalogue record for this publication is available from the British Library.

Library of Congress Cataloging-in-Publication Data
Names: Sjåfjell, Beate, editor. | Lynch Fannon, Irene, editor.
Title: Creating corporate sustainability : gender as an agent for change / edited by Beate Sjåfjell, University of Oslo, Irene Lynch Fannon, University College Cork.
Description: 1 Edition. | New York : Cambridge University Press, [2018] | Includes bibliographical references and index.
Identifiers: LCCN 2017057513| ISBN 9781108427111 (hardback : alk. paper) | ISBN 9781108447676 (pbk. : alk. paper)
Subjects: LCSH: Social responsibility of business. | Sustainable development. | Women executives.
Classification: LCC HD60 .C7396 2018 | DDC 658.4/08–dc23
LC record available at https://lccn.loc.gov/2017057513

ISBN 978-1-108-42711-1 Hardback

To Katarina, and to Zoë, Tim and Grace

CONTENTS

vii

CONTRIBUTORS

YUE S. ANG Yue S. Ang, LLB, LLM, PhD is a senior lecturer in law at Oxford Brookes University. Her research interests are in the areas of legal theory and normativity, vulnerability and the human condition of resilience, ethical outsourcing, female entrepreneurship, social enterprises, corporations and corporate spaces, corporate group governance and corporate social responsibility (CSR). Yue is a member of Daughters of Themis: International Network of Female Business Scholars and of the Sustainable Market Actors Network, which contributes to the international research project Sustainable Market Actors for Responsible Trade (SMART).

AIKATERINI ARGYROU Aikaterini Argyrou LLM, PhD is a postdoctoral researcher affiliated to the Utrecht Centre for Water, Oceans and Sustainability Law at Utrecht University (UCWOSL) and the Utrecht University Social Entrepreneurship Initiative. She is also a visiting research fellow at Nyenrode Business University. She obtained her bachelor of laws degree (LLB) from the Faculty of Law of the Kapodestrian University in Athens in 2009, her master of laws degree (LLM) from Utrecht University in 2011 and her PhD from Utrecht University in 2018 (2013–2018). She is a qualified corporate attorney in Greece and a member of the Athens Bar Association since 2012. Prior to her PhD studies (2011–2013), she was involved in many CSR research projects in the Netherlands, including the establishment of the 'ACCESS' CSR Conflict Management Center by the Hague Utilities for Global Organisations (HUGO) Initiative, and the development of the Good Governance Index by the Hague Institute of the Internationalisation of Law (HiiL). In the past, she worked as a trainee legal counsel for the Greek Embassy in The Hague and as a trainee attorney for two Greek-based legal firms (2009–2010). She is a member of the steering committee of Daughters of Themis (2016–2018).

VICTORIA SCHNURE BAUMFIELD Victoria (Tory) Baumfield is an assistant professor of law at Bond University, Australia, a PhD candidate

ix

in law at the University of Queensland, and a member of the New York Bar. Tory received her BA in international relations and French from the University of Pennsylvania in 1994 and her JD from Columbia Law School in 1997. Tory practiced as a commercial litigator at the Wall Street law firm Cahill Gordon & Reindel LLP for nine years before moving to Australia. Tory's research focuses on corporate law theory, regulation and corporate governance issues, in particular in the context of government-owned businesses (GOBs), public utilities, and the public/private divide. She is a member of the steering committee of Daughters of Themis (2017–2018).

ROSALIEN DIEPEVEEN Rosalien Diepeveen, LLM, is a lecturer and researcher at Nyenrode Business University. She obtained her master's degree from Utrecht University in 2014. She was involved in various research projects in the fields of corporate law, corporate governance, and CSR and still lectures about these themes. Her PhD focuses on gender diversity in corporate boards. Furthermore, she is the editorial secretary of *International and Comparative Corporate Law Journal*. She is a member of Daughters of Themis.

MARÍA ÁNGELES FERNÁNDEZ-IZQUIERDO Professor María Ángeles Fernández-Izquierdo received a PhD in financial economics and accountancy from the Universidad de Valencia in 1991. She is a full professor in finance and accountancy at Universitat Jaume I, and a member of the Spanish Institute of Financial Analysts. Her research focuses on efficiency, microstructure, and hedging in stock markets and their derivatives; ethical investment; and CSR. She has published scientific papers in high-impact international academic journals and is involved in several externally funded research projects such as Sustainable Market Actors for Responsible Trade (SMART). She is a member of Daughters of Themis.

IDOYA FERRERO-FERRERO Dr. Idoya Ferrero-Ferrero has a PhD in business management (2012) from the Universitat Jaume I. Currently, she works as a lecturer at the Finance and Accounting Department of the Universitat Jaume I. Her current research focus is on corporate governance, board diversity, sustainability assessment and reporting. She has taken part in several international congresses and published academic papers in international academic journals. She is involved in several externally funded research projects such as SMART. She is a member of the steering committee of Daughters of Themis (2017–2018).

TINEKE LAMBOOY Tineke Lambooy is a full-time professor in corporate law at Nyenrode Business University, where she is a member of the Research Centre for Entrepreneurship, Governance and Stewardship. She is also an associate professor in CSR with the Utrecht University Research Centre for Water, Oceans and Sustainability Law. Her research activities concentrate on corporate law, corporate governance, CSR, social entrepreneurship, and the role of business regarding ecosystems. In her PhD research, she analysed how legal and semi-legal frameworks support CSR (Kluwer, 2010), and in her inaugural lecture, she examined how corporate law can prompt leadership, entrepreneurship and stewardship. She is a Work Package leader in the project Sustainable Market Actors for Responsible Trade (SMART), and a member of Daughters of Themis.

CAROL LIAO Dr. Carol Liao is an assistant professor of the Peter A. Allard School of Law at the University of British Columbia, and a UBC Sauder Distinguished Scholar of the Peter P. Dhillon Centre for Business Ethics at the Sauder School of Business. She specializes in business law, corporate governance, law and economics, and the emerging field of social enterprise law. An award-winning scholar and teacher, her work has appeared in numerous journals and books, and has been widely cited in Canadian media. She is also the co-author of Canada's leading business law textbook, *Business Organizations: Practice, Theory, and Emerging Challenges, 2nd ed.* (Emond). Previously, she practised as a senior associate in the New York Mergers & Acquisitions Group of Shearman & Sterling LLP, a global law firm. She is a member of the steering committee of Daughters of Themis (2016–2018).

RAGNHILD LUNNER Ragnhild Lunner has a master's degree from the Faculty of Law, University of Oslo. She has worked as a research assistant at the Faculty's Department of Private Law, and wrote her master's thesis on human rights in public procurement, with Beate Sjåfjell and Anja Wiesbrock as her supervisors. Ragnhild has a bachelor's degree in journalism from Oslo and Akershus University College of Applied Sciences, and a background in development studies at the University of Oslo. She is the author of *Annual Meetings: A Handbook (Årsmøtehåndboka)*. In 2014, she was the Norwegian UN Youth Delegate on Post 2015 and Sustainable Development, representing the Norwegian Children and Youth Council. She is a member of Daughters of Themis.

IRENE LYNCH FANNON Irene Lynch Fannon is a professor at the School of Law at University College Cork. She has a BCL from Oxford University, a Doctorate in Juridical Science (SJD) from the University of Virginia, USA and is a Solicitor. Her research occupies two areas of corporate law, the first emanating from her comparative monograph *Working within Two Kinds of Capitalism* (Hart Publishing, 2003). She has written many book chapters and articles on corporate law and theory. She received funding from the Irish Research Council for projects on the role of women on corporate boards in 2013 and 2015. She also researches in the area of corporate insolvency and rescue law, having co-authored two editions of *Corporate Insolvency and Rescue* (Bloomsbury Professional, 1996 and 2012) and published many articles and chapters in this area of law. Her work has been cited in the Irish Supreme Court. She is involved in the EU funded Sustainable Market Actors for Responsible Trade (SMART), and is a member of Daughters of Themis. Over the course of her career she has been nominated to many regulatory review bodies established by the Irish Government and is currently a member of the Company Law Review Group in Ireland.

MARÍA JESÚS MUÑOZ-TORRES Professor María Jesús Muñoz-Torres has a PhD in agricultural economics from the Polytechnic University of Valencia (1994). She is a professor in finance in the Department of Finance and Accountancy at the Jaume I University. Her research currently focuses on sustainability assessment, socially responsible investing, sustainable efficiency of public financial support to companies and Sustainable Business Models. She has published scientific papers in high-impact international academic journals and is involved in several externally funded research projects such as Sustainable Market Actors for Responsible Trade (SMART). She is also a member of Daughters of Themis.

GILL NORTH Gill North is a professorial research fellow in the law school at Deakin University and is a member of its Centre for Comparative Corporate Governance. After completing a first-class honours law degree, she was awarded a doctorate in law from the University of New South Wales in 2011. Gill is a chartered accountant and experienced financial analyst, as well as a law academic. Prior to joining academia, she worked at multinational corporations and investment banks in the major financial centres (London, Tokyo, New York, and Sydney), where her roles included senior executive positions in the areas of corporate strategy, corporate finance, mergers and acquisitions, and funds management. Gill has advised and provided consultancy services to a broad spectrum of international and domestic entities, including governments, regulators, corporations, academics, lawyers, financiers, and consumer advocacy groups. Her primary areas of research include the law and practice of corporate governance, company disclosure, corporate sustainability, finance, and investment. Gill has published extensively on these areas in Australia and internationally, including two monographs, *Company Disclosure in Australia* and *Effective Company Disclosure in the Digital Age.*

ADAEZE OKOYE Dr Adaeze Okoye is a senior lecturer at the University of Brighton. She holds a PhD from the University of Hull and a master's degree in environmental law and policy from the University of Dundee, Scotland. She is an academic fellow of the Honourable Society of the Inner Temple and in 2015–2016 she was a visiting fellow at the Institute of Advanced Legal Studies, University of London. Her recent book, *Legal Approaches and Corporate Social Responsibility* (Routledge Research in Corporate Law, 2016) explores a Llewellyn law-jobs approach to the law and CSR relationship. She has also written about law and development, corporate governance, joint development agreements and environmental management systems in the oil industry.

EMMANUEL OSUTEYE Dr. Emmanuel Osuteye is a post-doctoral researcher with the Development Planning Unit, University College London. His PhD research and current research interests focus on the emergence and counterhegemonic activity of indigenous environmental movements to influence policy, as well as the interplay of formal and informal governance and planning structures on urban development in Africa. Emmanuel has significant in-country research and consultancy experience in a number of African countries including Ghana, Benin, Sierra Leone, Malawi, Tanzania and The Gambia.

CATHERINE O'SULLIVAN Dr. Catherine O'Sullivan is a lecturer at the School of Law at University College Cork (UCC). She is a graduate of UCC (BCL, LLM) and Osgoode Hall Law School (PhD). Her main research interests lie in criminal law, criminology, gender and the law, and law and popular culture. She has been instrumental in the promotion of criminology within UCC, being one of the founding members of the interdisciplinary MA in Criminology (2005) and BA in Criminology

(2014). She also contributes to the MA in Women's Studies. She was a founding member of the Centre for Criminal Justice and Human Rights, established in 2006, and served as co-director from November 2010 to February 2013. She is currently a director of the Sexual Violence Centre Cork (SVCC). The SVCC provides services for survivors of rape, sexual assault and sexual abuse, holds workshops for second- and third-level students, and advocates for law reform. She is a co-author of a leading student and practitioner text, *Criminal Law in Ireland: Cases and Materials* (2010), and of *Fundamentals of the Irish Legal System* (2016). Her articles have been published in various journals, including the *Irish Jurist*, the *Dublin University Law Journal*, the *Northern Ireland Legal Quarterly* and *Legal Studies*. She is one of the founding editors of the *Irish Journal of Legal Studies* (www.ijls.ie).

ROSEANNE RUSSELL Roseanne Russell is a lecturer in law at the University of Bristol. Her research interests include company law, employment law, and feminist legal theory. Before moving to academia, she held senior roles in private practice and in-house at the UK's former Equal Opportunities Commission. She is a member of the Law Society of England and Wales's Employment Law Committee, co-convenor of the Society of Legal Scholars Company Law Stream, and former consultative committee member for the UK Office of Tax Simplification's review of employment status. She is a member of Daughters of Themis, and was on its steering committee 2016–2017.

BEATE SJÅFJELL Dr. Beate Sjåfjell is a professor at the University of Oslo, Faculty of Law, and professorial research fellow at Deakin University School of Law. She is the head of the Oslo Faculty's Research Group Companies, Markets and Sustainability, a founding member of Daughters of Themis and chair of its steering committe. She coordinates the international research project Sustainable Market Actors for Responsible Trade (SMART), funded under the EU Framework Programme for Research and Innovation Horizon 2020, and has previously coordinated Sustainable Companies (2010–2014), funded by the Research Council of Norway. Her publications include the monograph *Towards a Sustainable European Company Law* (Kluwer Law International, 2009), the edited volumes *The Greening of European Business under EU Law: Taking Article 11 TFEU Seriously* (Routledge, 2015, co-editor Anja Wiesbrock), *Company Law and Sustainability: Legal Barriers and Opportunities* (Cambridge University Press, 2015, co-editor Benjamin Richardson), and *Sustainable Public Procurement under EU Law: New Perspectives on the State as Stakeholder* (Cambridge University Press, 2016, co-editor Anja Wiesbrock). Her scholarship include a number of papers on EU company and financial market law and the integration of sustainable development.

LORRAINE TALBOT Lorraine Talbot is professor of company law in context at Birmingham Law School. She previously held a chair in law at York University. Lorraine's work is concerned with the tension between labour and capital in the company and the conditions under which the company might become a force for social progress – also the topic of a two-year research fellowship from the Leverhulme Trust (2015–2017). Lorraine is a coordinating lead author in the International Panel for Social Progress, focusing on corporations, exploitation and social inequalities as well as barriers to innovation. Her previous work includes 'Why Shareholders Shouldn't Vote: A Marxist-Progressive Critique of Shareholder Empowerment' (*Modern Law Review*, 2013), 'Changing the World with Company Law? Some Problems' (*Legal Studies*, 2016), and book publications *Progressive Corporate Governance for the 21st Century* (Routledge, 2012), *Great Debates in Company Law* (Palgrave, 2014), and *Critical Company Law* (Routledge, 2007 and 2015). She is a member of the steering committee of Daughters of Themis (2017–2018) and a member of the Sustainable Market Actors Network.

FOREWORD

It has been forecast that global demand for resources will triple by 2050. We already consume some 1.5 globes worth of resources every single year and, following the estimates, would need around four planets full of resources to satisfy the demand by 2050 under business-as-usual scenario. There is just one problem with this: we only have one planet.

European economies cannot survive – let alone grow and prosper – unless we take some radical steps to increase our resource efficiency and move toward a true circular economy. We have to stop wasting precious resources and start using them more efficiently.

In this challenge there also lies a huge opportunity. The one who can deliver solutions for the resource efficiency dilemma is also the winner of the new economic race: this means solving the problem of doing more with less – creating more added value with less resources.

In a sustainable circular economy there is no waste, products are designed to be durable, repairable, reusable, and recyclable, and when they come to the end of their life, the resources contained in these products are pumped back into productive use again. The European Commission has calculated that increasing resource productivity by 30 per cent by 2030 would create 2 million new jobs while boosting our GDP by 1 per cent.

In order to support this change, however, we also need to change the rules of the game. Regulation is never neutral. Legislation is one of the essential drivers of the business revolution, as businesses and investors alike need a stable and predictable regulatory environment in order to change.

This regulation also needs to have a gender perspective.

Economic power is real power. Currently, women are underrepresented in positions where economic power is wielded, and globally they hold fewer economic resources than men do. Even in Europe, women have a lower purchasing power than their male counterparts.

The world is full of intelligent and capable girls and young women students. Women perform well academically and are known to be dedicated students. Over half of university graduates are women.

Somehow, however, fewer women than men make it to the top, to holding the decision-making positions in public or private enterprises. Somewhere along the way their path takes a different route to that of their male counterparts. Women account for only 7 per cent of board chairs and presidents and 6 per cent of chief executives in the largest companies. In 2014, a study by Harvard Business School of alumni who had indistinguishable goals in terms of work and career growth found that 57 per cent of men were in senior management positions, compared with 41 per cent women.

The World Economic Forum noted in November 2017 that at the current rate, women might expect to reach economic parity with men in 2234. We cannot wait that long.

Women are obviously not less intelligent or capable. It is a matter of different competencies, and of building appreciation for and acknowledging these competencies. Women have throughout history been innovators. We cannot let this innovation power go unutilized.

We have to actively harness women's potential and their agency. We need appropriate regulation to support this. We need quotas. We need social policies that provide a security net for working women, encompassing childcare, health services and opportunities to combine work with the role of informal carer, for example. We have to introduce ways to teach the skills of the future in a way that engages girls and women, to ensure that their interest in areas such as science, technology, engineering, mathematics and the digital economy is captured. We also need to build a supportive network that encourages and provides role models for girls and women.

Most importantly, we need to understand the forces that keep business on the unsustainable track it is on now. This volume offers important insights into these issues, to the (mainly insufficient) initiatives to realize the potential of women as agents for creating corporate sustainability, and crucial reflections on possible ways forward. As such, the volume is an invaluable contribution to the discussion we must have now: how to achieve the fundamental transition to a sustainable, circular, and just economy. We cannot afford not to have girls and women as partners in sustainable development, resource efficiency and circular economy – in painting the way for the future of our planet.

Sirpa Pietikäinen
Director of GLOBE EU
Member of the European Parliament

PREFACE

This volume springs out of the work of Daughters of Themis: International Network of Female Business Scholars. The success of this relatively new initiative reflects the idea that female business scholars from different disciplines and various backgrounds have a common desire for a 'room of our own' (to paraphrase Virginia Woolf). With annual international workshops as a forum where ideas can be discussed openly, across disciplinary and geographical boundaries, Daughters of Themis supports and encourages new ideas on some of the most pervasive issues in corporate law and the broader area of business scholarship.

While we reject the notion that women, as opposed to men, are inherently sustainability-oriented, we recognize that many of the members of Daughters of Themis are concerned with corporate sustainability challenges. We see that in research projects challenging mainstream corporate governance assumptions, female scholars, while otherwise in a distinct minority, are in equal numbers or even in a majority compared with male scholars – for example in the Sustainable Companies Project, 2010–2014, and the Sustainable Market Actors for Responsible Trade (SMART) 2016–2020, both coordinated by the University of Oslo. With much of the dominant theories and understandings being brought forward by men and male-dominated milieus, we present ourselves as a group of female scholars who, with a different perspective, may be a uniquely disruptive force. As this collection illustrates, women often experience issues from the perspective of the outsider, and we believe that this leads to innovation in the way we analyse current thinking.[1]

As editors of this volume, we have benefited tremendously from the insights of our contributors. Through the process of editing this

---

[1] That is not to say that we see innovation as the preserve of women, as is illustrated by our collaboration in various research projects, including the ongoing SMART Project. And although this volume originally was intended to have female contributors only, one of the contributions is co-authored by a male scholar.

interdisciplinary volume, we have learned so much that brings important nuances and challenges to preconceived notions about the role of gender in achieving corporate sustainability. We see interdisciplinarity as a necessary contribution to the fundamental understanding of business and finance and of the challenges posed to environmental, social and economic sustainability. We have a greater appreciation of how we can begin to shape the contours of the urgently required, and well overdue, shift from the current highly unsustainable state of corporate and business activity. We hope you, the reader, might be similarly inspired.

Many of the contributions in this volume were first presented as papers at the Second International Workshop of Daughters of Themis, in a secluded venue on the lovely island of Kea, Greece. We thank the participants for the supportive, helpful and critically constructive in-depth discussion of each topic presented. The warmth and companionship combined with high academic rigour that characterise our annual workshops facilitate fresh insights and encourage thinking beyond the frontiers of mainstream understanding. A number of the contributors, including the editors, are also involved in, or otherwise contribute to, the SMART Project, funded under the European Union's Framework Programme for Research and Innovation Horizon 2020, Grant Agreement No 693642.[2] We gratefully acknowledge this support.

Working together with the contributors to this volume has been a great pleasure. We are grateful to them for their insightful reflections and their patience with, and constructive responses to, our editorial suggestions. Our warmest thanks also go to Kim Hughes, Senior Commissioning Editor of Cambridge University Press, whose guidance and advice every step of the way from first idea to published book has been invaluable. We are grateful to the Department of Private Law of the Faculty of Law, University of Oslo, for dedicating resources in the form of research assistance for this volume, and we thank research assistants Hanne Bjørge Eriksen and Kaja Skille Hestnes for research assistance and diligent work on the footnotes.

Our thanks go also to our families for their understanding and support, and we dedicate this volume to our children, whose very presence reminds us every day of our duty to strive continuously for a better world.

Beate Sjåfjell and Irene Lynch Fannon

---

[2] Obviously, the volume is the sole responsibility of the editors and contributors, and do not necessarily reflect the views of the European Union.

1

Corporations, Sustainability and Women

IRENE LYNCH FANNON AND BEATE SJÅFJELL

1.1 Introduction

This volume of essays explores the relationship between three contemporary and significant intellectual ideas, namely, issues concerning unsustainable business practices and models, corporate law theory including corporate culture and governance, and the role of gender in relation to both. This collection includes contributions from female scholars who are lawyers, economists, sociologists and others who adopt a multidisciplinary approach. Our central focus is the corporation as the most influential business organisation of the twenty-first century, the actions of which affect human activities across the globe. Indeed, the corporation is not only an influential business organisation but also perhaps the most globally influential institution generally.[1] Corporations are propelled towards the pursuit of unsustainable business practices in a wide variety of ways, hence our focus on corporate law theory, corporate culture and governance. In considering the problems presented by activities of modern corporations, we have posed the question as to how issues relating to gender – and feminist theory more broadly described – interface with these problems. In answering this question, the authors in this collection consider a range of situations where corporate action,

---

[1] For a popularised presentation, see the film *The Corporation.com* (available at www.thecorporation.com). There has been considerable interest in business sustainability in recent years. For example, the Brookings Institute based in Washington, DC, has focussed on this issue as one of its key policy programs in its Global Economy and Development program; see www.brookings.edu/topic/sustainable-development-goals 'Multinational corporations with operations spanning the globe, and in some cases capacities and networks that match those of governments, have a particularly important role to play in helping to spread the opportunities of globalization and in mitigating some of its risks.'

Independent organisations are also engaged with this issue. The Sustainable Business Commission based in London presents availability of investment funds in sustainable business; see http://businesscommission.org.

unsustainable practices, and issues of gender have arisen in the particular contexts described in their contributions. Our contributors present an analysis of how issues relating to women and gender interweave with the central questions of corporate function and sustainability.

As contributors, none of us is limited in our scholarship to gender issues, and our focus in this volume is on business practice as it relates to our original disciplines of law, economics, sociology and so on. The question then became whether, in creating a more sustainable corporation, gender, or the actions of women, or feminist theory generally have acted as agents for change up to now and whether they have the potential to do so into the future. 'Corporate sustainability' in our collection rests on a specific understanding of sustainability and is intended to describe when corporations, and more generally, economic actors, create value in a manner that is (1) *environmentally* sustainable in that it ensures the long-term stability and resilience of the ecosystems that support human life, (2) *socially* sustainable in that it facilitates the respect and promotion of human rights and of good governance and (3) *economically* sustainable in that it satisfies the economic needs necessary for stable and resilient societies.[2]

Sustainable development, or sustainability, as it is now commonly referred to, is one of the most disputed and abused concepts of our time. For the concept to be meaningful, we argue that it must take as its starting point the recognition of ecological limits for human activity. We see this expressed in the concept of planetary boundaries as first expounded by Johan Rockström and colleagues,[3] which sets out and elucidates the physical limitations we now face as a result of continued human activity. As explained by Will Steffen, 'The concept of planetary boundaries challenges the belief that resources are either limitless or infinitely substitutable. It threatens the business-as-usual approach to economic growth.'[4] The second vital component of sustainability, as

---

[2] B. Sjåfjell, 'When the solution becomes the problem: the triple failure of corporate governance codes' in J. J. du Plessis & C. K. Low (eds.), *Corporate Governance Codes for the 21st Century* (Springer, 2017), p. 28.

[3] This concept was first adopted by J. Rockström et al. 'Planetary boundaries: exploring the safe operating space for humanity' (2009) *Ecology and Society*, 14(2), 32 (see https://www.ecologyandsociety.org/vol14/iss2/art32/) and subsequently updated by: W. Steffen et al. 'Planetary Boundaries: Guiding Human Development on a Changing Planet' (13 February 2015) *Science* 347(6223), 736

[4] S. Will, 'Rio+20: Another step on the journey towards sustainability' (29 June 2012) *The Conversation*.

reflected in the United Nations (UN) Sustainable Development Goals,[5] is the human dimension, where ongoing practices make it extraordinarily difficult for individuals to thrive. Our concern with unsustainable business practices therefore incorporates ideals of fair labour standards, sustainable manufacturing, sustainable consumer activity and ethical management. In 1987, the influential report *Our Common Future* (the Brundtland Report) emphasized that sustainability must encompass recognition of the environment as the basis of our existence, and must also include the goal of acceptable living conditions for people and the necessity of economic prosperity to provide for the former.[6] To date there has been a tendency in international and national policy-making to see economic prosperity, understood in the mainstream way as economic *growth*, as the overarching goal in relation to these additional aspirations. We see this reflected in the sustainable growth agenda of the European Union (EU) Commission which has been set out for 2020.[7]

With the aim of corporate sustainability in mind, it is our position that a different conception of corporate function and of the role of the corporate board and management can, and will, lead to change. Our case studies demonstrate that corporations can respond positively to calls for change, whether these are from those who are experiencing the effects of corporate action in their communities, from investors who have litigated

---

[5] UN General Assembly resolution 70/1, *Transforming Our World: The 2030 Agenda for Sustainable Development*, A/RES/70/1, (25 September 2015), see www.undocs.org/A/RES/70/1. Also see www.un.org/sustainabledevelopment/sustainable-development-goals.

[6] UN General Assembly, *Report of the World Commission on Environment and Development: Our Common Future* (1987). Transmitted to the General Assembly as an Annex to document A/42/427, *Development and International Co-operation: Environment*. [This is published as *World Commission on Environment and Development: Our Common Future* (Oxford University Press, 1987)]. Although criticised in some quarters for a variety of reasons, one of the strengths of the report is to regard poverty and social inequality as an aspect of sustainability. Critics have argued that the emphasis on economic growth is short sighted. See R. Heutig, 'The Brundtland Report: A Matter of Conflicting Goals' (1990) *Ecological Economics*, 2, 109–117, where the report is criticised for its emphasis on economic growth and for expressly linking poverty with unsustainability. J. Robinson 'Squaring the Circle? Some Thoughts on the Idea of Sustainable Development' (2004) *Ecological Economics*, 48, 369–384 notes criticisms of the report based on allegations of vagueness, and the criticism that the report is vulnerable to hypocritical interpretations and was accused of 'fostering delusions'. Nevertheless the same author seems to argue for a similar approach to sustainability which incorporates a 'recognition of the social construction of sustainable development'.

[7] European Commission, *EUROPE 2020 A Strategy for Smart, Sustainable and Inclusive Growth*, COM/2010/2020 final, and see further www.ec.europa.eu/europe2020/europe-2020-in-a-nutshell/priorities/sustainable-growth/index_en.htm.

to protect or bring about a different type of corporate action, or from policy makers. There is nothing inherent in the legal structure of a corporation which makes it necessarily resistant to changes regarding more sustainable strategies, or resistant to legal changes, such as increased reporting obligations, mandated diversity, or other regulations intended to improve the effects that the corporation has on society.

Consequently, we then move to a consideration of the modern corporation as it is understood in this context, and to a consideration of some initiatives which have already been implemented to render the modern corporation more accountable, including measures relating to diversity and sustainability reporting.[8] In general, we challenge these recent legislative initiatives as being limited and somewhat constrained in comparison with more radical measures we witnessed in relation to gender equality in the 1980s. We also consider alternative models of business which are presented as more sustainable alternatives to the corporation.[9] We then move to a critical assessment of core issues in corporate law and discuss how these principles can be affected by a refashioning of theory from a particularly feminist perspective. These three different areas of enquiry raise the question as to whether women really are agents for change, and our collection seeks to provide a thought-provoking but non-presumptive answer to that question. In other words, we do not rush to the conclusion that women really do act as agents for change; instead, we present the reader with more considered conclusions and with tentative starting points from which the enquiry can continue. By constantly connecting female experience with corporate law theory and sustainability, we present a new, holistic way of going beyond a topical or descriptive narrative. We wish to explore real potential for change derived from a more considered feminist perspective on the appropriate role of law, the effect of current corporate laws on corporate culture, and the combined impact of these understandings on sustainability.

1.2 Three Parts of Our Collection

1.2.1 Women as Influencers of Corporate Action

The first part of our collection includes descriptions of how women have interacted effectively to change particular corporate actions which were damaging their environments. A number of reports have described how

[8] Ch. 5.   [9] Ch. 9.

unsustainable corporate actions can impact more adversely on women, particularly in the destruction of natural resources such as water sources, forests and agricultural holdings.[10] The broader understanding of sustainability also includes unsustainable practices which affect the ability of humans to thrive because of unfair or non-existent labour standards, unsustainable manufacturing, or consumer activity.[11] The essays from Lorraine Talbot (on (un)ethical supply chain practices and female activism to secure fair labour conditions) and Adaeze Okoye and Emmanuel Osuteye (on women advocating for protection for their local communities in developing countries) consider the role of women acting outside established perceptions of what the corporation can and ought to be.[12] In these two chapters, we present interesting case studies on how women interacted successfully with corporations to effect change, sometimes in the face of cultural limitations which at times seemed more powerful than the resistance of the corporation. In both cases, women changed attitudes both within their own cultural context and within the culture of the corporation. The significance of these case studies is that they are placed within a theoretical framework which identifies the effect of change from 'below'. In other words, for corporations to act sustainably, it is not necessary that these changes are always initiated from the top, from senior decision makers or from board level, or from institutionalised policy decisions. Rather, our Ghanaian case study identifies with De Sousa Santos's ideas that challenge preconceived notions of the corporation and of social roles assigned on a gendered basis. The case study illustrates how change can occur in a 'spontaneous non-institutionalized' way.[13] We are asking the reader to consider that much change over time

---

[10] UN WomenWatch, *Women, Gender Equality and Climate Change* (2009), p. 3, see www.un.org/womenwatch/feature/climate_change; CEDAW, *Respect Rights of Rural Women, Recognize Their Vital Role in Development and Poverty Reduction, UN Experts Urge* (4 March 2016), press release see www.ohchr.org/EN/NewsEvents/Pages/Display News.aspx?NewsID=17148&LangID=E; See also Oxfam, *Impacts of Mining*, see www .oxfam.org.au/what-we-do/mining/impacts-of-mining, referred to in Ch. 3.

See also A. J. Sigot, 'Discourse on gender and natural resource management' in A. Sigot, L. A. Thrupp and J. Green (eds.), *Towards Common Ground: Gender and Natural Resource Management in Africa* (African centre for Technology Studies: Nairobi, 1995); referred to in Ch. 4.

[11] Ch. 2. See further the discussion on the concept of sustainability arising from the Brundtland Report in note 6.

[12] Chs. 2 and 4.

[13] B. D. S. Santos and C. A. Rodriguez-Garavito, *Law and Globalization from Below – Towards a Cosmopolitan Legality* (Cambridge: Cambridge University Press, 2005). B. D. S. Santos, *Towards a New common Sense: Law, Science and Politics in the*

does indeed occur in this way. Our description of how both workers and consumers can insist on the creation of ethical supply chains, using Bangladesh as an example, supports this argument. Finally, the consideration by Ragnhild Lunner of how women found a voice in relation to the extractive mining companies in the Lihir and Misima areas of Papua New Guinea shows how change is not the preserve of one particular stakeholder but sometimes results from a multi-faceted interaction within communities, and between corporations and communities, as women assert their non-traditional rights to represent themselves.[14] Chapter 3, based on a Habermasian[15] understanding of discourse, provides us with a theoretical framework in which we can understand that the inability to include, listen to and hear women's voices may deprive corporations of information, knowledge and opinions that may be vital to ensuring corporate sustainability. We present a theoretical framework in which to consider modes of discourse as a way of understanding how community activism can be more effective in achieving sustainable outcomes, and how such theories are reflected in institutionalised principles found in the international documents such as the United Nations Guiding Principles (UNGPs).[16] In terms of effecting real change, the actions described in these case studies illustrate how women changed cultural and corporate environments through activist measures.

We return to the interaction between culture, gender and the corporation in Part III.

1.2.2   Current Strategies for Corporate Sustainability

The theoretical analysis derived from Habermas in Part I is also applicable in Part II, which involves a geographical shift in focus to the liberal democracies of the west. This part includes essays on organisational change strategies, which are often initiated as legal responses to the types

---

Paradigmatic Transition (Routledge, 1995). O. Amao, *Corporate Social Responsibility, Human Rights and the Law* (Routledge, 2011).

[14] Ch. 3.

[15] J. Habermas, *Between Naturalism and Religion: Philosophical Essays* (Cambridge: Polity, 2008), pp. 44–49, referred to in Ch. 3.

[16] The Guidelines, with accompanying and explanatory commentaries, can be read in: United Nations, *Guiding Principles on Business and Human rights – Implementing the United Nations 'Protect, Respect and Remedy' Framework* (Office of the High Commissioner for Human Rights, 2011), referred to in Ch. 3.

of acutely unsustainable business practices outlined in Part I. The change strategies range from encouraging the participation of women on boards of listed companies to presenting alternative, and allegedly more sustainable, business models. In contrast to change coming from 'below' as described in Part I, these change strategies have the apparent allure of being the outcome of sophisticated policy initiatives, often from government or, as in the case of the B-Corporation in the United States, private entities which have adopted a 'quasi-governmental' approach to change.[17] We present a critique of these strategies as a distraction from real problems with current understandings of corporate function. We use the term 'liberal structuralism' to describe these changes to the corporation.[18] We argue that rules on gender diversity on boards fit into this category, as do legal reporting requirements.[19]

Many readers will be familiar with initiatives, whether voluntary or regulatory, to include women on boards, particularly as a partial solution to excessive risk-taking post financial crisis. The emphasis on female business leadership is also a popular subject for media analysis.[20]

---

[17] As described by Baumfield, the B-Corporation certification is the initiative of a private entity, B Lab, which has sought to promote an alternative to the traditional corporation (see Ch. 9, n. 35–39).

[18] In our concluding Ch. 14, we return to a discussion of several organisational change strategies derived from the work of K. Grosser.

[19] We consider rules described by Lynch Fannon in Ch. 6 such as the EU Draft Directive which has been passed by the European Parliament on gender quotas for non-executive board membership in European listed companies. See text of the European Parliament decision OJ C 436 24.11.2016, pp. 225–240. European Commission, *Proposal for a Directive of the European Parliament and of the Council on improving the gender balance among non-executive directors of companies listed on stock exchanges and related measures*, Draft Directive COM (2012) 614 final. A similar strategy is reflected in what are called 'triple bottom line' reporting requirements such as European Commission, EU Directive 2014/95/EU, see www.ec.europa.eu/finance/company-reporting/non-financial_reporting/index_en.htm; United States Securities Exchange Commission (SEC), *Report on Review of Disclosure Requirements in Regulation S-K* (December 2013) 42 (see www.sec.gov/News/PressRelease/Detail/PressRelease/1370540530982); Global Reporting Initiative (GRI), *About Sustainability Reporting*; and International Integrated Reporting Council, *Integrated Reporting*, see http://integratedreporting.org, all described in Ch. 5.

[20] For examples, see: J. Shankleman, '30 women shaping sustainable business' (28 March 2015) *GreenBiz*, see www.greenbiz.com/article/Apple-Nike-Google-30-women-shaping-sustainable-business; O. Balch, 'Women at the top is better for business and the environment' (27 April 2015) *The Guardian*, see www.theguardian.com/sustainable-business/2015/apr/27/women-top-better-business-environment-sustainable; and A. Learned, 'Where are the women leaders in sustainable business' (23 October 2013) *The Guardian*, see www.theguardian.com/sustainable-business/where-women-sustainable-business-leadership.

Ferrero-Ferrero et al. provide a powerful empirical analysis of the presence of women in leadership positions across a range of corporate sectors. The proposal for the EU Directive on Women on Boards, which was approved by the European Parliament in 2013, seeks to change the nature of corporate boards in EU listed companies. This initiative is based on the proposition that the corporation can be regulated to effect and reflect social change. This initiative is critiqued from a legal standpoint by Irene Lynch Fannon, as is the alleged 'business case' which supports this initiative.[21] Similarly, reporting obligations as introduced in a range of jurisdictions and described by Gill North present the same proposition[22] – that corporations can be regulated in large and small ways to effect the change we want. Whilst we are sceptical about some of the ambitious claims made for these sorts of changes, nevertheless our empirical studies show us that some, albeit mainly incremental, change has happened.[23]

Of interest to us regarding these initiatives are two bigger thematic questions. First we are concerned about resistance (often described in cultural terms) to even these small changes. We continue to be surprised at the strength of this resistance, encapsulated in the quote 'A Toad We Have to Swallow' in reference to women on boards.[24] The mandated inclusion of women's voices at sophisticated levels of business leadership in developed western economies is regarded with suspicion generated by a perception of over regulation, or is regarded as being unimportant. Similarly, scepticism about the efficacy of 'triple line reporting' surely reflects the reality of how these obligations are regarded in many corporations, rather than with the rules themselves. Our second thematic question raised in Part II concerns the potential for the role of legal rules and models in changing the corporation to achieve sustainability. We have certainly seen in western European countries and in countries such as Australia how corporations have been regulated to achieve inclusion of employees as stakeholders,[25] and we can similarly hypothesise that

---

[21] Ch. 6.   [22] Ch. 5.   [23] Ch. 7.   [24] Ch. 6.

[25] I. Lynch Fannon, *Working within Two Kinds of Capitalism* (Oxford and Portland, OR: Hart Publishing, 2003). For a discussion of the contest between regulation and regulatory resistance see M. T. Moore, *Corporate Governance in the Shadow of the State* (Oxford: Hart Publishing, 2013). I. Lynch Fannon, 'CSR and Law's Empire: Is there a Conflict?' (2007) *Northern Ireland Legal Quarterly*, 58, 1–21. I. Lynch Fannon, 'Corporate responsibility and European corporate governance, the view from now' in A. Beck and S. Skeffington (eds.), *The Impact of European Law on the Corporate World* (The Irish Centre for European Law, 2010).

reporting obligations may over time affect changes in mindsets. However, this presupposes that the reporting rules are taken more seriously and enforced by regulators, and that there is mandatory verification of the reported information. As the reporting rules are formulated now, they can justifiably be criticised as a compromise solution between those who wish to see a shift towards corporate sustainability and those who resist regulation.[26] Therefore, while law matters, we are concerned about the limited type of change expressed at present in liberal rules, which in part reflects regulatory capture by corporate lobbyists.[27] We can see that cultural resistance broadly understood is reflected in all aspects of our contributions.[28]

Similarly, Victoria Baumfield and Aikaterini Argyrou et al. turn a critical eye to the creation of legal frameworks for alternative business models, which we fear might serve as deflection devices avoiding necessary structural reforms of corporations.[29] Arguably, these strategies are not explicitly intended to avoid structural reform of the corporation. However, we are concerned that these policies as currently constructed serve as shallow 'quick fixes', or worse as the locus of shallow controversy which never engages with real change nor with the law's capacity to effect change. As described in Chapter 5 which considers 'triple bottom line' reporting and variants thereof, the real question is whether the role of corporations in society and their enormous and ongoing environmental and social impacts on the planet are sufficiently prioritised.[30] Policy reforms that require large companies to provide sustainability information are emerging, but are these reforms adequate and appropriately formulated to ensure that corporations ultimately act in the long-term best interests of the communities in which they operate?

In considering these kinds of changes to the corporation, or alternatives to the traditional corporation, one of the insights we present here is that women have not, in general, been significant leaders of change in the context of these particular initiatives. Whilst some women have been

---

[26] Ch. 5.

[27] See also B. Sjåfjell, 'Dismantling the legal myth of shareholder primacy: The corporation as a sustainable market actor', in N. Boeger and C. Villiers (eds), *Shaping the Corporate Landscape: Towards Corporate Reform and Enterprise Diversity* (Oxford and Portland, OR: Hart, 2018), ch. 4. See https://ssrn.com/abstract=2912141.

[28] Path dependency theory is also relevant to this discussion. See O. Hathaway, 'Path Dependence in the Law: The Course and Pattern of Legal Change in a Common Law System' (2001) 86 *Iowa Law Review* 601.

[29] Chs. 8 and 9.   [30] Ch. 5.

proponents of progressive corporate initiatives, women in equal numbers have taken the opposing view on initiatives such as quotas for women on boards or diversity reporting. We also see that women have not been at the fore in developing alternative business models or indeed in utilising alternative business models.

1.2.3 Feminist Theories and Corporate Sustainability

Part III includes contributions which focus on ethics and theory and which consider a gendered critique of corporate cultures and the ethics of sustainability. Specifically, Catherine O'Sullivan and Roseanne Russell identify and reject the gendered understanding of corporate ethics which has emerged in current corporate cultures and policy initiatives.[31] This critique of gendered construction of ethics illuminates the path to bringing ethics back to a centre stage position in the development of corporate law rules.

We also illustrate that there are creative ways of approaching established corporate law doctrines, both from a theoretical perspective and with a focus on real world outcomes. Yue Ang describes new approaches derived from feminist theory – such as the ethics of care[32] and spatial justice theories[33] – which provide a different theoretical framework in which we can reconsider the development of even fundamental corporate law doctrines such as corporate personality. This signposts a new theoretical foundation for changing corporate law to bring about effective ways in which we can obligate corporate respect for planetary boundaries, and thus shape corporate behaviour into a more sustainable pattern. Her piece is a unique contribution to the rethinking of corporate law theory.

The essays in Part III build on Part II, leading the reader to additional insights on how current legal frameworks can and ought to be changed to create a space in which the corporation and its primary actors (whether these are board members, management, investors or stakeholders such as employees), can act in ways which are driven by the overarching ethic of

---

[31] Chs. 11 and 12.

[32] Ch. 10. Also see Ang's powerful discussion of Kittay's ethic of care described in E. Kittay, *Love's Labor* (London: Routledge, 1999) and her consideration of spatial justice theories.

[33] A. Philippopoulos-Mihalopoulos, 'Law's Spatial Turn: Geography, Justice and a Certain Fear of Space' (2010) 7 *Law, Culture and the Humanities*, 188–189, referred to in Ch. 10.

sustainability. This is clearly as it should be. Parts I and II lead into this broader understanding of the ethical imperative.[34]

As a group of scholars, we understand what is at stake. Carol Liao indicates that gender (male) is linked to financial power, which in turn is protected by current conceptions of the corporation.[35] In her consideration of a number of feminist theories including those of Testy,[36] Liao makes the following observation which summarises very well the potential for this multidisciplinary scholarship:

> Intersectionality has gained in prominence as feminist scholars have promoted a more interconnected and multidimensional understanding of lived experiences; different social categorisations (including gender, race, class, sexual orientation, age, religion, disability/ability) are highly relevant in the context of power structures and different forms of privilege and oppression.[37]

In our concluding chapter, we bring the various contributions together to present the reader, and future researchers, with a road map for further thought.

1.3 Conclusion: Future Directions

The evolution of this text illustrates that women as participants in corporations, or indeed women as participants in other business models have not taken the leadership roles which one might have expected them to take. Other than in relation to the experiences of women activists described in Part I, this introductory chapter presents the view that women have not been particularly proactive in affecting corporate performance in sustainable ways. Indeed, our volume illustrates the significant intellectual pitfalls of identifying women in general as a force for effecting either positive corporate governance or performance. This is not intended to sound a pessimistic note, but simply to signpost a direction for future leadership opportunities. These leadership opportunities do not, however, belong exclusively to women, as we reject a gendered notion of good or bad corporate behaviour.

---

[34] Ref K. Testy, 'Capitalism and Freedom – For Whom?: Feminist Legal Theory and Progressive Corporate Law' (2004) 67 *Law and Contemporary Problems* 87 at 108.

[35] Ch. 13.

[36] K. Testy, 'Linking Progressive Corporate Law and Progressive Social Movements' (2002) 76 *Tulane Law Review* 1228, referred to in Ch. 13.

[37] See Ch. 13, n. 60–61.

We do present one underlying 'big idea' – which is an optimistic one – that there are indeed opportunities to change the way the corporation as we know it presents itself or is understood by those who work within its structures.

Change may happen from below, and when it does it can be supported by policy documents which identify the importance of meaningful discourse. Change can happen by improving our understanding of corporate function as it currently exists, by demonstrating the falsity of certain understandings around shareholder primacy and the 'profit imperative' and by shining a light on the nature of some resistance to regulation. As Baumfield illustrates in her contribution, notions of profit imperative are overstated and misunderstood even in the context of extremely well developed litigation such as that which has occurred in the United States.[38] Alternative models of business organisation may be a distraction from this 'big idea' but nevertheless, as Argyrou et al. illustrate, there are opportunities here to understand and illuminate different approaches to business sustainability.[39] Law has been a positive force in achieving equality for women in developed countries, and with this gold standard in mind we can be critical of the limited progress made to date regarding women in business leadership, and critical of opposition to even timid attempts to change corporations in relation to mandating some opportunities for women. Our understanding of the relationship between law and ethics allows us to see opportunities for a revival of the discussion of an ethical imperative in corporate decision making[40] together with a move away from a gendered understanding of ethics as described by Russell and O'Sullivan.[41] Finally, a powerful piece from

---

[38] Ch. 9. Contrast, as Baumfield does in the context of her discussion of the B-Corporation, the differing approaches to the complex issue of what shareholder primacy actually means in the decisions of the Chancery Court of Delaware in Newmark, *eBay Domestic Holdings, Inc v Newmark*, 16 A.3d 1 (Del. Ch. 2010) with the later and strictly speaking in terms of precedent, more authoritative decision of the US Supreme Court in *Burwell v Hobby Lobby Stores Inc*, 573 US ___ (2014); 134 S Ct 2751. See also the discussion in L. Johnson and D. Millon, 'Corporate Law after Hobby Lobby' (2015) 70 *The Business Lawyer* 1, 11. See further Ch. 14.

[39] Ch. 8.

[40] See I. Lynch Fannon, *The Ethical Corporation in Working within Two Kinds of Capitalism* (Hart Publications, 2003). See also W. Bratton, 'Confronting the Ethical Case against the Ethical Case for Constituency Rights' (1993) 50 *Washington and Lee Law Review* 1464. A. Berle, 'For Whom Corporate Managers are Trustees: A Note' (1932) 45 *Harvard Law Review* 1365.

[41] Chs. 11 and 12.

Ang demonstrates how legal theory can develop and change the way we think about fundamental concepts.[42] Change can happen by using existing legal and theoretical approaches and developing these in ways which have been enriched by the kind of scholarship we present in this volume.

Experience tells us that the corporation can be a vehicle for oppressive conduct until it is challenged, but when it is challenged there is nothing which acts as an imperative – either from the nature of the corporation, or from the laws which have created the corporation – preventing the corporation from responding positively to demands for change. Existing assumptions can be changed as we can see by the example of corporations which genuinely adopt broader social or sustainability agendas. Similarly, when faced with the type of pressure which was put on the corporations acting in Ghana or in Bangladesh,[43] none of the corporations were prevented from acting or responding on the basis of claims that the profit imperative constrained the changes which were made. Instead, obstacles to sustainable corporate conduct were created by cultural barriers in developing countries as they are here in western developed economies. The power of law – whether it is to create radically different labour standards, to incrementally change attitudes by insisting on new reporting obligations,[44] to create equal opportunities for women in terms of business leadership, or to change our understanding of corporate function – is that it responds to but also has the potential to effect change in cultures. Law has the potential to work as an agent for positive change. A theoretical framework driven by an ethical imperative serves as the basis for a critical analysis of existing legislative initiatives and will also provide ideas and inspiration for future, more radical change. We ask for sustainable and ethical corporate practices, and we also show how new ways of thinking (for example, the feminist ethic of care principle and spatial justice) allow us to see how legal rules can operate in ways which destroy current assumptions.[45] Even though there has been an ongoing critique of the corporation over the last three decades from progressive corporate scholars, there has been no unifying concept presented at its core. As Liao observes:

> there has been little developed under the flag of 'progressive corporate law' for some time now. The inability to find common terminology and consensus created a significant stumbling block to internal organisation

---

[42] Ch. 10.   [43] Chs. 2 and 4.   [44] Ch. 5.   [45] Ch. 10.

and cohesion. Other positions, such as more advanced versions of progressive corporate law theory emanating from a pragmatic European
perspective on corporate function, or the fact that nations have adopted
more stakeholder-based models of governance, have not been recognised
sufficiently in academic scholarship and have struggled to gain traction in
popular discourse in order to overtake these entrenched normative
beliefs.[46]

In describing the differing understandings of corporate function in a
comparative context some years ago, Lynch Fannon observed:

> Historically the corporation has presented itself as a private actor. This
> view has ... been underlined by the theoretical analysis of the law and
> economics school. In the ethical context the microeconomic paradigm
> sees the primary ethical problem as 'the threat that state regulation poses
> to individual autonomy and private wealth creation'.[47]

Not much has changed since the progressive corporate lawyers began this
discussion almost thirty years ago. Nevertheless, with new perspectives
derived from the urgency of sustainability and our awareness of the
potential impact of feminist theory, we propose that the corporation
can and ought to be changed. If we are in agreement that corporations
must act in more sustainable ways, the question remains as to how this
can be achieved. What strategies will affect corporate decision making
most effectively, whether these are made by corporate boards, managers,
shareholders, stakeholders or a combination of all three? Regulation, the
continued development of legal and cultural norms (including social
mobilisation and 'bottom-up initiatives') and the continued development
of new theoretical frameworks are all possible strategies.

In this collection, we present new feminist perspectives on this question. We describe the limitations of methods currently favoured by policy
makers but move on to examples where women, questions regarding
gender equality and feminist theories seem to have had influence in
effecting change. Our intention is to question current assumptions about
corporate function, about the regulation of corporations and about the
role of ethics. We show that the theoretical framework within which
the modern corporation operates can be expanded in innovative ways
to support change. Most importantly, we all agree that the reason the
corporation must change is to achieve a more sustainable future in the
broadest sense.

---

[46] Ch. 13.   [47] Lynch Fannon, *Working within Two Kinds of Capitalism*, 103.

PART I

Women as Influencers of Corporate Action

2

Reclaiming Value and Betterment for Bangladeshi Women Workers in Global Garment Chains

LORRAINE TALBOT*

2.1 Introduction

This chapter is concerned with the betterment of life for Bangladeshi women workers in the garment factories which form part of a global garment chain headed by western global corporations. It assesses the considerable cultural barriers women face in improving their working and living conditions and the paradoxical relationship between these barriers and the legal entitlements women possess qua workers under national and international law. It considers whether women's betterment is best pursued through the work of non-governmental organisations (NGOs) and other groups in pressuring global corporations to be more responsible or through their own political activity as organised labour. It concludes that while there is considerable scope for both, only women's political activity can substantially increase their betterment and enable them to claim more of the value they create.

Over the last forty years there has been a massive rise in the globalisation of production, distribution and profit claiming. The division of labour in production has become increasingly globalised as low-skilled work has relocated to the global South. In contrast, profit claiming has largely remained with the large corporations of the global North. This chapter is concerned with the labour and exploitation of Bangladeshi women working in the 'downstream', or the low skill, low value part of global apparel chains.

Bangladesh, like many developing countries, adopted an export-driven economy, supplying goods at low prices for western global brands. This economic strategy has increasingly relied on female labour. This shift in the gender composition of the workforce raises the possibility of increasing women's economic independence and betterment. However, evidence suggests that the cultural norms of female subordination in the home have been consciously reproduced in the workplace. The factories

* This chapter was written as part of a body of work funded by the Leverhulme Trust.

which produce these downstream products have sought the compliance and learned subordination of women in preference to male employees. As Kabeer puts it, 'factory organisation drew on, and indeed actively promoted, cultural norms of femininity which helped to legitimate employers' super-exploitation of their predominantly female workforce.'[1] This is a familiar pattern for women workers in the developing world, in both the formal and informal sectors. However, in Bangladesh, employers have found that a collective workforce can be an empowered workforce, and there is growing evidence of women seeking greater control over their working lives. The Rana Plaza tragedy prompted female-dominated protests against unsafe work conditions – a militancy in stark contrast with long-standing cultural norms of *purdah*.[2] Nevertheless, Bangladeshi women continue to face a great many barriers to their betterment, culturally and economically. While they possess reasonably progressive legal rights as workers, there is a widespread failure to recognise those rights. Abusive treatment in the workplace is the norm, and women who attempt to enforce their legal rights through unionisation suffer violence and intimidation.

In Section 2.2, the chapter considers the rise of global value chains and the position of developing countries in these. It provides some of the historical background to Bangladesh's entry into the global garment chain. Section 2.3 considers the cultural barriers to women's betterment together with Kabeer's complex picture of women's decision to work. In Section 2.4, the chapter considers the developmentally stagnant nature of the downstream garment industry, which potentially inhibits women's ability to reclaim value because their skills may be easily replaced. It then considers, as a key factor, their high degree of exploitation by both the factory owners and the 'chain leaders', the global corporations. Sections 2.5 and 2.6 consider the strategies for achieving women's betterment. First seeking global corporations to adopt more socially responsible polices in respect of their contractors. Second, seeking better law and better recognition of the law through collective

---

[1] N. Kabeer, *The Power to Choose – Bangladeshi Women and Labor Market Decisions in London and Dhaka* (London: Verso, 2002).

[2] *Purdah* refers to the practice in some muslim countries and by some muslims of screening women from men and strangers. This can be a literal screening through headwear, or by a curtain separating women from men in public areas, or it can be used more metaphorically to describe their separation from a life external from the family, such as formal work.

action. It concludes that Bangladeshi women's advancement falls to their own collective political organisation.

In order to understand the position of Bangladeshi women and the barriers to the betterment of their lives, I will engage a number of different theoretical approaches. This includes feminist criticism of legal norms as a way of understanding the particularities of women's social existence and cultural context. It uses Polanyi's notion of the dis-embedded market, which theorises the market as having an independent existence from the social context of the economy which is both dominant and conflicting.[3] And finally, as a way of understanding the limits of legal rights, particularly as a means to advance the position of women, the chapter uses Pashukanis's notion of the legal subject presupposing the market subject.[4]

2.2   Global Value Chains and the Rise of the Bangladeshi Garment Industry

Corporate reach and global outsourcing has been an ongoing feature of capitalism. However, from the 1970s, as capitalism rapidly globalised, the term 'commodity chain' and then 'global commodity chain'[5] or the 'global supply chain' was coined as a more accurate way to describe the many inputs contained in commodities which were increasingly sourced from many parts of the world. Later, the term 'global value chain' was introduced by Gereffi[6] to encompass the services and ideas which com-posed a commodity as well as the physical inputs.[7]

Gereffi distinguished 'producer-driven chains' from 'buyer-driven chains' to indicate where the power resided and where the most value was extracted. Producer-driven chains are generally those in high tech sectors like pharmaceuticals where the power is situated at the Research and Development end of the chain, so that it is this that drives the

---

[3] K. Polanyi, *The Great Transformation: The Political and Economic Origins of Our Time* (Boston: Beacon Press, 2001).

[4] E. Pashukanis, *Law and Marxism: A General Theory towards a Critique of the Fundamental Juridical Concepts* (London: Pluto Press, 1989).

[5] G. Gereffi, 'Global value chains in a post-Washington Consensus world' (2014) *Review of International Political Economy*, 21(1), 9–37.

[6] Ibid.

[7] Other scholars have introduced the idea of a global value network to describe the non-linear nature of the inputs into commodities.

design and assembly of the commodity. The ubiquitous example of this form of chain is Apple Inc, where production and assembly lie at the low value part of the chain and most profits are claimed by the intellectual property–owning corporation. In buyer-driven chains, it is the retailer which drives and controls production, and the retailer which claims most of the value in the chain. Retailers source from numerous countries either through their own corporate network or through outsourcing or both. The ubiquitous example here is Walmart Inc. The commodities which are sold in the buyer-led chain are generally low tech goods where the productive part of the chain is composed of low-skilled, replaceable and low-paid workers. The value is claimed at the marketing and retail end and the brand is the prized and protected part of the chain. The apparel industry, examined here, is a buyer-led chain.

Key to modern global corporate wealth is the ability to claim the valuable parts of the chain while outsourcing the less valuable. Multinationals have ensured that they retain the part of production to which accrues the main bulk of profits, the part which economists call 'rents'. Rents are those things which are either naturally scarce, or can be constructed as scarce (by legal mechanisms such as copyrights and patents, and by excluding others from access to the resource). This form of value extraction began to become popular in the 1970s but dominated by the mid-1990s as global value chains became truly global, covering all aspects of manufacturing, food supply, energy and services such as call centres. And they were growing fast. By 2013, The United Nations Conference on Trade and Development (UNCTAD) reported that global value chains shaped by multinational corporations accounted for some 80 per cent of global trade, estimated to be worth $20 trillion in trade each year.[8] The developing country input into global value chains has rapidly increased over the last twenty-five years, from 20 per cent in 1990 to 30 per cent in 2000 to over 40 per cent in 2013.[9] This does not, of course, reflect developing countries' claim to the value in the chain; they claim a small percentage of actual value. The percentage increase reflects their inputs.

---

[8] UNCTAD, *Global Value Chains and Development: Investment and Value Added Trade in the Global Economy* (2013), see http://unctad.org/en/PublicationsLibrary/diae2013d1_en.pdf.

[9] Ibid.

The origins of the Bangladeshi garment industry[10] lie in the new international division of labour which began with East Asia's rapid development of export-orientated manufacturing. Plentiful cheap labour and government support made East Asian manufactured goods highly competitive, and the prospect of manufacturing there became very attractive for western capitalists who were increasingly obliged to share the wealth of production with their domestic labour force. East Asia gave business in the global North the opportunity to sidestep domestic workers – who had succeeded in securing strong labour rights and well-paid employment – and relocate production to East Asia with its cheap, compliant workforce. Labour-intensive industries like lower-end garment production was particularly drawn to the export-orientated economies.

But many businesses did not relocate, and their business was under threat from cheaper global production. To counter this, an international agreement, The Multi-Fibre Arrangement 1974,[11] limited imports from developing countries (including western companies that had relocated production there) to developed countries through quotas. It was designed as a short-term measure to allow western business to adjust to this new global production, but in the event, these protectionist measures remained in place until 2004. However, one of its effects was to bring a small number of factories from East Asia to Bangladesh because Bangladesh was exempt from the Arrangement. These were the early seeds of low-skill manufacturing in Bangladesh. It coincided with rapid political, economic and cultural changes in Bangladesh. The war of independence had left its people and economy devastated. Bangladeshi industries were nationalised to provide a socialist solution to its problems but just three years after independence, Bangladesh was in the grip of a year-long famine. In 1976, Bangladeshi leader President Rahmen was assassinated in a military coup. For rural communities, the ability to survive from agriculture alone became impossible and it became common for men to manage several different jobs. The number of people in poverty rose from

---

[10] The production of fine fabrics in Bengal goes back many centuries. It was suppressed by British imperialism from the eighteenth century to enable the advancement of the British textile industry.

[11] WTO Trade Topics, *Textiles Monitoring Body (TMB) The Agreement on Textiles and Clothing*, see www.wto.org/english/tratop_e/texti_e/texintro_e.htm.

around 40 per cent in the 1960s to nearly 80 per cent by the end of the 1970s.[12] In urban areas, more educated men took up the white-collar work opportunities offered by the growing Bangladeshi state. Women remained in home-based, informal and now downgraded agricultural work. They were economically vulnerable in a way which was both new and pervasive.

The Government's New Industrial Policy of 1982 increased privatisation and encouraged foreign investment in textile manufacturing. As a result, the few garment factories introduced in the 1970s mushroomed. By the 1990s, the garment industry was a major component of the Bangladesh GDP. Garment factories preferred women while women sought release from the deprivation of the 1970s and the devastating effect it had on their status and prospects. Women were drawn from rural communities to the big city factories and some of the lowest pay the world had to offer. The industry continued to grow, today representing 85 per cent of Bangladesh's exports.[13]

2.3 Cultural Barriers and Reclaiming Value

Women workers are certainly exploited. Yet Bangladesh's garment factories have, at least, enabled women from the lower classes to gain more formally paid employment. Qua recognised workers they can, in principle, claim the rights and protection of Bangladesh's labour law and its greater rights in regards to pay, length of working day, sickness and maternity pay than they would expect from work in the home or other informal employment. However, the law does not operate as a decontextualized framework of rules, and this works against women workers. As Ackerly and Attansai argue, engaging the lens of law or other international standards distorts the lived experience of women in developing countries. Women, they argue, are embedded within the cultural and social norms of these societies, and these contexts are the most 'powerful forces of injustice'.[14] Legal norms, like the universal views of injustice held by mainstream international feminists like Nussbaum and Okin, do not sufficiently contextualise women within their local conditions. Their 'focus on the global obscures the realities of local

---

[12] Kabeer, *The Power to Choose.*
[13] See www.worldstopexports.com/bangladeshs-top-10-exports.
[14] B Ackerly and K Attansai, 'Global Feminisms: Theory and Ethics for Studying Gendered Injustice' (2000) *New Political Science* 31 (4), 543, 550

diversity and experience and the necessity of understanding these par-
ticulars for a feminist argument that will affect their material reality'.[15]

However, this embeddedness is complex and changing. Women do
not have homogenous experiences, nor do they interpret the world
through the same interpretive lens. Furthermore, women exist in a world
that is not static, and the embedded cultural norms of Bangladeshi
society have been wracked by huge political and economic events. In
Kabeer's account of women's entry into the labour market, she shows
that women are a heterogeneous group, making choices in circumstances that were not of their choosing. Up until the 1980s, around
95 per cent of women worked around the home and in subsistence
farming. By the 1970s, this family economy had failed, leaving women
dependent on their families or husbands. It was around this time, argues
Kabeer, that 'demand dowries' became the norm. Women were viewed
as economic burdens to potential husbands, who started to require
substantial payments for shouldering responsibility for their upkeep.
Commodifying women through a dowry explains the rise in extreme
violence suffered by Bangladeshi women, argues Kabeer. Typically,
violence occurs because a dowry was unpaid. However, there are many
examples of a woman and her children being abandoned by her husband
so he can acquire another wife and more dowry. 'Dowry violence' is
commonly associated with disfiguring or fatal acid attacks. It is these
pressures – either for unmarried women whose families lack the means
for a dowry, or married women who have been abandoned – that drive
women to garment factory work. For them, the factory represents
survival and independence. So while they may be despised culturally
and condemned for their wanton independence and abandonment of
the modesty and protection of *purdah*, they continue to seek employment.[16] In other words, subordination and *purdah* do not define their
experiences as workers; instead, their choice to work is an abandonment
or re-interpretation of the cultural norms they have known. As Kabeer
shows in her interviews with Bangladeshi women, they do not feel they
have abandoned *purdah*. Indeed, many have reconceptualised it to
accommodate their financial imperative to work given that a patriarchal
society built around the family no longer protects and provides for them.
Many women feel they have been forced by circumstance to work
outside the home. They have been forced to be modern, and it is not

[15] Ibid, p. 550.   [16] Kabeer, *The Power to Choose*, p. 82.

they who have failed to meet their cultural obligations. It is the protection implicit in a patriarchal society that has failed to materialise.

> It is in this perceived erosion of the patriarchal contract, and the increasing inability of men to sustain the model of the male breadwinner, that the genesis of women's entry into factory employment has to be understood. It made it possible, and necessary, for them to abandon old ways of behaving as passive occupants of predestined roles and to find new forms of agency which would allow them to anticipate the consequences of patriarchal risk and to take full advantage of the opportunities that came their way.[17]

Taking control to avoid destitution is not the only draw to the factories. Kabeer also noted that better-off urban women have also become factory employees, often with the consent or approval of their husbands, in order to pay for additional goods, or their children's education; aspiration not desperation.

The more complex picture of choice presented by Kabeer's work notwithstanding, the broad statistics indicate that female subordination remains the overriding norm. A review of women's position by UNICEF in 2007[18] showed that three quarters of Bangladeshi women were married before they were 18 and one third before they were 15. Maternal mortality was high because 85 per cent of births were at home and only 25 per cent had medical attendance. Half of married women's access to health was controlled by their husbands. Girls and women were generally the last in the family to be fed, and consequently illnesses through malnutrition were high. UNICEF found that over half of married women had experienced domestic violence, while the later study from the Bangladesh Bureau of Statistics[19] puts this figure at 85 per cent. Adolescent girls were often harassed or molested on the streets. Since 1999 there have been over 3,000 reported incidents of acid attacks against women, often cases of dowry violence. Child labour is very common.[20] A recent survey showed that around 8 per cent of children under ten were working, rising to 45 per cent by the age of fourteen.

---

[17] Ibid, p. 140.
[18] UNICEF, *The State of the World's Children 2007. Women and Children, The Double Dividend of Gender Equality*, see www.unicef.org/sowc07/docs/sowc07.pdf.
[19] Reported in UNSTATS, *Measuring Gender-Based Violence: Results of the Violence against Women (VAW) Survey in Bangladesh*, see https://unstats.un.org/unsd/gender/Mexico_Nov2014/Session%203%20Bangladesh%20paper.pdf.
[20] Overseas Development Institute, *Child Labour and Education A Survey of Slum Settlements in Dhaka* (2016), see https://www.odi.org/publications/10654-child-labour-and-education-survey-slum-settlements-dhaka.

The garment industry was 'a major employer of children, accounting for two thirds of female child labour'.[21] Other work included invisible domestic servitude and sex work. Child workers generally have no access to education.

The experience and position of women is part of a dynamically changing environment in which social norms exist in a dialectical relationship with market norms. The expansion of the market has tended to dis-embed the economy – Polanyian-wise – from the particular social context of these countries.[22] Women workers are paid poverty wages but they do occupy the role of a financial provider. They must enter contracts with their employer, not as subordinates but as (formally) free individuals capable of entering this legal arrangement.[23] Contract relies on the legal assumption of equality between the contract makers and while this is substantively inaccurate, it delivers a measure of autonomy to workers. The normative implications of this assumption and the material benefits of a legal claim to wage conflict with the high levels of social subordination of women in Bangladesh.

Problematically for women's betterment is that their implicit claims as autonomous workers have caused more violence against women as a whole. As Polanyi showed, the dis-embedding effect of the market results in a 'double-movement'.[24] Society reacts against the market's otherness, its conflict with understood social and cultural norms. The double movement is an attempt to re-embed the market within activities and institutions which reflect and reassert long-standing social and cultural norms. In Polanyi's study of the dis-embedded English working class, much of the reaction was against the dis-embedding of the market from long-standing social systems of support.[25] However, in Bangladesh the market dis-embeds long-standing cultural norms of female subordination and dependence, prompting a double movement to reassert male domination. This means that although the labour market created by global garment chains has provided new opportunities for women, society constantly seeks to reinforce the cultural norms of male dominance and female subjugation by subjecting women to physical and sexual violence. This is a dynamic process; as the market dis-embeds women

---

[21] Ibid, p. 9.   [22] Polanyi, 'The Great Transformation'.
[23] This assumption is discussed more fully in Section 2.6.
[24] Polanyi, 'The Great Transformation', p. 136.   [25] Ibid, p. 175.

from their subordinate position, women have sought to assert themselves and act against the cultural norm. This is then countered by violence from men within and outside the workplace. So, as Section 2.6 notes, women who have sought to assert their rights through organised labour have suffered violence and intimidation from the combined and connected interests of factory owners and the political elite who are either factory owners themselves or integrated with factory employers in other ways. This raises the question of how women can claim their true value in the workplace, given the cultural and economic forces aligned against them.

2.4   Claiming Value in Sectors with Developmental Limitations

Nineteenth-century capitalism in the global North spearheaded industrial and technological development and increased labour productivity. It first replaced skilled craftsmanship with unskilled factory labour but then frequently replaced unskilled factory labour with work that required new specialist skills. One of the outcomes of this process was the development of a skilled workforce that was not easily replaced and therefore possessed substantial bargaining power used to enhance wages and work conditions. The story is not quite the same for labour in global capitalism, and it is certainly not the same for labour at the low-skilled end of a global value chain of a low-tech product. Bengal was once renowned for the beauty of its fabrics and the skill of its fabric makers. The industry was destroyed in the nineteenth century because of, among other things, cheaper fabrics made by factory methods in England. In other words, the industry in Bengal did not become more productive, requiring new skills which then increased the bargaining power of its workers. Instead it was overridden by international production and those new skills were developed in England. Now Bangladesh has its new sector of low-skilled factory work, but there is little chance that it will follow the trajectory of England and other western economies. The following account explores why there is no dynamic in the Bangladesh export economy that will render women more skilled and thus able to enhance their betterment and claim to value.

Recent studies show that global value chains have become generally more networked and long – indicative, as will be shown, of increases in skilled work within the chain. Statistics from the Organisation for Economic Co-operation and Development (OECD) show that most global trade is in intermediate inputs – over 50 per cent of goods trade and almost 70 per cent of services trade[26] – and this intermediate part of the chain, the middle, continues to grow. This may be partly attributed to the general reduction in the trade costs that attach to the product from producers to consumers, such as freight costs (large container shipping has massively reduced these costs), insurance, land transport and tariffs and duties.[27] But, it is also attributable to organisational and managerial techniques which reduce the risks and transaction costs attached to bringing in cheap labour higher up in the chain.[28] De Backer and Miroudot also show that the inputs from different countries have been changing, thus changing the shape of global value chains. Many countries whose specific function in the chain was of a low-value, low-skilled or downstream nature are increasingly engaging in higher-skilled, higher 'upstream' value. They measure this by distance to final demand in the chain. Their analysis of the studies of value chains undertaken by the OECD shows that the developing economies of Chile, China, Taiwan, Hong Kong, Malaysia, the Philippines, Singapore and Thailand have increased their 'upstreamness'. But so too have the developed economies of Austria, Germany, Ireland and Luxembourg. The increase in the length of the global value chain correlates with a tendency for greater upstreamness: 'on average, most countries' move upstream is consistent with the overall increase in the length of [global value chains]'.[29]

However, several economies have seen a decrease of chain length. Cambodia, Romania, the Slovak Republic and Slovenia – countries that specialise in downstream goods and services – remain primarily downstream producers.[30] This is because the lengthening of global value chains is more likely with chains in high-tech goods.[31]

---

[26] OECD, *Trade in Value Added*, see http://oe.cd/tiva.

[27] K. De Backer and S. Miroudot, 'Mapping Global Value Chains', Working Paper Series no 1677, European Central Bank (May 2014).

[28] Talbot, 'Operationalising Sustainability in Corporation Law Reform through a Labour-Centred Approach: A UK Perspective' (2014) *European Company Law* 11 (2) 94 at 95–96.

[29] Backer and Miroudot, 'Mapping Global Value Chains'.

[30] Ibid, 'Mapping Global Value Chains', p. 14.

[31] China is different in this respect. Gereffi shows that China is rapidly encompassing more of the upstream parts of the chain in these commodities and there is a tendency to consolidation in these chains rather than lengthening, a focus on the domestic market and re-orientation of power to top Chinese manufacturers evidenced in 'China's supply chain cities which integrate all aspects of GVC from design production to showrooms for global buyers.' G. Gereffi, 'Global Value Chains in a Post-Washington Consensus World' (2014) *Review of International Political Economy* 21(1), 9–37, 17.

However, for the low-tech, buyer-led retail chains, there is little additional value to be made by lengthening the chain. For countries like
Bangladesh, which has specialised in the low-tech apparel industries, the
opportunities to go upstream are limited. In garment chains, raw materials are imported mainly from the United States, Pakistan and Australia,
into manufacturing centres like Bangladesh (and also in China, Cambodia and Thailand). The cotton is made to the retails brands' specifications
in the estimated 5,600 garment factories in Bangladesh and then bought
and shipped to western high streets.[32] This sector is overwhelmingly
important to Bangladesh's economy. Bangladesh is now the second-
largest exporter of apparel, second only to China. This has consequences
for women's betterment in the garment sector, where the more than
4 million female workers constitute over 85 per cent of the workforce.
Whereas the higher-tech industries offer professional development to
their workers, the garment chain is, more or less, stagnant. Workers here
will not become more skilled and they will not be able to exercise more
bargaining power in respect of that skill. They are more easily replaceable. Women cannot rely on the capitalist dynamics which shaped
development in the West and which delivered the opportunities for
bargaining that labour could exploit.

On the other hand, women workers receive a tiny proportion of the
value of the garments they make, which gives them considerable scope to
demand more for their labour. The degree of their exploitation may be
demonstrated in the now well known values breakdown of a Hennes &
Mauritz (H&M) T-shirt, discussed (among others) by Tony Norfield.[33]
The shirt is sold for 4.95 euros. The factory owner sells each shirt for
1.35 euros. The women, who are paid around 3 euros a day (given the
minimum wage), produce 250 shirts an hour in a 10–12-hour day. H&M
makes 0.60-euro profit per shirt – that is, they make approximately 1,500
euros from the shirts one female worker makes in one day. She is paid
3 euros for her day's work while H&M makes 1,500 euros from that same
day's work. So while the success of western corporations is often attributed to western laws and corporate governance and to corporations'

[32] These brands include Walmart, H&M, Tesco, C7A, Mango Primark, Arcadia Group,
Aristocrate Distributor Ltd, Bebe Clothing (UK) LTD, BHS Ltd, Bonmarche Brand Co
Management Ltd, Character World Danielle Group plc, Debenhams, Edinburgh Woollen
Mill and Fat Face. Many of these retailers are signatories of the Bangladesh Accord. See
http://bangladeshaccord.org/signatories.
[33] Tony Norfield, *T-Shirt Economics Labour in an Imperialist World*, see http://column
.global-labour-university.org/2012/08/t-shirt-economics-labour-in-imperialist.html.

superior business acumen and expert (highly paid) executives, the reason is much simpler. The people who make the goods are paid an infinitesimal portion of the value they create. It is also worth noting that H&M's annual turnover for 2015 was $20.92 billion, a tenth of the whole of Bangladesh's GDP in the same year.[34]

This super-exploitation reveals women's latent power. The global industry is dependent on their labour. The global industry is one from which women can reclaim a great deal more of the value they create. The question then remains as to strategy.

Value is extracted from the point the product leaves the garment makers, first from the factory owners and second from the global retailer. In the H&M T-shirt example, the factory owners are paid 1.35 euros for each T-shirt and have already paid 0.40 euro for the 400g of cotton bought from America for each shirt. The 0.95 euro for each shirt they receive after deducting the cost of cotton covers the cost of running the factory including wages. The poor working conditions and ultra-low wages indicate that a substantial proportion of that sum is profit. That being so, organised and unionised labour could claim more value for its workers (either more pay, fewer hours or both), thereby reducing the factory owners' profits; an outcome which factory owners resist.

The second tranche of value extraction is the costs to H&M of getting the garments shipped to the consumer (in the following example, Germany) and the costs associated with the high-street shops. As noted previously, this leaves H&M with 0.60-euro profit for each T-shirt. The strategy for reclaiming value for women workers must aim to make the global corporation divest some of that profit for those workers. The mechanism for achieving this – given the corporation is not the women's employer – could normally only be based in non-legal mechanisms such as corporate social responsibility.[35]

The next section will examine the possibility of reclaiming value and women's betterment through making corporations more socially responsible. It is followed in the proceeding section by a consideration of the possibilities provided by collective and individual legal rights.

---

[34] H&M, *Annual Report 2015*, see https://about.hm.com/content/dam/hmgroup/groupsite/documents/masterlanguage/Annual%20Report/Annual%20Report%202015.pdf and World Bank figures on Bangladesh GDP 2015, see http://data.worldbank.org/country/bangladesh.
[35] For a discussion of possible emerging trends, see Ch. 10.

2.5   Women's Betterment from Outside: International Pressure and Corporate Social Responsibility

A great deal of international spotlight has been shone by human rights groups, NGOs and academic researchers on the exploitative and dangerous working conditions of Bangladeshi women workers. Their important work in highlighting these issues has resulted in a number of initiatives designed to make upstream companies take some responsibility for the conditions of downstream workers, to be more cognisant of their working conditions and to take steps to redress inhumane practices. The practice of corporate social responsibility (CSR) has grown exponentially over the last twenty years, pushed in large part by these social and environmental activists. Corporations have shown an increased enthusiasm for demonstrating their adherence to social concerns as well as meeting their legal obligation to enhance shareholder value, a shift known as pursuing the 'triple bottom line' rather than the bottom line. A new profession of CSR experts and consultants have emerged. Companies compete to be the most CSR cognisant.[36] Even the most inherently unsocially responsible companies, such as those selling tobacco (a product with surely no social benefits) boasts glossy CSR reports from their own CSR committees of CSR experts. British American Tobacco's last publicly available Annual Report (2015) reviewed its activities in addressing human rights risks and promoting the interests of tobacco farmers, sustainable agriculture and the success and global reach of its Youth Smoking Prevention Initiative.[37]

In contrast to Milton Friedman's famous claim that the social responsibility of companies was to make profit for shareholders and not to consider the wider community (responsibility for which lay elsewhere), companies are finding that good CSR means good business. Many corporations market products accredited as socially responsible, such as those certified by the Fair Trade Association[38] because consumers increasingly prefer products with a CSR pedigree. A good CSR image protects corporate reputation and brand, that part of the global value chain which claims the majority of the profit. The value of brands, of

---

[36] National CSR Awards, see https://nationalcsrawards.co.uk.

[37] BAT, *Annual Report 2015*, see www.bat.com/group/sites/uk__9d9kcy.nsf/vwPagesWebL ive/DO9DCL3B/$FILE/medMDA87PVT.pdf?openelement at pp. 64–65.

[38] Fair Trade Association, *Monitoring the Scope and Benefit of Fairtrade*, Sixth Edition (2014), see www.fairtrade.net/fileadmin/user_upload/content/2009/resources/2014-Fair trade-Monitoring-Scope-Benefits-final-web.pdf.

course, makes the corporate watchers and activists particularly strong, enabling them to pressure corporations into adopting socially responsible policies. Reports of human rights abuses, child labour or environmental destruction can have a direct impact on consumer preferences and thus the bottom line.

So international pressure has had a significant impact on corporations' alleged adoption of CSR, but does CSR benefit Bangladeshi women workers? Because their work sits at the downstream of global value chains, CSR's 'beyond the law' approach arguably has the potential to impose responsibility where the law holds that none applies. The companies upstream of the garment chain, the chain leaders, do not own the factories of Dhaka and they do not employ its workers because in law the companies are buyers contracting with the factory owners. They negotiate the purchase of goods which the factories manufacture at an agreed price, and they have no immediate legal responsibility for the factory workers. In the absence of the buyers having a legally enforceable relationship with workers, CSR acting 'beyond the law' may provide workers with some protection. It may be in the company's interest to apply, or to be seen to apply, business ethics that are closer to those of its domestic jurisdiction and those of its main consumers. There may be a strong business case for adopting policies which benefit the producers' workers and provide visibility and proof of good corporate citizenship.

This justification for CSR reveals the failure of the law in this respect.[39] In construing the relationship as arms-length contracting, the law radically misconstrues and misrepresents the real relationship of power between suppliers and purchasers. The buyers are global retail brands, and some are the largest in the world. They are heavily integrated into the production process and have a powerful hold over the conditions and pay of the producers' workers. They can ensure that producers cut costs to the bone, supress wages, enforce overtime and ignore health and safety problems.

However, this real power that global brands can assert over its suppliers can be positive if they do, in fact, adopt CSR initiatives that achieve women's betterment. So do they? Primark and Hennes & Mauritz AB

---

[39] For a discussion of the relationship between CSR and law, see I. Lynch Fannon, 'CSR and Law's Empire: Is There a Conflict?' (2007) *Northern Ireland Legal Quarterly* 58, 1–21; B. Sjåfjell, 'Why Law Matters: Corporate Social Irresponsibility and the Futility of Voluntary Climate Change Mitigation' (2011) *European Company Law* 8(2–3), pp. 56–64.

(H&M) are major garment purchasers from the factories of Dhaka and provide useful illustrations of the effectiveness of CSR.

Primark, a UK public limited company owned by Associated British Foods, adopted an industry-derived CSR code from the Ethical Trading Initiative (ETI), called the ETI Base Code. This code requires members to submit annual reports to the ETI board showing how they are dealing with labour conditions in their supply chains and how they have complied with ETI Base Code principles, which include prohibitions on forced and child labour, the freedom of association for workers, a living wage and safe working conditions.[40]

H&M, a Swedish public limited company, adopted its own CSR and ethical principles. It prides itself on having a direct relationship with its 820 independent suppliers who employ around 1.6 million people.[41] It is also a family-controlled business. The Persson family own 68.6 per cent of the shares through an intermediary company, Ramsbury Invest AB. Most of the shares are owned by Karl-Johan Persson.[42] In other words, the Persson family possess unencumbered power to design sound and effective CSR polices without the need to mollify shareholders.

However, it appears that the social responsibility of both Primark and H&M did not extend to the Bangladeshi garment workers supplying thousands of their global stores. These two global retailers were supplied by the small factories in the Rana Plaza in Dhaka. Yet their social responsibility and ethics codes did not stop them (and other brands) ensuring that suppliers competed on price, making savings through low wages, job insecurity and hazardous working conditions. Indeed, they were often the sole customers of these factories, making specific requirements of their management in respect of the workforce and often managing directly. Primark's sole supplier in Rana Plaza was New Wave Bottoms,[43] one of the largest factories in the building. Primark was its main buyer.

The Rana Plaza was a tragedy waiting to happen. Dhaka's Capital Development Authority, which approves building permits for factories,

---

[40] ETI Base Code Principles, see www.ethicaltrade.org/resources/eti-base-code.
[41] H&M, *Corporate Governance Report 2015*, see https://about.hm.com/en/about-us/corporate-governance/corporate-governance-report.html.
[42] H&M, *Annual Report 2015*, p. 77.
[43] Primark, *Rana Plaza Long Term Compensation*, see www.primark.com/en-ie/our-ethics/news/rana-plaza.

granted a permit for the Rana Plaza building to build six floors. It did not undertake any follow-up monitoring which would have revealed that eight floors had been built in an already weak structure. The building was filled with thousands of workers and heavy machinery and electricity generators. When the walls showed significant cracking, days before the buildings collapse, workers were ordered to stay and continue working with threats of violence and assurances of dismissal. The death of 1,134 workers has been called mass industrial homicide.[44] Not an accident but the inevitable result of the combined greed of factory owners and upstream retail corporations.

These global brands first tried to distance themselves from the tragedy, hiding behind the corporate veil as blameless purchasers equally shocked by the deaths and injuries caused by the hazardous conditions.[45] However, local people, trade unions and local and international activists successfully challenged their interpretation and ultimately pressured them to demonstrate their contrition through a more stringent CSR programme, the Bangladesh Accord 2013. This initiative legally binds companies that sign the Accord (signatory companies) to various agreements to improve the safety of the working environment and to commit to a fire and building safety programme for five years. Currently, the Accord covers 215 signatory companies, 1,600 factories and around 2 million workers in Bangladesh. An H&M representative is one of the Steering Committee members (together with other company representatives). The other members are drawn from national and international unions.[46]

The agreement covers all suppliers of signatory companies[47] and requires suppliers to submit to rigorous levels of inspection. For major suppliers, if, following an inspection (by a qualified safety inspector) they fail to meet agreed standards of safety, each signatory company must contribute funding to support such repairs as are needed in proportion to their use of the factory and up to a maximum of $500,000 per year. Corrective action must be performed within a designated timetable and,

---

[44] T. Hoskins, 'Reliving the Rana Plaza factory collapse: a history of cities in 50 buildings, day 22' (23 April 2015) *The Guardian*, see www.theguardian.com/cities/2015/apr/23/rana-plaza-factory-collapse-history-cities-50-buildings.

[45] M. Strydom, D. Nelson and D. Bergman, 'Primark 'shocked' by Bangladesh building collapse' (25 April 2013) *The Telegraph*, see www.telegraph.co.uk/finance/newsbysector/retailandconsumer/10017011/Primark-shocked-by-Bangladesh-building-collapse.html.

[46] Bangladesh Accord Steering Committee, see http://bangladeshaccord.org/governance.

[47] A list of signatory companies is available at http://bangladeshaccord.org/signatories.

should the factory be closed during that period, workers' employment and pay must be maintained by the supplier for up to six months. Similarly, signatory companies must make 'reasonable efforts' (not defined) to ensure that any worker who loses their job is offered alternative and safe employment elsewhere.

Whether this happens depends on both the signatory company and supplier factory conforming to the terms of the Accord. If the supplier factory does not conform, this can result in the termination of their business relationship with the signatory company – a substantial incentive to comply. The problem is making the signatory company perform. If the signatory company does not perform, the supplier may bring the dispute to the Accord's Steering Committee for adjudication (this is available for both parties in respect to non-compliance with the Accord). If the signatory company wants to appeal a decision found against it, arbitration is available to it (and to all parties). If the arbitration process also finds against the signatory company, then the supplier factory may enforce the decision through the courts of the signatory company's domestic jurisdiction.[48]

Of course, it is highly unlikely that a run-down factory in Dhaka will pursue payment from a court in (usually) the global North. The costs and complications alone would likely preclude this. However, the most significant criticism of this arrangement is that it ignores the power relationship between a factory which is dependent on the large retailer's order and the large retailer who can find a supplier elsewhere. Supplier factories are therefore highly unlikely to risk losing their main or only buyer by pursuing a dispute. What this means is that for all its attempts to be more hard law, the Accord, as with all CSR initiatives, relies on the corporation's assessment about what is good for business. If fulfilling their obligation under the Accord is good for business, they will do it; if it is not, they will not.

That said, the Accord has seen a marked improvement in factory conditions. Its 2015 Annual Report stated that '50,405 of the 97,458 total safety hazards from initial inspections had been verified or reported as repaired, representing 51 per cent of remediation completion'.[49] So it is

---

[48] Bangladesh Accord, *Dispute Resolution System as Agreed by Steering Committee 2014*, see http://bangladeshaccord.org/2014/04/dispute-resolution-process-agreed-steering-committee-10th-april-2014.

[49] Bangladesh Accord, *Annual Report 2015*, see http://bangladeshaccord.org/wp-content/uploads/Annual-Report-Bangladesh-Accord-Foundation-2015.pdf.

important to recognise the efforts of the trade unions and other stakeholders in ensuring that safety issues are pursued. However, given the legal and economic obstacles to ensuring compliance from an unwilling signatory company, this can only be achieved with those companies' willingness and their calculation that it is in their best interests to do so. Their adoption of and compliance with the Accord was driven by the supercharged business case presented by the Rana Plaza tragedy – the fire at Tazreen Fashion's factory a few months earlier provoked no such reaction.[50] Customer protests outside high-street shops made it clear that companies were facing an unprecedented commercial threat to their brand. The Bangladesh Accord 2013 provided the swift rehabilitation to brands that they needed. Confident that this has now been achieved, H&M, a key corporate actor in this initiative, felt able to boast about being instrumental in reducing poverty in Bangladesh.[51]

The Accord has a limited scope in terms of the betterment of women. It does not deal with safety issues relating to forced overtime, working while sick, working with a late-term pregnancy or working soon after giving birth. All these are employment rights issues. The Accord certainly does not extend to improved wages and job security. Women still work for extremely low wages and are frequently dismissed when they have children to avoid paying maternity payments. As Oxfam (2016) notes, 'firms are consistently using their dominant position to insist on poverty wages. Between 2001 and 2011, wages for garment workers in most of the world's 15 leading apparel-exporting countries fell in real terms.'[52]

2.6   Women's Betterment through the Law and Collective Action

While CSR soft law protections are reliant on the (self-interested or otherwise) goodwill of global corporate retailers, domestic labour law

---

[50] Organisations like the Clean Clothes Campaign have sought to keep the issue alive. See https://cleanclothes.org/news/press-releases/2015/11/18/three-years-after-tazreen-factory-fire-walmart-still-refuses-to-pay.

[51] H&M, *Annual Report 2015*, stated 'In Bangladesh, which has been an important sourcing market for H&M for many years, the export-led growth in the textile industry is said by the World Bank to be the main contributory factor to poverty having been halved in the country since 1990.'

[52] Oxfam Report, *An Economy for the 1 Per Cent*, (2016) see www.oxfam.org/sites/www.oxfam.org/files/file_attachments/bp210-economy-one-percent-tax-havens-180116-en_0.pdf.

(individual and collective) may provide ways of bettering the position of
women once they become part of the formal labour force. Such rights
have been enhanced following Rana Plaza, as Bangladesh's political elite
were under both national and international pressure to raise labour
standards and safety at work. Consequently, in 2013 Bangladesh
amended its labour laws and increased the numbers of labour and
building inspectors.[53] The 2013 reforms provided some protection for
those engaged in collective labour rights. For example, government officials are no longer obliged to send the names of union leaders to
employers at the time of registering a trade union, and workers can get
outside advice when engaging in collective bargaining.[54] However, despite these reforms, government officials continue to collude with employers at the expense of employees. Evidence from the International Labour
Rights Forum's (ILRF) study showed that factory workers viewed government administrators as 'part of the network of social relations of
intimidation and violence that hold them back when they seek to organize unions to defend their rights and protect their safety' and that
'sometimes administrators abuse the law to deny and silence workers
who stand up for their rights.'[55] In particular the Joint Directorate of
Labour (JDL), the agency empowered to register unions and file complaints in labour courts for unfair labour practices, has blocked numerous
valid applications for unions. Workers who want to set up unions must
get signatures from 30 per cent of the workforce,[56] a difficult task given
the constant threat of violence against labour activists. In addition, the
JDL has been shown to share these hard-earned signatures with employers, leading to abuse, intimidation, violence and loss of jobs for the
signatories.[57] The ILRF undertook a number of interviews and surveys
of women working in garment factories in which women testified to
violent attacks following their attempts to assert their legal rights as
workers, from employers (generally by paid thugs), male employees
and even more alarmingly, state officials and the police.[58]

---

[53] The Bangladesh Labour Law (Amendment) Bill 2013, see www.ilo.org/wcmsp5/groups/
public/—ed_protect/—protrav/—ilo_aids/documents/legaldocument/wcms_229274.pdf.
[54] Human Rights Watch, *Bangladesh: Amended Labor Law Falls Short* (July 2013), see
www.hrw.org/news/2013/07/15/bangladesh-amended-labor-law-falls-short.
[55] International Labor Rights Forum (ILRF), *Our Voices, Our Safety. Bangladeshi Garment
Workers Speak Out* (December 2015), see http://laborrights.org/sites/default/files/publica
tions/Our%20Voices%2C%20Our%20Safety%20Online_1.pdf, p. 31.
[56] Since the 2013 reforms, this is only 10 per cent for public-sector workers.
[57] ILRF, *Our Voices, Our Safety.*   [58] Ibid.

Aleya Akter, who had worked for Lufa Garments since she was nine years old, told how she was badly beaten up on three separate occasions, once while management and the police looked on.[59] Extreme violence was directed at her solely because she wanted to form a labour union in her workplace. Eventually, her employers capitulated, and she is now the General Secretary of the Bangladesh Garment and Industrial Workers' Federation. From child labourer, to abused woman, to general secretary in a union she fought to have established is an empowering and inspiring journey for all exploited and abused workers.

However, it remains a common experience for women that the abuse and subordination they experience in the domestic sphere is reproduced in the public sphere of work. Their wages are too low to be empowering ($68 per month minimum wage). The ILRF study showed that in most cases women are obliged to hand their wages to husbands who exercised total control over finances.[60] In the workplace women are insulted and forced to meet impossible deadlines and work long hours without breaks. They are beaten and sexually harassed. Those women who voice their discontent with their working conditions by organising unions, like Aleya, become targets of repression. Women testified that 'Factory owners use their networks of political, financial, and social relations that extend from the factory to workers' communities to develop their retaliatory capacity against workers who seek to organize and form unions.'[61]

These networks of oppression against women – which include, as noted, politicians and state officials – reflect the generally integrated nature of Bangladesh's business and political elite. Like most developing countries (including, for example, England in the nineteenth century) there is a high degree of integration of these groups. At least 10 per cent of seats in parliament are held by factory owners or their close families, and the social connections go much further. This is again a gendered hierarchy. Of the 350 members of parliament, only 72 are women. It is mainly men that are both members of parliament and factory owners.[62]

Women seeking to exercise their legal rights to organise collectively in the workforce and to enforce their collective labour rights have felt the

---

[59] Ibid, p. 11.   [60] Ibid, p. 39. 79 per cent of a sample of 100 women interviewed.
[61] Ibid, p. 21.
[62] List of members of parliament in Bangladesh, see www.parliament.gov.bd/index .php/en/mps/members-of-parliament/current-mp-s/list-of-10th-parliament-members- english.

full impact of the Polanyian double-movement.[63] Their experience is
little different when women have sought to enforce their *individual*
labour rights. For women, the formal rights of the law are often overridden by cultural norms of patriarchy which do not consider them to be
rightful claimants of universal rights. For example, the law provides that
a woman should receive eight weeks of maternity pay calculated
according to her usual pay and paid in cash.[64] It further provides that
if an employer dismisses a woman employee in the period six months
before her delivery or eight weeks after, without sufficient cause, she will
not be deprived of any maternity benefit to which she would have
become entitled.[65] However, it is most women's experience that they
are removed from their position when they leave to have their baby and
then re-employed on new, lower grade contracts. Very few women
receive maternity pay and those that do only receive a portion of what
they are entitled.[66] The law also provides that no adult worker shall
ordinarily be required or allowed to work in an establishment for more
than eight hours in any day,[67] but she can work an extra two hours of
overtime at double pay.[68] However, it is widely reported that garment
workers routinely work twelve hours a day, seven days a week. The law
also provides that no woman shall, without her consent, work in an
establishment between the hours of 10.00 PM and 6.00 AM.[69] But
factories operate twenty-four hours a day, and women have little choice
but to give their consent,[70] even though the late hours they are obliged to
work makes them more vulnerable to physical and sexual attacks when
leaving the workplace to go home. The Bangladesh Labour Act provides
for compulsory rest and food breaks,[71] but women cannot enforce this

[63] Polanyi, 'The Great Transformation'.
[64] The Bangladesh Labour Act 2006, Section 46 and 48 respectively.   [65] Ibid, Section 50.
[66] J. Burke, 'Bangladesh garment workers suffer poor conditions two years after reform vows' (April 2015) *The Guardian*, see www.theguardian.com/world/2015/apr/22/gar ment-workers-in-bangladesh-still-suffering-two-years-after-factory-collapse.
[67] The Bangladesh Labour Act 2006, Section 100.   [68] Ibid, Section 108.
[69] Ibid, Section 109.
[70] War on Want states that women 'are forced to work 14–16 hours a day, seven days a week, with some workers finishing at 3am only to start again the same morning at 7.30am. On top of this, workers face unsafe, cramped and hazardous conditions which often lead to work injuries and factory fires.' See www.waronwant.org/sweatshops-bangla desh.
[71] The Bangladesh Labour Act 2006, Section 101.

and often employers deprive workers of breaks as a punishment. Female child workers experience the same disregard for their legal rights.[72] The strongly entrenched cultural subordination and repression of women and girls subverts the written law. There is a great deal of cultural resistance to women, qua workers, becoming juridical persons and rights bearers. In this, the legal norms of market exchange conflict with the cultural norms of female subordination.

This is not to say that the law does not frequently bolster cultural norms, or that the law is good while culture is bad. Nor that the law does not frequently seek to minimise workers' rights. There is much in Bangladesh's labour law which is repressive. For example, although the International Labour Organisation (ILO) recommends that only 10 per cent of employees in a workplace should be signed up to qualify for a union, Bangladesh law insists upon a prohibitive 30 per cent (since 2013, public sector workers require only 10 per cent). Trade unions may not be formed at all in export-processing zones and other service sectors. Employers have huge scope under the Labour Act to dismiss workers. They may serve formal disciplinary notice to workers for 'wilful disobedience, whether alone or in combination with others to any lawful or reasonable order of a superior'.[73] Furthermore, the 2013 amendments to the Labour Act empower the government to stop a strike if it would cause 'serious hardship to the community' or be 'prejudicial to the national interest'.[74] These terms are so wide as to cover almost any industrial action if the government so wishes. Furthermore, workers at any factory which is either a joint enterprise with foreigners or is owned by them outright are barred from striking in the first three years of the factory's establishment.[75]

International standards are traditionally seen as a way of bringing wayward states in line with internationally accepted norms. However, in Bangladesh, international standards have been formally adopted but they are rarely observed in practice. For example, Bangladesh has ratified parts of the ILO Convention, the International Covenant on Civil and Political Rights (ICCPR), the International Covenant in Economic, Social and Cultural Rights (ICESCR), the Convention on the Elimination of Discrimination Against Women (CEDAW) and the Convention of the Rights of the Child (CRC). Many of these principles have been

---

[72] Overseas Development Institute, *Child labour and Education.*
[73] The Bangladesh Labour Act 2006, Section 23 (4) (a.
[74] The Bangladesh Labor Law (Amendment) Bill 2013.   [75] Ibid.

incorporated into the law or ratified in the constitution. Specifically, ILO Conventions 29 (1930) and 105 (1957) on forced labour were ratified in 1972 and relevant ICCPR articles were ratified in 2000. However, there are many accounts of employees being locked in factories and forced to meet deadlines. Indeed, it was locked factories which resulted in workers being trapped and killed in the fire at Tazreen Fashions. The state seemed to accept this at the time; however, amendments to the Labour Act in 2013 specifically prohibiting the locking of factory exits may indicate a shift in thinking.

Non-discrimination under ILO Conventions 100 (1951) and 111 (1958) was ratified in 1998 and 1972 respectively. Equality for women under CEDAW was also ratified, so the constitution now prohibits discrimination by the state on the grounds on gender (among other criteria) and provides for maternity leave under labour law.[76] Yet in practice, sexual harassment and discrimination is endemic in factories and maternity leave, as already noted, is generally not granted. Labour law also prohibits child labour following the ratification of ILO Conventions 138 and 182 in 2001. However, in practice child labour is common in the garment industry.[77] In 1972, Bangladesh ratified ILO Conventions 87 (1948) and 98 (1949) on Freedom of Association and Collective Bargaining, and Article 176 of the Bangladesh Labour Act gives workers the right to form unions.[78] The Act prohibits unfair labour practices on the part of employers, such as dismissing a worker for joining a union.[79] However, as shown earlier, in practice employers intervene to discourage employees from forming unions.

Perhaps even more disconnected from practice is the Bangladesh constitution's provision that a worker must receive a reasonable wage and that one person may not be exploited by another (following ratification of ILO Conventions 25 and 131 on a Living Wage). Bangladesh workers are some of the lowest paid in the world; the minimum wage is set at just $68 a month for fulltime work, and working more than the

---

[76] Convention on the Elimination of All Forms of Discrimination against Women (CEDAW), *The Eighth Periodic Report of The Government of the People's Republic of Bangladesh: Submitted Under Article 18* (May 2015), see http://mowca.portal.gov.bd/sites/default/files/files/mowca.portal.gov.bd/page/762c7e6e_69ce_4979_817c_f7dbc2b561ed/8th%20Periodic%20Report-%20CEDAW.pdf.

[77] Overseas Development Institute, *Child labour and Education*.

[78] Amendment to Section 176 of Act No. 42 (Bangladesh Labour Act) of 2006.

[79] The Bangladesh Labour Act 2006, Article. 195, Unfair Labour practices on the part of the employers.

legal maximum hours is the norm.[80] Bangladesh also ratified ILO Convention 155 on Safe Working Conditions; Article 51 of the Labour Act also provides for this. In short, Bangladesh has happily ratified many of the relevant conventions to protect workers and then allowed them to be flouted with impunity.[81]

The problems inherent in law as a way of achieving social betterment have been formulated by both Marxist legal theorists and relational feminists. Marxist legal theorist Pashukanis argues that under capitalism (unlike most other social-economic systems) discriminatory law is not the primary location of inequality and exploitation.[82] Indeed, discriminatory legal practices were likely to diminish under capitalism in time as their roots lay in latent feudal practices. New economies and their cultural and moral norms evolve from old economies and their different accompanying and validating norms. The notion of a master and servant relationship, reflecting semi-feudal norms, attached to the labour contract in early industrialising Britain[83] and for a period this benefited employers. However, over time these outdated norms were compelled to give way to labour demands for greater rights and greater recompense, and the law gradually reflected the norms of non-discrimination. Likewise, in Bangladesh, the cultural norms of female subordination from the old economy will eventually give way in the face of organised female labour, once they have established sufficient political strength.

Bangladesh differs from the British experience because it already possesses an impressive raft of anti-discriminatory law. There is, however, a chasm between what the law currently claims for female workers and what is delivered in the workplace. Only women workers can bridge this chasm because only women have self-interest in doing so. In contrast, female subordination greatly enriches their immediate employers and the companies they supply. Thus, in Bangladesh, political resistance is about making the law a lived reality for women workers rather than forcing legal change per se. However, from the perspective of Marxist legal theory and relational feminists even this achievement would only

---

[80] Following ratification of ILO Convention 1 in 1972.
[81] For example an ITV documentary showed young girls of 13 being forced to work 11-hour days in foul and dangerous conditions, producing garments for British retailers. They were filmed being 'kicked, slapped and hit with a used fabric roll as well as abused with physical threats and insults'., See www.theguardian.com/world/2014/feb/06/bangladesh-garment-factories-child-labour-uk.
[82] Pashukanis, *Law and Marxism*, pp. 141–142.
[83] Fox, *Beyond Contract: Work, Power and Trust* (Faber and Faber, 1974).

perfect the commodification of labour. It would create a ceiling to worker (and female) liberation, not a floor from which greater claims can be met. For Pashukanis, the achievement of equal rights and the construction of people as individual rights holders was a necessary condition for their exploitation as workers. Legal equality was necessary for people to enter legally binding arrangements to exchange commodities – the central mechanism to deliver profit. In short, to organise economic inequality, it was necessary to have legal equality. The legal capacity to exchange enables the exchange of labour for a wage, as the capacity to labour becomes a property with exchangeable value. The market transforms labour from a social relationship (usually one of subordination) into a commodity, 'a reified form in that the products of labour are related to each other as values'.[84] The worker, as the bearer of value (her own commodified labour), acquires the 'capacity to become a legal subject and a bearer of rights'.[85] For exchange to take place, the worker must be able to exercise rights as an autonomous legal subject.

The law which guides exchange is quintessentially contract law. Exchange relations are posited on the exchange of equivalents between two equal and free individuals. It concretises the myth of equivalent exchange that underpins the relationship between labour and capital and the exchange of labour for wage. The reality of that exchange is that it is not equal, or politically neutral, but a system designed to capture value from labour. That labour is exploited in this way is obvious when observing the factories in Bangladesh. However, if workers successfully gained equal rights, or the 'living wage' (the goal of many activists), it would be progress, but it would not be the annihilation of worker exploitation. The exchange between labour and capital would still be highly unequal, as the T-shirt example makes abundantly clear. Aligning lived reality with existing labour rights, though desirable, would not annul the central exploitative relationship encompassed in the labour contract.

From a relational feminist perspective, the abstraction of value and rights from the worker is a form of alienation that is a peculiarly male construct[86] – a classic liberal construct of the abstract, autonomous, equal, self-serving individual. From this perspective, achieving legal rights for women misunderstands the problem. The problem is male bias in the dominant social systems. Addressing this involves reconstructing

---

[84] Pashukanis, *Law and Marxism*, p. 111.   [85] Ibid, p. 112.
[86] R. West, 'Economic Man and Literary Woman: One Contrast' (1988) 39 *Mercer Law Review*, 867.

systems to reflect the more socially self-defining women described by Gilligan.[87] Female liberation is not the commodification of female labour, albeit on improved terms. It is the creation of social systems that enable women to live as a multifaceted community members.

From both Marxist and feminist perspectives, the achievement of legal equality is not the end game, for this merely enables the commodification of humanity into exchangeable labour units. The possession of rights to enter binding contracts operationalises the market, and it is the market which is built on and so perpetuates economic inequality.

2.7   Conclusion

Women face huge counter forces against their attempts to achieve betterment and to claim the value which they have created in the workplace. The cultural norms of *purdah* and female subordination have exacerbated this violent abuse following the economic pressures of war and famine in the 1970s. This has continued through women's entry into the workforce from the 1980s; indeed, work has become a focus for abuse. This chapter has considered the various motivations for women entering the workplace to demonstrate that women workers do not lack agency, although they are undoubtedly exploited to extreme degrees. We have considered the latent power that women possess in the workplace, not as skilled irreplaceable workers (because of the nature of garment work), but as an important source of value to the global North. As workers at the downstream of global value chains, these women lack many of the political and legal powers of those further up the chain. However, without their work the chain would fail to profit as it does, and clothes could not be made as cheaply. This chapter has focused on the direct appropriation of value by corporations, but that is not the entire story. It should also be noted, if not discussed in detail, that citizens of the global North enjoy the benefits of a welfare state derived in part from taxes on imports from Bangladesh. In the T-shirt example, the German state imposes 19 per cent value-added tax (VAT), or nearly 0.80 euro per shirt, even more than H&M's profit per shirt. There is a great deal of dependency on the exploited women of Bangladesh, and therein lies their power. This chapter has considered the strategies for women workers to exercise that power and claim some for the huge value they create.

---

[87]   C. Gilligan, *In a Different Voice: Psychological Theory and Women's Development* (Cambridge, MA: Harvard University Press, 1982).

First we considered the potential for making upstream corporations take more responsibility for these workers. Absent a legal relationship, this falls to CSR initiatives. The willingness for corporations to take on CSR has traditionally resulted from the work of activists in highlighting exploitative corporate behaviours such as child labour or wanton destruction of the environment. Most global corporations now report on their extensive CSR practices. The chapter notes that these practices did not prompt corporate buyers from Bangladeshi factories to intervene over their hazardous working conditions. It notes the success of the Bangladesh Accord 2013 in achieving more 'hard law' concessions from corporations, but concludes that such is the power relationship between the supplier factory and the corporate retailer that the former was unlikely to be able or willing to pursue legal action. Adherence to the Accord, like all CSR initiatives, therefore depends on the corporation's calculation that it is in their best interest to do so.

Section 2.6 considered the role of national and international law as mechanisms to enable female betterment. It finds that the law provides little for women if the cultural and political environment does not allow them to enforce their legal rights. Indeed, legal rights in themselves have severe limitations when they exist in a society that rejects female betterment and equality. Thus, the primary mechanism for female betterment is political collective action to enforce existing laws and to insist on social change to protect and promote women's interests. Bangladeshi women workers are finding that collective political organisation is a difficult but essential route to betterment. There are currently around 120 registered garment trade unions, the largest being the National Garment Workers' Federation, and more are being established in factories every day. However, the rights of unions and the right to establish unions are at the will of the state which continues to be dominated by men.

The chapter also notes that full recognition of women's legal rights is not the end game. Indeed, recognition as equal legal autonomous individuals is an almost inevitable consequence of capitalism, which is based on exchange relations in the productive sphere. While legal rights do represent progress for women, this is limited to a recognition of women as owners of their own labour power. Women's political activity must go beyond that. And it must certainly go beyond what global corporations and Bangladeshi society want to give. Women are agents of their own destiny, and whether they reclaim their value as workers or shape institutions that recognise the holistic and social person, it falls to their own political activity.

3

Access to Voice

Meaningful Participation of Women in Corporate Consultations

RAGNHILD LUNNER[*]

3.1 Introduction

Companies potentially have a large economic, social and environmental impact on local societies and countries in which they invest or establish business. The UN acknowledges that 'private business activity, investment and innovation are major drivers of productivity, inclusive economic growth and job creation.'[1] However, corporate activity may also have severe negative environmental and social impacts. Even though companies are 'engines of economic production and development', according to Sjåfjell, 'the existing system of corporate regulation, governance and control does not deliver sustainable economic activity'.[2] Discussing these issues through the lens of corporate sustainability may be helpful. 'Corporate sustainability' is a wide concept of corporate action that takes into account these impacts. According to Sjåfjell, corporate sustainability is achieved

---

[*] I would like to thank Professors Beate Sjåfjell and Irene Lynch Fannon for guidance, for believing in my ideas, and for bringing me on board on this important book project. Professor Anne Hellum and Associate Professor Ingunn Ikdahl for valuable input, and for encouraging me to 'get it out there'. Thank you to the wonderful Daughters of Themis. And thank you to Adrian Farner Rogne, Sunniva Sivsdatter Hartmann and Åshild Marie Vige for reading and commenting on the draft.
[1] UN General Assembly resolution 70/1, *Transforming Our World: The 2030 Agenda for Sustainable Development*, A/RES/70/1, (25 September 2015), p. 29, see www.undocs.org/A/RES/70/1.
[2] B. Sjåfjell, 'Bridge Over Troubled Water: Corporate Law Reform for Life-Cycle Based Governance and Reporting', University of Oslo Faculty of Law Research Paper No. 2016–23, see https://ssrn.com/abstract=2874270.

when business in aggregate creates value in a manner that is (a) environmentally sustainable in that it ensures the long-term stability and resilience of the ecosystems that support human life, (b) socially sustainable in
that it facilitates the respect and promotion of human rights and of good
governance, and (c) economically sustainable in that it satisfies the economic needs necessary for stable and resilient societies.[3]

According to one estimate, 80,000 transnational enterprises as well as
'10 times as many subsidiaries and countless millions of national firms,
most of which are small and medium-sized enterprises' affect people's
lives every day.[4] This chapter will consider socio-economic and other
examples of unsustainable corporate activity with a focus on extractive
mining industries. It will consider how such activities affect women and
men in local communities in very different ways due to the different
gender roles in these communities. Efforts have been made to encourage
companies to conduct consultations with groups who may be potentially
affected by their corporate activities, through international soft law
instruments such as the *United Nations Guiding Principles on Business
and Human Rights* (UNGP).[5] However, gaining access to such consultations may be difficult for some women. In this chapter, I will use
Habermas's ideas of law and discourse to analyze these experiences and
how consultations may be conducted in a meaningful way.

Following this introduction, in Section 3.2 I will elaborate on how
women and men *are* affected differently by unsustainable corporate
activities, and I will briefly consider how they may have different access
to decision-making.

Companies operate within a complex regulatory framework consisting
of local, national and international law, social norms and politics.
The legal instruments seeking to regulate corporate behaviour are
multifaceted, fragmented, diverging and have different enforcement

---

[3] B. Sjåfjell, 'When the solution becomes the problem: the triple failure of corporate
governance codes' in J. J. du Plessis & C. K. Low (eds.), *Corporate Governance Codes for
the 21st Century* (Basel: Springer International Publishing, 2017), p. 28.

[4] UN Human Rights Council, *Report of the Special Representative of the Secretary-General
on the issue of human rights and transnational corporations and other business enterprises,
John Ruggie*, A/HRC/17/31, (21 March 2011), p. 5, see www.ohchr.org/Documents/Issues/
Business/A-HRC-17-31_AEV.pdf.

[5] The Guidelines, with accompanying and explanatory commentaries, can be read in:
United Nations, *Guiding Principles on Business and Human Rights – Implementing the
United Nations 'Protect, Respect and Remedy' Framework* (New York and Geneva: Office
of the High Commissioner for Human Rights, 2011), see www.unglobalcompact.org/
library/2. Hereinafter referred to as UNGP.

mechanisms of varying levels. In Section 3.4, I will consider the UNGP as a soft-law instrument which has been developed to mitigate unsustainable corporate behaviour. The Guiding Principles seek to ensure the protection of and respect for human rights. They represent a 'global standard of expected conduct for all business enterprises wherever they operate'.[6] More specifically, they encourage companies to conduct consultations with groups whose human rights are potentially adversely affected, cf. Principle 18b. We know that industrial mining, and other industrial activity, may cause both direct and indirect gendered effects (see Section 3.2.1). Therefore, it is even more important to be aware of, and disclose, gender issues when dealing with fundamental human rights. The purpose of this chapter is to examine some potential obstacles and opportunities that lie within the operationalisation of UNGP Principle 18b. This will be done through a socio-legal analysis of the UNGP as a soft-law instrument in the light of social anthropological research and perspectives of legal philosophy.

The UNGP principle on consultation can be read in the light of Habermas's writings about what constitutes meaningful dialogue within a society. Therefore, Habermas's approach to communication, rational discourse, legitimate argumentation and decision-making will be presented in Section 3.3.

Section 3.4 has meaningful consultations as its main topic. A 'meaningful consultation' entails meaningful participation by relevant stakeholders. Two cases from Papua New Guinea and the mining industry, which illustrate lack of meaningful consultation, are presented in Section 3.4.1, followed by a discussion of the content of Principle 18b in Section 3.4.2. Here, I will discuss the potential of Principle 18b to promote women as agents of change in light of the two cases and the perspectives of Habermas. Section 3.4 aims to show that awareness of potential obstacles to participation is essential to ensure real and meaningful participation from women in consultation processes conducted by companies. As this chapter illustrates, women may experience unequal access to decision-making processes from the local to the national level. Lack of female voices may deprive companies of information, knowledge and opinions that may be vital to ensuring corporate sustainability.

If women are not consulted and their interests not represented, they are arguably subject to a 'double discrimination', firstly because they are

---

[6] UNGP, p. 13.

not represented in local communities, and secondly because they are not included in consultations, leading to a lack of consideration of their specific interests.[7] Conversely, if women are included, the potential of gender as an agent for corporate sustainability in terms of corporate activity may be realised. In line with this, in Section 3.5 I will discuss the potential for increasing real and meaningful participation of women in consultations, while Section 3.6 concludes with reflections on how aware-ness of local power structures is vital to realise the potential within Principle 18b of the UNGP.

3.2   Unequal Voice and Participation

3.2.1   Gendered Effects of Unsustainable Corporate Activity

Research conducted by Oxfam shows that industrial mining is not gender neutral. Oxfam has identified the following issues as examples of ways in which women are especially vulnerable to industrial mining activities:

- women aren't consulted when companies negotiate access to land, compensation or benefits
- when mining damages the environment, it undermines women's ability to provide food and clean water for their families and can increase their workload
- compensation and benefits are paid to men 'on behalf of' their families, denying women access to mining's financial benefits and potentially increasing their economic dependence on men
- women can lose their traditional status in society when mining creates a cash-based economy
- a transient male work force can bring increased alcohol, sex workers and violence into a community, which can affect women's safety
- women mine workers often face discrimination, poor working condi-tions and unequal pay for equal work.[8]

The findings of Oxfam are similar to the research conducted by The North-South Institute in 2002: a decreased ability to act as environmental caretakers, loss of female traditional knowledge and decreased ability to provide food and water, as well as domestic violence and sexual

---

[7] Not in the meaning of 'intersectional', double discrimination.
[8] Oxfam, 'Impacts of Mining', see www.oxfam.org.au/what-we-do/mining/impacts-of-mining.

harassment were amongst the 'gendered impacts' of mining.[9] Oxfam also reports 'rape and sexual assault by company or state-employed security'.[10]

As caretakers, women may 'typically assume responsibility ... for their partners and children who suffer from the health impacts of coal.'[11] In some countries, women also have the main responsibility of collecting water and wood used for fuel.[12] Pollution of water and deforestation are two examples of potential consequences of mining.[13] Changes in access to water or wood due to corporate activities such as pollution or deforestation may lead to longer walks for women in search of these natural resources, and less time for social and economic activities. UN Women-Watch writes that

> as a result, women have less time to fulfil their domestic responsibilities, earn money, engage in politics or other public activities, learn to read or acquire other skills, or simply rest. Girls are sometimes kept home from school to help gather fuel, perpetuating the cycle of disempowerment.[14]

Another issue is that women may not have legal rights to or be registered as land owners, even though they manage the household and live on, or de facto own, the land.[15] This may in turn lead to them not being taken

---

[9] G. Whiteman and K. Mamen, *Meaningful Consultation and Participation in the Mining Sector? A Review of the Consultation and Participation of Indigenous Peoples within the International Mining Sector* (Ottawa: The North-South Institute, 2002), pp. 16–17 and 21.

[10] C. Hill, C. Madden and M. Ezpeleta, *Gender and the Extractive Industries: Putting Gender on the Corporate Agenda* (Oxfam, 2016), p. 3, see www.oxfam.org.au/what-we-do/mining/the-gendered-impacts-of-mining.

[11] K. Gomez and G. Regaignon (eds.), *Digging Deeper: The Human Rights Impacts of Coal in the Global South* (Dejusticia and Business and Human Rights Resource Centre, 2015), p. 36, see www.media.wix.com/ugd/c04a21_3e6e58c1b5804082bf31ac72699d0c53.pdf.

[12] UN WomenWatch, 'Women, Gender Equality and Climate Change' (2009) p. 3, see www.un.org/womenwatch/feature/climate_change; A. Hellum, P. Kameri-Mbote and B. van Koppen, 'The human right to water and sanitation in a legal pluralist landscape: perspectives of southern and eastern African women', in A. Hellum, P. Kameri-Mbote and B. van Koppen (eds.), *Water is Life – Women's Human Rights in National and Local Water Governance in Southern and Eastern Africa* (Harare: Weaver Press, 2015), p. 3.

[13] Gomez and Regaignon, *Digging Deeper*, p. 31 and 34; G. D. Peterson and M. Heemskerk, 'Deforestation and Forest Regeneration Following Small-Scale Gold mining in the Amazon: the Case of Suriname' (2001) *Environmental Conservation*, 28 (2), 117–126 at 117.

[14] UN WomenWatch, 'Women, Gender Equality and Climate Change', p. 2.

[15] K. Bhanumathi, 'The status of women affected by mining in India', in I. Macdonald and C. Rowland (eds.), *Tunnel Vision – Women, Mining and Communities* (Victoria: Oxfam, 2002), pp. 19–24 at 21, see www.oxfam.org.au/wp-content/uploads/2011/11/OAus-TunnelVisionWomenMining-1102.pdf.

into account when negotiating expropriation or resettlement deals when mines are established in a local area.[16] The Committee on the Elimination of Discrimination Against Women (CEDAW) has urged the international community to ensure 'protection of rural women from the negative consequences of acquisition of land by . . . extractive industries and megaprojects'.[17]

These sources provide several examples of gendered effects of corporate activity. Unsustainable corporate action may directly or indirectly impede on the human rights of people in local areas where they conduct business. Such impediments may, for example, be the right to safe drinking water or adequate food, the right to health and land rights.[18] Even though both genders may be affected by breaches of human rights in general, these examples show why it is important to put the 'gender glasses' on when conducting consultations with local communities.

3.2.2 Missing Voice: Lack of Voice and Obstacles to the Participation of Women

A large number of reports find that women and men have unequal access to policy- and decision-making processes, from the local to the national level.[19] CEDAW has identified that 'in many countries, [women's] specific needs are not adequately addressed in laws, national and local policies and budgets. They remain excluded from leadership and

---

[16] S. Kavilu and J. Wanzala, 'Kenyan Women Step Up Fight for Land Destined for Coal Mine', (17 January 2017) *Reuters*, see www.reuters.com/article/us-kenya-women-land rights-idUSKBN15121H.

[17] CEDAW, 'Respect Rights of Rural Women, Recognize Their Vital Role in Development and Poverty Reduction, UN Experts Urge', press release (4 March 2016), see www.ohchr.org/EN/ NewsEvents/Pages/DisplayNews.aspx?NewsID=17148&LangID=E.

[18] United Nations, *The Corporate Responsibility to Respect Human Rights: An Interpretive Guide* (Office of the High Commissioner for Human Rights, 2012), p. 13, 21, 28, 44, 53, 83 and 88, see www.ohchr.org/Documents/Publications/HR.PUB.12.2_En.pdf; Gomez and Regaignon, *Digging Deeper*, p. 21 and 27–28; Hill, Madden and Ezpeleta, *Gender and the Extractive Industries*, p. 2.

[19] See for example Oxfam, 'Impacts of Mining'; R. de Silva de Alwis, Women's Voice and Agency: The Role of Legal Institutions and Women's Movements, Women's Voice, Agency, & Participation. *Research Series 2013 no. 5* (Washington, DC: World Bank, 2014), p. 5, see http://documents.worldbank.org/curated/en/468221468154150146/ Women-s-voice-and-agency-the-role-of-legal-institutions-and-womens-movements; Also, as an illustrative example: As of 1 May 2017, only two parliaments in the world have a percentage representation of women that exceeds 50 per cent; Rwanda and Bolivia, see www.ipu.org/wmn-e/classif.htm.

decision-making positions at all levels'.[20] According to UN Women-Watch, 'women are often excluded from decision-making on access to and the use of land and resources critical to their livelihoods'.[21] The report *Digging Deeper* found that in some communities women were 'often marginalized in decision-making structures, particularly traditional ones'.[22] Exclusion of women thus may be regarded from the perspective of social dominance theory, where culturally rooted hierarchies are based on gender, age and/or ethnicity.[23] An illustrative experience from South Africa was that 'traditional societal structures ... excluded women in decision-making, with coal companies reinforcing such structures through payments to traditional male leaders'.[24]

When conducting consultations within the UNGP framework, companies must be aware that women often may not participate in, or may be restricted from, participation and leadership from the local to the global level. This may be caused by a number of factors, including 'discriminatory laws, practices, attitudes and gender stereotypes, low levels of education, lack of access to health care and the disproportionate effect of poverty on women'.[25] However, the reason for non-participation may also be practical, such as timing or availability of translators.[26]

Women's participation is covered by the UN's new Sustainable Development Goals. In *Transforming Our World: The 2030 Agenda for Sustainable Development*, it is recognized that 'women and girls must enjoy equal access to quality education, economic resources and political participation as well as equal opportunities with men and boys for employment, leadership and decision making at all levels.'[27] The lack of representation may lead to a lack of knowledge about activities violating women's human rights. This is an especially

---

[20] CEDAW, 'Respect Rights of Rural Women'.

[21] UN WomenWatch, 'Women, Gender Equality and Climate Change', p. 2.

[22] Gomez and Regaignon, *Digging Deeper*, p. 36.

[23] Hans Morten Haugen, Kampen om utviklingen – Teorier, strategier og globale utfordringer [The battle for development – Theories, strategies and global challenges] (Oslo: Cappelen Damm Akademisk, 2015), p. 128.

[24] Gomez and Regaignon, *Digging Deeper*, p. 7.

[25] UN General Assembly, *Women and Political Participation*, A/RES/66/130, (19 December 2011), p. 2, see www.undocs.org/A/RES/66/130.

[26] D. Kemp and F. Vanclay, 'Human Rights and Impact Assessment: Clarifying the Connections in practice' (2013) *Impact Assessment and Project Appraisal*, 31 (2), 86–96 at 92.

[27] UN General Assembly, *Transforming Our World*, p. 10.

important issue within the field of extractive industries, since the effects of such industrial activities may be severe.

3.3 Meaningful Voice: A Habermasian Perspective on Communication and Legitimate Decisions

The UNGP underlines companies' responsibility to respect human rights. In order to address potential and adverse human rights impacts, the Guiding Principles encourage companies to conduct *human rights due diligences* – in short, to identify and assess any actual or potential adverse human rights impact of their activities (see Section 3.4.2). Consultations with potentially affected groups, as promoted by Principle 18b, may be a part of a due diligence process. The development of soft-law instruments to ensure participation and representation in consultations can be viewed in the light of Habermas's theories of the fourth phase of legalisation. He describes a development in society where social and democratic values enhance positions and the rights of citizens, specifically targeting vulnerable groups.[28] Habermas's theory of *communicative rationality* is of relevance when analysing the guidelines in the context of the relationship between companies and people potentially affected by their actions. Although his work mainly relates to the political public sphere, his analysis of communicative action and what constitutes a *rational discourse* is relevant to the topic of consultation meetings between a company and local stakeholders.

In short, the function of a society is partly based on a functioning social integration, where dialogue between citizens is steered by a specific form of rationality.[29] Through *communicative action*, consensus is reached based on open dialogue and arguments, which are accepted by the other participants in the dialogue. But the arguments must be based on certain criteria, for them to be considered valid.[30] It is through this rational discourse that the best arguments and acceptable actions may be made. As Habermas points out,

> What is convincing is what we can accept as rational. Rational acceptability depends on a procedure that does not shield 'our' arguments from

[28] Jørgen Dalberg-Larsen, 'Jürgen Habermas og den moderne stats krise' [Jürgen Habermas and the crisis of the modern state], in *Retssociologi – klassiske og moderne perspektiver* [*Sociology of law – classical and modern perspectives*] (Copenhagen: Hans Reitzels Forlag, 2013), p. 305.

[29] Ibid., p. 303.   [30] Ibid.

anyone or anything. The process of argumentation as such must remain open to any relevant objections and any improvements in our epistemic conditions. This kind of maximally inclusive and continuous practise [and discursive process] increases the responsive potential by which rationally accepted claims to validity prove their worth.[31]

Habermas emphasizes that it is the process that *leads to* a decision that makes the decision legitimate. He further underlines that 'if the process of argumentation is to live up to its meaning, communication in the form of rational discourse must allow, if possible, all relevant information and explanations to be brought forth and weighed so that the stance participants take can be inherently motivated solely by the revisionary power of free-floating reasons'. Further, in order for argumentation to count, it must meet 'certain pragmatic presuppositions', i.e., criteria for valid arguments and rational discourse.[32] Habermas identifies the four most important presuppositions of argumentation, in order for it to be valid and a form of rational discourse. These provide an idealistic framework for measuring the quality of consultations between companies and local societies. The first is *publicity and inclusiveness*, which entails that 'no one who could make a relevant contribution concerning a controversial validity claim must be excluded'. The second is *equal rights to engage in communication*, meaning that 'everyone must have the same opportunity to speak to the matter at hand'. Thirdly, there must be an *exclusion of deception and illusion*, meaning that 'participants must mean what they say'. The fourth states the importance of *absence of coercion*, meaning that 'communication must be free from restrictions that prevent the better argument from being raised and determining the outcome of the discussion'.[33]

Habermas claims that the process of argumentation is 'self-correcting' if it is not in line with the four presuppositions. By this he means that an 'unsatisfactory discussion spontaneously ... generates reasons for an "overdue" liberalization of the rules of procedure and discussion, for changing an insufficiently representative circle of participants [and] for expanding the agenda or improving the information base'.[34] The creation of guidelines such as the UNGP may be seen as such 'reparation'. In other words, it may be regarded as an instrumental response to the

---

[31] Jürgen Habermas, *Between Naturalism and Religion: Philosophical Essays* (Cambridge: Polity, 2008), p. 44.
[32] Ibid., p. 49.   [33] Ibid., p. 50.   [34] Ibid., p. 51.

emerging realization that the representation of all relevant voices and arguments is not sufficiently ensured. The development of procedural rights for participation in consultations may in the light of communicative rationality be viewed as a form of procedural legitimization of decisions. Consultations within the UNGP framework may ensure rational discourse (through allowing more arguments), and corporate decisions based on such rational discourse may again be regarded as more legitimate.

The four presuppositions are of course idealisations, but may nevertheless give a useful starting point for discussing the execution of consultations and human rights due diligences. Habermas's perspective can be used as a tool, both for companies and other stakeholders, to evaluate and control whether consultations are undertaken in a meaningful way. In this light, the next section presents two cases about gender issues and industrial mining in Papua New Guinea, illustrating obstacles to meaningful participation by women. Thereafter, informed by the Habermas perspective and the cases, the UNGP will be discussed with regards to how consultations can be undertaken in a meaningful way, with a gender perspective.

3.4   Ensuring Meaningful Participation in Consultations

3.4.1   Lack of Voice: Two Cases of Mining in Papua New Guinea

It may be easy to blame companies for not being sufficiently inclusive, but a report from Oxfam also shows that the lack of women representatives in consultations with extractive industry companies is not entirely due to international mining companies alone. In *Tunnel Vision – Women, Mining and Communities*, Martha Macintyre argues that it is an oversimplification of the political complexities of the projects that 'multinational companies regularly [are] portrayed as ruthless foreign boards of directors'.[35] The following presentation of the cases builds on the findings in the report.

Macintyre conducted socio-anthropological research at Papua New Guinea in the eighties where she followed the establishment of two mines, one in Misima and one in Lihir. In the time before the establishment of the mine in Misima, local consultations took place between the

---

[35] M. Macintyre, 'Women and mining projects in Papua New Guinea: problems of consultation, representation and women's rights as citizens', in *Tunnel Vision*, pp. 26–27.

representatives of the mining company and representatives from the local community. The mining industry was not new in Papua New Guinea, as there had been mining there for 100 years before the Misima case. Therefore, provisions in the Papua New Guinea Mining Act specifically addressed consultations and granted legal participatory rights to women. Women had raised concerns about food security, declining soil fertility, increased land clearance and limited job opportunities. According to Macintyre, they were overlooked, as 'the voices of the women who foresaw the problems of sustainability were drowned in the wave of enthusiasm for a role in the cash economy'.[36] During her field work, Macintyre observed that even though women were able to raise their concerns about the mining practices on a lower level, they were not consistently, or at all, included in the more formal and established fora for consultations and meetings between the relevant agents in the process.

Another case, from Lihir, illustrates a similar situation. The US company Kennecott aimed at establishing a mine in the area, and arranged meetings between consultants from the company and local village leaders. Several social impact studies (which may be regarded as a forerunner to the human rights due diligence practice that the UNGP encourages) were conducted over the course of ten years. Negotiations were arranged in order to discuss social support projects and monetary compensation. The participants were representatives of relevant stakeholders. Macintyre observed that even though a governmental official was assigned the task of controlling that all regulations intending to protect local interests were being followed up, 'the participatory process ... proved to be inequitable as women were excluded from the formal negotiation process'. Macintyre also observed that 'although they were occasionally consulted by the company's community relations department, women were not represented on the relevant committees and were forced to rely on men to represent their interest'.[37] When confronted with a proposal for including women in the relevant committees, a representative of the boards of directors had claimed that it was 'utterly contrary to Lihirian custom and that men were adequate representatives of women's interests'.[38] Macintyre links this opinion to the Papua New Guinean men's views of tradition and the customary role of

---

[36] Ibid., p. 27.   [37] Ibid., p. 27.   [38] Ibid., p. 28.

women, grounded in the women's traditional role as 'breadwinners', used in this context to describe their main responsibility of providing food.[39]

Lack of inclusion of women as described here may arguably be regarded as a form of double discrimination, or non-inclusiveness. Firstly, when women are not included in the local communities' public sphere. Secondly, and perhaps consequently, when women are not included in the 'pool of representatives' in companies' consultations. Macintyre shows us that local power structures, and the view on women in the public political sphere, may constitute an obstacle to the representation and participation of women.[40]

3.4.2   Inviting Voice: A Gender Perspective on Consultations within the UNGP Framework

Several international legal instruments, conventions and guidelines have been developed in the last decades to ensure that local communities and indigenous peoples are being heard before corporate action is taken.[41] Similarly, unsustainable corporate activity and possible human rights breaches are met with new efforts to include local community members in corporate decision-making processes. A key soft-law instrument is the UNGP, which is meant to function as a framework of expected norms for all the business enterprises[42] in the world.

According to one of the three pillars of the UNGP, the role of companies is to 'respect' human rights. This can be seen in relation to

---

[39]   Ibid., p. 27. As readers will know, the use of the term 'breadwinners' in western society is usually used to refer to men as having the earning power in a family. The different use of the term in this context is a real example of the construction of gendered roles by social expectations discussed by a number of contributors to this collection. Talbot, O'Sullivan, Russell, Lynch Fannon inter alia.

[40]   Interestingly, the Lihir mine website offers a 'Sustainability report' for 2015, showing increased efforts to take sustainability issues into account. While the report does mention consultations with stakeholders as a measure of risk management, the specific mentions of 'gender' and 'women' relates mostly to statistics and employment efforts towards women in the workforce of the mine. Newcrest Mining Limited, *Sustainability Report 2015*, pp. 9 and 37, see www.newcrest.com.au/sustainability/current-sustainability-report.

[41]   Examples given: ILO Convention 169, the United Nations Declaration on the Rights of Indigenous People (UNDRIP) article 10 and the UN REDD (Reducing Emissions from Deforestation and Forest Degradation) programme.

[42]   The terms 'business enterprises', 'companies' and 'corporations' are used interchangeably in the commentaries to the Guidelines. In this chapter, the term 'companies' will mostly be used.

the duty of states to 'protect' human rights (the first pillar). This differentiation is in accordance with fundamental principles of international law; states are subject to principles of international law, companies are not. According to Principle 11, respect 'means that they should avoid infringing on the human rights of others and should address adverse human rights impacts with which they are involved'.[43] UNGP Principle 17 sets the framework for the businesses' approach to 'respecting', and not infringing upon, human rights. The principle states that in order to 'identify, prevent, mitigate and account for how they address their adverse human rights impacts', business enterprises should carry out a human rights due diligence.[44] The process and essential components of a human rights due diligence is elaborated on in Principles 18–21. It follows from Principle 18 that

> In order to gauge human rights risks, business enterprises should identify and assess any actual or potential adverse human rights impacts within which they may be involved either through their own activities or as a result of their business relationships.[45]

Furthermore, according to Principle 18b, this process should

> involve meaningful consultation with potentially affected groups and other relevant stakeholders, as appropriate to the size of the business enterprise and the nature and context of the operation.[46]

Following from this, one aspect of human rights due diligence is to conduct consultations with potentially affected groups and other stakeholders.

The largest obstacle to meaningful consultations is of course consultations not being undertaken at all. The nature of the UNGPs makes them dependent on companies operationalising them of their own accord (or national legislators implementing them or similar formulations with binding legal provisions).[47] According to Kirsch, 'with the spread of neo-liberal political and economic policy, states have become markedly less effective as regulatory bodies, often transferring the responsibilities

---

[43] United Nations, *The Corporate Responsibility*, p. 9.   [44] UNGP, p. 17.
[45] UNGP, p. 17.   [46] UNGP, p. 19.
[47] A rare example of this is the adoption of a law in France in 2017 that imposes a duty of 'reasonable vigilance' for the largest multinational companies, to protect human rights in supply chains. See M. B. Taylor, 'Due Diligence: A Compliance Standard for Responsible European Companies' (2014) *European Company Law*, 11 (2), 86–89.

for monitoring and compliance to the corporations under review'.[48] This leaves the implementation of the responsibility to respect human rights up to the companies, through human rights due diligence, a situation which may be compared to leaving the fox to watch the geese. Even when voices of concern and objections are raised, the companies may ignore them.[49] To ensure that consultations take place, and that they are effective, remedy mechanisms and access to court for dispute settlement is of vital importance.[50] The success of the second pillar of the UN Guiding Principles must thus therefore be seen in conjunction with both the first and the third pillar of the Guiding Principles framework: the obligation of states to protect against human rights abuse and ensuring access to remedy.[51] I will not go further into the larger debate about whether voluntary measures is the better option for ensuring corporate sustainable choices through human rights due diligence, remedy and arbitration procedures. Suffice it to say, in agreement with Taylor, that there may be a gap between global soft-law norms which specify the human rights responsibilities of companies, and national norms which regulate their responsibilities.[52]

In our context, what requires further discussion in Principle 18b is the meaning of who may constitute 'potentially affected groups', and what constitutes a 'meaningful consultation'. The aforementioned challenges with gendered effects of corporate activity and lack of women's participation and representation inform the discussion.

3.4.2.1   Potentially Affected Groups

The term 'group', as in 'potentially affected groups', may be interpreted in different ways. Examples include local societies, direct employees or other workers in the supply chain.[53] The UNGP is meant to cover a wide spectrum of potentially affected stakeholders, not just indigenous peoples, women or other specified groups. This is evident by the wide scope given to the word 'potentially affected groups' in the commentary, and the reference in the UNGP to a concrete evaluation of who may be affected by human rights issues.[54] According to the UNGP Interpretive

---

[48] S. Kirsch, 'Mining and environmental human rights in Papua New Guinea', in J. G. Frynas and S. Pegg (eds.), *Transnational Corporations and Human Rights* (New York: Palgrave Macmillan, 2003), pp. 115–136 at 115.

[49] Ibid., pp. 122 and 128.   [50] Ibid., p. 127.   [51] UNGP, p. 27.

[52] Taylor, 'Due Diligence', p. 86.   [53] United Nations, *The Corporate Responsibility*, p. 37.

[54] UNGP, p. 19.

Guide for companies, who is to be regarded as 'vulnerable', and thus part of a potentially affected group, may depend on the context.[55] Therefore, women may in one context be potentially affected or vulnerable with regards to human rights issues, while they in another context may not be so. The wide potential for interpretation may lead to difficulties in clarifying who may be the target audience for the company's endeavour to consult and to disclose human rights issues.

An interpretation of the term 'groups' points towards the word not only referring to *one* local community or proficiency; it may also refer to marginalized individuals *within* larger groups, such as women, children or elders.[56] In the process of establishing the UNGP, the UN Secretary General emphasised the importance of seeing potentially marginalized groups within other groups, for example women within local communities and indigenous populations, as they may 'face a heightened risk of overall social and economic marginalization'.[57] The UNGP Interpretive Guide underlines that 'in some situations women from marginalized groups may be doubly vulnerable: because they are marginalized and because they are women'.[58]

3.4.2.2   What Is a Meaningful Consultation?

Habermas's arguments about the communicative *process* align with the underlying premise of the international guidelines for consultations with stakeholders. Informing the soft-law instruments, in preambles and commentaries, there is a notion that corporate decisions will be better and more legitimate if potentially affected groups are allowed to contribute with their concerns, perspectives and information about, for example, human rights issues. A successful consultation which fulfils the four requirements may contribute to corporate sustainability, through including relevant voices and facilitating proper and sustainable responses to human rights issues.[59]

An inadequately directed due diligence may be an obstacle to a meaningful consultation. If companies only focus on human rights issues *within* the physical boundaries of the factory or mining site, or only

---

[55] United Nations, *The Corporate Responsibility*, p. 11.   [56] Ibid., p. 11.
[57] UN Working Group on the issue of human rights and transnational corporations and other business enterprises, *Human rights and transnational corporations and other business enterprises – Note by the Secretary-General*, A/68/279 (United Nations General Assembly, 7 August 2013), p. 23, see https://documents-dds-ny.un.org/doc/UNDOC/ GEN/N13/420/90/PDF/N1342090.pdf?OpenElement.
[58] United Nations, *The Corporate Responsibility*, p. 11.   [59] Ibid., p. 47.

facilitate negotiations with employees, they may overlook human rights impacts elsewhere.[60] If women are excluded from consultations, either due to lack of awareness or local power structures, as seen in the Lihir and Misima cases, an essential element of the foundation for a rational discourse is not present. Even though men may be adequate representatives for womens interests, 'it is rare that a community has unified interest and is able to speak with one voice.'[61] The corporate actions made may not be considered valid, in Habermas's perspective, because 'all relevant information and explanations' simply are not brought forth.

Accordingly, because of failure to address the right 'potentially affected group' the consultations may risk not being sufficiently 'meaningful', from the perspective of the UNGP. This illustrates the link between UNGP Principle 17 and Principle 18b; a human rights due diligence that does not sufficiently consider women as a specific segment of the potentially affected group in cases where it is relevant may in itself constitute an obstacle to corporate sustainability. If gender-specific consequences are being analysed with emphasis on potential breaches of human rights, concerns such as those of the women in the Lihir case may be given more weight in consultations. This may in turn lead to social and environmental aspects of corporate sustainability being given more weight than the economic, in cases where this is necessary in order to ensure respect for human rights. However, including women specifically in consultations may not lead to a fully meaningful consultation. As Julia Byford points out,

> having a position on a committee does not automatically mean that you feel able to speak, to be heard, or to affect outcomes. Participation does not automatically include those who were previously left out of such processes and is only as inclusive as those who are driving the process choose it to be, or as those involved demand it to be.[62]

Understanding of the local context or local communities is crucial to ensure that the consultations are 'meaningful'. For example, the energy company Repsol hired an anthropologist with knowledge of the specific community of indigenous peoples in order to ensure that the company possessed sufficient knowledge about the community to be able to conduct valuable meetings.[63] A consultation that manages to *include* the

---

[60] Ibid., p. 41.   [61] Macintyre, 'Women and mining projects', p. 28.
[62] J. Byford, 'One day rich', in *Tunnel Vision*, p. 32.
[63] A. Egeland, 'Berørt, men blir de hørt? - Selskapers involvering av rettighetsbærere i henhold til FNs veiledende prinsipper om næringsliv og menneskerettigheter (UNGP)' ['Affected, but are they heard? Companies' involvement of rights holders in line with the

potentially affected groups and give *equal* rights to participation may not be 'meaningful' if it does not succeed in bringing forth the relevant information. It is the *quality* of the discursive procedure that is central, according to Habermas.[64] The consultation will not be free of 'coercion' if traditional or cultural power structures impede women from speaking up. Meaningfulness also implies an element of follow up. Only talking about human rights issues and potential adverse impact is not enough to ensure legitimate corporate decisions if action is not taken to prevent infringement on the rights. Therefore, Principle 19 calls for taking 'appropriate action' within the company.[65] Being aware of these potential obstacles and having a strategy to cope with them may increase the meaningfulness. I will return to this in Section 3.5.

3.4.2.3   The Issue with Representativeness

A gender perspective may be vital in order to achieve the purpose of the consultations undertaken under the UNGP. It can provide insights from voices that may not be reached through traditional patriarchal power structures or consultation procedures where one person is considered an appropriate representative for the whole group of the indigenous community. A man may convey different issues than a woman. Women may have different knowledge and experiences than men, such as the concern for food security or sexual violence. By excluding women from consultation processes, vital knowledge about consequences for women may be lost as well as their *opinions* on corporate activities.

Deciding who the companies should identify as potentially affected groups or representative individuals may not always be straightforward. For example, in a case from Colombia, Repsol identified eighteen societies of indigenous people potentially affected by their business.[66] Choosing representatives from and between these groups may prove a challenge, even without a gender perspective. When electing representatives for consultations, one must ask whether these will be fully representative for all minorities within the potentially affected group.[67] Increased inclusiveness will ideally contribute to more legitimate decisions, because of the increased dialogue and inclusion of relevant arguments.

UN Guiding Principles on Business and Human Rights (UNGP)'] Master Thesis, University of Oslo (2015), p. 28.
[64] Habermas, *Between Naturalism and Religion*, p. 51.   [65] UNGP, pp. 20–21.
[66] Egeland, 'Berørt, men blir de hørt?', p. 24.   [67] Ibid., p. 24.

Another complicating factor is that women may identify with or be discriminated against because of multiple identities or interests, as well as or instead of their gender. Examples given are age, religious or ethnic backgrounds or class.[68] Seeing women only as representative of 'women's issues' or 'indigenous issues' may lead to misinterpretations of the information they provide. Substantial differences or interests may also exist *between* groups of women or individual women.[69] Differences in class, access to resources and access to power may be as large between women as between women and men. A resourceful woman may have more status, power and ability to make herself heard than a marginalized man, or other genders. Such nuances are important when conducting human rights due diligences and deciding who should get a seat at the table. Furthermore, women may influence the processes in other ways than participating in formal consultations,[70] for example informally through their husbands or brothers.[71] Even though it may seem difficult for a company to handle such complex conditions and power structures, it is equally important to be aware of them and act upon this knowledge. Marginalized women may not be the ones who get a seat at the table. At the same time, these might be the ones who are *most* vulnerable and exposed to human rights violations.

3.5   Claiming Voice: Increasing Participation through Empowerment

In order to facilitate meaningful participation by women, companies must be aware of the power structures in the society where they plan to do business. This may ensure that the presuppositions of rational discourse can be realised, especially the equal right to engage in communication.

In Amartya Sen's words, women's movements have changed from focusing on women's *well-being*, implying a passive state of women to receive welfare, to a focus on women's *agency*, regarding women as

---

[68]   A. Hellum, J. Stewart, S. Sardar Ali and A. Tsanga, 'Paths are made by walking: introductory thoughts', in A. Hellum, J. Stewart, S. Sardar Ali and A. Tsanga (eds.), *Human Rights, Plural Legalities and Gendered Realities: Paths Are Made by Walking* (Harare: Weaver Press, 2007), p. xviii.

[69]   Hellum et al., 'The human right to water and sanitation', 26; United Nations, *The Corporate Responsibility*, p. 45.

[70]   Kemp and Vanclay, 'Human Rights and Impact Assessment', p. 92.

[71]   Macintyre, 'Women and mining projects', p. 28.

'active agents of change: the dynamic promoters of social transform-
ations that can alter the lives of *both* women and men'.[72] How, then, can
one realise the potential of women as agents for corporate sustainability?
A broad body of reports and literature suggests action on a number of
levels.

Oxfam suggests conducting a 'gender impact assessment'.[73] This can
be done as part of the human rights due diligence. They underline the
importance of understanding context, 'including the differences between
women's and men's access to and control of resources' and 'the influencing roles of state, market and community institutions and how they
may perpetuate gender inequality'. They also propose developing a
'gender risk awareness strategy' and undertaking 'community based
gender audits or reviews'.[74] These suggestions show that in order to fulfil
the four presuppositions of legitimate argumentation and give room for
meaningful consultations, the framework for rational dialogue must be
put into place by companies understanding the context in which the
dialogue takes place.

Macintyre claims, based on her field work in Papua New Guinea, that
the 'best opportunity for women to get around the bargaining table is
during the initial negotiation phase, when mining companies are most
susceptible to local demands'.[75] Companies may be reluctant to include
women in consultations because they may risk offending custom, or
affecting perceptions of themselves and their role within the community
(i.e., reputation).[76] Macintyre encourages pressure on governments to
protect the rights of its citizens, as 'mining companies should not be
allowed to take on the role of the State by setting out the rights and
responsibilities of citizens in decision-making processes'.[77] Ideally, being
aware of participatory and informational rights and being able to realise
them will support empowerment, because 'having a right' and being able
to access it may not be the same thing.[78] Kemp and Vanclay warn against
conducting consultations on human rights issues in jurisdictions where
discussing human rights is forbidden or inhibited because of political

---

[72] A. Sen, *Development as Freedom* (Oxford: Oxford University Press, 2001), p. 189.
[73] M. Scaife (ed.), *Women, communities and mining: The gender impacts of mining and the
role of gender impact assessment* (Oxfam, 2009), p. 4,, see https://policy-practice.oxfam
.org.uk/publications/women-communities-and-mining-the-gender-impacts-of-mining-
and-the-role-of-gende-293093.
[74] Scaife, *Women, communities and mining*, pp. 4–5.
[75] Macintyre, 'Women and mining projects', p. 28.   [76] Ibid., p. 28.   [77] Ibid., p. 28.
[78] Hellum et al., 'Human rights, plural legalities and gendered realities', p. xxi.

context, and where individuals or groups could face persecution because of it. They underline that '[human rights] assessment teams must be vigilant about ensuring that individuals and groups are not put at risk by virtue of human rights assessment itself'.[79]

A report by Norwegian civil society organizations presents a number of case studies and strategies to ensure, amongst several goals, increased participation by women. The report builds on civil society efforts to 'mainstream gender',[80] but the findings may nevertheless be relevant for companies aiming to ensure participation. The report addresses the need to 'change discriminatory institutional structures and legalisation' through mainstreaming gender in projects and empowering women to claim their rights.[81] Several organizations promote political civil society training and education on women's and human rights as a means of ensuring increased participation of women, thus also increasing the *publicity and inclusiveness*.[82] Companies may or may not meet a fully mature civil society in societies where they are present. Presuming not all women in a local community can be invited to consultations, but nevertheless should be given the opportunity to voice their opinions, a strong civil society provides for a group of allies that may help convey the specific gender issues at stake. Arguably it is disproportional and beyond the UNGP responsibility to 'respect' human rights to expect companies to help build or strengthen a civil society in connection with the corporate activities. Nonetheless, the UNGP framework constitutes a point of departure. It certainly does not prevent companies from taking even further action, especially if it can contribute to consultations being truly meaningful. Inclusive projects conducted by the World Bank, PwC and Dell have allegedly sought to enhance women's participation in consultation processes, in recognition that women's empowerment and participation may benefit the companies as well.[83]

---

[79] Kemp and Vanclay, 'Human rights and impact assessment', p. 92.

[80] Understood as how the organizations through activities and programs work with the topic of gender equality, by focusing on women issues and empowerment.

[81] C. Wiik and L. Begby (eds.), *Promoting Gender Equality and Women's Empowerment Internationally. The Norwegian Civil Society Experience* (The Gender Network, 2012), p. 6.

[82] Ibid., pp. 8, 14 and 18.

[83] United Nations Global Compact, *Making the connections: Women, Corporate Sustainability and Sustainable Development*, (29 February 2012), p. 2, see www.unglobalcompact.org/library/3331.

The Norwegian Church Aid (NCA) underlines that gender equality should be a policy commitment of the organization with managers accountable for providing resources, budgets, staff and time. They encourage employment of gender advisory staff and use of sex disaggregated data for projects.[84] Consultations may thus be based on such data as a starting point for discussions, and may be a valuable addition to the personal stories and opinions of women. Women and men may, for example, have different priorities on implementation of sanitary systems in a local area.[85] Being aware that potential stakeholders may be illiterate, and mitigating this through adapting the consultations accordingly, may contribute to consultations being more public and inclusive, as well as fulfilling the requirement of *the equal right to engage in communication.*[86]

Ensuring that projects that work with empowerment bring men on board, to ensure anchoring of the efforts with both genders, is also noted as an important strategy.[87] Cooperative for Assistance and Relief Everywhere (CARE) underlines in relation to the engagement of men and boys, the importance of recognizing that 'men are also constrained and controlled by the dominant gender norms'.[88]

The holistic approach that these sources take supports the argument that in order to conduct 'meaningful consultations' with 'potentially affected groups' and produce a valuable human rights due diligence, sensitive gender issues need to be considered. In order to deal with the issues of power structures and traditional views on women's participation in consultations, an opportunity may lie in conducting specific human rights due diligence consultations with women alone, by interviewing them separately, as representatives of their 'group within a group'.[89] Conducting gender-specific consultations in order to unveil different risks, priorities and experiences is in accordance with the UNGP commentary's recommendation to 'ensure special attention to any particular human rights impacts on individuals from groups or populations that may be at heightened risk of vulnerability or marginalization'.[90] However, one must be mindful of potential differences between women as well.

More empirical research is also needed with regards to what degree women's voices actually *are* underrepresented in local fora and

---

[84] Wiik and Begby, *Promoting Gender Equality*, p. 16.   [85] Ibid., p. 16.   [86] Ibid., p. 10.
[87] Ibid., p. 8.   [88] Ibid., pp. 8–9, see also Ch. 11.
[89] Egeland, 'Berørt, men blir de hørt?', p. 24.   [90] UNGP, p. 20.

consultations within the UNGP framework. There is potential for the UNGP leading to more sustainable corporate behaviour. But the recommendations should not be used uncritically, without undertaking a critical risk analysis through human rights due diligence about who might or might not be heard in the consultation process.

3.6   Conclusion

Unsustainable corporate activities by companies have gendered effects. Women and men may experience unequal access to corporate consultations. Lack of participation by women may not only be caused by lack of corporate will but also by local power structures, both between women and men and between women, which may impede equal participation and representation. Building on awareness of this knowledge, women's participation and access to voice may be increased. The chapter has highlighted some potential obstacles and opportunities to meaningful participation by women and shows how women's agency is affected by multifaceted factors on all levels of society, structural as well as practical. Local efforts have to be adjusted to context and conducted in combination with building a resilient civil society and putting pressure on governments to ensure that human rights are being protected.

Inspired by Habermas's approach, it is argued that increased participatory processes may lead to more legitimate decision making by companies. Even though women may be marginalized when it comes to access to decision-making processes and consultations, companies, along with other actors, have a key role to play in advancing gender equality across the workplace, in the marketplace and in the community. Being aware of the gendered effects and differences in access to voice, and acting upon a strategy to eliminate these differences, may realise women's full potential as bearers of specific knowledge and opinions. In turn, this may lead to promotion of the human rights and welfare of both genders. It may also contribute to realising the full potential of Principle 18 through meaningful consultation with potentially affected groups and to increased corporate sustainability.

Ascertaining Corporate Sustainability from 'Below'

The Case of the Ghanaian Rural Mining Communities

ADAEZE OKOYE AND EMMANUEL OSUTEYE

4.1 Introduction

This chapter examines a unique bottom-up perspective of corporate sustainability in context. The role of corporate sustainability and corporate social responsibility (CSR) in driving for improvements in the environmental and social performance of large companies in the extractive industry has been both topical and controversial.[1] This has often involved issues of the company,[2] the environment[3] and torts,[4] amongst others. It has drawn attention to the issue of corporate legitimacy and the 'social licence to operate'.[5]

Yet these issues are often examined from a top-down perspective, that is, changes that companies can make environmentally and socially to affect communities. This chapter introduces corporate sustainability as perceived and influenced from below and utilizes the Ghanaian empirical example to focus on women at the grassroots level. The word 'below' is used in the Santos sense, which identifies subaltern cosmopolitan studies

---

[1] J. G. Frynas, *Beyond Corporate Social Responsibility: Oil Multinationals and Social Challenges* (Cambridge: Cambridge University Press, 2009).

[2] C. Villiers, 'Corporate law, corporate power and corporate social responsibility' in N. Boeger, R. Murray and C. Villiers, *Perspectives on Corporate Social Responsibility* (Cheltenham: Edward Elgar, 2008) p. 85–112; and P. Ireland, P and R. G. Pillay, 'Corporate social responsibility in a neo-liberal age' in P. Utting and J. Marques (eds.), *Corporate Social Responsibility and Regulatory Governance* (Basingstoke: Palgrave-Macmillan, 2009) p. 77–104.

[3] F. Edoho, 'Oil Transnational Corporations: Corporate Social Responsibility and Environmental Sustainability' (2008) *CSR & EM*, 15 (4), 210–222.

[4] S. Joseph, *Corporations and Transnational Human Rights Litigation* (Oxford: Hart Publishing, 2004)

[5] G. Palazzo, and A. G. Scherer, 'Corporate Legitimacy as Deliberation: A Communicative Framework' (2006) 66 *Journal of Business Ethics*, 71–88.

of global concepts.[6] It highlights fresh research about the environmental challenges in the extractive industry in Ghana and considers the responses from women in rural communities. These are responses which challenge preconceived and accepted social roles, especially those of gender. It considers the potential of this spontaneous non-institutionalized dimension of the local environmental movement in Ghana, to contribute a rethink of the discourse in this area of corporate sustainability.

Definitions of corporate sustainability and CSR are contested.[7] Nevertheless, these terminologies will be used in this chapter as a summation of various aspects of business-society relationships. The European Commission in its renewed strategy document put forward a broad definition of CSR as 'the responsibility of enterprises for their impacts on society'.[8] CSR defined in this way suggests that businesses move towards a triple bottom-line of 'people, planet and profits'.[9] Sustainability is also concerned with the social, the environmental and the economic and achieving a balance of all three.[10] It involves 'the principle of ensuring that our actions today do not limit the range of economic, social and environmental options open to future generations'.[11]

Delineating exactly what the CSR role represents is the current battle-ground for its conceptual relevance to sustainability and human development. Therefore, in this chapter, the terms 'CSR' and 'corporate sustainability' will be used as an 'umbrella construct'[12] for corporate actions and responses to the economic, social and environmental aspects of society.

---

[6] B. D. S. Santos, *Towards a New Common Sense: Law, Science and Politics in the Paradigmatic Transition* (New York: Routledge, 1995).

[7] A. Okoye, 'Theorising Corporate Social Responsibility as an Essentially Contested Concept: Is a Definition Really Necessary?' (2009) *Journal of Business Ethics*, 89 (4), 613–627.

[8] European Commission, *A renewed EU strategy 2011–2014 for Corporate Social Responsibility Brussels*, COM (2011) 681 Final.

[9] J. Elkington, *Cannibals with Forks: The Triple Bottom Line of 21st Century Business* (Oxford: Capstone, 1997); M. Hopkins, *The Planetary Bargain: Corporate Social Responsibility Matters* (London: Earthscan, 2003).

[10] J. L. Caradona, *Sustainability* (Oxford University Press, 2014), p. 8.

[11] Elkington, *Cannibals with Forks*, p. 20.

[12] R. Strand, R. E. Freeman and K. Hockerts, 'Corporate Social Responsibility and Sustainability in Scandinavia: An Overview' (2015) *Journal of Business Ethics*, 127 (1), 1–15. They utilise these concepts as umbrella constructs in the sense of Hirsch & Levin. See P. M. Hirsch and D. Z. Levin, 'Umbrella Advocates versus Validity Police: A Life-Cycle Model' (1999) *Organization Science*, 10(2), 199–212.

The importance of the role of corporate action is seen in the UN Sustainable Development Goals and the emphasis on a crucial role for the private sector.[13] Furthermore, for developing countries there is a vital link between CSR and sustainable development. The link can be demonstrated in the drive for investment and economic sustainability while recognising the tensions which this may have with environmental and social sustainability as well. The tensions which exist within corporate sustainability and CSR objectives are symptomatic of newer concepts driven by globalisation, where contradictory objectives often exist side by side.

Although globalisation is often defined in a linear sense, Santos rightly points out that the 'process of globalisation is highly contradictory and uneven'.[14] He exemplifies this assertion in this way:

> The first I would call globalized localism. It consists of a process where a given local phenomenon is successfully globalised, be it the world-wide operation of TNCs [Trans-National Corporations], the transformation of English into lingua franca, the globalisation of American fast food or popular music or the world-wide adoption of American copy-right laws on computer software. The second form I would call localized globalism. It consists of the specific impact of transnational practices and imperatives on local conditions that are thereby destructured and restructured in order to respond to transnational imperatives. Such localised globalisms include: free trade enclaves; deforestation and massive depletion of natural resources to pay for foreign debt.[15]

Thus while CSR is an Anglo-American concept that has spread globally, it has taken on the inherent tensions of globalization, partly because as a concept it has remained fluid and difficult to pin down, but also because it is significantly driven by the business agenda.

The concept of power is central to CSR. Multinational companies have grown in power and influence and this has given rise to corresponding demand for responsibility. Yet the hegemonic power of companies can and does shape the CSR agenda. This is apparent in the attempt to justify a business case for assumption of social responsibility.[16] Nevertheless,

---

[13] M. J. D. Hopkins, *Corporate Social Responsibility and UN Sustainable Development Goals: the Role of the Private Sector* (April 2016), see www.csrfi.com/wp-content/uploads/2013/10/CSR-and-the-United-Nations-SDGs.pdf.

[14] Santos, *Towards a New Common Sense*, p. 262.   [15] Ibid, p. 263.

[16] K. C. Davis, 'The Case for and against Business Assumption of Social Responsibilities' (1973) *Academy of Management Journal*, 16(2), 312–322.

CSR still allows significant room as a site of counteractions and contention so as to give expression to other actors in the CSR relationship.

Our emphasis on corporate sustainability from below seeks to address the fact that issues in this context have often been examined from a top-down perspective. This captures corporate actions or inactions in the areas of environmental and social performance or questions corporate action or inaction in particular spheres like mining. It is also shaped by corporate policy and often disseminated by the company. This had led to assertions that companies have sought to 'de-radicalize' or 'green-wash' CSR and counter-assertions of a re-radicalization through stronger 'accountability' elements.[17]

However, studies from below identify actions and responses from within the affected communities. This is 'a key part of our bottom-up approach'.[18] This will involve 'amplifying' the voices of the affected persons as part of subaltern cosmopolitan studies of global concepts. Through this, one can reflect on the capability of communities. That is, what they can do or have done as well as the limitations of their actions.

The interplay between communities' demands for social responsibility, companies' assumption of social responsibility and the drive for sustainability can play out in a legal environment that is seen either as detrimental, enabling or passive. This contextual examination permits an exploration of this interplay through the case study of the Dumasi women.[19] The chapter asserts that this contribution from below is a vital aspect, if CSR is to aim for holistic sustainability. It will also consider the responses and changes in the environmental consciousness of women from within the Dumasi mining community as expressions of corporate sustainability. The assertion of this chapter is that actions and responses from within the community are an integral and interesting element of corporate sustainability. These actions and responses play a key role in the contextualisation of CSR and in the broadening of its agenda. This offers huge potential for such communities to contribute to the CSR agenda and to shape it in novel, sustainable ways.

---

[17] R. Shamir, 'Corporate social responsibility: A case of hegemony and counter-hegemony' in B. D. Santos and C. A. Rodriguez-Garavito (eds.), *Law and Globalisation from below: Towards a Cosmopolitan Legality* (Cambridge: Cambridge University Press, 2005), pp. 92–117.

[18] Santos and Rodriguez-Garavito, *Law and Globalisation from below.*

[19] One of the authors, Osuteye conducted fieldwork and interviews in the area in 2012.

This chapter will examine the context of Dumasi and gold mining (Section 4.2), then analyse the flash-point between the mining industry in this case and the women. That flash-point is water (Section 4.3). The chapter thereafter examines the results of this interaction in context as a case for ascertaining corporate sustainability from below (Section 4.5). The conclusion reflects on the potential of grassroots responses challenging the African CSR status quo in four main ways (Section 4.6).

4.2 Dumasi as the Local Context for Gold Mining Activity

4.2.1 The Local Community: Geography and People

The Prestea-Huni Valley district of the Western Region of Ghana is about 335 km from the capital, Accra, and houses some of Ghana's most popular mining towns, including the Prestea, Bogoso and Tarkwa towns. In between these relatively larger industrial towns are several smaller communities and villages, one of which, Dumasi, is the focus of this study.

This area of the district is covered by gold- and diamond-bearing rocks that are known in West African geological parlance as the 'Birimian and Tarkwaian' rocks that are also predominantly found in other West African countries such as Cote D'Ivoire, Burkina Faso, Mali, Niger, Guinea, Senegal and Liberia. According to Wright et al,[20] the 'Birimian' and 'Tarkwaian' rocks are metamorphic rock formations found in West Africa that usually occur in close association with each other, with the latter being more known to contain gold deposits.

Interestingly, the nomenclature of these West African rocks originates from the Birim region and the Tarkwa town in Ghana, as these were the first areas in West Africa to have the rocks thoroughly studied and classified. This indicates the significance of the Prestea-Huni Valley district to the mining industry in Ghana and the wider West Africa region, not only in terms of actual mining explorations but also for the study and understanding of precious mineral deposits in West Africa.

---

[20] J. B. Wright, D. A Hastings, W. B. Jones and H. R. Williams, *Geology and Mineral Resources of West Africa* (London: George Allen and Unwin, 1985), p. 10.

Ghana was known as the Gold Coast until independence in 1957, and Botchway[21] stresses that this was a name descriptive of its resources and importance.

The district has several active mines scattered through it, some of which are in very close proximity to villages and populated communities. Collectively it has the highest concentration of mines in any single district on the continent, most of which is owned by the largest corporations in the mining industry.[22] It also lies in the part of the country that receives the highest amount of rainfall annually and has vestiges of the ever-dwindling tropical rain forests in Ghana. The soil profile is well drained, and the arable land makes it conducive for the cultivation of cash crops such as cocoa and oil palm that the residents of the local communities often engage in. Operations of mineral exploration, particularly in large surface mining concessions, therefore interfere with the farming and livelihood activities of the residents of the local communities. There has been a shift from traditional labour-intensive underground mine shafts to modern open-cast mines.[23] However, this has involved a move towards heap leaching and carbon in leaching processes.[24] The use of cyanide in the heap leaching technique of extraction of metals from the ore is a significant feature in the Ghanaian mining industry and a major source of conflict between companies and local communities.[25]

About 35km from the town of Tarkwa is the Bogoso/Prestea mine concession owned by the Canadian company Golden Star Resources Limited (GSR). The company has a visible presence in the mineral exploration industry in other African countries such as Cote D'Ivoire, Burkina Faso, Niger and Sierra-Leone, as well as other properties in South America, notably in Brazil, Suriname and French Guiana.[26]

---

[21] F. Botchway, 'Land Ownership and Responsibility for the Mining Environment in Ghana' (1998) 38 *Natural Resources Journal*, 509–536, 510.

[22] T. Akabzaa, 'Research for advocacy on issues on mining and the environment in Africa: A case study of Tarkwa mining district in Ghana' in Third World Network Africa (ed.) *Mining, Development and Social Conflicts in Africa* (Accra: Combert Impressions, 2001).

[23] Akabzaa, 'Research for advocacy'; W. Tsuma, *Gold Mining in Ghana: Actors, Alliances and Power* (Munster: Lit Verlag, 2011).

[24] Ibid.

[25] Ibid.; M. Anane, 'Ghana: Cyanide Spill Worst Disaster Ever in West African Nation' (2001) *Corp Watch*, see www.corpwatch.org/article.php?id=744.

[26] Golden Star Resources Limited (GSR), *Corporate Information*, see www.gsr.com/corpor ate. The latest operation information for the Bogoso/Prestea area can be found via

4.2.2 The Company

GSR was established in 1992 and by the end of 2011 had produced over 2 million ounces of gold from its global operations. It operates the Bogoso/Prestea mines under the locally registered name of Golden Star Bogoso/Prestea Limited (GSBPL). The Bogoso/Prestea property is a mine complex that consists of several active gold mines and gold prospecting concessions scattered between the towns of Bogoso and Prestea. At present, the mines are all open-surface pits with the exception of one deep shaft pit in Prestea, which reaches a depth of about 1.5km. This pit is a very large one, covering an approximate distance of 85km in length. GSBPL also operates a refractory processing plant at the Bogoso end of the property.[27]

Both Bogoso and Prestea have been historically known as gold mining towns in Ghana, with the deep shaft mine in Prestea established by the colonial administration in 1873. Gold mining in Bogoso began in the early twentieth century and in both cases the mining operations were characterized by deep shaft mines. Ownership of the mines in these towns has changed hands since the government of Ghana took over from colonial rule in the 1950s and decided to privatize mining operations to cut back losses and increase profits, because of a lack of the required financial capital to invest in prospecting and modernizing operations. A series of macroeconomic reforms under a World Bank Structural Adjustment Programme in the early 1980s facilitated a massive inflow of foreign investment estimated at about $5 billion over two decades, resulting in a phenomenal growth of the mining sector.[28]

GSR entered the Ghanaian market in 1999 with the 90 per cent take-over of the Bogoso properties, and a subsequent take-over of the Prestea

www.gsr.com/operations/reserves-and-resources/default.aspx. The company Vice President (Investor Relation & Corporate Affairs) confirms that the Bogoso is no longer a mine and is on care and maintenance since 2015 – Email communication 9 June 2017.

[27] GSR, *Corporate Information*.

[28] A. Kumah, 'Sustainability and Gold Mining in the Developing World' (2006) 14 *Journal of Cleaner Production*, 315–323.

See further, B. Babut, R. Sekyi, A. Rambaud, M. Potin-Gautier, S. Tellier, W. Bannerman and C. Beinhoff, 'Improving the Environmental Management of Small-Scale Gold Mining in Ghana: A case Study of Dumasi' (2003) 11 *Journal of Cleaner Production*, 215–221.; A. Darimani, 'Mining boom and enclave economy: development impact and challenges in mining areas' in G. Hilson (ed.) *Enclaves of Wealth and Hinterlands of Discontent: Foreign Mining Companies in Africa's Development* (Accra: Third World Network-Africa, 2010).

concession in 2001. Gold production had been extensive, especially in the light of rising gold prices on the international market. In 2011, GSR produced 140,504 ounces of gold from its activities in just the Bogoso/ Prestea properties. The company discovered new gold deposits and built a 2.7 million tonne refractory plant in 2007. In between Bogoso and Prestea are several small communities and villages that are separated by large tracts of farmland, mining pits and waste rock dumps. These communities live in such close proximity to mining activities that they have been affected in diverse ways by it. From Osuteye's interaction with community residents and NGOs that work with them, the overall sentiments on the effects of mining on their livelihood and quality of life has been a negative one.[29] The impacts include the areas of economics, health, environment (pollution) and human rights.

Dumasi is one of the communities between Bogoso and Prestea which is home to the GSR Dumasi pit, a surface gold mine. The community of about 4,000 residents is located adjacent to the Bogoso plant and historically and predominantly comprised of cocoa and oil palm farmers. The effects of mining as they occur in the wider district are also evident in Dumasi, especially in recent years when there has been such growth and expansion in surface mining activities, with an open pit gold mine literally in the backyard of the community. This close proximity to mining activities has led to grave concerns and widespread discontent amongst residents regarding the operations of the present owners of the mine. It contextualises the situation that contributed to and motivated a social response, which is central to this case study.

4.3   Water at the Centre of Discontent

Dumasi, in common with other mining sites, shares economic, environmental, health and human rights abuse concerns,[30] which culminates

---

[29] E. Osuteye carried out field trips in 2011–2012.

[30] T. Akabzaa, 'Research for advocacy'; B. N. A. Aryee, B. K. Ntibery and E. Atorkui, 'Trends in Small-Scale Mining of Precious Minerals in Ghana: A perspective on Its Environmental Impact' (2003) *Journal of Cleaner Production* 11, 131–140; Kumah, 'Sustainability and gold mining in the developing world'; T. Akabzaa, J. S. Seyire and K. Afriyie *The glittering Façade: Effects of Mining Activities on Obuasi and Is Surrounding Communities* (Accra: Third Wold Network-Africa, 2007); G. Hilson, 'Child Labour in African Artisanal Mining Communities: Experiences from Northern Ghana' (2010) *Development and Change*, 40 (3), 445–473; G. M. Hilson and E. Maconachie, 'Good Governance and the

in what Sassen[31] describes as part of a wider problem of the displacement and *expulsion* of poor and marginalized groups.[32] However, in Dumasi, a particular concern centred on the quality of and access to clean water. This was because of the impact on the water sources by corporate activities of GSR. Mining companies were given absolute rights to the water resources found within their concessions, and this was sanctioned by the country's 2006 Minerals and Mining Act,[33] which puts the interests of the mining companies ahead of those of the host communities. Section 17 of the 2006 Minerals and Mining Act clearly states that

> Subject to obtaining the requisite approvals or licenses under the Water Resources Commission Act 1996 (Act 552), a holder of a mineral right may, for purposes of or ancillary to the mineral operations, obtain, divert, impound, convey and use water from a river, stream, underground reservoir or watercourse within the land the subject of the mineral right.

This provision puts a lot of power in the hands of mining companies to use water resources at their discretion, and consequently local communities suffered when water sources were polluted or destroyed. There is a requirement for mineral licence holders to obtain necessary approvals and permits from the Environmental Protection Agency (EPA) for protection of public health and environment (Section 18 of the Act), but this does not grant direct rights of remedy to the community. The central body vested with environmental protection is the Ghanaians EPA which lacks a strong record of regulatory enforcement.

4.3.1   The Community and Access to Water

Access to water and issues of water pollution were the most important concerns of the Dumasi community mainly for two reasons. The first reason stems from the traditional views that rural communities have about 'nature', which makes water pollution an essential issue, and secondly, the

Extractive Industries in Sub-Saharan Africa' (2009) *Mineral Processing and Extractive Metallurgy Review*, 30 (1), 52–100.
[31] S. Sassen, *Expulsions: Brutality and complexity in the Global Economy* (Cambridge, MA: Harvard University Press, 2014).
[32] In poor countries, complex contracts and legal provisions serve as a 'channels for expulsion' and allow the authorized removal of local communities and rural economies from their land. See Sassen, *xpulsions: Brutality and Complexity in the Global Economy*, p. 2.
[33] Ghana Minerals and Mining Act 2006 [No. 703].

practical difficulties that the absence of safe water supply has on the livelihoods and the execution of everyday tasks for the local community. To the local dwellers, water is not seen merely as another natural resource that can drive the local economy and support basic livelihood. They hold an almost sacred view of water sources as being the source of life, forming part of the very general view of humanity, conceived as an integration of nature and the universe. Out of this general belief arises the tenet that nature cannot be violated without endangering life in totality. This view of human existence being intertwined with nature has resulted in several African communities having evolved some traditional environmental ethics of care for nature.[34]

4.3.2   The Ethic of Care

Traditional communities are in awe of the beauty and power of nature, often regarding the elements of nature as having some form of mystical powers worthy of respect and often times worship.[35] This leads to the formulation of a host of practices and regulations that ensure that the integrity and rhythm of nature is preserved. It is very common to see communities name and deify rivers, lakes and streams as having spirits and souls, offering sacrifices or having shrines that commemorate festivals and ceremonies to both celebrate the good of nature and give thanks for all the benefits the natural world bestows.

In essence, this ethic of care is manifested in the various practices that ensure a sustainable use of nature. For instance, the Akan tribe, which is the largest tribe in Ghana covering most of the Western Region, including the people of Dumasi, has traditional laws regulating the exploitation of nature, enforced by the performance of rituals and ceremonies that mark periods whereby rivers, lakes and forests under constant use are temporarily closed to public access to enable species diversity in the ecosystem to re-generate and reproduce.[36] For instance there were 'days of rest' also known as 'taboo days' during which the land and rivers were expected to rest, and breaking this rule was considered a bad omen. The

---

[34] G. P. Hagan, 'Traditional laws and methods of Conservation and sustainable use of biodiversity' in D. S. Amlalo, L. D. Atsiatorme, and C. Fiati (eds.) *Biodiversity Conservation: Traditional Knowledge and Modern Concepts* (1998), Proceedings of the third UNESCO MAB Regional seminar on biosphere reserves for biodiversity and sustainable development in Anglophone Africa, Cape Coast, Ghana (9–12 March 1997).

[35] W. Maathai, *The Challenge for Africa* (London: Arrow Books, 2009).

[36] Hagan, 'Traditional laws and methods of Conservation'.

spirit of the land and the rivers, as they believed, deserved to rest on these days and not be disturbed.[37] These rest days and periods were essential for ecosystem regeneration and invoking an ethic of care and consideration in the use of the environment. Reverence for the elements of nature that were regarded as having spirits of their own was so high that on some occasions their disturbance or use would be accompanied by the offering of prayers and rituals to, as it were, appease the spirit of nature. Busia[38] captures the practice of Ashanti wood carvers as follows;

> An Ashanti craftsman will endeavour to propitiate certain trees before he cuts them. He will offer an egg, for example, to the Odum tree saying, 'I am about to cut you down and carve you; do not let me suffer harm'.

The carver offers this prayer to the spirit of the prized 'Odum' tree (*Chlorophora exelsa*) as a sign of respect and consideration before cutting even a single tree down, bearing in mind that any careless treatment of the tree could result in the sprit bringing bad fortune on him. Therefore, without recourse to the scientific basis or methods of conservation, such traditional beliefs went a long way to promote a form of cultural conservation of nature.

In addition to this strong ethic of care, the second consideration of the practical difficulties posed by water stress was also seen in the example of Dumasi, making the combination of these two factors a strong basis for subsequent collective action. This community was not connected to the main treated water pipeline network and was fully reliant on six streams that flowed through and around it for their water needs. However, the operations of the GSR led to a pollution of all six water sources, making them unfit for human consumption or use in agriculture. The six streams, namely the Apopre, Worawura, Nana Nyaboa, Akyesua, Benya and Abodwese are very small streams that on average are about 2–3m wide and just about 1m deep. And out of these six, two of them, the Apopre, which flows from the east to the west of the community, and the Worawura, which flows from north to south, served as the main sources of drinking water because of their purity and clarity, while the other streams were used mainly for agricultural purposes.

---

[37] B. A. Abayie-Boaten, 'Traditional conservation practices – Ghana's example' in *Biodiversity Conservation*.
[38] K. A. Busia, 'The Ashanti of the Gold Coast in African World Studies' in D. Forde (ed.), *The Cosmological Ideas and the Social Values of African People* (London: Oxford University Press, 1951).

4.3.3   Environmental Degradation

The tailings dam of the Bogoso mine properties was constructed very close to the source of the streams and over time cyanide leaked into the water source, causing severe pollution. This initial problem of cyanide pollution became evident in 1992, before ownership of the dam was transferred to GSR, with visible fish kills and several complaints of skin rashes after using the water for bathing. A borehole was constructed in the community to compensate for the pollution and as a means of using ground water sources instead of the open streams for human consumption. By the early 2000s, the population's demand on the single borehole had grown so much that some residents had resorted to using the polluted Apopre stream for other domestic activities.

Additionally, research conducted by some environmental NGOs that had begun an outreach programme in the community showed that the levels of iron, mercury and other heavy metals were dangerously high and a clear indication that besides the open streams, the very water table in the community had now been polluted from the years of mining activities. The situation had become so bad that the farmers also reported crop failure and low yields as a result of using the polluted streams for crop cultivation.

Frustrated by the lack of potable water, the residents appealed to GSR, the present owners of the mines, to come to their aid and provide them with safe drinking water. As a result, in 2003, two plastic water tanks were made available to the community, with GSR committing to employ the services of water tanker trucks from the bigger towns of Bogoso or Tarkwa to refill them anytime the water ran out. Within a year, the community realized that the two tanks were not enough to meet their needs. This was more apparent because of other major cyanide spillage events, such as one in October 2004, which put the residents completely off using the streams for any kind of domestic activities and made them fully reliant on the water tanks.

After some persistence and persuasions, GSR agreed to provide two additional tanks to meet the community's needs. However, over the next seven years the community struggled to meet its water needs even with the four tanks as its population grew. But more especially, they struggled because GSR was not regular and punctual in its refilling schedule, making the community go for days without water when the tanks run out. Some had no other choice than to resort to using polluted water as they agonizingly waited for the refilling of the tanks.

By mid-2011, the community began advocating for a more permanent solution to their water stress and lobbied through the local chief to get GSR to provide an extra tank as a temporary measure. Neither negotiations for a permanent water supply nor for an additional tank were making any progress, and it was difficult to get access to the mine authorities to discuss issues. Security guards operated all access points. The residents struggled to cope with limited water supplies, and living conditions had become even more difficult since the refill schedule had become increasingly irregular.

These frustrations underscored the organisation of what would be a landmark public protest by the Dumasi women to collectively register their discontent and demand prompt remedy from GSR.

4.4 Women as Pivotal: 'The March for Water'

The water crisis in Dumasi had affected every aspect of community life. However, the women in the community, who were traditionally required to keep the household running, felt the burden even more strongly. The execution of domestic chores such as cooking, washing and caring for children were made very difficult without access to safe water sources. Some resorted to a difficult commute to the neighbouring town seven miles away for borehole water, and others somehow made do with the polluted streams.

The burden of the women was not merely a physical one in terms of the increased difficulty in accessing water for domestic use; it also came with associated emotional distress, especially when the difficult decision to use the polluted water brought about an additional range of health concerns. There was an apparent rise in the incidence of skin ailments that was attributed to the use of polluted water for bathing or cooking. This created an extra chore of women having to care for the sick, especially children. Furthermore, the women interviewed shared the distress they felt when it appeared that the men of the community, who were leading the efforts of negotiating the solution for the water crisis and making no headway, vented their frustrations on their women in the home setting.

4.4.1 Female Activism

Over time, it appeared to the women that the men had almost given up on the situation and become near apathetic in accepting that water stress was now a part of community life. Through the community capacity-building outreach work of Wacam, a mining advocacy NGO, a female resident of Dumasi was encouraged and supported to stand for election as the Assembly member to represent the Dumasi electoral area on the district assembly. This effort in March 2011 was successful, and for the first time, Dumasi had a female Assembly member. Assembly members form part of the wider District Assembly. They are responsible for advocating for the needs for their communities at that level,[39] which amongst others would include some developmental projects that could be financed by the District Assembly common fund through the Local Government Ministry. However, in most cases the District Assemblies were not adequately resourced to become effective vehicles of change in the respective communities they covered.

The Assembly Woman, when interviewed, described the period between July and December 2011 as the worst for the community, when the refilling service was the least regular, and inadequate in meeting the needs of community's population. During that period, attempts by the men and opinion leaders to secure an additional tank and regular refilling service stalled. Having had enough of the struggle and distress, the women mobilized themselves to take action with the new Assembly Woman taking the lead. Information was spread by word of mouth that there was a need to take the matter into their own hands, and all the plans were kept away from the men of community. Very early in the morning of 12 December 2011, a group of more than 200 women gathered at the community centre where the tanks were situated. The women were clad in red and black coloured traditional funeral clothes to symbolize their grave displeasure, almost to say that they were in mourning. They each carried empty buckets and 'gallons'[40] as symbols of their grievance and embarked on a march to the main entrance of GSR singing and chanting songs. The women blocked the main road that led to the corporate offices on the mining site and prevented vehicles from entering, disrupting the commencement of normal operations for the day. Besides the blockade that

---

[39] District Assemblies are the pivotal administrative and developmental decision-making organs of the Local Government. They have deliberative, legislative and executive functions and are the planning authority for the districts, including key developmental planning in the areas of health, education etc., although central policy comes from the local government ministry, Friedrich-Ebert-Stiftung Ghana, *A Guide to District Assemblies in Ghana* (2010), see http://library.fes.de/pdf-files/bueros/ghana/10487.pdf.

[40] Plastic water drums with screw-caps commonly used to store water in Ghana.

prevented staff from getting to work, the entire demonstration was peaceful and did not involve the destruction of any property.

Another woman who was at the front of the march described her surprise at how the security guards at the mine premises and gate, who had been a source of intimidation, did not react violently to their protest. There was no direct clash with any security official even though they were on site and kept their ground at the gates. At about 1 PM, after a standoff of about of about five hours, a representative from GSR came to address them and invited the leadership to come into a meeting with the Corporate Affairs Manager. On the spur of the moment, five women were nominated as leaders for this meeting. This was a turning point for the women, who regarded this invitation as success in its own right. They had initially gotten the impression that GSR was ignoring their protest and hoped that they would leave after a short while. But they had resolved to stay and render the mine non-operational by blocking any vehicular traffic in or out. They were prepared to stay for as long as it would take and come every day if need be because of how frustrating the water situation was for them.

The outcome of the meeting was an agreement by the management of GSR to allow the women to discuss and document their concerns and return at a later date to subsequently present their request. Following on this opportunity, the women, through their five delegated leaders, then drafted a petition requesting a permanent solution to the water crisis, which they submitted a week later on 19 December 2011. To their delight, GSR responded and agreed to their request, promising prompt action to bring a permanent solution to the water crisis. The progress in the negotiation process and the response of GSR was considered a huge success on the scale that men and opinion leaders in the community had not been able to achieve, earning the women a considerable amount of respect.

4.4.2   Corporate Action and Inaction

As much as the promises for a permanent supply of water were good news, two months quickly passed from the time of the assurances with no tangible steps that the community could see. This led to another petition being sent on 28 February 2012 and a request for two additional tanks as a temporary measure while the company worked out the modalities of permanent water supply. This second petition received an immediate response that very day from a newly appointed Corporate Affairs

Manager of GSR, who also invited the leadership of the women for further discussions, and gave assurances that the situation would be addressed.

The additional tanks were provided as a temporary step, and plans to provide the community with safe drinking water were laid out. The company had employed the services of a geologist who confirmed that the ground water sources in the heart of the Dumasi community where the first borehole had been dug had become contaminated with unsafe levels of heavy metals. Feasibility studies in the wider area discovered an area in the outskirts of the community far away from the tailings pond where ground water was not affected by mining activities and as such was safe for human consumption. The plan was to construct a mechanized borehole that would be piped into the community to a number of taps that would be situated at vantage points. This plan appeared to sit very well with the community as the best solution.

The only challenge was that the area that was identified as a safe zone for the construction of this borehole was private land under cultivation, and as such, GSR had to enter negotiations with the owners and agree on adequate compensation before the project could commence. The company has provided an update which indicates that aspects of the project are still ongoing.[41]

4.5   CSR from Below: Potential

The case of Dumasi not only represents an example of a non-institutionalized response to environmental-related concerns, but also presents some evidence of a paradigm shift that confronts the widely accepted traditional views of rural women in Africa and is unique in a number of ways. The use of the descriptor 'non-institutionalized

---

[41] Vice President [Investor Relations & Corporate Affairs], GSR provided the following update: 'I have spoken to our corporate responsibility team at Bogoso/Prestea and they responded that in January 2012 we were contacted by some women in Dumasi who were concerned that the pumps serving their borehole and their water supply was restored. However we also discussed a longer term solution to their water supply issue and a project was designed and approved and is now in the process of being implemented. A new borehole has been drilled and installed with a submersible pump and an electrical powerline contract has been awarded. The plan is to pump water from the new borehole to the existing Dumasi water treatment system and to restore all the old water distribution lines so that water can be supplied through the existing and the planned new stand pipes for the Dumasi community. It is estimated that the project will be completed by end of July 2017.' Email correspondence 9 June 2017.

movement' in talking about the Dumasi case as part of the wider environmental movement in Ghana evokes the idea of loose, temporary collectives that aggregate for collective action and act as agents of social change.[42] The observed paradigm shift from the Dumasi case also underlines our classification of the gender dimension of the movement. In other words, the classification of a gender dimension is not solely because of the mere participation of women, but more so because of the championing of issues that directly affect women and the creation of an inadvertent shift in the traditional roles of gender.

In rural African traditional communities, women are responsible for managing the home. This responsibility involves a plethora of women-exclusive chores that often puts a disproportionate burden of work on women in the traditional home. Home management duties range from fetching and providing water, cooking, cleaning and childcare. Practically, they are also responsible for every other task that forms part of the process of meeting the house management chores. For instance, in order to cook, women are actively engaged in the process of getting fuelwood or producing charcoal, which is predominantly used in rural communities.[43]

Rural women are additionally involved in farming, often undertaken for subsistence purposes, which thereby plays a major role in the local food production process. They are engaged at all levels of this process, from the clearing of land, through planting, harvesting and more importantly, the processing of harvested crops.[44] Women are not normally paid for any of these tasks and so despite their efforts and hard work, they often do not gain any financial independence.

Most traditional African societies are dominantly patrilineal in nature and have laws that exclude women from the ownership of property, and as such, women are marginalized when it comes to access to and control

---

[42] R. Eyerman and A. Jamison, *Social Movements: A Cognitive Approach* (Cambridge: Polity Press, 1991). See further, E. Osuteye 'Environmentalism in Ghana: The rise of environmental consciousness and movements for nature protection', PhD Thesis, University of Kent (2015), see https://kar.kent.ac.uk/47995.

[43] B. K. D. Dovie, E. T. F. Witkowski and C. M. Shackleton, 'The Fuelwood Crisis in Southern Africa; Relating Fuelwood Use to Livelihoods in a Rural Village' (2004) 60 *GeoJournal*, 123–133; Programme for the Promotion of Household and Alternative Energy sources in the Sahel (PREDAS), 'Women and household energy in Sahelian countries' (2009) Issue 56 *Boiling Point*.

[44] A. J. Sigot, 'Discourse on gender and natural resource management' in A. Sigot, L. A. Thrupp and J. Green (eds.), *Towards Common Ground: Gender and Natural Resource Management in Africa* (Nairobi: African centre for Technology Studies, 1995).

of resources, and their inputs are usually not commensurate to the personal benefits that they could derive.[45] The result of this system is the creation of power relations that ascribe controlling powers to men and a subordination role for women. Women are consequently excluded from decision-making power, leadership and authority in the communities. In short, women are often silently discriminated against and exploited;[46] 'silently' in terms of the cultural acceptance that makes such discrimination go on unchallenged.

In view of this, one then understands why the water problems of Dumasi were handled solely by the male traditional opinion leaders up until the point of the demonstration. The men were culturally mandated and reasonably expected to take the lead in all the initiatives necessary for decision making. Hence, the onset of male apathy and acceptance of the crisis as their new way of life had a damaging effect on the possibility of a future solution.

The traditional roles of women provoked a female response in Dumasi in two ways. Firstly, the women saw themselves as some form of last resort since their expectations of men were not being met. The idea of considering themselves as a last resort rests comfortably with the cultural fabric that places women in the background of the responsibility of handling social affairs. In essence, the 'last resort' mentality stirred up a new sense of responsibility that hitherto had not been exercised or invoked.[47]

Secondly, by virtue of the indispensable nature of water to the fulfilment of the domestic responsibilities of women, the water crisis meant that there was a disproportionate burden that was felt by women as they were unable to perform their culturally assigned duties. Although they had endured for several years, this burden reached its tipping point when it became apparent that the men had shirked their responsibilities and become increasingly apathetic. In our opinion, this 'last resort' mentality and the disproportionate burden of domestic chores on the women

---

[45] Sigot, 'Discourse on gender'; S. Opare, 'Engaging Women in Community Decision Making in Rural Ghana: Problems and Prospects' (2005) *Development in Practice*, 15(1), 90–99.

[46] Maathai, *The Challenge for Africa*.

[47] See further, E. E Anugwum and K. N. Anugwum 'The Other Side of Civil Society Story: Women, Oil and the Niger Delta Environmental Struggle in Nigeria' (2009) 70 *GeoJournal*, 333–346 and A. Ikelegbe, 'Engendering Civil Society: Oil, Women Groups and Resource Conflicts in the Niger Delta Region of Nigeria' (2005) *Journal of Modern African Studies*, 43 (2), 241–270.

accounts for the paradigm shift that challenged the status quo and provoked the women's movement.

Yet there are several limitations, revealed in the interplay between communities and companies. Titles for minerals and the grant of licences are vested in the government (Section 1 and 2, Minerals and Mining Act 2006).[48]

4.5.1   CSR and Power Relationships

The communities are in a weak bargaining position, as they are not power holders. The lacunas in legal provisions, which currently protect power-holders, are pushing actors such as the women in Dumasi to adopt other forms of action.[49] At first glance, it again appears as if this CSR push is asking for action 'beyond' the law, but it actually has potential to give dynamism to the law. It is pushing in the direction of alternative legal dispute resolution through negotiation. It is prompting corporations like GSR to appoint corporate affairs managers which place community issues at the forefront of their agenda, broadening the sphere of director's responsibilities. This in itself is a pre-emptory move because the social aspects of company operations are no longer fully external to the corporations, although the current corporate mining laws and regulations may still focus squarely on the economic agenda. Human actors such as the Dumasi women continue to push their social concerns forward as a direct correlation of company action. The drive for responsibility here is from a subaltern position in a Gramscian sense.[50] This is because it refers to a 'group of people in a particular society suffering under hegemonic domination of a ruling elite class that denies them the basic rights of participation in the making of local history and culture as

---

[48] Section 1: Minerals Property of Republic: Every mineral in its natural state in, under or upon land in Ghana, rivers, streams, water-courses throughout the country, the exclusive economic zone and an area covered by the territorial sea or continental shelf is the property of the Republic and is vested in the President in trust for the people of Ghana. Section 2: Compulsory Acquisition of Land: Where land is required to secure the development or utilization of a mineral resource, the President may acquire the land or authorise its occupation and use under an applicable enactment for the time being in force.

[49] Even where there is a requirement for Environmental Impact assessments through the EPA, the provisions requiring environmental protection are often couched in non-prohibitive terms.

[50] See A. Gramsci, *Selections from a Prison Notebook*, ed. and trans. Q. Hoare and G. N. Smith, (London: Lawrence & Wishart, 1971).

active individuals of the same nation'.[51] The women were excluded from legal title and rights to the land as title was vested in the government; they were also initially excluded from community-company dialogue because of the role of patrilineal authority. However, the social conditions forced a response from these women which inadvertently changed their traditional roles.

CSR and sustainability must be viewed from below to understand the complex relationships, interplays and responses. For there to be a significant change in the CSR role towards environmental and social sustainability, the evolving dialogue between companies and communities (women in Dumasi) must play a more central role in setting the CSR agenda. The dialogue may choose to evolve towards negotiated legal agreements or contracts. This aspect of CSR is still embryonic and it is in the nature of counter-hegemonic struggles that such experiments may or may not succeed. Nevertheless, the dialogue should evolve if CSR is to go beyond a corporate agenda and aspire for wider sustainability.

4.6 Conclusion

This study from the perspective of the Dumasi women brings out the potential of grassroots responses challenging the African CSR status quo in four main ways.

Firstly, the potential for social change: Dumasi women demonstrate the potential to utilise the negotiated space available to them under the mining company's CSR attempts to push for wider change and to inadvertently contribute to societal change, breaking down old barriers and unintentionally realising leadership potential which can shape their community and the company relationship for the better.

Secondly, although CSR is still dominantly company-driven action, its content and responsiveness is open to contest. It often mirrors the power positions in any given society, but in this case has revealed room for a counter-position and change. The direct engagement and responses, including the appointment of internal lines of responsibility and a link to the corporate governance structure, indicate the potential such interaction can bring.

---

[51] E. Louai, 'Retracing the Concept of the Subaltern from Gramsci to Spivak: Historical Developments and New Developments' (2012) *Africa Journal of History and Culture*, 4 (1), 4–8.

Thirdly, through publicising such examples and the networks and partnership with NGOs, other communities may have potential to amplify the voice of their communities and sustain their struggles, making Dumasi more than a one-off event. This potential to concretise and scale-up the Dumasi lessons could serve as a means for communities to contribute to corporate sustainability and wider sustainability.

Finally, the role of the law in counter-hegemonic positions such as this is often grey. The relationship between law and authority can result in situations where law can coincide with the interests of power holders in society. Yet the nature of law as a tool or instrument can still leave room for its utilisation towards experimental objectives which may benefit interests of the subaltern. It is in some ways reflective of power and authority but can also be a tool for countering power. This is especially pertinent as newer forms of law and legal concepts are being developed at local, national and international levels. This creation and development of law within the broader context of globalisation creates multiple potential sites of engagement. These developments reveal the pluralistic nature of law emerging at various levels. They include non-judicial forms of dispute resolution, negotiations, reporting, monitoring, and even cultural expressions of local law. These interactions and exchanges may be able to shape the future of CSR and corporate sustainability in non-traditional legal ways.

PART II

Current Strategies for Corporate Sustainability

Company Reporting of Environmental, Social and Gender Matters

Limitations, Barriers and Changing Paradigms

GILL NORTH

5.1 Introduction

In this chapter, the author draws on her experience as a legal academic and researcher, and prior work as a financial analyst, to highlight the limitations of current reporting frameworks and the barriers faced by stakeholders[1] seeking quality information on financial and non-financial sustainability matters. The chapter examines the accepted rationales for company reporting and disclosure regimes, the minimal access rights that stakeholders of listed companies other than shareholders (such as employees, environmentalists, and women's rights advocates) have to information,[2] the political nature of company reporting policy and practice, and the highly variable quality of corporate information available in public domains.

The author contends that existing policy rationales and scholarly theories supporting corporate reporting regimes no longer reflect reasonable societal expectations because they are motivated largely by economic and commercial concerns. Company reporting rules were introduced into law to enable shareholders to make well-informed decisions, and this remains the primary purpose of reporting regimes today. While rules

---

[1] There is no accepted definition of 'stakeholders'. For the purposes of this chapter, the term applies to groups or individuals that contribute to, or are influenced or impacted by, a company's activities.

[2] In this chapter, the term 'sustainability reporting' is assumed to encompass corporate sustainability reports, corporate social responsibility reports, corporate citizenship reports and integrated reports, as these reports include similar environmental, social and governance content regardless of the report title. For an overview of the role and purpose of sustainability reporting, see Global Reporting Initiative, 'About Sustainability Reporting' at www.globalreporting.org/information/sustainability-reporting/Pages/default.aspx.

have developed across many parts of the world that encourage or require listed companies to provide information to other stakeholders, many of these are bound by financial risks and share price performance, so are primarily directed at shareholders, with the needs of other stakeholders viewed merely as secondary.

The author draws attention to corporate communication structures that provide differentiated information through private and public channels and that prioritise corporate disclosure and engagement with preferred institutional participants. She suggests these tiered reporting structures adversely impact the quality of publicly available company information. Published research on company reporting continues to highlight concerns when companies ignore sustainability and public interest factors within their reports, deal with them relatively superficially, or disclose environmental, social and gender information merely as a public relations exercise.[3] These findings reflect the compromises made during legislative processes and the open-ended nature of many reporting rules. To illustrate this, the author reviews the progress of three company reporting reforms within the European Commission (Commission), with a special focus on gender equality policy.

While the chapter acknowledges the many limitations of disclosure regulation, it calls for these regimes to be structured to work as well as possible. There are positive trends in company reporting, including an increasing number of companies providing sustainability information, and concerted efforts by a wide range of participants to improve the management and reporting of sustainability risks and impacts. Nevertheless, bolder and more sophisticated debate is needed on the purpose, structure and law of corporate reporting and engagement in modern society.

---

[3] See, e.g., K. Bondy, J. Moon and D. Matten, 'An Institution of Corporate Social Responsibility (CSR) In Multi-National Corporations (MNCs): Form and Implications' (2012) 111 *Journal of Business Ethics* 281; D. Hess, 'The Future of Sustainability Reporting as a Regulatory Mechanism' in D. Cahoy and J. Colburn eds., *Law and the Transition to Business Sustainability* (Cham: Springer International Publishing, 2014). See also L. Moerman and S. Van Der Lan, 'Social Responsibility in the Tobacco Industry: All Smoke and Mirrors?' (2005) 18 *Accounting, Auditing & Accountability Journal* 374; D. Hess, 'The Three Pillars of Corporate Social Reporting as New Governance Regulation: Disclosure, Dialogue and Development' (2008) 18 *Business Ethics Quarterly* 447, 464–465; M. Mitchell, A. Curtis and P. Davidson, 'Can Triple Bottom Line Reporting Become a Cycle for "Double Loop" Learning and Radical Change?' (2012) 25 *Accounting, Auditing & Accountability Journal* 1048.

Section 5.2 considers the current state of company reporting, with a primary focus on sustainability reporting law and practice. Section 5.3 discusses structural barriers and concerns that limit the benefits derived from corporate reporting regimes, that undermine the overall quality and usefulness of the information provided, and that minimise accountability mechanisms which prompt corporations to consider and act on environmental, social and gender matters.

Section 5.4 discusses the progress of three European company reporting reforms to highlight the political nature of corporate disclosure policy. Section 5.5 concludes.

5.2   Company Reporting Today

Listed company disclosure regulation in developed countries and in many emerging nations includes periodic reporting requirements and rules that require timely disclosure of material information on a continuous or ad hoc basis between reporting periods.[4] Most jurisdictions have reporting regimes that require listed companies to publicly release financial statements and notes at least twice a year. The annual reports generally contain the most comprehensive information on both financial and non-financial matters. Financial statements convey only a limited picture of a company's position and prospects, so commentary in the form of management discussion and analysis (MD&A) is generally required to enable shareholders and stakeholders to make well-informed decisions.[5] Outside of the United States, the nature and scope of mandated MD&A is limited, and as highlighted in Section 5.3.3, the quality of MD&A is a continuing issue in many jurisdictions.

International debates concerning corporate sustainability models and reporting have developed and intensified over the last decade, leading to a growing number of corporations that provide disclosures on environmental, social and gender matters in their annual report, in a standalone

---

[4] For more details, see G. North, *Effective Company Disclosure* (Alphen aan den Rijn: Kluwer Law International, 2015) pp. 99–169. North's book provides an overview of the periodic reporting and continuous disclosure regimes in the United States, Canada, Germany, the United Kingdom, Japan, Hong Kong, Australia and Singapore.

[5] See, e.g., European Parliament, Directive 2014/95/EU; European Commission, http://ec .europa.eu/finance/company-reporting/non-financial_reporting/index_en.htm; United States Securities Exchange Commission (SEC) Report on Review of Disclosure Requirements in Regulation S-K: (December 2013) 42, see www.sec.gov/News/PressRelease/ Detail/PressRelease/1370540530982.

sustainability report,[6] in an integrated report,[7] and/or on the company website. Indeed, sustainability reporting by large corporations is now mainstream in most parts of the world.[8] The form and quality of this sustainability reporting varies markedly, but generally includes content on: the company's activities and its impact on the environment, suppliers, employees, workplace safety, community relationships and human rights.

The employee content in the annual reports of corporations often includes one or more gender equality metrics and some commentary. The nature of this reporting is increasingly determined by legal parameters, with many countries requiring the inclusion of a gender diversity report or commentary on a company's diversity policies. These diversity reporting rules, which are discussed further in Sections 5.4.2 and 5.4.3, may be prescribed in domestic legislation, corporate governance codes, or securities exchange listing rules.

Users of corporate sustainability disclosures are interested in the substance of information provided rather than its form. Institutional investors and others are seeking information in a consistent and standardised manner that enables comparative and aggregated analysis of: a company's short, medium, and longer term goals; its risk management structure; its performance against the identified goals; 'hypothetical scenario' analysis;[9] and these classes of information across the company's supply chains (regardless of legal boundaries).[10] However, as indicated in

---

[6] Global Reporting Initiative (GRI), 'About Sustainability Reporting'.
[7] International Integrated Reporting Council, Integrated Reporting, see http://integratedreporting.org.
[8] KPMG International, *The KPMG Survey of Corporate Responsibility Reporting* (2013) 9–10, see https://home.kpmg.com/bm/en/home/insights/2016/07/the-kpmg-survey-of-corporate-responsibility-reporting-2013.html. The KPMG survey reviewed corporate responsibility (CR) reporting across the 100 largest companies in 41 countries. This report notes that most of the world's largest 250 companies report on CR, with 78% of these companies referencing the GRI guidelines. It suggests that the debate has well and truly moved on from whether companies should report on CR and the important issue now is the quality of such reporting and the best means to reach relevant audiences.
[9] 'Scenario analysis is a process for identifying and assessing a range of outcomes of future events under conditions of uncertainty. Scenarios are hypothetical constructs. ... Scenario analysis can be qualitative, relying on descriptive, written narratives, or quantitative, relying on numerical data or models, or some combination of both.' Taskforce on Climate Related Financial Disclosures, *Recommendations of the Taskforce on Climate-related Financial Disclosures* (14 December 2016) 27.
[10] See, e.g., Ceres, 'Investors Ask Fossil Fuel Companies to Assess How Business Plans Fare in Low-Carbon Future: Coalition of 70 Investors Worth $3 Trillion Call on World's

Sections 5.5.3–5.5.5, investors and others indicate that many companies fail to satisfy these benchmarks at present.

There are positive signs that engender some optimism regarding the response of corporations to sustainability challenges. Many corporate leaders acknowledge the need for businesses to operate responsibly and on a sustainable basis. For example, one study found that 93 per cent of chief executive officers interviewed across 103 countries regard sustainability as important to the future success of their businesses, and 87 per cent believe the *United Nations 2030 Agenda for Sustainable Development and the Sustainable Development Goals* provides an opportunity to rethink approaches to sustainable value creation.[11] It is likely that these executive responses reflect the mounting evidence of associations between sound corporate management and reporting of sustainability risks and enhanced commercial outcomes.[12] A growing number of institutional investors are committed to responsible investment principles and practices,[13] and are proactively using market and legal mechanisms to promote improvements in the management and reporting of

Largest Oil & Gas, Coal and Electric Power Companies to Assess Risks Under Climate Action and 'Business as Usual' Scenarios' (Oct. 24, 2013), see http://waldenassetmgmt .com/wp-content/uploads/2017/10/CarbonAssetRiskPressRelease_Final_102113.pdf; Ceres, 'Inadequate Carbon Asset Risk Disclosure by Oil and Gas Companies' (Letter to Mary White, Chair of United States Securities and Exchange Commission, April 1, 2015); Taskforce on Climate Related Financial Disclosures, *Recommendations.*

[11] United Nations Global Compact-Accenture Strategy CEO Study, see www.accenture.com/ au-en/insight-un-global-compact-ceo-study.

[12] For a summary outline of studies that examine the links between commercial outcomes and the sustainability practices and reporting of corporations, see G. North, 'Corporate Sustainability Practices and Regulation: Existing Frameworks & Best Practice Proposals' in J. du Plessis and C. K. Low (eds), *Corporate Governance Codes for the 21st Century* (Cham: Springer Publishing, 2017).

[13] See Principles for Responsible Investment (PRI), 'About the PRI', at www.unpri.org/ about. The PRI states that it 'works to understand the investment implications of environmental, social and governance (ESG) factors and to support its international network of investor signatories in incorporating these factors into their investment and ownership decisions'. It notes that it 'acts in the long-term interests of its signatories, of the financial markets and economies in which they operate and ultimately of the environment and society as a whole.' It is supported by, but is not part of, the United Nations. The PRI has 1,700 signatories from over 50 countries representing $62 trillion (USD). Signatories of PRI agree to: incorporate ESG issues into investment analysis and decision-making processes; be active owners and incorporate ESG issues into ownership policies and practices; seek appropriate disclosure on ESG issues by the entities in which they invest; promote acceptance and implementation of the Principles within the investment industry; work together to enhance their effectiveness in implementing the Principles; and report on their activities and progress towards implementing the Principles.

sustainability matters and to reallocate capital to companies with superior sustainability features.[14] To enhance their influence, these investors
are forming coalitions and mobilising their efforts on a global scale, and
these efforts are increasingly supported by well-resourced and influential
international bodies.[15] Corporate regulators across the globe acknowledge the high levels of investor activism around sustainability risk
management, and are seeking to improve the quality of environmental
and social reporting by providing standards, benchmarks, and best practice guidance.[16] Notably, there are companies that are genuinely
attempting to integrate sustainable development goals and the principles
of the United Nations Global Compact[17] within their business models,
practices, and reporting, and some of these entities are striving for upper
echelon sustainability management and reporting standards. Some corporations are also grappling with the complex challenges of inclusiveness
and diversity within corporate boards and executive ranks. The levels of
women on corporate boards and in senior management are rising across
the globe, albeit typically from a low base.[18] Interestingly, specialist
portfolios that invest in gender diverse companies have developed as a

---

[14] See, e.g., BlackRock, 'How BlackRock Investment Stewardship Engages on Climate Risk'
(March 2017), see www.blackrock.com/corporate/en-gb/literature/market-commentary/
how-blackrock-investment-stewardship-engages-on-climate-risk-march2017.pdf.

[15] There are many multinational bodies associated with corporate sustainability management and reporting, including the GRI, the International Integrated Reporting Council,
the Sustainability Accounting Standards Board, the UN Sustainable Stock Exchange
Initiative, the UN Global Compact Principles, and the UN Sustainable
Development Goals.

[16] See, e.g., Sustainable Stock Exchanges Initiative, 'Model Guidance on Reporting of
ESG Information to Investors' (2015), www.unglobalcompact.org/docs/issues_doc/Finan
cial_markets/SSE-model-guidance-on-reporting-ESG.pdf; The World Federation of
Exchanges Ltd, 'WFE Sustainability Working Group Exchange Guidance & Recommen-
dation' (October 2015), see www.world-exchanges.org/home/index.php/news/world-
exchange-news/world-exchanges-agree-enhanced-sustainability-guidance; London Stock
Exchange Plc, 'Revealing the Full Picture Your Guide To ESG Reporting - Guidance For
Issuers On The Integration Of ESG Into Investor Reporting And Communication'
(February 2017), see https://www.lseg.com/sites/default/files/content/images/Green_
Finance/ESG_Guidance_Report_LSEG.pdf

[17] United Nations Global Compact (GCP), 'The Ten Principles of the UN Global Compact'
(9 March 2017), see www.unglobalcompact.org/what-is-gc/mission/principles. The GCP
is the most prominent corporate sustainability initiative, with 9,000 companies and 4,000
non-businesses signatories.

[18] M. Lin and S. Poon, 'Gender Diverse Portfolios as New Asset Class' (Working Paper,
April 10, 2017) 3–4, see Lin, Ming-Tsung and Poon, Ser-Huang, Gender Diverse Portfolios as New Asset Class (August 9, 2017), see https://ssrn.com/abstract=2958134.

new asset class in the United States, and empirical evidence suggests this diversity improves a company's sustainability performance.[19]

In summary, while the structural barriers and concerns discussed in the next section are well entrenched, influential financial market actors are challenging traditional corporate reporting practices and standards. Consequently, the future form, content, and quality of listed company reporting are likely to depend on the capacity, influence, and fortitude of these private actors, and of policy makers and regulators.

5.3   Company Reporting: Structural Barriers and Concerns

The utility of existing corporate reporting frameworks is undermined by significant structural barriers and concerns. These include the narrowly framed rationales supporting company reporting regimes; the large asymmetries between public and private communication structures; disordered reporting rules that result in poor quality disclosure; widespread misconceptions about the role and benefits of effective disclosure law and practice within financial markets; and poor business cultures, decision making and conduct. While these barriers and concerns are discussed in turn, they are interconnected and cumulative, so achieving effective corporate sustainability reporting is challenging, even in jurisdictions with mandatory reporting rules.

5.3.1   Rationales for Existing Company Reporting and Disclosure Regimes

The notion that companies should explain themselves to the world is longstanding. Theodore Roosevelt noted in 1901 that

> great companies exist only because they are created and safeguarded by our institutions; and it is our right and our duty to see that they work in harmony with these institutions. The first requisite is knowledge, full and complete; knowledge which may be made public to the world.[20]

Since this statement was made, transparency has remained a constant theme within financial market and corporate policy debates. Disclosure policy that requires the release of information within public domains can be a powerful tool to promote good governance and conduct. When designed well, these regimes support and strengthen other governance

---

[19] Ibid.   [20] T. Roosevelt, State of the Union Message to Congress (3 December 1901).

mechanisms that ensure companies remain accountable to persons and groups most influenced and impacted by their activities.[21]

Company reporting rules have existed since the legal inception of corporations. For example, representative governance rules and reporting requirements were included in the Parishes Acts of the early nineteenth century in Europe, and these were extended and applied when the Joint Stock Companies Act of 1856 was enacted in the United Kingdom.[22] This early legislation required companies to post a full and fair balance sheet to all registered shareholders at least seven days prior to a shareholders' meeting,[23] and these rules were designed to provide shareholders with an opportunity to deliberate and engage with a company's directors and senior executives about their business decisions and financial performance.[24]

National reporting rules that apply to listed companies across developed nations today are underpinned by similar policy rationales.[25] These rationales are strongly influenced by international corporate governance and securities law principles, including those established by the Cadbury Committee, the G20 and Organisation for Economic Co-operation and Development (OECD),[26] and the International Organization of Securities Commissions (IOSCO).

The 1992 Cadbury Report is often viewed as the pioneer of the modern corporate governance movement and codes.[27] However, the foundations it establishes for company reporting are ambiguous and incomplete. The Cadbury Report suggests that company directors are primarily accountable to shareholders and reporting is a means to provide investors with

---

[21]   C. Villiers, *Corporate Reporting and Company Law* (Cambridge: Cambridge University Press, 2009), p. 233.

[22]   See, e.g., C. Cordery, 'The Annual General Meeting as an Accountability Mechanism' (Working Paper No. 23, School of Accounting and Commercial Law, Victoria University, Wellington, New Zealand, 2005), p. 11, citing Proceedings of the Business Archives Council (Great Britain), Annual Conference, 1994. See also G. North, 'Public Company Communication, Engagement and Accountability: Where Are We and Where Should We Be Heading?' (2013) 31 *Company and Securities Law Journal* 167.

[23]   Joint Stock Companies Act 1856 (UK), ss 70, 72.

[24]   Joint Stock Companies Act 1856 (UK), ss 73.

[25]   North, *Effective Company Disclosure*, pp. 111, 125, 131, 137, 143, 153.

[26]   The G20 (or Group of Twenty) is an international forum for the governments and central bank governors from 20 major economies.

[27]   *Report of the Committee on the Financial Aspects of Corporate Governance* (1 December 2012), see www.ecgi.org/codes/documents/cadbury.pdf.

information to enable them to exercise their responsibilities as owners.[28] The broader principles of corporate openness with others who have contributed to the success of the business are arguably presented as merely aspirational or voluntary principles.

The G20/OECD corporate governance principles (OECD Principles) provide the primary international standards for modern corporate governance. The preamble of the OECD Principles indicates that they are intended to support economic efficiency, sustainable growth and financial stability. It suggests that 'the corporate governance framework should recognise the rights of stakeholders established by law or through mutual agreements and encourage active co-operation between corporations and stakeholders in creating wealth, jobs, and the sustainability of financially sound enterprises.'[29] Regardless of these ambitions, Part IV of the OECD Principles merely references existing rights and protections that stakeholders may have under national law and does not add anything further.[30]

IOSCO is the primary international body that develops standards and guidance in the area of securities regulation and it represents 95 per cent of securities exchanges around the world.[31] IOSCO indicates in its materials that company reporting and disclosure regimes are for the benefit of investors. For example, its document entitled 'Objectives and Principles of Securities Regulation' notes that the primary rationales for corporate disclosure regimes are protecting investors; ensuring fair, efficient, and transparent markets; and reducing systemic risk.[32] Its guidance on periodic reporting also states that these reports facilitate investor decision making and monitoring of the markets by making it possible for investors to compare the performance of the same company over regular intervals, and by enabling investors to make useful comparisons among different companies.[33]

---

[28] Report of the Committee on the Financial Aspects of Corporate Governance (1 December 2012) [3.4].

[29] G20/OECD Principles of Corporate Governance (2015), p. 34, see www.oecd.org/corpor ate/principles-corporate-governance.htm.

[30] G20/OECD Principles of Corporate Governance, pp. 34–36.

[31] International Organization of Securities Commissions (IOSCO), 'About IOSCO', see www.iosco.org/about/?subsection=about_iosco.

[32] IOSCO, 'Objectives and Principles of Securities Regulation' (June 2010) p. 3, see www.iosco.org/library/pubdocs/pdf/IOSCOPD323.pdf.

[33] Technical Committee of the International Organization of Securities Commission, *Principles for Periodic Disclosure by Listed Entities Final Report* (February 2010), p. 4, www.iosco.org/library/pubdocs/pdf/IOSCOPD317.pdf.

Thus, the leading international bodies that set company reporting law principles and standards are predominantly focused on investor interests and economic factors. Regulation that deals with the position and rights of other stakeholders to access company information and engage in responsive dialogue with corporate executives is poorly defined or lacking, leaving the role and accountability of corporations in society in a state of limbo.

5.3.2   Public vs Private Reporting and Engagement

The stated rationales for company reporting regimes are severely undermined by disclosure and engagement frameworks that combine private and public forums and that operate across many parts of the world on a distinctly tiered basis. Private exchanges between senior company executives and select participants (who may or may not be shareholders) have occurred for many decades, and for many listed companies, are the communication channel of choice.[34] Importantly, the scale and perceived legitimacy of these private briefings continue to rise. As one director notes:

> Institutional investors have unparalleled access to management through briefings, one-on-one meetings, broker conferences, site visits and strategy days throughout the year. ... Where companies have issues, fund managers are not backward in seeking an audience with the chairman and managing director to ensure their views are heard.[35]

Company executives and the largest institutional participants are highly motivated to exchange information privately. Private communication models allow company executives to carefully control and manage the content disclosed, the disclosure recipients, and the public face of the organisation, and the invited attendees prefer privately obtained information because it improves their competitive advantages vis-à-vis other market participants. In some instances, the publicly disclosed content is a mere shadow of the information provided privately, and in extreme cases, the reported picture of the company

---

[34] E. Soltes, 'Private Interaction between Firm Management and Sell-side Analysts' (2014) 52 *Journal of Accounting Research* 245; S. Johnson, 'FSA Crackdown on Cash for CEO Access', FT.com, 4 March 2013, see www.ft.com/content/084a4bdc-84db-11e2-891d-00144feabdc0.

[35] V. Geddes, FIRST Advisers, 'Opinion Restoring the Relevance of AGMS' *Company Director* 1 August 2010.

is so idealised, insipid, or opaque that its value for readers is limited. While most countries have rules that require listed companies to publicly disclose materially price-sensitive information,[36] the private briefings can be legitimised by deeming the information exchanges during these sessions as discussion and explanation of the publicly disclosed information.[37]

5.3.3   Disordered Reporting Regimes

Company reporting regimes around the world are piecemeal and disordered, and increasingly so as incremental rules are added. This messiness stems from a diverse range of factors, including unresolved ambiguities around the purposes and audiences of specific company reports and the inclusion of sustainability matters that differ in intent, design, content, and regulatory support from prior financial reporting models.[38] Disclosure rules are presently contained within domestic legislation, corporate governance codes, and securities exchange listing rules, often without adequate regard for how these rules operate on an integrated basis.[39] Many of these rules are ambiguous in terms of required form and content, and the supporting monitoring and enforcement structures are weak. These various issues impact the overall quality of company reporting significantly, particularly of environmental, social, and gender disclosures.

The primary goals of corporate sustainability reporting are for companies to explain how they create value over the long term and their use of capital and other resources to do so. These are laudable aims, but there is a significant gulf between these aspirations and the realities of current reporting. For example, the quality of MD&A disclosures is especially important when considering the efficacy of sustainability reporting, as much of this information cannot be adequately disclosed in numerical form alone. Despite the criticality of this form of reporting, investors and

---

[36] North, *Effective Company Disclosure*, pp. 101–169
[37] See, e.g., Australian Securities and Investments Commission (ASIC), "Heard It on the Grapevine . . .." Draft ASIC Guidance and Discussion Paper. *Disclosure of Information to Investors and Compliance with Continuous Disclosure and Insider Trading Provisions* (November 1999), p. 20.
[38] North, 'Corporate Sustainability Practices and Regulation'.
[39] North, *Effective Company Disclosure*, pp. 99–169, 239–263.

regulators suggest that the usefulness of corporate MD&A is a continuing issue.[40] As one regulator notes, MD&A in reports is 'sometimes so formulaic that it communicates very little to the reader.'[41] Outside of the United States, MD&A rules are generally broad and non-prescriptive, leaving companies with considerable discretion around the scope and form of the commentary and analysis provided. Most of these MD&A obligations are limited to disclosure of matters deemed material, with materiality typically defined either explicitly or impliedly as the effect on the company's financial position and prospects or its share price.[42] Consequently, the fulcrum that many companies use to determine whether to provide MD&A, and how to disclose it, is often weighed largely by financial concerns. Yet even when narrow financial materiality thresholds are applied, there are quality concerns. A survey of institutional investors found that only 7 per cent of respondents thought companies provided sufficient information to assess financial materiality and less than 28 per cent agreed that sustainability reporting is linked to business strategy and risks.[43] Many investors and scholars also highlight the tendency for companies to provide information in a manner that paints the company in a positive light.[44] For example, companies often carefully select the type and duration of the key indicators they report on,

[40] For summary outlines of company disclosure studies, see North, *Effective Company Disclosure*, pp. 34–39, 64–67, 89–94, 188–189, 190–193, 196–197, 207–210, 213. See also Hess, 'The Three Pillars', p. 462; B. Comyns, F. Figge, T. Hahn and R. Barkemeyer, 'Sustainability Reporting: The Role of "Search", "Experience" and "Credence" Information' (2013) 37 *Accounting Forum* 231; KPMG, 'Survey of Corporate Responsibility Reporting' (2013), pp. 9–10, see https://assets.kpmg.com/content/dam/kpmg/pdf/2015/08/kpmg-survey-of-corporate-responsibility-reporting-2013.pdf.

[41] B. Gibson, 'Facilitating Capital Raising for Corporate Australia' (Speech delivered at the Corporate Finance World Australia 2009 Conference, 10 November 2009), p. 8.

[42] North, *Effective Company Disclosure*, pp. 101–169.

[43] G. Serafeim, 'Integrated Reporting and Investor Clientele' (2015) 27 *Journal of Applied Finance* 34, citing a survey by Eurosif and the Association of Chartered Certified Accountants in 2013 on 'What Do Investors Expect from Non-Financial Reporting?'

[44] J. Peloza, 'Using Corporate Social Responsibility as Insurance for Financial Performance' (2006) 48 *California Management Review* 52; Hess, 'The Three Pillars', pp. 462–463; I. Castello and J. Lozano, 'Searching for New Forms of Legitimacy through Corporate Responsibility Rhetoric' (2011) 100 *Journal of Business Ethics* 11; D. Minor and J. Morgan, 'CSR as Reputation Insurance: Primium Non Nocere' (2011) 53 *California Management Review* 40; Comyns et al, 'Sustainability Reporting', pp. 232–234, 241. See also North, *Effective Company Disclosure*, pp. 16, 189–193.

with most third-party assurance reports referencing only the reported indicators.[45] Although external assurance of reported sustainability information is increasingly provided by corporations, and audit standards are emerging, the integration and usefulness of these verification processes are questioned by many commentators.[46]

5.3.4 Company Disclosure Misconceptions

Poor quality reporting from corporations sometimes arises because of differing perspectives and understandings of the role and benefits of disclosure by company executives and their advisers, regulators, shareholders, and other stakeholders. Most regulators suggest that the primary aim of company disclosure is to provide clear, concise, and accurate information to enable sound investment decisions.[47] Similarly, most disclosure recipients indicate they want relevant, timely, complete, and useful information that is readily understandable.[48] Fortunately, there are corporate executives and representative bodies that comprehend the importance of effective communication with all stakeholders. For

---

[45] H. Jenkins and N. Yakovleva, 'Corporate Social Responsibility in the Mining Industry: Exploring Trends in Social and Environmental Disclosure' (2006) 14 *Journal of Cleaner Production* 271; P. Clarkson, Y. Li, G. Richardson and F. Vasvari, 'Revisiting the Relation Between Environmental Performance and Environmental Disclosure: An Empirical Analysis' (2008) 33 *Accounting, Organizations and Society* 303; P. Soyka and M. Bateman, 'Finding Common Ground on the Metrics That Matter' (Investor Responsibility Research Center, 2012), see https://irrcinstitute.org/wp-content/uploads/2015/09/IRRC-Metrics-that-Matter-Report_Feb-20121.pdf; K. Chotruangpraset, 'Global Reporting Initiative Indicator Selection Decisions: A Case Study' (Working Paper, Accounting Department, Schulich School of Business, York University, 2013); G. Sarfaty, 'Regulating Through Numbers: A Case Study of Corporate Sustainability Reporting' (2013) 53 *Virginia Journal of International Law* 575, 582; S. Merry, 'Measuring the World: Indicators, Human Rights, and Global Governance' (2011) *Current Anthropology* 52 (S3), 583, 584.

[46] See, e.g., A. Gurtuck and R. Hahn, 'An Empirical Assessment of Assurance Statements in Sustainability Reports: Smoke Screens or Enlightening Information?' (2016) 136 *Journal of Cleaner Production* 30; C. Villiers and J. Mähönen, 'Accounting, Auditing, and Reporting: Supporting or Obstructing the Sustainable Companies Objective?' in B. Sjåfjell and B. J. Richardson (eds.), *Company Law and Sustainability: Legal Barriers and Opportunities* (Cambridge University Press, 2015).

[47] See, e.g., C. Cox, Chairman SEC, 'Plain Language and Good Business' (Speech delivered to the Center for Plain Language Symposium, Washington DC, 12 October 2007); B. Gibson, ASIC Commissioner, 'Disclosure and the Role of ASX and ASIC' (Speech delivered at the Listed Companies Conference, 26 March 2008), p. 6.

[48] See, e.g., A. Lawrence, 'Individual Investors and Financial Disclosure' (2013) 56 *Journal of Accounting and Economics* 130.

example, Arcus, the prior chief executive of the Institute of Directors in New Zealand suggests that good governance practice requires reporting that is open and meaningful.[49] He notes that:

> '[g]ood corporate reporting supports good corporate governance and the underlying principles of accountability, transparency, probity and long-term business sustainability. Thoughtful reporting focused on performance also promotes shareholder and stakeholder confidence and trust.'[50]

Other companies (and legal advisers and scholars) view disclosure matters as largely dichotomous, with company boards and executives in one group and investors and other stakeholders in the other. While the underlying motivations of these commentators are generally left ambiguous, stated rationales to support the dichotomy model include the costs of disclosure, potential liability, and personal concerns.

Many executives (and others) publicly characterise demands from investors and stakeholders for useful information as merely a business cost and burden.[51] When the costs of disclosure regulation are discussed, the cost items are often limited to the direct costs borne by a company to produce and disseminate relevant reports or announcements. Such analysis is short-sighted and incomplete, as cost-benefit analyses should include the upfront costs and the long-term benefits derived from public disclosure frameworks. These costs and benefits should then be compared to the longer-term costs borne by companies, investors, and other stakeholders when listed companies fail to provide important information, selectively release information, or their public disclosures are incomplete, unclear, imbalanced, or late.

Some company directors and executives and their legal advisors indicate that they make disclosure decisions with a focus on limiting potential liability, with a corresponding reluctance to disclose prospective information or matters that are still uncertain.[52] Reporting of useful

---

[49] Institute of Company Directors (NZ), 'Response to NZX Review of Corporate Governance Reporting Requirements' (25 February 2016), p. 9, see www.iod.org.nz/Portals/0/Governance%20resources/IoD%20submision%20to%20NZX%20Feb%202016.pdf.

[50] Institute of Company Directors (NZ), 'Response', p. 1.

[51] European Commission, 'Report from the Commission Staff Working Paper Impact Assessment' (SEC(2011)1280 final), see www.ipex.eu/IPEXL-WEB/dossier/document/SEC20111280.do.

[52] C. Glassman, United States Securities Exchange Commissioner, 'Does the SEC Disclosure Eschew Obfuscation? Res Ipsa Loquitor' (Speech presented at the Plain Language Associations International's Fifth International Conference, Washington DC, 4 November 2005).

sustainability information requires a company to explain its future strategies, plans, and targets, and these processes involve assumptions, forecasts, and judgments. However, most jurisdictions provide companies and their directors with legal protections when disclosing forward-looking information.[53] The author is not aware of any instance where liability has attached to a listed company or its directors in jurisdictions with these protections when it had in good faith provided forward-looking information on a reasonable basis.[54]

Perhaps understandably, some corporate directors and managers are most concerned with personal interests, such as their reputation and remuneration, and minimising accountability.[55] These concerns should be considered in light of legal obligations to act in the best interests of the corporation and available evidence on the benefits of clear and comprehensive reporting. Findings from country-specific and global empirical studies of financial markets consistently highlight associations between high corporate disclosure standards, sound corporate governance and sustainability practices, and improved performance for corporations that satisfy these criteria, including superior commercial outcomes and higher levels of investor and public trust.[56] Regardless of their motivations, company directors and executives that are not aware of, or do not accept, the documented benefits of high quality reporting often show a propensity for boiler-plate public disclosures, with more substantive information provided to institutional participants privately.

It is challenging for companies to provide clear, concise, and effective sustainability disclosures. Integrating sustainability factors into business strategies and operations requires high-level skills and considerable commitment because these factors are multifarious, interconnected, involve long durations, and require forward planning and assumptions. Effective communication of the company's sustainability processes, decisions, and outcomes requires additional skills and a willingness to engage openly and fully with shareholders and other stakeholders.[57] Notwithstanding these many challenges, a company's board and executives need to clearly communicate their objectives, priorities, plans, and performance

---

[53] See, e.g., Private Securities Litigations Reform Act of 1995 (US).
[54] The author would welcome evidence to the contrary.
[55] North, *Effective Company Disclosure*, pp. 15–20.
[56] North, *Effective Company Disclosure*, pp. 34–39, 64–67, 89–94, 188–189, 190–193, 196–197, 207–210, 213. See also North, 'Corporate Sustainability Practices'.
[57] North, *Effective Company Disclosure*, pp. 216–217.

effectively for outsiders to construct a complete picture of a company and assess its sustainability structures and achievements.[58]

5.3.5   Poor Business Cultures, Decision Making, and Conduct

Sometimes low quality corporate reporting is intentionally opaque, but the author suggests that more commonly, it reflects a poor business culture; a lack of business vision, understanding, or clarity in the minds of the directors and senior managers; and/or ineffective leadership. When a company's board and senior managers are not fully cognisant of their business strategy and direction, these failings inevitably flow through to its reporting. In extreme instances, the quality of company reporting is so poor and the content so generic and vague that it is hard for readers to fully discern the core nature of the company's businesses and its goals and longer-term performance. When these companies include environmental, social, and gender disclosures in an ad hoc and disconnected fashion, the overall story and messages of the company can become even more confused, unfocused, and voluminous, especially when glossy pictures are included for marketing purposes.

There are critical connections between the motivations, skills, and quality of a company's board and executives, its business culture and modus operandi, and the content and quality of its reporting, and these require deeper consideration by business, policy makers, and scholars.

5.4   Relevant European Company Reporting Developments

This section does not seek to comprehensively discuss all law governing listed company reporting in Europe. Instead, it briefly discusses two European directives and a proposal for a third to illustrate the highly political nature of company reporting policies and related issues. The three reforms discussed are the Transparency Directive 2004/109/EC, the Non-Financial Reporting Directive 2014/95/EU, and the Gender Balance on Corporate Boards Proposal. The Transparency Directive provides the minimum periodic reporting obligations for companies listed on

---

[58] See D. Langevoort, 'Investment Analysts and the Law of Insider Trading' (1990) 76 *Virginia Law Review* 1023, 1028, 1054. See also Paul Davies et al, 'European Company Law Experts' Response to the European Commission's Green Paper "The EU Corporate Governance Framework"' (22 July 2011), p. 1, see http://ec.europa.eu/internal_market/consultations/2011/corporate-governance-framework/individual-replies/ecle_en.pdf.

regulated markets in Europe. The Non-Financial Reporting Directive requires larger listed companies to report on environmental, social, and diversity matters. The Gender Balance on Corporate Boards Proposal would require larger listed companies to establish objectives and procedures to reach a minimum level of 40 per cent female (and male) directors on their boards by 2020. However, enactment of this proposal appears to have stalled, with the European Council (Council) unable to reach agreement on its terms.

5.4.1 Transparency Directive

The Transparency Directive was adopted and implemented by the Commission in 2004[59] and includes the primary disclosure obligations that apply to listed companies trading on a regulated market in member states.[60] The Transparency Directive was reviewed in 2009,[61] leading to amendments that were enacted on 26 November 2013, with two years allowed for implementation.[62] These amendments abolished the requirement for companies to publish interim management statements or quarterly reports and extended the deadline for publishing half-yearly reports to three months after the end of the reporting period. The periodic reporting obligations for companies listed on European exchanges are therefore limited to a relatively scant half-year report and an annual report.[63] Member states are only permitted to require companies to publish additional information if this is not financially burdensome and the information is proportionate to factors influencing investment decision making.[64] This is unusual for Directives of the EU, which are

---

[59] Directive 2004/109/EC, Europa.eu, 'Transparency of Information about Issuers of Securities', see http://europa.eu/legislation_summaries/internal_market/single_market_ser vices/financial_services_transactions_in_securities/l22022_en.htm#.

[60] European Parliament Directive 2013/50/EU amending European Transparency Directive 2004/109/EC and European Commission Directive 2003/71/EC.

[61] See European Commission, Report from the Commission. See also Mazars, *Transparency Directive Assessment Report 90*, at www.mazars.co.uk/Home/News/Our-publications/Gen eral-publications/Transparency-Directive-Assessment-Report.

[62] Directive 2013/50/EU Official Journal of the European Union Volume 56, 6 November 2013, L294.

[63] For discussion on the passage of this directive and its effects, see North, *Effective Company Disclosure*, pp. 180–185.

[64] European Parliament, Directive 2013/50/EU amending 2004/109/EC and Directive 2003/71/EC, [5–6]. See also *Official Journal of the European Union* Volume 56, 6 November 2013, L294/14.

typically designed to create a 'floor' of obligations rather than a ceiling. The regulated information must be disseminated using processes that ensure the information is accessible to as wide an audience as possible, with the timing of release across Europe as close to simultaneous as possible.[65] There is no centralised public repository of listed company disclosures in Europe currently,[66] but the Amending Directive indicates that the Commission proposes to develop technical standards to enable pan-European access to regulated information.[67]

The revised Transparency Directive confirms that the primary purpose of company reporting in Europe is to enable investors to make well-informed decisions, yet it restricts the regularity and timeliness of publicly available information from listed companies. These end results highlight the considerable power of the business sector on reporting policy determinants.[68]

5.4.2   Non-Financial Reporting Directive

On 22 October 2014, the European Parliament and Council adopted the Non-Financial Reporting Directive.[69] The Non-Financial Reporting Directive required EU Member States to enact legislation by 6 December 2016 requiring larger listed companies with more than 500 employees to disclose relevant and useful information in their management report on policies, main risks, and outcomes regarding environmental matters; social and employee-related aspects; respect for human rights; anti-corruption and bribery issues; and diversity on the board of directors.

It is too early to properly assess the efficacy of this reform, but the author is cautious about its incremental effects on the quality and

[65] Directive 2004/109/EC Article 21(1); Implementation of certain provisions of Directive 2004/109/EC, Article 12(2), see http://eur-lex.europa.eu/legal-content/EN/TXT/?uri=CELEX:32007L0014.

[66] European Commission, Revised Directive on Transparency Requirements for Listed Companies (Transparency Directive) – Frequently Asked Questions, Memo/13/544 4.

[67] European Commission, COM (2011) 683 final 2011/0307(COD) Amending Directive 2004/109/EC& 2007/14/EC, 8.

[68] For discussion and critique of the review process and its recommendations, see North, *Effective Company Disclosure*, pp. 180–185; G. North, 'Listed Company Disclosure and Financial Market Transparency: Is This a Battle Worth Fighting or Merely Policy and Regulatory Mantra?' (2014) 6 *Journal of Business Law* 486.

[69] European Parliament, Directive 2014/95/EU; European Commission, see http://ec.europa.eu/finance/company-reporting/non-financial_reporting/index_en.htm.

usefulness of company reporting in Europe.[70] The Non-Financial Reporting Directive requires legislative change in Member States, but the mandated content is broadly framed and the delivery mechanisms for disclosure are discretionary.[71] For example, the Non-Financial Reporting Directive requires larger listed companies to publish a general diversity policy, or explain its omission in the corporate governance statement, but lacks supporting obligations that require companies to report on specific diversity objectives, targets, and progress. Given the highly generic and relatively undemanding nature of these obligations, the impact of this reform is likely to be muted.[72]

5.4.3 Gender Balance on Corporate Boards Proposal

Gender diversity reporting rules are sometimes used as an initial soft-policy approach to nudge companies to be more inclusive and diverse in their hiring policies, particularly when they appoint directors and senior executives. When this regulatory approach disappoints or fails, some countries consider tougher policies. For example, in late 2013, the European Parliament voted by a large majority for the introduction of the Gender Balance on Corporate Boards Proposal requiring larger listed

---

[70] See Sarfaty, 'Regulating through Numbers', pp. 599–600 for European country outlines. For discussion on the comparative regulation more broadly, see C. Williams, 'Corporate Social Responsibility and Corporate Governance' in J. Gordon and W. G. Ringe (eds.), *Oxford Handbook of Corporate Law and Governance* (Oxford: Oxford University Press, 2016).

[71] For discussion on the passing of Directive 2014/95/EU, see D. Kinderman, 'The Struggle Over the EU Non-Financial Disclosure Directive' (2015) 6 *WSI-Mitteilungen*. Kinderman suggests the final text was weakened significantly as a result of opposition from business, with Germany being the most outspoken opponent.

[72] For a deeper analysis of the EU's non-financial reporting rules, see C. Villiers and J. Mähönen, 'Article 11: Integrated Reporting or Non-Financial Reporting?', in B. Sjåfjell and A. Wiesbrock, *The Greening of European Business under EU Law* (Oxon: Routledge, 2015), pp. 274–311. For discussion of various approaches to gender balance on boards, see B. Sjåfjell, 'Gender Diversity in the Boardroom and Its Impacts: Is the Example of Norway a Way Forward?' (2014) 19 *Deakin Law Review* 25; A. Dhir, *Challenging Boardroom Homogeneity: Corporate Law, Governance, and Diversity* (Cambridge: Cambridge University Press, 2015); S. Terjesen, R. Aguilera and R. Lorenz, 'Legislating a Woman's Seat on the Board: Institutional Factors Driving Gender Quotas for Boards of Directors' (2015) 128 *Journal of Business Ethics* 233. For a summary of the European regulation around gender representation on company boards, see Frank Bold and Cass Business School, 'Corporate Governance for a Changing World: Report of a Global Roundtable Series' (2016), p. 84 fn 164, see www.purposeofcorporation.org/corporate-governance-for-a-changing-world_report.pdf.

corporations to set a quantitative objective to reach a minimum of 40 per cent female (and male) non-executive directors by 2020. The Gender Balance on Corporate Boards Directive will not, if adopted, mandate that Member States impose quotas. Instead, Member States will need to enact legislation that requires the relevant companies to establish procedures to reach the 40 per cent thresholds, with Member States able to choose the means by which this objective is implemented. The Commission announced in November 2014 that it had made progress but had not been able to reach agreement.[73] It indicated that it was confident that a compromise could be found, however at the time of writing, no further announcement had been made. The reasons why agreement within the Commission has not been forthcoming are unclear, but business resistance may be a significant concern.[74]

The three company reporting reform examples highlight the intensely political nature of reporting law and the progressive compromises that arise. These compromises commonly result in reporting rules that provide corporations with high levels of discretion around the tone and content of public disclosures and that are difficult for public supervisors to monitor and enforce. Such regimes often lack sufficient substance, specificity, and supervisory teeth to disrupt the entrenched power and information imbalances between corporations, investors, and members of society.

5.5   Conclusion

Company reporting rules have existed since the legal inception of corporations. These regimes were introduced to enable investors to monitor and assess the performance of their companies and hold company boards and senior executives to account. When structured appropriately, reporting frameworks can be a powerful tool to enable investors and other stakeholders of a company to monitor and respond to its developments and impacts (both financial and non-financial). Notably though, mere technical compliance with disclosure rules does not result in meaningful disclosures; indeed, it can result in verbiage.

---

[73] Press release from the 3357th European Council Meeting, Employment, Social Policy, Health and Consumer Affairs, 11 December 2014, see www.consilium.europa.eu/uedocs/ cms_data/docs/pressdata/en/lsa/146172.pdf.

[74] For an in-depth analysis, see Ch. 6. See also Sjåfjell, 'Gender Diversity'; Dhir, *Challenging Boardroom Homogeneity*.

The ultimate test of effective company reporting is whether the substance and form of the disclosed content matter is useful for its readers.[75] However, empirical research of corporate disclosures regularly highlights issues with the variability, quality, and usefulness of publicly available information, especially the standards of environmental, gender, and social reporting.[76] The factors contributing to these reporting quality concerns are many. The presently accepted rationales for reporting regimes are largely driven by shareholder interests and these narrowly constructed models are undermined by private communication structures. The development of reporting law is highly political and business resistance can lead to piecemeal or entangled legal frameworks that give company boards and executives considerable discretion around the form of disclosure and the disclosed content. Such loosely framed regimes are more difficult to monitor and enforce, and corporate regulators often lack the motivation and capacity to proactively supervise the legality and quality of company reporting beyond the financial statements.

The role and purpose of reporting regimes within financial markets need to be fit for modern purposes. Corporate reporting today is no longer about merely sending an occasional report to shareholders, and listed companies need to provide high-quality information on a continuing basis through non-discriminatory channels. Digital forms of communication

---

[75] The Kay Review of UK Equity Markets and Long-Term Decision Making: *Final Report* (July 2012), p. 72, see www.ecgi.org/conferences/eu_actionplan2013/documents/kay_review_final_report.pdf.

[76] Across the recognised corporate sustainability areas, management and reporting of climate-related risks appear to be the most advanced, particularly programs to reduce greenhouse gas emissions: see e.g., Corporate Knights Capital, 'Measuring Sustainability Disclosure: Ranking the World's Stock Exchanges' (October 2014), see www.corporateknights.com/reports/2017-world-stock-exchanges/; Carbon Disclosure Project, 'Out of the Starting Blocks: Tracking Progress on Corporate Climate Action' (October 2016), see www.cdp.net/en/research/global-reports/tracking-climate-progress-2016; Taskforce on Climate Related Financial Disclosures, *Recommendations of the Taskforce on Climate-related Financial Disclosures* (December 14, 2016), www.fsb-tcfd .org/publications/final-recommendations-report/; G. North, 'Climate Change Risk Mitigation, Liability and Reporting: The Temperature Is Rising for Corporations' (Working Paper, Deakin University, Jan 2018).

In contrast, the sustainability area that corporations indicate is the most challenging to address and report on is human rights. See United Nations Global Compact, Guide to Corporate Sustainability: Shaping a Sustainable Future (no pagination), see www.unglobalcompact.org/library/1151.

are now predominant, and many societal groups expect to have direct and equitable access to corporate information that is timely, specific, clear, accurate, and balanced. Consequently, there are growing calls from diverse bodies for more inclusive and effective company reporting structures and content.

The journey towards better quality disclosure of sustainability matters is continuous and evolving and there are positive developments that sustainability advocates can build on. Committed institutional investors are engaging in concerted activism to prompt corporations to comprehensively report their actions and outcomes in a manner that enables investors and others to better assess a company's risk management framework, performance, and impacts.[77] These participants contend that sustainability risks need to be proactively identified and managed by corporations because they affect a company's ability to create long-term value.[78] Efforts by these investors and others have gained considerable traction and are receiving increasing support from businesses, multilateral bodies, civic groups and supervisors. Many corporate leaders acknowledge that business models fit for modern challenges require a long horizon, an emphasis on sustainability, and communication structures that are inclusive and effective.[79] Nonetheless, further shifts in the attitudes of global leaders and decision makers concerning the role and purpose of corporations in society and the priorities afforded to the environmental, gender, and social impacts of companies will be required to raise overall reporting standards.

Women are making some strides as potential agents for change in corporate spheres, with increasing levels of female participation in decision-making forums and positions that influence business sustainability outcomes. However, as discussed in other chapters of the book, the overall capacity and influence of women in global business is still low and the barriers to entry are many. To influence business outcomes more

---

[77] North, 'Climate Change Risk Mitigation, Liability and Reporting'
[78] See, e.g., Sustainable Stock Exchanges Initiative, *2016 Report on Progress* (2016), p. 32, see www.sseinitiative.org/2016rop/; BlackRock, 'BlackRock Investment Stewardship', see www.blackrock.com/corporate/en-au/about-us/investment-stewardship.
[79] Frank Bold and Cass Business School, 'Corporate Governance for a Changing World', pp. 18, 52. Participants agreed on the importance of environmental, social and governance reporting by corporations. Further, they suggested that 'the role of corporate governance is not only to protect the corporation but to ensure that a corporation is able to create value for society at large.'

substantively, continued growth in the numbers of women in corporate board rooms and senior executive ranks, and in key roles across the finance, asset management, accounting, and public sectors, is essential. Enactment of carefully tailored and specific gender reporting rules, and subsequent robust monitoring and enforcement of these regimes, could assist with this aim.

6

'A Toad We Have to Swallow'

Perceptions and Participation of Women in Business and the Implications for Sustainability

IRENE LYNCH FANNON*

6.1 Introduction

In November 2013 the EU Parliament voted to support a Commission Directive mandating quotas for women on boards of EU listed companies.[1] The Directive proposed to mandate a target of having at least 40 per cent of women non-executive directors on the boards of listed EU companies by 2020. Gender equality has been a cornerstone of EU policy since the 1950s, when the Treaty of Rome 1957 specifically

---

* Thanks are due to the Irish Research Council for funding for this project and to my colleagues at the Daughters of Themis Workshop, held in Greece, May 2016.
[1] See text of the European Parliament decision OJ C 436 24.11.2016 p. 225–240. Draft Directive COM (2012) 614 final, Proposal for a Directive of the European Parliament and of the Council on improving the gender balance among non-executive directors of companies listed on stock exchanges and related measures. See also staff working documents SWD (2012) 348 final and SWD (2012) 349 final and COM (2012) 615 final Communication from the Commission, *Gender Balance in Business Leadership: A Contribution to Smart, Sustainable and Inclusive Growth*. By the end of 2014 it was clear that this proposal has been 'stalled' at Council level. However, a Directive requiring reporting on diversity was presented and passed: European Parliament and Council Directive 2014/95 of 22 October 2014 amending Directive 2013/34/EU concerning disclosure of non-financial and diversity information by certain large undertakings and groups, OJ 2014 L330/1 (see further Ch. 5). In addition, in relation to bank and financial institutional governance specifically, the Capital Requirements Directive emphasised the importance of diversity including gender diversity in bank boards to combat what is described as 'groupthink'. See further Council Directive 2013/36, of the European Parliament and of the Council of 26 June 2013 on Access to the Activity of Credit Institutions and the Prudential Supervision of Credit Institutions and Investment Firms, Amending Council Directive 2002/87 and repealing Council Directives 2006/48 and 2006/49, O.J. 2013 (L 176) 338.

included an Article on the provision of equal pay for men and women.[2] The specific policy focus reflected in this Directive was to include more women in decision-making roles in Europe's biggest corporations. The business sector had been identified by the European Commission as lagging behind other sectors in this regard. When the Parliament voted by a significant majority[3] in favour of the draft Directive, it was described as 'a toad we have to swallow'[4] by Michael Fuchs, a 'pro-business' EU Parliamentarian, adumbrating the surprising level of resistance which the proposal would meet in subsequent months. To date it has not become law. However, the European Commission Work Programme for 2016 has included the Directive as a 'Priority Pending Proposal.' These are described as 'existing proposals which merit speedy adaption by the co-legislators'.[5]

This chapter considers a number of inter-related issues surrounding the EU (draft) Directive in the context of our broader enquiry regarding the role of gender in the creation of corporate sustainability. It will initially examine what is described in the literature as 'the business case' for increasing female membership of corporate boards. There have been numerous articles and reports supporting the business case for the inclusion of women on boards of companies, many of which are presented in glossy, media-friendly formats. The chapter takes a sceptical approach to the business case 'movement' from the perspective of corporate governance scholarship. More profoundly this chapter rejects the idea that a proposition which focusses on the inclusion of women as participants in economic life must be justified solely by reference to the shallowly described business needs of a corporation. In doing so, some unfortunate limitations in the current directive will be identified, derived

---

[2] Formerly Article 119 of the Treaty establishing the European Economic Community, Rome, 25 March 1957, in force 1 January 1958 and now Article 141 of the Treaty on European Union, Maastricht, 7 February 1992, in force 1 November 1993. There are a range of relevant directives emanating from this broad commitment, including directives on equal pay, on the implementation of the principle of equal treatment for men and women as regards access to employment, vocational training and promotion, working conditions and so on.

[3] The EU Parliament recorded a vote of 459 in favour, 148 against and 81 abstentions in November 2013.

[4] Tony Barber, 'Quotas for female board members looks like a toad too far.' (9 January 2014) *Financial Times*.

[5] European Commission Work Programme, *No Time for Business as Usual: Annex III*, COM (2015) 610 final. See also European Commission, *Strategic Engagement for Gender Equality 2016–2019*, SWD (2015) 278 final, p. 27. The Directive is still at Council level. Interinstitutional File: 2012/0299 (COD) as of May 2017.

from a critique shared by collaborators in this collection that these so-called innovations, which are driven by what we have described as 'liberal structuralism', tend to mask much more entrenched difficulties with current corporate models and systems of work. There are also difficulties with an overtly gendered approach to corporate management. Instead of the business case approach, this chapter will explore a second type of economic argument supporting the mandated quota initiative. This argument is embedded in the much broader EU gender equality agenda as it has developed since the 1950s. There is an additional case presented in EU policy documents for such legislation which is derived from traditional European ideals such as inclusiveness and sustainability. These ideals have now been reiterated in specific policy goals, in particular the goal of achieving 'smart, sustainable and inclusive growth' outlined in EU policy documents which look forward to 2020, and so this chapter places this particular initiative in this broader EU policy context.[6] It will present an argument based on the author's previous research that a particular understanding of corporate function, rooted in European political philosophy, leads to the conclusion that it is appropriate that corporate actors would be engaged with by the European Union and its member States in delivering particular social goods, such as gender equality, and even more significantly, 'sustainable growth and inclusion'. Finally, the idea of mandating particular levels of participation by women on boards will be explored in the broader context of a discussion of the function of law. The chapter proceeds as follows: Section 6.2 explores the business case through the prism of current corporate governance scholarship and explores the difficult question as to how we measure the relationship between good corporate governance and corporate performance. Section 6.3 considers alternative arguments for mandated gender diversity, arguments which are particularly apt in the context of European achievements in relation to gender equality and relevant to the focus of this collection on corporate sustainability. Section 6.4 discusses corporate law theory and the concept of corporate function in relation to legal instruments to achieve particular social goals. Section 6.5 returns to the question of why this Directive has led to such controversy and

---

[6] European Commission, *EUROPE 2020 A strategy for smart, sustainable and inclusive growth*, COM (2010) 2020 final. This document includes seven flagship initiatives including 'An agenda for new skills and jobs' to modernise labour markets and empower people by developing their skills throughout the lifecycle. This goal of inclusivity intersects with the EU equality agenda. (See Section 6.3.4).

hypothesises pessimistically that the modern corporation has become less adaptive and innovative, even in the face of small incremental changes of which this Directive is an exemplar.

6.2   The Business Case

6.2.1   Introduction

The 'business case' argument is based on an assertion that the presence of women on boards, even as non-executive directors, will improve the quality of corporate governance generally, corporate decision-making at board level specifically, and hence corporate performance. This is an ambitious argument by any measure. Judged from the perspective of corporate governance scholarship[7] of the last two decades, it seems

---

[7] It is difficult to summarise the conflicts within corporate law and corporate governance scholarship at this point, but it is fair to state that orthodox views on the nature of the market – and the consequent grounding of corporate governance scholarship and corporate law theory in neo-liberal law and economics analysis – have been re-assessed following the global financial crisis. Corporate law theorists and corporate governance scholars even disagree as to the relationship between governance and the financial crisis. K. J. Hopt, 'Corporate Governance of Banks and Other Financial Institutions after the Financial Crisis,' 13 *Journal of Corporate Law Studies* 237–238 concludes that '[T]he clear majority view is that the role of bank governance failures in the financial crisis was rather limited' yet, the OECD took a different view stating that 'The financial crisis has also pointed in a large number of cases to boards of financial companies that were ineffective and certainly not capable of objective, independent judgement.' OECD, *Corporate Governance and the Financial Crisis: Key Findings and Main Messages* (OECD, June 2009), 41, www.oecd.org. See also on the Irish banking crisis and the difficulties presented by poor governance in the banking system, I. Lynch Fannon, 'The End of the Celtic Tiger: A Case Study on the Failure of Corporate Governance and Company Law' (2015) 66 *Northern Irish Legal Quarterly* 1–22. In terms of board composition, there has been considerable focus on the role of independent directors on boards. S. LeMire and G. Gilligan, 'Independence and Independent Company Directors' (2013) 13 *Journal of Corporate Law Studies* 443–475. See also M. U. Gutierrez and M. L. Saez, 'Deconstructing Independent Directors' (2013) 13 *Journal of Corporate Law Studies* 63–84, where the authors argue that voluntary regulations on directorial independence are a substitute for state action in the legislative arena. Many authors have also argued that there is a trade-off or balancing act between appointing independent directors and losing the necessary skill and experience of institutionally knowledgeable directors. M. T. Moore: 'The Neglected Value of Board Accountability in Corporate Governance' (2015) 9 *Law and Financial Markets Review*, 10–18. Bainbridge has described the preoccupation with independence of directors as a fetish S. Bainbridge, '*Corporate Governance and Financial Crisis*' (Oxford: Oxford University Press 2012), p. 102. Other, very respected scholars have argued for a rethink of fundamental principles of corporate function. L Stout, *The Shareholder Value Myth*, (San Francisco: Barrett-Koehler Publishers, 2012); C. Meyer, *Firm Commitment, Why the Corporation Has Failed Us and How to Restore Trust in It* (Oxford University Press, 2013). See also

impossibly difficult to assess on its merits in any clear way, particularly on an empirical basis.[8] The global financial crisis left corporate governance scholarship with even more uncertainties, and so the complexities of this assertion cannot be overstated.

There have been many studies published in recent years advocating the benefits of increasing female membership on corporate boards. These include a major study conducted by Credit Suisse in 2012[9] surveying over 2,360 companies globally. Others had preceded this study, and yet others followed it.[10] In the range of studies emanating from institutions in the private sector which seek to establish or at least describe this business case, a number of commonalities emerge. First, it has been established that in Europe and Norway there is an overall higher proportion of women on boards than in other regions (some European countries, including Norway – which was the first country to have a mandatory quota[11] – already have quota systems in

---

M. Moore, *Corporate Governance in the Shadow of the State* (Oxford and Portland, OR: Hart Publications, 2013) for an excellent discussion of the principle debates in corporate governance scholarship. See also L. Talbot, *The Great Debates in Company Law* (Suffolk: Palgrave Great Debates Series, 2014).

[8] A significant empirical study was conducted by Sanjai Bhagat and Bernard Black in 1999 on the significance of independent directors to corporate performance. The authors state that empirical evidence suggested that firms with supermajority independent directors performed worse than other firms with more inside directors but only marginally so. S. Bhagat and B. Black, 'The Uncertain Relationship between Board Composition and Firm Performance' (1999) 54 *Business Law*. See also C. M. Daily et al., 'On the Measurement of Board Composition: Poor Consistency and a Serious Mismatch of Theory and Operationalization' (1999) 30 *Dec. Sci.* 83 on the challenges of accurate measurement of issues to underpin empirical study in this field. See further chapters in this collection.

[9] Credit Suisse, *Gender Diversity and Corporate Performance* (2012).

[10] For other similar studies see McKinsey, *Women Matter* (2007, 2008, 2010). Catalyst, *The Bottom Line, Connecting Corporate Performance and Gender Diversity* (2004). This latter organisation supports women in business generally. Other similar reports include: KPMG, *Cracking the Code* (March 2014); Recruitment and Employment Confederation (REC), *Room at the Top: Women and the Role of Executive Search* (March 2014); Accenture, *Career Capital* (February 2014); McKinsey, *Forward Looking Boards* (February 2014); PwC, *Mining for Talent* (February 2014), Financial Reporting Council, *Developments in Governance 2013, The Impact and Implementation of the UK Corporate Governance and Stewardship Codes* (December 2013); Government Equalities Office, *Think Act Report: Two Years On* (December 2013); 30% Club, *Mothers on Boards* (August 2013). See Davies Report 2014, 2015 UK Government Department of Business, Innovation and Skills, at https://www.gov.uk/government/collections/women-on-boards-reports.

[11] This legislation has been the subject of some criticism in Norway. It is claimed that there is a small cohort of women who populate the non-executive positions on boards of listed

place[12]), with some regions (Asia) indicating particularly low representation. Generally, larger companies tend to have more women on boards, and the fastest rates of change in relation to female participation on boards occurred in Europe (again this is not surprising given the move towards quotas in EU Member States). These findings lead to the important question as to whether companies with a higher proportion of women on the board perform better – in other words, does the business case hold up to scrutiny? As already observed, this is a particularly difficult question to answer, not only in terms of identifying correlation between the presence of women on the board and good corporate governance and performance, but also regarding identification of a specific causative connection to corporate performance.

There are two kinds of assumptions underlying the business case approach. The first is that gender-diverse boards are more representative of the population, and that consequently the board, and the corporation, is thus more responsive to the general business environment. Although intuitively acceptable, the idea that women exert influence on the board and in the corporation which is generally effective and responsive to business needs is very difficult to empirically prove.[13] The second

---

companies, sometimes referred to as the 'golden skirts.' Nevertheless, others note that mandated quotas have had a beneficial effect on the earnings of female board members, have widened the pool of potential female board members and have impacted favourably on women from within the firm being asked to join the board. 'While only 43 percent of women on ASA boards pre-reform had earnings above the 90th percentile in their cohort and degree group, that share went up to 51 percent post-reform; there was no change for men (61 percent pre-reform vs. 62 percent post-reform). There is also an 8 percentage point increase in the share of women coming from top positions in their firm after the reform – the change for men is only 3 percentage points. Also, interestingly, the fraction of women who have spouses on a board of directors fell post-reform, from 12% to only 7%. While this could in part reflect the mechanical drop in the number of male board members, it also suggests the possibility that firms went beyond their traditional networks when trying to fill their quota.' M. Bertrand, S. E. Black, S. Jensen and A. Lleras-Muney, 'Breaking the Glass Ceiling? The Effect of Board Quotas on Female Labor Market Outcomes in Norway' (June 2014) 8266 *IZA DP* . See also B. Sjåfjell, 'Gender Diversity in the Board Room & Its Impacts: Is the Example of Norway a Way Forward?' (2015) 20 (1) *Deakin Law Review*, 25–52. See https://ssrn.com/abstract=2536777 or http://dx.doi.org/10.2139/ssrn.2536777.

[12] See further D. Ahern and B. Clarke, '"Listed Companies' Engagement with Diversity: A Multi-Jurisdictional Study of Annual Report Disclosures', Law Working Paper 221/2013, European Corporate Governance Institute (2013).

[13] R. B. Adams, 'Women on Board. The Superheroes of Tomorrow?', ECGI Working Paper Series 466/2016 (March 2016), observes that 'The literature faces three main challenges: data limitations, selection and causal inference.'

assumption is even more complex, and that is that women as either executive or non-executive directors make decisions differently from men and that the difference in approaches to decision making (for example, a tendency for women to be more risk averse, which seemed to be a particularly attractive trait post financial crisis) represents a move towards better corporate governance. In the case of both types of assumptions, there is an additional logical leap from asserting that improved corporate governance, specifically improved board governance derived from gender diversity, leads to better corporate *performance*.[14]

Some studies provide detailed information on corporate performance by reference to stock market performance and financial performance.[15] Other studies indicate that board diversity counteracts a tendency towards 'groupthink', this phenomenon having been particularly signifi-cant in the period leading to the financial crisis.[16] Choudhury has identified that the presence of women changes the nature of board decision-making from attendance right through to the attention paid by all members on the board to documentation, the discussion and outcomes.[17] Again, the research shows that companies with women on the board tend to behave in 'relatively defensive' ways. In other words, these companies tend to behave more cautiously or less aggressively in relation to risk. The adoption of an argument such as the business case argument, which depends on characterising certain kinds of decision making as male or female, particularly in a formal business context, is very problematic. Other contributors to this collection will present a more in-depth critique of this gendered approach to behaviours and values. For example, Roseanne Russell cautions against the adoption of

[14] M. McCann and S. Wheeler, 'Gender Diversity in the FTSE 100: The Business Case Claim Explored' (2011) *Journal of Law and Society* 38, 542–574.

[15] In its survey of stock market data, the Credit Suisse study spanned the period from December 2005–December 2011. Two regional datasets for the United States and Europe show that companies with women on boards outperformed companies without women over this period in these regions. Interestingly this success is attributed to relatively defensive decision making by these companies.

[16] The problem of 'groupthink' has been identified as a contributing factor in relation to the behaviour of banking executives and boards during the financial crisis. See n. 23. See also n. 12.

[17] B. Choudhury, 'New Rationales for Women on Boards' (2014) 34 *Oxford Journal of Legal Studies*, 511–542; D. Ferreira, 'Board Diversity' in H Kent Baker and R. Anderson (eds.), *Corporate Governance: A Synthesis of Theory, Research and Practice* (Hoboken, NJ: John Wiley and Sons, 2010), p. 233; 'Corporate Directors Contribute to Board Deliberations' in S. Vinnicombe et al. (eds.), *Women on Corporate Boards of Directors: International Research and Practice* (Cheltehnham, UK: Edward Elgar Publishing, 2006), p. 127.

this kind of analysis in her very compelling piece. Similarly, Catherine O'Sullivan illustrates how gendered understandings of ethics constrain the potential for ethical action generally, confining this sort of action to a specifically female domain.[18] Even more challenging is the issue of causality as distinct from correlation inherent in the claim that having women on the board improves corporate governance and corporate performance. The Credit Suisse report acknowledges that 'none of our analysis proves causality; we are simply observing the facts'.[19]

6.2.2   Proving the Impossible: Causality

Previous research from this author disputed the alleged connections (in terms of better corporate performance) between the US model of corporate governance in relation to labour market regulation issues specifically and the European social model.[20] At the time, the European social model had been described as being in decline in opposition to the rise of the Anglo American model. Writers such as Hansmann and Kraakman famously claimed superiority for the latter.[21] Two decades later, both claims of superiority and the accompanying claim of the inevitable convergence of other models towards the 'superior' Anglo American model are becoming increasingly muted.[22] Without dwelling too long on the contours of this scholarly debate, the challenge has always been to

---

[18] Chs. 11, 12.

[19] There is also scholarship which supports the idea that in fact women are appointed to boards as saviours to clean up a pre-existing disaster which has been hidden to this point. M. K. Ryan and S. A. Haslam, 'The Glass Cliff: Evidence That Women Are Over-Represented in Precarious Leadership Positions' (9 February 2005) *British Journal of Management* 16, 81–90. S. Adams, 'Are Female Executives Over-Represented in Precarious Leadership Positions?' 20 (1) *British Journal of Management*, 1–12. This is a very interesting area of scholarship including the assertion that women are often intended to be identified as scapegoats following financial failures.

[20] I. Lynch Fannon, *Working within Two Kinds of Capitalism* (Oxford and Portland, OR: Hart Publications, 2003).

[21] H. Hansmann and R. Kraakman, 'The End of History for Corporate Law' (2001) 89 *Georgetown Law Journal* 371. Discussed extensively in M. T. Moore, *Corporate Governance in the Shadow of the State* (Oxford and Portland, OR: Hart Publications, 2012).

[22] For a multijurisdictional assessment of Hansmann and Kraakman's views see Welsh, Spender, Lynch Fannon and Hall, 'The End of the End of History for Corporate Law' (2014) *Australian Journal of Corporate* Law. See Kraakman, Davies, Hansmann et al., *The Anatomy of Corporate Law: A Comparative and Functional Approach* 3rd ed. (Oxford: Oxford University Press, 2016).

identify empirical evidence to support claims regarding effective corporate governance and the causal connection to corporate performance.[23]

Accordingly, despite the quality of the many surveys on this issue, the following difficult questions remain:

First and foremost; can we honestly describe male and female decision-making patterns in clear-cut gendered terms?

Does the presence of women alone lead to more conservative/risk-averse decision making? (Also bearing in mind that risk aversion may not always be a desired strategy.) If so, how could the presence of only one or two women make such a difference?

Are the outcomes driven by male decision making in the presence of women? In other words, is it the nature of male decision making which is still driving the corporate culture? Some studies indicate that board diversity counteracts a tendency towards 'groupthink', this phenomenon having been particularly significant in the period leading to the financial crisis.[24]

Are the outcomes a result of a particular corporate culture which led to the decision to have women on the board in the first instance? Could it be the case that these particular corporations are displaying a generally more socially responsive and responsible approach to corporate decision making which also led to a more responsive and responsible approach to the financial crisis? In effect, are the efforts which particular corporations make to appoint women to their boards simply a signal of a more deep-seated corporate culture which has proven to be more resilient through the financial crisis?

---

[23] Lynch Fannon, *Working within Two Kinds of Capitalism*.

[24] The author has written about this phenomenon in I. Lynch Fannon, 'The End of the Celtic Tiger'. This work refers to reports at that time concerning the situation in Ireland, including the Honohan and Nyberg Reports. In a section entitled 'Herding and Groupthink' the Nyberg Report makes the following observation at paragraph 1.6.5: 'Groupthink occurs when people adapt to the beliefs and views of others without real intellectual conviction. A consensus forms without serious consideration of consequences or alternatives, often under overt or imaginary social pressure. Recent studies indicate that tendencies to groupthink may be both stronger and more common than previously thought. (Barron, R: 2005) One consequence of groupthink may be herding, if the views in question relate to institutional policies, but this need not be the case.' *Misjudging risk: causes of the systemic Banking crisis in Ireland: Report of the Commission of Investigation into the Banking Sector in Ireland* (The Nyberg Report, March 2011). *The Irish Banking Crisis: Regulatory and Financial Stability Policy 2003–2008* (The Honohan Report, May 2010). K. Regling & M. Watson, *A Preliminary Report on the Irish Banking Crisis* (May 2010). Irish Government Publications Office, Molesworth Street, Dublin.

The argument put forward in this chapter is that these questions are almost impossible to answer without indulging in a stereotyping of the way all women decide, how all men decide, and how groups decide.[25] This approach lacks credibility, as will be further discussed in other contributions to this book. The answers will not yield a strong argument hitherto described as the business case for mandating women membership on boards. For these reasons, this author maintains a stance of deep intellectual scepticism regarding the so-called business case for inclusion of women on boards.

6.2.3 A Final Word on the Business Case

Whilst the scepticism expressed in the preceding paragraphs derives from a corporate governance scholarship perspective, it must be said that other parts of the academy, in particular colleagues in management theory, are more convinced by the business case for having women on corporate boards. An interesting study by Professor Katherine Phillips on the nature of group dynamics in decision making indicates that a more diverse group presents positive challenges to each group member which generate a more intensive scrutiny of factors leading to particular decisions.[26] To quote one study,[27] 'there is unusually strong consensus within academic research that a greater number of women on the board improves performance on corporate and social governance metrics. ... The more gender diverse boards were more likely to focus on clear communication to employees, to prioritize customer satisfaction, and to consider diversity and corporate social responsibility.'[28]

---

[25] See B. Choudhury, 'New Rationales for Women on Boards', pp. 511–542 for an interesting discussion of empirical studies regarding the dynamics of boardroom behaviour when women are members of boards. See D. C. Langevoort, 'Behavioral Approaches to Corporate Law' in C. A. Hill & B. H. McDonnell (eds.), *Research Handbook on the Economics of Corporate Law* (Northampton, MA: Edward Elgar, 2012), pp. 442–455.

[26] Professor Katherine Phillips, Columbia Business School, see www8.gsb.columbia.edu/cbs-directory/detail/kp2447.

[27] D. A. H. Brown et al. (2002) 'Not Just the Right Thing, but the Bright Thing' The Conference Board of Canada, Toronto, 2002, referred to in the Credit Suisse study at p. 18. C. L. Dezső and D. G Ross 'Does Female Representation in Top Management Improve Firm Performance? A Panel Data Investigation' (2012) 9 *Strategic Management Review* 33, which found positive links between female board membership and firm performance but only in firms where innovation was a key part of strategy.

[28] A common theme in the research on financial performance and the presence of women on boards is that women tend to be more risk averse regardless of the financial position of the company. Professor Nick Wilson of the Leeds University Business School showed that

The Communication from the EU Commission in relation to the direct-ive refers, for example, to 'a well-established economic and business case for increasing the presence of women in business leadership positions'.[29] Even if studies demonstrate a correlation between the presence of women on boards and improved corporate performance, correlation is not the same as causation. The difficulties inherent in identifying the exact causes of good corporate performance will bedevil this issue as it has bedevilled corporate governance and corporate performance for more than twenty years.[30]

The business case movement is thus an intellectually suspect argument to justify an initiative which has a much deeper and more defensible social goal.

6.3   The Alternative (and Better) Arguments Based on Broader Economic and Social Goals

6.3.1   Policy Objectives of the European Union

In its introductory documents to the Directive on Women on Boards, the European Commission places the Directive squarely within the EU gender equality agenda. The history of the EU equality agenda is

---

at least one female director on the board appears to reduce the likelihood of insolvency by 20%. Note that the Credit Suisse study itself illustrates correlation between female board membership and lower levels of gearing.

[29] European Commission, *Gender balance in business leadership; a contribution to smart, sustainable and inclusive growth*, COM (2012) 615/final 14.11.2012, p. 5. Further on in the Communication there is a reference to the following studies: Credit Suisse, *Gender Diversity and Corporate Performance* (Research Institute, August 2012); Catalyst, *The Bottom Line Connecting Corporate Performance and Gender Diversity* (2004); McKinsey Reports, *Women Matter* (2007, 2008 and 2010).

[30] K. Farrell and P. Hersch, 'Additions to Corporate Boards: The effect of gender.' *Finance Department Faculty Publications*, Paper 18. The authors found in a study of 300 Fortune 1000 companies that 'Despite finding a positive relation between return on assets and the likelihood of adding a woman to the board, event study results fail to detect any significant market reaction to female additions. Therefore, although better performing firms tend to have more women on the board, we cannot conclude that more gender diverse boards generate better firm performance.' See http://digitalcommons.unl.edu/financefacpub/18. Adams and Ferreira, 'Women in the Boardroom and Their Impact on Governance and Performance.' (2009) 94 *Journal of Financial Economics*, 291–309, found in a study of 1,939 US stocks between 1996 and 2003, statistically significant negative effects following the appointment of women to the board, although their study did record that the presence of women on boards improved attendance records for all directors!

described in terms of particular milestones and achievements, beginning with the reference in the original Treaty of 1957 to gender equality. The Explanatory Memorandum to the Directive notes that the original Treaty of 1957 specifically referred to the need for men and women to be paid equally and to have equality of opportunity,[31] in addition to the many legal instruments which have been enacted to ensure these promises are acted upon as they relate to equal pay, equality of access and opportunity.

Many specific directives have followed. The Directive on Women on Boards is part of the modern European agenda on equality. European Commission documents make it clear that even now, particular obstacles still exist for women in corporate and business life. The Communication from the Commission to the Council, the Parliament and the Committees (referred to in this text as 'the report')[32] identifies the following factors:

Firstly, the persistence of traditional gender roles in education. The report notes that women are still under-represented in STEM subjects: sciences, technology, engineering and mathematics.

Secondly, once in the labour market, the report notes that women tend to concentrate in a small number of occupations which are often less well-paid and less valued. Women make up almost 83 per cent of those working in health and social work, over 71 per cent of those in education and over 62 per cent of those in retailing.

Thirdly, the report notes that only ten EU Member States have met the Barcelona objectives regarding childcare coverage.[33]

The report goes on to state that even where women overcome the difficult obstacles presented by these factors (i.e., under-representation in their industry, isolation as they continue to work in male-dominated

---

[31] 'Equality between women and men is one of the Union's founding values and core aims under Articles 2 and 3(3) in the TEU. In accordance with Article 8 TFEU the Union shall aim to eliminate inequalities, and to promote equality, between men and women in all its activities. There are several important legal measures in place to promote equal treatment and equal opportunities of men and women in matters of employment and occupation, including self-employment.' See Explanatory Memorandum, Draft Directive, COM (2012) 614 final, Directive of the European Parliament and of the Council on improving the gender balance among non-executive directors of companies listed on stock exchanges and related measures, p. 6.

[32] European Commission, *Gender balance*, pp. 9–12.

[33] European Commission, *Gender balance*, p. 10, which specifically refers to the objectives of the Barcelona European Council 2002 stating that 'Only ten EU Member States have met the Barcelona objective of 33% childcare coverage rate for children under three, while only nine Member States have met the Barcelona objective of a 90% coverage rate for children between three years old and the mandatory school age.'

sectors and child care issues), the glass ceiling still exists. In describing the nature of the glass ceiling, the report refers to phenomena such as prejudice, specifically referring to 'subtle barriers including the perception that women are either not interested or incapable of performing certain tasks', and protectionism, evidenced by a lack of transparency in recruitment and promotion practices.

6.3.2   The Economic Aspects of Equality

Emphasis on the EU equality agenda brings us closer to the real economic argument facing Europe. This concerns efficient use of social capital and a planned realisation of the benefits of a significant level of public investment in education. In recent documents which have revisited issues of gender equality, the European Commission in its Report entitled Strategic Engagement for Gender Equality has focussed on five strategic issues:

- equal economic independence for women and men;
- equal pay for work of equal value;
- equality in decision-making;
- dignity, integrity and ending gender-based violence; and
- promoting gender equality beyond the EU.

Three out of five of these strategic issues are economic in character.

The issue of equality in decision making includes the role of women on boards of EU companies. As the report notes, there are concerns about continued non-participation of women in labour markets thereby undermining their economic independence. The report specifically refers to continued gender pay gaps and continued non-progression of women into senior business positions, and goes on to refer to issues of poverty and social exclusion for older women. Recent EU policy documents have focussed on growing concerns regarding the impoverishment of women in particular as they age.[34] This chapter therefore argues that the really authentic economic argument in support of quota legislation emanates from the equality agenda generally. This economic argument is derived from the nature of European political structures which both support continued state, publicly funded investment in education at all levels including tertiary education and which also supports the inclusion of

---

[34] European Commission, *Strategic Engagement for Gender Equality 2016–2019*, p. 8. (Formerly, SWD (2015) 278 final, Brussels, 3 December 2015).

women as economic actors. These economic issues are different in character from an exclusively business-oriented argument, as they do not place the corporation centre stage, but rather the concerns of the state and society. A close reading of EU documents on various issues, including the documents referred to here, clearly indicate that this economic argument has two aspects: the continued undermining of women as economic actors, leading to a lack of economic independence and in some cases poverty and social exclusion, and the continued loss to the labour market and Europe's economy of a sustained publicly funded investment in the educational accomplishment and talent of women. The report states that 'despite . . . investment in education young women are still twice as likely as young men to be economically inactive'. Because girls and women are treated equally in terms of state funding during their educational experiences throughout the EU, the commitment to equality is underpinned economically and must be followed through to eliminate situations where women begin to experience obstacles and difficulties, the nature of which has been described in the EU documents. The previously referenced communication notes that 'despite representing around 45% of people employed in the EU and 56% of people in tertiary education, women only represent 13.7% of board members in the major publicly listed companies in the EU'.[35] There is therefore a loss of both educated and experienced business leaders. Not only is there the actual loss to the labour market of skilled and experienced business people, but there is also the loss of leadership which would be more likely to provide a positive impact regarding the participation of women generally and the support of women as economic actors generally.

This chapter emphasises that the single most important economic argument for ensuring female participation on boards of European companies in significant numbers derives from the substantial loss of leadership, talent, professionalism and skill which the alternative and current scenario presents. In a European context, the provision of publicly funded third-level education (in contrast to the privately funded nature of such education in the United States) makes this case all the more immediate in economic terms. It is a substantial loss of public

---

[35] European Commission, *Gender balance*, p. 7. Interestingly, the accompanying figures show that even though women occupy over a quarter of seats on boards of companies in Finland, Latvia and Sweden and over a fifth in France there are fewer than 10% of women on boards in Ireland, Italy, Greece, Portugal and Hungary.

investment in education if this potential is not used. It has economic benefits which are in the first instance about reaping the rewards of substantial investment in education of girls and women, and in the second instance about ensuring the participation of skilled and educated people in corporate and business life. What is most interesting regarding this Directive is the level of resistance to it which is expressed in crude terms as per the German representative of the business lobby quoted in the title of this chapter, but also in more subtle ways by an exhortation of a retreat to voluntarism. It is clear that the heyday of EU equality achievements is a distant memory in the face of such allegedly 'pro-business' lobbying.

6.3.3   Equality and Social Justice

In addition to the economic argument based on investment in education and the realisation of the full potential of such investment and appropriate participation of women in the labour market, there is also the underlying equality argument, namely that equality is inherently a societal good.[36]

In keeping with the thematic identification of liberal structuralism and its flaws in this collection, this section concludes that the best justification for supporting legislation mandating women on boards derives from concern with the equality of women as economic actors. This is by far the most coherent justification as compared with the business case, which seeks to embed the justification for legislation in benefits to the corporation. Viewing a question as important as equality through such a narrow lens has proven to be incoherent in its own terms, thereby giving rise to justified scepticism and shallow political rejection.

6.3.4   Gender Balance and 'Smart, Sustainable and Inclusive Growth'

As European policy in the area of sustainable and inclusive growth has developed, the European Commission and other institutions

---

[36] This idea is expressed very strongly in EU Social Policy documents and of course is central to liberal political theories. See further M. McCann and S. Wheeler, 'Gender Diversity in the FTSE 100: The Business Case Claim Explored' (2011) *Journal of Law and Society* 38, 542–574.

have also acknowledged the interconnectedness of the gender equality agenda and the newer policy goals regarding sustainable and inclusive growth. The Communication of the Commission from 2012[37] sends a very clear signal even in its title, 'Gender Balance in Business Leadership: A Contribution to Smart, Sustainable and Inclusive Growth'. The document clearly connects gender equality with inclusiveness, encouraging better labour market participation and further support for women in decision-making roles. It also presents the argument that diversity, and in this case gender balance particularly, will lead to different and better approaches to business growth and success:

> There is an economic and business case for gender diversity on boards, including recent research. Gender diversity in the boardroom has been shown to lead to innovative ideas, increased competitiveness and performance, and improved corporate governance. It is a sign of openness to more viewpoints and respect for differences among stakeholders — shareholders, investors, employees and customers — signalling the company's recognition of the complexity of world markets and its preparedness to compete effectively at the global level.[38]

While the Communication continues on to provide a very useful summary of the obstacles which still face the integration of women into decision-making positions, it is short on the explicit linkages between further inclusiveness and sustainability particularly. Nevertheless, the recognition of the need for businesses to move towards both inclusivity and sustainability is important and significant.

6.4   Regulating the Corporation to Achieve Equality

In this section a key question is considered. If we are convinced by any or all of the three justifications for increasing the participation of women on boards of large corporations (i.e., the 'business case' or the real economic argument derived from existing investment in the broader equality agenda or indeed the argument derived from supporting 'sustainable and inclusive growth'), the question still remains: Is the State entitled to interfere in internal corporate governance affairs through legislation of a mandatory nature to achieve business, economic or social goals?

---

[37] COM (2012) 615 final.   [38] COM (2012) 615 final, Para 5., p. 13.

6.4.1   Corporate Law Theory

As has been well documented, from the mid-1990s corporate governance scholars, and in particular academics on both sides of the Atlantic who were corporate law scholars interested in corporate law theory, adopted a particular school of thought in relation to the function and regulation of corporate actions. The theoretical view of the corporation was driven by a law and economics analysis which focussed on the idea (which has always been accepted as a fundamental principle) that the function of the limited liability corporation is to externalise business risk.[39] As a driver of capitalist entrepreneurialism and business growth, the limited liability corporation functions to shift the taking of business risk to external holders of that risk, in particular creditors whether these are lenders or suppliers.

The Chicago-based law and economics school effectively provided a theoretical justification for a market-driven approach to regulating the corporation as a risk externalisation machine. More importantly for the purposes of this chapter, in the later years of its hegemony the law and economics school of thought also provided a theoretical justification for limiting the state's role in regulating corporations, particularly in the area of internal corporate governance.[40] For approximately the ten or fifteen years prior to the crash of 2008, the law and economics driven understanding of corporate function and governance was also supported by attempts to correlate the Anglophone approach to these matters with superior economic performance at both the level of the corporation and in overall macroeconomic terms. During this period, Hansmann and Kraakman published their article which described the European social model of corporate governance as a failed model.[41] Even as late as 2006, when the UK was on the brink of enacting a major piece of legislation which reformed UK company law (the Companies Act 2006), there was a considerable shift away from a more European understanding of corporate function to a more market-driven approach. This was also

---

[39] R. A. Posner, 'The Rights of Creditors of Affiliated Corporations' (1975/76) 43 *University of Chicago Law Review*, at 499 et seq; B. D. Baysinger and H. N. Butler, 'The Role of Corporate Law in the Theory of the Firm' (1985) 28 *Journal of Law and Economics* 179, 183–184; S. Bainbridge and M. Todd Henderson, *Limited Liability: A Legal and Economic Analysis* (Edgar Elgar Publishing, 2016).

[40] H. Hansmann and R. Kraakman, 'The End of History for Corporate Law' (2001) 89 *Georgetown Law Journal* 371. M. T. Moore, *Corporate Governance in the Shadow of the State* (Hart Publications, 2012).

[41] Hansmann and Kraakman, 'The End of History', 371.

exemplified by the enactment of the Enterprise Act in 2002 in the UK which liberalises some aspects of company law, including removing state intervention in relation to the protection of some state creditors, specifically the revenue authorities.[42]

Whilst this version of the theory of company law, corporate performance and corporate governance rode the wave, as it were, in the Anglophone world, in Europe things were very different. The view of the corporation as a public actor and therefore amenable to regulation or indeed participation in the achievement of broader economic and social goals was much more embedded in the European view of corporate function. This difference in the European approach to corporate function and regulation compared with a more Anglophone approach has been attributed by this author (and others) to a different political philosophy concerning the relationship of the corporation to the State.[43] As documented in their survey of the approach of European countries to this matter, Deirdre Ahern and Blanaid Clarke[44] describe how the issue of increasing female participation on boards of European companies has been addressed through the use of quotas in a number of EU countries and so it is possible that the directive may yet be passed, if for the sole reason of levelling the European playing field. However, the Ahern and Clarke study also highlighted pipeline issues such as the idea that it is insufficient to simply focus on a rather crude quota mechanism at the top level without taking steps to ensure gender equality at other levels in the corporation.[45] Accordingly, they argued that reporting instruments which require reporting of efforts at various levels might be equally effective to achieve the desired outcome. Currently, this seems to be the focus of the EU initiative in this area.[46]

---

[42] See generally L. Sealy and S. Worthington, *Cases and Materials in Company Law*, 10th edn. (Oxford: Oxford University Press, 2013).

[43] This part of the argument is adumbrated in I. Lynch-Fannon, *Working within Two Kinds of Capitalism.* J. Plender, *Going off the Rails: Global Capital and the Crisis of Legitimacy* (Chichester: John Wiley & Sons Ltd, 2003) for a very readable consideration of the role of capital in governance structures. For an inspiring article on this subject see W. T. Allen, 'Contracts and Communities' (1993) 50 *Washington and Lee Law Review* 1.

[44] See further D. Ahern and B. Clarke, 'Listed Companies' Engagement with Diversity'. Note that in this study where reasons were requested for promoting diversity the business case received less endorsement from companies than equality and human rights reasons, even in jurisdictions such as Australia where companies endorsed the business case at quite high levele.

[45] Ibid.

[46] In this collection Gill North considers reporting and disclosure obligations. See Ch. 5.

6.4.2   The European Reality

One of the issues arising from these differences concerns the role of
the state as a regulator and the corporation as the focus of state
regulation to achieve particular goals. This is a central issue for the
matters which concern us in this chapter and collection. The corporation as the proper focus of state regulation to achieve particular goals
has always been at the centre of European understandings of the
position of the corporation. Therefore, it is appropriate to enlist
corporations in achieving broad social goals such as sustainable and
inclusive growth, and goals which can be described as economic in a
broader sense in the European understanding.[47] Not all laws are
definitively related to the operation of the market. For example,
consumer protection and environmental protection legislation as we
know it would never necessarily be delivered either by what law and
economic theorists call a perfect market or an imperfect market. The
function of legislation can be viewed through different philosophical
prisms, but unfortunately many current debates about corporate and
business regulation are firmly rooted in what could be described as a
law and economics, neo-liberal philosophy which, although still
almost hegemonic in certain academic quarters, is not necessarily the
only way of looking at corporate law. The argument here is that it is
appropriate to regulate the corporation as an actor in and as part of
society so that the corporation can assist with the attainment of
equality, inclusion and sustainability.

6.4.3   A Final Word on Corporate Function

The case for a legislative approach to ensuring women participate in
business leadership is made in the EU documents. The Treaty basis for
the legislation is also referred to, with the Report specifically outlining
the competence of the EU in this area by referring to Article 157(3)
TEFU. It is as if the EU Commission is most anxious to make the case
for the legislation in its own right by referring to the underlying
competence of the European Union in the area of gender equality as
an added extra justification. The statements as to EU competence to
legislate are stronger than simply a formulaic statement as to legal

---

[47] See n. 26.

competence but more a positive claim to the EU's role as a policy driver in this area in particular.[48]

6.5   A Storm in a Tea Cup: What Resistance to Mandated Quotas Tells Us about Corporations, Women and Broader Sustainability Goals

When the EU Commission Directive was presented, it was greeted with outright hostility, as exemplified by the 'Toad we have to Swallow' statement, and with a more considered and more powerful resistance which relied on pressing the case for voluntary achievement of a quota of 30 per cent of women on boards of listed companies, as exemplified by the work of Lord Davies in the UK[49] and the establishment of the 30% Club. Because of this hostility and resistance, the Directive remains as a draft at the time of writing. However, it was placed on the European Commission's work programme for 2016. As a consequence of the opposition mandated standards of this kind now face, the Directive now represents a fairly timid requirement that Member States should insist through legislation on a target of 40 per cent women in *non-executive* directorial positions in EU listed companies by 2020. The differences in executive positions versus non-executive positions are ignored, as are governance issues in the very significant non-listed sector.

There are two key arguments. The first is that the Directive is now extremely limited in its scope and reach and so cannot be regarded as a beacon of achievement. It is a good example of the liberal structuralist approach to incremental change within corporations which does not really achieve much, leaving the corporation unchanged and unchallenged insofar as the progression of women as economic actors and regarding the achievement of any inclusivity goals are concerned.

---

[48] M. Sydlo, 'Constitutional Values Underlying Gender Equality on Boards of EU Companies' (2014) *International & Comparative Law Quarterly*, pp. 167–196, where the author argues that the underlying rationale for imposing quotas or creating other legislative instruments regarding gender equality on corporate boards must be accurately placed within the EU legal order.

[49] In the latest and final report issued by Lord Davies (October 2015) it was indicated that FTSE 100 companies are now displaying 79.3% men, 23.7% women board membership. Note that the accompanying press release stated that 'Lord Davies has concluded 5 years of outstanding work on gender equality by proposing a series of recommendations including a bold new target of all FTSE 350 boards having 33% female representation by 2020 – around 350 more women in top positions.' Lord Davies, *UK Department of Business, Innovation and Skills*, see www.gov.uk.

The second key point made in this chapter is that corporate and public resistance is the single most interesting aspect of this initiative. Unfortunately, such resistance, emanating from so many different quarters, is a sad reflection on how little is understood about the support women need through this kind of legislation to make their way in public and corporate life. In the past, the EU has been much more proactive in meeting resistance and conservatism head on, with bold legislation relating to mandated equal pay, equal opportunities legislation and legislation mandating significant leave rights including maternity and parental leave rights. In the period around the presentation of this directive and subsequently, resistance emerging from so-called pro-business lobbyists is much stronger. Even more disappointingly, many women seem to agree with this approach.[50] It seems to this author that perhaps women in particular underestimate how much such laws are needed, as the historic need for regulation is beyond their own experience. Much more importantly, in the broader context of creating sustainable corporations, there is a complete failure to understand how law can and has shaped our culture and society in positive ways. In particular, there is huge potential for law to change what we now think of as the modern corporation.

6.5.1   Voluntarism, Self-Regulation and Mandated Quotas

Resistance to the directive was expected by the EU Commission.[51] There are very specific statements in the preparatory EU documents behind the Directive regarding previous attempts at a self-regulatory or voluntary

---

[50]   The initiative from the UK Government headed by Lord Davies issued its final Report in 2015. Other than Lord Davies, the other three signatories to the Report are women. In its summary, it points out that the UK ranks 6th in terms of including women on boards, noting that other countries ahead of it all have mandatory quotas. These observations lead to the following conclusion in the Report: 'Voluntary Approach Working Albeit More to Be Done. The national call for action and voluntary, business-led approach is continued for a further five year period, ensuring substantive and sustainable improvement in women's representation on Boards of FTSE 350 companies into the future.' Similarly, the founder and chair of the 30% Club, which is specifically against mandatory quotas in this area, are both women, and the club has significant numbers of pro-business women as members. See https://30percentclub.org.

[51]   During the 2013 European Corporate Governance and Company Law Conference sponsored by the EU during the Irish Presidency (Dublin, May 2013). See www.corpgov2013.com where Clarke and Ahern presented their research, discussed previously, it was indicated that the majority of those attendees surveyed prior to the conference disagreed with the imposition of mandatory minimum levels as the only way to achieve appropriate diversity on boards. In addition, in this survey there was

approach not working. This is both a literal justification as to the level of action now being sought, pre-emptively addressing any disagreements there may be on the issues of subsidiarity and proportionality, as well as a broader, policy-oriented statement as to the merits of voluntarism and self-regulation compared with a regulatory approach:

> Figures show that legislative measures yield more substantial progress compared to voluntary initiatives, especially if they are accompanied by sanctions. This is most clearly demonstrated by the impact of the now well-established Norwegian legislation, which imposes a legally binding quota of 40% with the dissolution of the company as sanction in case of non-compliance, and – within the EU – by the situation in France where a legally binding quota of 20% within 3 years (2014) and 40% within 6 years (2017) is in force.[52]

In a fairly damning indictment of voluntary approaches to this specific issue, and perhaps to corporate governance issues generally, it is noted in a short briefing accompanying the Directive that following the introduction in March 2011 of a voluntary code by Commissioner Reding entitled 'Women on Board – A Pledge for Europe'[53] (which called for a commitment to raise female membership of boards to 30 per cent by 2015), only twenty-four companies had commited to the pledge.[54] The documents go on to describe

significant resistance to the role of law in improving corporate governance generally with the following result: 'Opinion was sharply divided on whether corporate governance could be legislated for (with 44% agreeing and 48% disagreeing) whereas a clear majority (77%) believed that EU initiatives on Corporate Governance should aim at a new drive to encourage general adoption of best practises in Corporate Governance in all Member States rather than imposing detailed legislation. In this regard, one respondent suggested that external evaluations be made mandatory to ensure that Boards continuously sought to improve their effectiveness'.

[52] European Commission, 'Women on Boards: Commission proposes 40% objective', press release, Brussels, 14 November 2012, p. 2.

[53] European Commission, EU Justice Commissioner Reding challenges business leaders to increase women's presence on corporate boards with 'Women on the Board Pledge for Europe', Memo 11/24, Brussels, 1 March 2011, see http://europa.eu/rapid/press-release_MEMO-11-124_en.htm.

[54] This is noted in both the Communication of the Commission to the Parliament, Council and the Committees, Gender Balance in Business Leadership n. 30 at p. 13. And the Memo from the European Commission, dated Brussels, 14 November 2012, p. 1, where it is stated that 'Due to the slow progress of self-regulatory initiatives, several EU Member States have already started to act and have introduced legally binding laws for company boards.'

a scattered and 'legally fragmented' approach at the national level which include measures of 'varying scope, ambition and effectiveness'.[55]

In the overall theme of this collection, the specific issues arising regarding voluntarism speak to the limitations of corporate social responsibility measures in the context of sustainability.

Nevertheless, post global financial crisis, mandated standards in relation to some aspects of corporate governance are enjoying more favour than hitherto. Examples include mandated rules on approval of executive remuneration such as what are known as 'say on pay' provisions mandating shareholder approval for executive pay, exemplified by the approach in the EU Shareholder Rights Directive.[56] In addition, the Disclosure of Financial Interests Directive includes mandatory disclosure of significant shareholder interests.[57] Similarly, we now see mandated requirements regarding independence of directors in banks under the Capital Requirements Directive IV.[58] Overall, the movement represents an acceptance that better governance can be delivered through mandated standards, but not sadly when it comes to including women.[59] As discussed in the next section, this contrasts strangely with the position regarding the inclusion of women on boards of companies and the fate of the directive.

6.6   Conclusion

This chapter highlights the difficulties in building a case for legislative instruments supporting mandated standards that affect corporations, in particular when the purpose of the legislation may not be directly related to corporate performance. The consideration of the fate of the quota

---

[55] Ibid., p. 14.

[56] See COM/2014/0213 final which includes the EU proposals to amplify the Shareholders' Rights Directive (Directive 2007/36/EC). This proposed Directive was approved in March 2017 by the European Parliament.

[57] Directive (EU) 2015/849 on the prevention of the use of the financial system for the purposes of money laundering or terrorist financing and amending Directive 2009/101/ EC, and see the proposal to further amend this Directive. COM (2016) 450 final. Even though the directive is overtly designed to 'counter the financing of terrorism' it will also 'ensure increased transparency of financial transactions and of corporate entities under the preventive legal framework in place in the Union, namely Directive (EU) 2015/849'.

[58] Directive 2013/36/EU, Articles 76–91.

[59] European Commission, *European company law and corporate governance: A modern legal framework for more engaged shareholders and sustainable companies*, COM (2012) 740 final.

Directive since its acceptance by the European Parliament indicates the strong resistance which exists towards change in the corporation even regarding what this author would consider to be a rather non-controversial agenda concerning female participation. This story exemplifies exactly how limited these liberal structuralist measures are as change mechanisms when faced with sustained business-oriented corporate lobby groups. Much more important is the bigger problem below the surface. It is this author's view that the position of women always shines a light on the enormity of the obstacles facing those of us who would like to see change in so many different areas of corporate activity, some of which have been discussed in this volume and many of which concern core issues of sustainability. If indeed countenancing the idea of a small piece of legislation mandating that less than half of the positions of *non-executive* directors on listed companies in Europe be women is so problematic, what does this say for the future changes necessary to achieving authentic corporate sustainability? In this sad context, the role of women in corporations simply shines a light on a rather dark and unoptimistic story.

Gender Diversity on Corporate Boards

An Empirical Analysis in the EU Context

IDOYA FERRERO-FERRERO, M. ÁNGELES FERNÁNDEZ-
IZQUIERDO AND M. JESÚS MUÑOZ-TORRES

7.1 Introduction

Gender diversity on boards of directors is high on the European political agenda. Since 2010, the European Commission has strongly encouraged gender equality in decision-making positions, starting with its own internal policy[1] and including this issue in legislation. In spite of increasing awareness and initiatives to achieve gender equality, women are still underrepresented, particularly in decision-making positions. There are only 21 per cent female board members and 7 per cent female chairpersons on the boards of the largest publicly listed companies registered in the EU countries.[2] These figures show that further action is clearly needed in order for the EU objective of finding at least '40 per cent of the under-represented sex among non-executive directors on boards of listed companies'[3] to become a reality. Academics may contribute to improved practice and policy by exploring the effectiveness of the

---

[1] European Commission, Communication from the Commission to the European Parliament, the Council, the European Economic and Social Committee and the Committee of the Regions. *Gender balance in business leadership: a contribution to smart, sustainable and inclusive growth*, COM (2012) 615 final; European Commission, *Proposal for a Directive of the European Parliament and of the Council on improving the gender balance among non-executive directors of companies listed on stock exchanges and related measures*, COM (2012) 614 final; European Commission, *Gender balance in decision-making positions, database, board members*, 2015, see http://ec.europa.eu/justice/gender-equality/gender-decision-making/database/business-finance/supervisory-board-board-directors/index_en.htm.

[2] European Commission. *Gender balance in decision-making positions, database, board members.*

[3] European Commission. *Proposal for a Directive of the European Parliament and of the Council on improving the gender balance.*

implemented measures, trends, barriers and drivers to progress towards a better gender balance on corporate boards.

In the literature, academics have not yet established a widely accepted definition of 'gender diversity'. Nonetheless, it could be understood as a balanced mix of feminine and masculine qualities in a team, which may be expressed in behaviours, competences or views. Theoretically, gender diversity improves decision making on boards for several reasons. The first is due to differences in ethical behaviour between women and men.[4] Allegedly, men make decisions quicker and are focused on the economic consequence, while women better explore the implications of the decision for multiple stakeholders, foresee negative consequences and make more ethical decisions.[5] A second argument is that gender diversity improves understanding of the market and more easily satisfies the different needs of society. Another stream of the literature analyses gender as a social construct where gender ascription is rooted in normative behaviour. In this case, a combination of stereotypes, occupational discrimination, caring and domestic responsibilities act as impediments to women achieving senior positions of responsibility.[6] Our aim is not to address the social construct issue, as regardless of these issues there are many reasons for ensuring gender balance in business leadership. For instance, women are as qualified as men in terms of education and, therefore, where women are underrepresented, it limits the talent pool.[7]

The role that corporate governance plays in sustainability is well recognised;[8] however, the number of studies that have explored the impact of gender diversity on sustainability are limited. Although other contributors to this volume dispute the ascription of gender-constructed

---

[4] J. Kennedy, J. and L. Kray, 'Who Is Willing to Sacrifice Ethical Values for Money and Social Status? Gender Differences in Reactions to Ethical Compromises' (2014) 5 (1) *Social Psychology and Personality Science*, 52–59.

[5] A.J. Hillman, 'Board Diversity: Beginning to Unpeel the Onion' (2015) 23(2) *Corporate Governance: An International Review*, 104–107.

[6] M. Susan, and D. Patton, 'All Credit to Men? Entrepreneurship, Finance, and Gender' (2005) 29(6) *Entrepreneurship Theory and Practice*, 717–735. See also Ch. 13.

[7] See Ch. 6.

[8] I. Ferrero-Ferrero, M. A. Fernández-Izquierdo and M. J. Muñoz-Torres, 'Integrating Sustainability into Corporate Governance: An Empirical Study on Board Diversity' (2015) 22 (4) *Corporate Social Responsibility and Environmental Management*, 193–207.

C. de Villiers, V. Naiker, and C. J. van Staden, 'The Effect of Board Characteristics on Firm Environmental Performance' (2011) 37(6) *Journal of Management*, 1636–1663.

C. Post, N. Rahman and E. Rubow 'Green Governance: Boards of Directors' Composition and Environmental Corporate Social Responsibility' (2011) 50(1) *Business & Society*, 189–223.

approaches, from another point of view, there are studies that assume differences between women and men to foster the role of gender as an important agent for promoting sustainability strategies in corporations. For instance, Huse and Solberg[9] and Bear et al.[10] argue that female directors differ in leadership styles since women are more diligent, committed, sensitive to social and ethical issues and stakeholder-oriented and less self-interest-oriented than male directors. In empirical literature, some studies find that gender diversity may play an insignificant role in sustainability issues,[11] but a substantial number of recent studies show a positive impact of gender diversity on sustainability reporting quality, voluntary disclosure of greenhouse gas emissions, corporate social responsibility engagement and ethical policy making.[12] Notwithstanding these reasons, boards remain mainly populated by men. Facing this reality, in recent years, a variety of practices have emerged to promote women in decision-making positions, but their effectiveness has not previously been clearly tested and their implementation causes controversy. To enhance understanding of the effectiveness of board diversity practices, further research about the conditions of board diversity is clearly needed. There are a limited number of studies which have explored different factors in gender board diversity, such as board and firm size, sector or country.[13]

---

[9] M. Huse and A. G. Solberg, 'Gender-Related Boardroom Dynamics: How Scandinavian Women Make and Can Make Contributions on Corporate Boards' (2006) 21 (2) *Women in Management Review*, 113–130.

[10] S. Bear, N. Rahman and C. Post, 'The Impact of Board Diversity and Gender Composition on Corporate Social Responsibility and Firm Reputation' (2010) 97(2) *Journal of Business Ethics*, 207–221.

[11] See, e.g., J. Galbreath, 'Are There Gender-Related Influences on Corporate Sustainability? A Study of Women on Boards of Directors' (2011) 17(1) *Journal of Management & Organization*, 17–38.

[12] H. Al-Shaer and M. Zaman, 'Board Gender Diversity and Sustainability Reporting Quality' (2016) 12(3) *Journal of Contemporary Accounting & Economics*, 210–222; M. Harjoto, I. Laksmana and R. Lee, 'Board Diversity and Corporate Social Responsibility' (2015) 132(4) *Journal of Business Ethics*, 641–660; L. Liao, L. Luo and Q. Tang, 'Gender Diversity, Board Independence, Environmental Committee and Greenhouse Gas Disclosure' (2015) 47(4) *The British Accounting Review*, 409–424; M. Jizi, 'The Influence of Board Composition on Sustainable Development Disclosure' (2017) 26, *Business Strategy and the Environment*, 640–655.

[13] J. Grosvold, S. Brammer and B. Rayton, 'Board Diversity in the United Kingdom and Norway: An Exploratory Analysis' (2007) 16(4) *Business Ethics: A European Review*, 344–357.

This chapter presents research that responds to two questions: Which are the factors that affect gender board diversity? Are companies adopting gender diversity policies 'substantially' or 'symbolically'? This study analyses a range of factors from suborganisational to macro societal levels that may have affected gender diversity on boards of directors for a sample of EU listed companies for the period 2002–2013. This research provides interesting insights to identify obstacles and facilitators to gender diversity in the EU context. The main results reveal that board size, firm size, industry, country, time and effective programs of equal opportunity in the workforce have become relevant factors to explain the variability in the percentage of women on boards. In contrast, the corporate policy and actions for maintaining well-balanced boards do not facilitate additional recruitment of women to boards. It seems that firms may adopt a balanced board policy in a symbolic way, without a clear objective to achieve a more balanced gender representation on their boards.

This work is divided into five sections. After this introduction, Section 7.2 presents the theoretical framework. Section 7.3 includes information on the sample, variables and methodology used in estimating the models. Section 7.4 presents the results and Section 7.5 offers discussion and the main conclusion.

7.2 Theoretical Framework

An important strand of the literature sees institutional theory[14] as a focal point for explaining the difference in female presence on the board between countries, industries and firms. Institutional theory posits that organisational structure and processes reflect institutional pressures, rules and norms present in the organisational environment. In this regard, Scott[15] proposed a multilevel institutional framework which addresses three pillars: a regulatory pillar concerning rules and laws; a normative pillar referring to social norms, behaviour and societal influences; and a cultural-cognitive pillar regarding cultural, innate and subjective views of institutions. Based on institutional theory, this study

---

[14] J. W. Meyer and B. Rowan, 'Institutionalized Organizations: Formal Structure as Myth and Ceremony' (1977) 83 *American Journal of Sociology*, 340–363.

W. R. Scott, *Institutions and organizations* (Thousand Oaks, CA: Sage, 1995).

[15] Scott, *Institutions and organizations*.

explores a range of factors from suborganisational to macro societal levels that may affect gender diversity on boards of directors.

At the suborganisational level, several studies[16] have explored the link between gender diversity and board characteristics. Various elements have been analysed and board size has emerged as a key factor based on the assumption that larger boards facilitate wide and real community representation.[17]

However, there is an unexplored factor in the literature which may have significant impact on gender diversity on boards, and which may be supported by institutional theory of the firm. The regulations that are emerging in the EU aim at facilitating the development of internal policies of companies, that is, the commitment of a company to develop and implement policies for recruitment of women to managerial positions and boards to ensure their participation in decision-making areas. The European Commission[18] is working on the promotion of gender diversity for those companies that fail to meet the requirement of 'at least 40 per cent of the under-represented sex among non-executive directors'. With the aim of establishing additional measures in order to meet the objective in the next few years, the Commission has considered equality in decision making as one of the priorities of the Strategic Engagement for Gender Equality (2016–2019).[19] Complementing this initiative, the Commission attempts to raise awareness though the dissemination of information, promotes the exchange of good practices and supports stakeholders in designing and implementing activities that improve gender equality in decision-making positions. The expectation is that firms that adopt policies that emphasise diversity in boards of directors will have a more gender-balanced representation on its boards in the future.

---

[16] S. Brammer, A. Millington and S. Pavelin, S., 'Gender and Ethnic Diversity among UK Corporate Boards' (2007) 15 *Corporate Governance: An International Review*, 393–403; M. J. Conyon, and C. Mallin, 'Women in the Boardroom: Evidence from Large UK Companies' (1997) 5(3) *Corporate Governance: An International Review*, 112–117; J. I. Siciliano, 'The Relationship of Board Member Diversity to Organizational Performance' (1996) 15(12) *Journal of Business Ethics*, 1313–1320.

[17] Siciliano, 'The Relationship of Board Member Diversity', 1313–1320.

[18] European Commission, *Proposal for a Directive of the European Parliament and of the Council on improving the gender balance*.

[19] European Commission. *Strategic engagement for Gender Equality* (2016–2019). SWD (2015). 278 final. 2016. See http://ec.europa.eu/anti-trafficking/eu-policy/strategic-engagement-gender-equality-2016–2019.

At the organisational level, as mentioned in previous studies,[20] larger and more visible organisations are more vulnerable to public pressure and arguably have a better ability to understand and respond to societal expectations. Therefore, larger organisations are subjected to greater public scrutiny to comply with corporate governance recommendations, such as the recommendations in the Davies Report[21] or Good Corporate Governance Code in Spain,[22] including a balanced gender representation in their upper levels of command.

Another factor that affects gender diversity is the company's commitment and effectiveness towards maintaining diversity and equal opportunities in its workforce. Grosvold et al.[23] note that the implementation of equal opportunity programmes at the top management level, broadly speaking, could be problematic due to the homogeneous and small pool of suitably qualified candidates to become managers. In spite of this argument, it is expected that in those firms with an effective equal opportunity programme, the internal pool of talent will be greater and the gender balance will be better embedded in the corporate culture and business philosophy.

At the sectoral level, there are different arguments within institutional theory that could explain the variation of board diversity across the different sectors of economic activity. First, governments may adopt different regulatory frameworks that may influence corporate governance practices.[24] Second, sectors vary in terms of female employment base. For instance, according to the British Workplace Employment Relations Survey of 2004, the sectors with a larger proportion of female employees

[20] A. J. Hillman, C. Shropshire and A. A. Cannella, 'Organizational Predictors of Women on Corporate Boards' (2007) 50(4) *Academy of Management Journal*, 941–952; A. Saeed, Y. Belghitar and A. Yousaf 'Firm-level Determinants of Gender Diversity in the Board-Rooms: Evidence from Some Emerging Markets' (2016) 25(5) *International Business Review*, 1076–1088.

[21] Davies Report, *Women on Boards: An Independent Review into Women on Boards*. Department for Business Innovation and Skills (BIS), London. 2011, see https://www .gov.uk/government/uploads/system/uploads/attachment_data/file/31480/11-745-women-on-boards.pdf.

[22] CNMV (Comisión Nacional del Mercado de Valores). *Good Governance Code of Listed Companies*, see www.cnmv.es/DocPortal/Publicaciones/CodigoGov/Good_Govern anceen.pdf.

[23] Grosvold et al., 'Board Diversity in the United Kingdom and Norway'.

[24] J. Grosvold, 'Where Are all the women? Institutional Context and the Prevalence of Women on the Corporate Board of Directors' (2011) 50(3) *Business & Society*, 531–555.

are financial services, hotels and restaurants, wholesale and retail, and other business services.[25] In this regard, those sectors that have a relatively low proportion of female workers tend to promote male candidates in management roles, given the criterion of industry experience, which means that a limited number of women have been recruited for these types of companies and have the requisite deep knowledge of the industry.[26] However, other research results do not support the converse. In sectors with more women in the workforce, like education, Fernández Izquierdo et al.[27] show poor performance in terms of female representation at top-level decision making. Third, board diversity is higher in consumer-oriented sectors which predominantly serve end consumers, such as consumer goods manufacturing, retail, banking, utilities and media[28]. At the country level, companies are dependent on the regulatory framework, societal values and norms and cultural characteristics of the context that shapes board-level decision making and processes. These characteristics are especially relevant at the national level, since a country tends to have shared gender stereotypes and beliefs given the national history, including the political orientation of governments, national corporate governance codes, a common gender equality policy in education and a common awareness about the role of women in the economy.[29]

Over time, institutions develop distinct regulations and norms that may influence the firm's behaviour and, consequently, gender diversity on the board.[30] In this regard, focusing on the EU context, the promotion of gender equality is a fundamental value and objective, and considerable progress has been made in the recent years.[31] Therefore we may expect increased gender diversity over time.

---

[25] Brammer et al., 'Gender and Ethnic Diversity'.

[26] Brammer et al., 'Gender and Ethnic Diversity'; Hillman et al., 'Organizational Predictors '.

[27] M. A. Fernández Izquierdo, M. J. Muñoz-Torres, I. Ferrero-Ferrero and L. Bellés-Colomer, 'Gender and Sustainability in the Governance of Spanish Universities' (2017) 12 (2) *ICCLJ*, 61–79.

[28] Brammer et al., 'Gender and Ethnic Diversity'.

[29] Grosvold et al., 'Board Diversity in the United Kingdom and Norway'; Grosvold, 'Where Are all the Women?'.

[30] Grosvold, 'Where Are all the Women?'.

[31] European Commission, *Strategic engagement for Gender Equality (2016–2019).* SWD (2015). 278 final. 2016. See http://ec.europa.eu/anti-trafficking/eu-policy/strategic-engagement-gender-equality-2016–2019.

7.3   Sample, Variables of the Model and Methodology

This section explains the sample, variables of the model and methodology used to empirically identify factors that explain the evolution of the percentage of women on boards.

7.3.1   Sample

The sample consists of companies listed in the stock exchanges of the EU Member States for the period 2002–2013. The information was obtained from the Thomson Reuters ASSET4 database, which uses only publicly available information. As Schäfer et al.[32] state, Thomson Reuters Asset4 database provides transparent, objective, auditable, comparable and systematic economic, environmental, social and governance information, offering a comprehensive platform for establishing benchmarks for the assessment of corporate performance. Firms from Slovenia, Slovakia, Romania, Malta, Lithuania, Latvia, Estonia, Croatia and Bulgaria were not considered because the database did not contain information about gender board diversity for the firms of these countries. The sample consists of an incomplete data set in the panel of 1,013 companies and 8,811 firm-year observations. The final sample for the regression is 7,685 firm-year observations for the period 2002–2013.

7.3.2   Variables of the Model

Percentage of Women on the Board:	This is the dependent variable of interest in this study and it is measured as the percentage of women on the board of directors divided by 100.
Board size:	This study measures board size as the logarithm of the number of board members.
Policy:	This variable is coded 1 if a firm has a policy for maintaining well-balanced membership of the board and 0 otherwise.[33]
Implementation:	This variable is coded 1 if a firm describes the implementation of its balanced board structure policy and 0

---

[32] H. Schäfer, J. Beer, J. Zenker and P. Fernandes, *Who Is Who in Corporate Social Responsibility Rating? A Survey of Internationally Established Rating Systems That Measure Corporate Responsibility* (Gütersloh: Bertelsmann Foundation, 2006).

[33] This variable has been created according to the indicator of Asset4 'Board Structure/ Policy'.

otherwise. This variable is lagged one period with the aim of capturing the causal effect on the dependent variable.[34]

Improvements: This variable is coded 1 if a firm has the necessary internal improvement and information tools to develop balanced board structure and 0 otherwise. This variable is lagged one period with the aim of capturing the causal effect on the dependent variable.[35]

Firm size: This study measures firm size as the logarithm of the total assets. The use of this mathematic transformation is used to smooth the time series and to make data easier to handle and interpret. Workforce Opportunity: This variable is a score that uses values from 0 to 1. The variable measures a company's management commitment and effectiveness towards maintaining diversity and equal opportunities in its workforce. It reflects a company's capacity to increase its workforce loyalty and productivity by promoting an effective life-work balance, a family-friendly environment and equal opportunities regardless of gender, age, ethnicity, religion or sexual orientation.[36]

Industry Dummies:[37]   This study considers industry variation including dummy variables, according to the sector classification of the Industry Classification Benchmark (ICB). In the regression model, the omitted variable is the sector Construction and Materials.

Country Dummies: This study uses country dummies to reflect the differences between countries due to regulatory context, norms and national culture. In this case, the omitted variable is the country United Kingdom. In the regression model, Cyprus has been also deleted due to the small number of observations compared with the number of independent variables.

---

[34] This variable has been created according to the indicator of Asset4 'Board Structure/ Implementation'.

[35] This variable has been created according to the indicator of Asset4 'Board Structure/ Improvements'.

[36] This variable has been created according to the indicator of Asset4 'Workforce/Diversity and Opportunity'.

[37] Dummy variable: is one that takes the value 0 or 1 to indicate the absence or presence of some categorical effect that may be expected to shift the outcome (dependent variable). To work with this type of variable, we need to select one category, for example one industry, as the omitted one, in order to compare the behaviour of the rest of the variable categories with the omitted one.

Year Dummies: The data span from 2003 through 2013; this study includes dummy variables to control for year-fixed effects. In the regression model, the omitted variable is year 2003.

7.3.3   Methodology

In order to explore how the variables affect gender board diversity, this study estimates the linear regression model presented in Equation 7.1.

Consistent with previous research, Equation 7.1 contains the percentage of women on the board of directors as the dependent variable which is explained by factors from suborganisational to macro societal levels. Note that the policy, implementation, improvements and workforce opportunity variables will have an effect on te percentage of women in the future, so this study lags these variables one period.

$$
\begin{aligned}
PERCENTAGE\_&\ WOMEN\_\ BOARD_{i,t} \\
= \beta_0 &+ \beta_1 \cdot BOARD\_\ SIZE_{i,t} + \beta_2 \cdot POLICY_{i,t-1} \\
&+ \beta_3 \cdot IMPLEMENTATION_{i,t-1} + \beta_4 \cdot IMPROVEMENTS_{i,t-1} \\
&+ \beta_5 \cdot FIRM\_\ SIZE_{i,t} + \beta_6 \cdot WORFORECE\_\ OPPORTUNITY_{i,t-1} \\
&+ \sum_{K=1}^{38} \delta_K \cdot INDUSTRY_i + \sum_{L=1}^{17} \alpha_L \cdot COUNTRY_i + \sum_{J=1}^{10} \lambda_J \cdot YEAR_t + \eta_i + \upsilon_{it}
\end{aligned}
$$

$$(Eq.\ 7.1)$$

This study uses a panel data methodology given the relation shown in Equation 7.1 is explored for a group of firms over time (cross-sectional and time series data). There are two relevant advantages of panel data compared with either purely cross-sectional or time series data.[38] Firstly, panel data allows studying dynamic relationships and, secondly, it takes into account the differences among subjects (firms in this study). This heterogeneity, idiosyncrasy or uniqueness of subjects may introduce serious bias into the model estimators if omitted, since it may be correlated with other explanatory variables.

---

[38] E. W. Frees, *Longitudinal and panel data: Analysis and applications in the social sciences* (Cambridge University Press, 2004).

Traditionally, panel data provides two techniques for controlling heterogeneity of individuals: fixed effect and random effect. In this context, the fixed-effect estimation would be inconsistent because this technique assumes that the individual heterogeneity is invariant over time. Pathan[39] argues that for this type of study, the random-effect method is more suitable than the fixed-effect, since the important variables, such as board size, do not vary much over time; and the number of years is large (11 years). Therefore, with the aim of addressing the presence of individual heterogeneity, this study estimates Model 1 using the generalized least square random effect (GLS-RE) technique.

Additionally, the problem of collinearity (i.e., when two or more explanatory variables are highly correlated, which could undermine the statistical significance of an explanatory variable) has been explored by means of the variance inflation factors for the independent variables. This study tests the presence or absence of the collinearity problem using variance inflation factors (VIF), which quantifies how much the variance of the estimated coefficients are inflated when the problem of collinearity exists. Collinearity is not a problem due to the VIF results.[40]

7.4   Empirical Results

This section presents the empirical results of the model. First an analysis of descriptive statistics is included, then the main results analysis is provided.

Table 7.1 shows the mean and standard deviation of the variables 'Percentage of women on the board', 'Policy', 'Implementation', 'Improvements', and 'Workforce opportunity', as well as these statistics by year, country and sector. A preliminary result is that the mean of the 'Percentage of women on the board' is 10.26 per cent for the sample, a result that differs substantially from year, country and sector and is far from desirable from a sustainability point of view. This result strongly contrasts with the large number of companies that have a policy for maintaining well-balanced membership on the board (97.17 per cent) and those that describe the implementation of its balanced board structure policy (87.86 per cent). In contrast, only 37.67 per cent of the firms

---

[39] S. Phatan, 'Strong Boards, CEO Power and Bank Risk-Taking' (2009) 33 *Journal of Banking and Finance*, 1340–1350.

[40] L. C. Hamilton, *Statistics with Stata: Updated for Version 10* (Belmont: Duxbury Press, 2009).

Table 7.1 *Descriptive statistics*

Variable	PERCENTAGE OF WOMEN ON THE BOARD		POLICY		IMPLEMENTATION		IMPROVEMENTS		WORKFORCE OPPORTUNITY	
	Mean	S.D.	Mean	S.D.	Mean	S.D.	Mean	S.D.	Mean	S.D.
Whole sample										
	0.1026	0.1085	0.9717	0.1657	0.8786	0.3267	0.3783	0.4850	0.5821	0.3062
Obs.	8,783		8,811		8,811		8,811		8,811	
By year										
2013	0.1826	0.1132	0.9964	0.0596	0.9668	0.1793	0.6240	0.4847	0.6260	0.3000
Obs.	843		843		843		843		843	
2012	0.1561	0.1121	0.9966	0.0585	0.9623	0.1906	0.6160	0.487	0.6194	0.3010
Obs.	875		875		875		875		875	
2011	0.1292	0.1082	0.9920	0.0890	0.9576	0.2013	0.5753	0.4946	0.6222	0.3029
Obs.	876		876		876		876		876	
2010	0.1117	0.1053	0.9930	0.0838	0.9476	0.2231	0.5128	0.5001	0.6282	0.3008
Obs.	858		858		858		858		858	
2009	0.0971	0.1018	0.9964	0.0601	0.9385	0.2404	0.4948	0.5003	0.6020	0.3072
Obs.	829		829		829		829		829	
2008	0.0891	0.1025	0.9950	0.0706	0.9275	0.2595	0.4488	0.4977	0.5815	0.3118
Obs.	799		800		800		800		800	
2007	0.0833	0.1008	0.9923	0.0874	0.8912	0.3116	0.3137	0.4643	0.5557	0.3117
Obs.	779		781		781		781		781	

149

Table 7.1 (*cont.*)

Variable	PERCENTAGE OF WOMEN ON THE BOARD		POLICY		IMPLEMENTATION		IMPROVEMENTS		WORKFORCE OPPORTUNITY	
	Mean	**S.D.**	**Mean**	**S.D.**	**Mean**	**S.D.**	**Mean**	**S.D.**	**Mean**	**S.D.**
2006	0.0773	0.0996	0.9712	0.1672	0.8026	0.3983	0.1464	0.3537	0.5247	0.3037
Obs.	760		765		765		765		765	
2005	0.0685	0.0937	0.9595	0.1973	0.7647	0.4245	0.1020	0.3028	0.5411	0.2978
Obs.	759		765		765		765		765	
2004	0.0571	0.0854	0.9188	0.2734	0.7719	0.4200	0.1250	0.3310	0.5533	0.3057
Obs.	636		640		640		640		640	
2003	0.0550	0.0789	0.8982	0.3028	0.7176	0.4508	0.0738	0.2618	0.5241	0.2992
Obs.	389		393		393		393		393	
2002	0.0437	0.0693	0.8135	0.3900	0.6244	0.4849	0.0285	0.1666	0.5225	0.3015
Obs.	380		386		386		386		386	
By country										
Austria	0.0575	0.0823	0.9588	0.1994	0.6907	0.4634	0.0000	0.0000	0.5319	0.3390
Obs.	192		194		194		194		194	
Belgium	0.0839	0.0957	0.9640	0.1866	0.9209	0.2704	0.4389	0.4971	0.4005	0.2967
Obs.	278		278		278		278		278	
Cyprus	0.0819	0.0253	1.0000	0.0000	1.0000	0.0000	0.3333	0.5164	0.3846	0.0791
Obs.	6		6		6		6		6	

Czech Republic									
0.0900	0.0713	1.0000	0.0000	1.0000	0.0000	0.2273	0.4290	0.5214	0.2123
Obs. 22		22		22		22		22	
Denmark									
0.1191	0.1092	0.9494	0.2196	0.5798	0.4946	0.1790	0.3841	0.4660	0.3228
Obs. 257		257		257		257		257	
Finland									
0.2003	0.1196	0.9928	0.0845	0.8710	0.3359	0.0896	0.2861	0.5021	0.2836
Obs. 279		279		279		279		279	
France									
0.1243	0.1148	0.9684	0.1751	0.8969	0.3042	0.2694	0.4439	0.7138	0.2791
Obs. 979		980		980		980		980	
Germany									
0.0884	0.1040	0.9939	0.0780	0.7094	0.4543	0.0600	0.2373	0.6735	0.3070
Obs. 817		819		819		819		819	
Greece									
0.0653	0.0840	0.8035	0.3982	0.3887	0.4885	0.0830	0.2764	0.3941	0.3130
Obs. 223		229		229		229		229	
Hungary									
0.0389	0.0483	1.0000	0.0000	0.8095	0.4024	0.0000	0.0000	0.6676	0.2840
Obs. 21		21		21		21		21	
Ireland									
0.0764	0.0768	1.0000	0.0000	0.9662	0.1813	0.5338	0.5006	0.3430	0.2700
Obs. 148		148		148		148		148	
Italy									
0.0508	0.0747	0.9705	0.1695	0.7264	0.4463	0.2736	0.4463	0.5792	0.3350
Obs. 507		508		508		508		508	
Luxembourg									
0.1177	0.1408	1.0000	0.0000	0.8846	0.3226	0.3270	0.4737	0.3596	0.2042
Obs. 52		52		52		52		52	
Netherlands									
0.1138	01185	0.9781	0.1464	0.9618	0.1921	0.2978	0.4579	0.6289	0.2984
Obs. 365		366		366		366		366	
Poland									
0.1141	0.1236	1.0000	0.0000	0.7900	0.4091	0.0420	0.2015	0.2501	0.2329
Obs. 119		119		119		119		119	
Portugal									
0.0209	0.0390	0.9091	0.2887	0.6777	0.4693	0.2231	0.4181	0.5058	0.2869
Obs. 120		121		121		121		121	

Table 7.1 (cont.)

Variable	PERCENTAGE OF WOMEN ON THE BOARD		POLICY		IMPLEMENTATION		IMPROVEMENTS		WORKFORCE OPPORTUNITY	
	Mean	S.D.	Mean	S.D.	Mean	S.D.	Mean	S.D.	Mean	S.D.
Spain	0.0792	0.0870	0.9412	0.2355	0.9333	0.2500	0.2647	0.4416	0.6983	0.3220
Obs.	501		510		510		510		510	
Sweden	0.2245	0.1270	0.9132	0.2818	0.9168	0.2764	0.2532	0.4352	0.5755	0.2774
Obs.	551		553		553		553		553	
United Kingdom	0.0910	0.0933	0.9931	0.0826	0.9842	0.1248	0.6420	0.4795	0.5751	0.2780
Obs.	3346		3349		3349		3349		3349	
By sector										
Aerospace & Defence	0.0678	0.0968	0.9412	0.2370	0.8824	0.3246	0.3382	0.4766	0.6259	0.2912
Obs.	68		68		68		68		68	
Alternative Energy	0.1161	0.1132	1.0000	0.0000	0.5714	0.4994	0.2679	0.4469	0.6797	0.3056
Obs.	55		56		56		56		56	
Automobiles & Parts	0.0864	0.0936	1.0000	0.0000	0.7500	0.4345	0.2095	0.4083	0.7948	0.2508
Obs.	148		148		148		148		148	
Banks	0.1134	0.1196	0.9501	0.2180	0.7874	0.4095	0.2738	0.4462	0.6322	0.3401
Obs.	617		621		621		621		621	
Beverages	0.1161	0.1070	0.9559	0.2069	0.7941	0.4074	0.1765	0.3841	0.3659	0.2395
Obs.	68		68		68		68		68	

Chemicals	0.1022	0.1019	0.9890	0.1048	0.8011	0.4003	0.1050	0.3074	0.6945	0.2743
Obs.	181		181		181		181		181	
Construction & Materials	0.0950	0.1030	0.9668	0.1795	0.8761	0.3299	0.2175	0.4132	0.6018	0.3217
Obs.	331		331		331		331		331	
Electricity	0.0994	0.1228	0.9677	0.1772	0.8925	0.3106	0.2151	0.4120	0.7108	0.3016
Obs.	185		186		186		186		186	
Electronic & Electrical Equipment	0.0977	0.1045	1.0000	0.0000	0.9462	0.2268	0.2581	0.4400	0.4419	0.2802
Obs.	93		93		93		93		93	
Financial Services	0.0927	0.0956	0.9800	0.1404	0.8250	0.3809	0.2200	0.4153	0.3643	0.3182
Obs.	200		200		200		200		200	
Fixed Line Telecommunications	0.1058	0.1111	0.9787	0.1448	0.9007	0.3001	0.3333	0.4731	0.7406	0.2555
Obs.	141		141		141		141		141	
Food Producers	0.0670	0.0951	0.9907	0.0962	0.8519	0.3569	0.1574	0.3659	0.3870	0.2822
Obs.	107		108		108		108		108	
Food & Drug Retailers	0.1342	0.1553	0.9090	0.2886	0.7803	0.4156	0.2045	0.4049	0.6160	0.2042
Obs.	131		132		132		132		132	
Forestry & Paper	0.1921	0.0702	0.9286	0.2607	0.9762	0.1543	0.4048	0.4968	0.7178	0.1970
Obs.	42		42		42		42		42	
Gas, Water & Multiutilities	0.0719	0.0874	0.9912	0.0941	0.9115	0.2853	0.1947	0.3977	0.8181	0.2152
Obs.	113		113		113		113		113	
General Industrials	0.0597	0.0857	0.9634	0.1889	0.7927	0.4079	0.2439	0.4321	0.5191	0.3244
Obs.	82		82		82		82		82	

Table 7.1 (*cont.*)

Variable	PERCENTAGE OF WOMEN ON THE BOARD		POLICY		IMPLEMENTATION		IMPROVEMENTS		WORKFORCE OPPORTUNITY	
	Mean	S.D.	Mean	S.D.	Mean	S.D.	Mean	S.D.	Mean	S.D.
General Retailers	0.1822	0.1770	0.9651	0.1846	0.6512	0.4794	0.1279	0.3360	0.5346	0.3378
Obs.	86		86		86		86		86	
Health Care Equipment & Services	0.1124	0.1086	0.9375	0.2430	0.7734	0.4203	0.0938	0.2926	0.3931	0.2637
Obs.	128		128		128		128		128	
Household Goods & Home Construction	0.2518	0.1280	0.8688	0.3404	0.7050	0.4599	0.1148	0.3214	0.4883	0.3130
Obs.	61		61		61		61		61	
Industrial Engineering	0.1284	0.1077	0.9702	0.1705	0.8172	0.3873	0.1194	0.3249	0.5364	0.2872
Obs.	267		268		268		268		268	
Industrial Metals & Mining	0.1074	0.1205	0.9272	0.2608	0.8940	0.3088	0.1788	0.3845	0.4185	0.2483
Obs.	150		151		151		151		151	
Industrial Transportation	0.0943	0.1046	0.9208	0.2707	0.6782	0.4683	0.1287	0.3357	0.5924	0.3216
Obs.	202		202		202		202		202	
Leisure Goods	0.0867	0.1059	1.0000	0.0000	0.6207	0.4938	0.0690	0.2579	0.3786	0.2216
Obs.	29		29		29		29		29	

Life Insurance	0.1183	0.0978	0.9855	0.1204	0.7391	0.4423	0.5507	0.5011	0.7653	0.2633
Obs.	69		69		69		69		69	
Media	0.1263	0.1239	0.9790	0.1439	0.8404	0.3668	0.2290	0.4208	0.5826	0.3289
Obs.	332		332		332		332		332	
Mining	0.1281	0.1031	1.0000	0.0000	0.9615	0.1961	0.3846	0.4961	0.5932	0.3428
Obs.	26		26		26		26		26	
Mobile Telecommunications	0.2072	0.1269	1.0000	0.0000	0.8529	0.3568	0.2647	0.4444	0.5766	0.3207
Obs.	68		68		68		68		68	
Nonlife Insurance	0.1171	0.1270	0.9796	0.1419	0.7687	0.4231	0.1497	0.3580	0.6799	0.3244
Obs.	147		147		147		147		147	
Oil Equipment & Services	0.0780	0.1069	0.9539	0.2115	0.9231	0.2685	0.3692	0.4864	0.4028	0.2795
Obs.	65		65		65		65		65	
Oil & Gas Producers	0.0895	0.1073	0.9355	0.2465	0.8194	0.3860	0.2258	0.4195	0.6159	0.2983
Obs.	154		155		155		155		155	
Personal Goods	0.1196	0.1049	0.9726	0.1638	0.8082	0.3951	0.3014	0.4604	0.6851	0.2939
Obs.	144		146		146		146		146	
Pharmaceuticals & Biotechnology	0.0999	0.0855	0.9037	0.2957	0.7754	0.4184	0.2567	0.4380	0.5668	0.3186
Obs.	183		187		187		187		187	
Real Estate Investment Trusts	0.0674	0.0886	0.9510	0.2170	0.8824	0.3238	0.2353	0.4263	0.5531	0.3123
Obs.	102		102		102		102		102	
Real Estate Investment & Services	0.1197	0.1291	0.9470	0.2250	0.8030	0.3992	0.0379	0.1916	0.4211	0.3255
Obs.	131		132		132		132		132	

Table 7.1 (*cont.*)

Variable	PERCENTAGE OF WOMEN ON THE BOARD		POLICY		IMPLEMENTATION		IMPROVEMENTS		WORKFORCE OPPORTUNITY	
	Mean	S.D.	Mean	S.D.	Mean	S.D.	Mean	S.D.	Mean	S.D.
Software & Computer Services	0.0834	0.1058	1.0000	0.0000	0.7718	0.4211	0.1410	0.3491	0.5291	0.3140
Obs.	148		149		149		149		149	
Support Services	0.1454	0.1292	0.9231	0.2676	0.7308	0.4457	0.1154	0.3210	0.5554	0.2808
Obs.	104		104		104		104		104	
Technology Hardware & Equipment	0.1175	0.1170	0.9130	0.2830	0.8609	0.3476	0.2783	0.4501	0.6072	0.3153
Obs.	114		115		115		115		115	
Tobacco	0.2021	0.1540	0.9412	0.2425	1.0000	0.0000	0.3529	0.4926	0.5436	0.2991
Obs.	17		17		17		17		17	
Travel & Leisure	0.1035	0.1248	0.9281	0.2592	0.8366	0.3710	0.3333	0.4730	0.6768	0.3257
Obs.	150		153		153		153		153	

Note: Obs. – number of observations

156

have internal improvement and information tools to develop balance board structure and, focusing on the commitment and effectiveness towards maintaining equal opportunity in the workforce, the mean of the score is 58.21 per cent. Accordingly, there is still much room for improvement.

Regarding the evolution of gender diversity and the efforts to develop balanced board structures, Table 7.1 presents growing means year by year, which represents slight progress during the last years, probably as a consequence of the EU and national regulatory initiatives. Concerning countries, the highest (22.45 per cent) and the lowest (2.09 per cent) mean of the percentage of female board members are obtained in Sweden and Portugal, respectively.[41] In relation to sectors, the result of gender diversity is closely linked with the proportion of female employees in a specific sector. For instance, the lowest proportion of women on the board (5.97 per cent) corresponds to the General Industrials sector, which includes male-dominated branches of economy such as industrial companies and producers and distributors of containers and packaging. In contrast, the best results of gender diversity (25.18 per cent) are observed in the Household Goods and Home Construction sector, which considers producers and distributors of durable and non-durable house-hold products, furniture and home construction – areas where women are substantial in the workforce and represent an important group of consumers.

Table 7.2 shows the results of GLS-RE estimation of Model 1. The regression is well-suited for the dependent variable with an overall R-squared[42] of 35.17 per cent. In line with the results of previous studies,[43] a positive relationship is evident between gender diversity and board size (0.0018, p-value < 0.001). Regarding the efforts of a firm to improve gender diversity on the board, the results reveal an insignificant

---

[41] Note that Norway, which is not an EU Member State and therefore not included in this analysis, is an exception because of the change in the Companies Act that mandated a minimum of 40 per cent of each gender on the board of public companies. For further information, see: B. Sjåfjell, 'Gender Diversity in the Board Room & Its Impacts: Is the Example of Norway a Way Forward?' (December 11, 2014). *Deakin Law Review*, 20 (1) (2015), pp. 25–52.

[42] R- squared is a measure on a scale of 0 to 100 that indicates the proportion of the variance in the dependent variable that is predictable from the independent variables. It is a goodness-of-fit measure in multiple-regression analysis.

[43] Conyon and Mallin, 'Women in the Boardroom', 112–117; J. I. Siciliano, 'The Relationship of Board Member Diversity to Organizational Performance' (1996) 15(12) *Journal of Business Ethics*, 1313–1320.

Table 7.2

ESTIMATION OF PERCENTAGE OF WOMEN ON THE BOARD	
BOARD SIZE$_{i,t}$	0.0018*** (0.0004)
POLICY$_{i,t-1}$	−0.0071 (0.0050)
IMPLEMENTATION$_{i,t-1}$	0.0035 (0.0031)
IMPROVEMENTS$_{i,t-1}$	−0.0036 (0.0024)
FIRM SIZE$_{i,t}$	0.0045** (0.0014)
WORKFORCE OPPORTUNITY$_{i,t-1}$	0.0147*** (0.0037)
AEROSPACE & DEFENCE	−0.0174 (0.0324)
ALTERNATIVE ENERGY	0.0812* (0.0323)
AUTOMOBILES & PARTS	−0.0079 (0.0236)
BANKS	0.0213 (0.0159)
BEVERAGES	0.0407 (0.0297)
CHEMICALS	0.0202 (0.0212)
ELECTRICITY	0.0320 (0.0199)
ELECTRONIC & ELECTRICAL EQUIP.	0.0019 (0.0260)
FINANCIAL SERVICES	−0.0023 (0.0199)
FIXED LINE TELECOMMUNICATIONS	0.0271 (0.0223)
FOOD RETAILERS	0.0403† (0.0242)
FOOD PRODUCERS	0.0171 (0.0254)
FORESTRY & PAPER	−0.0290 (0.0392)
GAS, WATER & MULTIUTILITIES	−0.0118 (0.0244)
GENERAL INDUSTRIALS	−0.0206 (0.0293)
GENERAL RETAILERS	0.1143*** (0.0277)
HEALTH CARE EQUIPMENT & SERVICES	0.0052 (0.0238)
HOUSEHOLD GOODS & HOME CONSTRUCTION	0.1066*** (0.0311)
INDUSTRIAL ENGINEERING	−0.0188 (0.0194)
INDUSTRIAL METALS & MINING	−0.0116 (0.0218)
INDUSTRIAL TRANSPORTATION	0.0160 (0.0204)
LEISURE GOODS	−0.0461 (0.0444)
LIFE INSURANCE	0.0315 (0.0296)
MEDIA	0.0442* (0.0177)
MINING	−0.0250 (0.0403)
MOBILE TELECOMMUNICATIONS	0.0855** (0.0302)
NONLIFE INSURANCE	0.0242 (0.0235)
OIL EQUIPMENT & SERVICES	−0.0094 (0.0307)

Table 7.2 (*cont.*)

ESTIMATION OF PERCENTAGE OF WOMEN ON THE BOARD	
OIL & GAS PRODUCERS	−0.0059 (0.0216)
PERSONAL GOODS	0.0292 (0.0227)
PHARMACEUTICALS & BIOTECHNOLOGY	0.0032 (0.0207)
REAL ESTATE INVESTMENT TRUSTS	−0.0315 (0.0261)
REAL ESTATE INVESTMENT & SERVICES	−0.0050 (0.0224)
SOFTWARE & COMPUTER SERVICES	−0.0031 (0.0219)
SUPPORT SERVICES	0.0366 (0.0238)
TECHNOLOGY HARDWARE & EQUIPMENT	0.0028 (0.0246)
TOBACCO	0.0310 (0.0540)
TRAVEL & LEISURE	0.0267 (0.0229)
SWEDEN	0.1209*** (0.0172)
SPAIN	−0.0425** (0.0160)
PORTUGAL	−0.1092*** (0.0243)
POLAND	−0.0538** (0.0202)
NETHERLANDS	0.0084 (0.0177)
LUXEMBOURG	−0.0409 (0.0346)
ITALY	−0.0724*** (0.0167)
IRELAND	−0.0326 (0.0228)
HUNGARY	−0.1504*** (0.0417)
GREECE	−0.0468* (0.0200)
FRANCE	0.0093 (0.0153)
FINLAND	0.1217*** (0.0195)
DENMARK	0.0071 (0.0201)
CZECH REPUBLIC	−0.0786* (0.0347)
BELGIUM	−0.0245 (0.0196)
AUSTRIA	−0.0365† (0.0208)
GERMANY	−0.0288† (0.0159)
2013	0.1424*** (0.0044)
2012	0.1176*** (0.0044)
2011	0.0907*** (0.0043)
2010	0.0707*** (0.0043)
2009	0.0561*** (0.0043)
2008	0.0476*** (0.0042)

Table 7.2 (*cont.*)

ESTIMATION OF PERCENTAGE OF WOMEN ON THE BOARD	
2007	0.0412*** (0.0041)
2006	0.0328*** (0.0040)
2005	0.0239*** (0.0040)
2004	0.0101* (0.0043)
CONSTANT	0.0588 (0.0200)
Wald (X^2 statistics)	3,751.65*** [71]
R^2 within	0.3297
R^2 between	0.3275
R^2 overall	0.3517
Obs.	7,685

This table presents the results of the GLS-RE estimates of Model 1.
Standard errors are in brackets. Statistically significant at $^{\dagger}p < 0.10$; $^{*}p < 0.05$; $^{**}p < 0.01$; $^{***}p < 0.001$.
The subscript '*i*' refers to the *i*th firm
The subscript '*t*' refers to the time, therefore '*t*−1' denotes the value of the variable one time before time t.

effect of policy for maintaining well-balanced boards. Likewise, the fact that a company describes the implementation of this policy or the existence of internal improvement and information tools to develop the policy on the percentage of women on the board also have an insignificant effect on the percentage of women on the board. A possible explanation for this unexpected outcome is that the firms may adopt a balanced board policy in a symbolic way, without a clear objective of achieving a more balanced gender representation on their boards. Focusing on the organisational level, this study supports the expected positive relationship between gender diversity on boards and firm size (0.0045, *p*-value < 0.01) and effectiveness towards maintaining equal opportunities in the firm's workforce (0.0147, *p*-value < 0.001), given the *p*-value of both variables is below 0.05.[44] This result supports the institutional theory, because those firms that are effective in developing and implementing equal opportunities programmes in their workforces foster a diversity and plurality culture and help mitigate subsequent homosocial

---

[44] In econometrics, when p-value is small (*p*-value < 0.05), we could say that we have strong evidence on the significance of the variable for explaining the dependent variable.

reproduction and male-dominance in the firm, leading to a higher percentage of women on boards.

With reference to the sectorial and country levels, the results support the conclusions of previous studies.[45] Those sectors with a larger proportion of female employees and those oriented to end consumers such as General Retailers, Household Goods and Home Construction, Media and Mobile Telecommunications are positively correlated to the proportion of women on the boards. Regarding countries, this study shows that the institutional environment in Spain, Portugal, Poland, Italy, Hungary, Greece and the Czech Republic is worse than the institutional environment established in the UK in terms of promoting gender diversity on boards. However, in Sweden and Finland the institutional environment is better than that established in UK. This result is in line with the arguments of Grosvold et al.,[46] since these relationships are explained by the different institutional pressures for improved gender diversity as well as the variations in social and cultural characteristics among the countries of the EU. Finally, this study observes progress in gender diversity on boards more evident during 2012 and 2013. Nonetheless, much work needs to be done to ensure well gender-balanced boards and achieve the objectives of the EU.

7.5   Discussion and Conclusion

This study advances the understanding of gender diversity by exploring the factors that may affect the percentage of women on the corporate board. To that end, this chapter uses multilevel factors from institutional theory and tests their significance to explain board gender diversity. This chapter uses a panel of listed firms from the EU during the period 2002–2013 and applies GLS-RE estimator, which takes into account the idiosyncrasy of each firm in the estimation. The main results are in line with previous studies, identifying board size, firm size, industry, country, time and effective programs of equal opportunity in the workforce as significant variables to explain the variability in percentage of women on the board. However, as an unexpected result, this study finds that corporate policy and additional efforts for maintaining well-balanced

---

[45] Grosvold, 'Where Are All the Women'; Grosvold et al., 'Board Diversity in the United Kingdom and Norway'; Brammer et al., 'Gender and Ethnic Diversity'; Hillman et al., 'Organizational predictors'.

[46] Grosvold et al., 'Board Diversity in the United Kingdom and Norway'.

boards do not affect the gender composition of the board in the next year. This finding puts in doubt the effectiveness of gender diversity policy at board level and sheds suspicion on the possibility that firms adopt a balanced board policy in a symbolic manner.

The result of this study could explain the mixed findings in previous research about the relationship between gender diversity and corporate sustainability, as many of these analyses use percentage of women on the board as a proxy of effective gender diversity.

As long as women have true participation, engagement and a greater voice in decision-making processes, the presence of women adds quality to board discussions and decision making, facilitating better understanding of the business environment and addressing the demands of different stakeholders. However, this substantive and effective participation of women requires corporate policies and commitment to maintaining gender diversity in top positions. Those firms that adopt gender diversity with minimal structural change to the corporation (liberal structuralism approach) – where the presence of women on the board is only a symbolic practice, with progressive marginalisation and devaluation of women in decision-making processes – will not be able to gain the gender diversity benefits.

This study proposes to combine additional variables such as the existence and implementation of a policy for maintaining well-balanced membership and the existence of internal tools for improving the percentage of women on boards. Nonetheless, this study finds that, in the EU during the period 2002–2013, these variables do not lead to the enhancement of the percentage of women on boards. The study also shows the ineffectiveness of corporate efforts to improve female representation, evidencing minimal structural change as a response to legal requirements instead of a solution to real problems.

An explanation of these findings could be that during the sample period a 'male-centric' environment persisted in firms, which is associated with a lack of fit between feminine stereotypes and leadership qualities. Therefore, with the aim of fostering gender as an agent for change towards corporate sustainability, it is not important that firms not only adopt the minimal normative requirements in term of policies or gain in women's numeric representation on top positions, but that they also have voice, authority and access to the necessary resources to establish sustainable strategies.

As with every empirical research, the findings should be viewed in light of potential limitations, which also might open new areas for future research. One limitation of this study is that empirical findings are conditioned by the sample and the availability of information. A larger sample, extending this study to non-EU countries, will make it possible to test the robustness of the results. The results of this study might also be limited by the variables used, which are related to diversity in the broad sense (age, background, nationality, etc.) other than the dependent variable. Future studies should use more accurate measurements of gender diversity on boards and their effectiveness. Another limitation is the assumption of only a year between the policy adoption and its consequence on the percentage of board of directors, which should be overcome in further works considering longer periods of time to examine the cause-effect relationship.

Finally, this study concludes that although the EU and national initiatives have already produced encouraging results, much remains to be done with respect to improving the effectiveness of the diversity policy on boards and their consequent effect on corporate sustainability.

Social Entrepreneurship: (The Challenge for) Women as Economic Actors?

The Role and Position of Women in Dutch Social Enterprises

AIKATERINI ARGYROU, ROSALIEN DIEPEVEEN AND
TINEKE LAMBOOY

8.1 Introduction

This chapter provides a discussion concerning an empirical study and its gender-related results with respect to the role and position of women in Dutch social enterprises. The objective of the chapter is to discuss to what extent Dutch social enterprises are catalysts to promote the role and position of women in their organisational structure and functioning. As several social enterprises pursue as their societal goal the improvement of the position of women in society, or certain groups of (marginalised) women, this chapter analyses – on the basis of the empirical results – whether the role and position of women in Dutch social enterprises may indicate a change to sustainable organisational practices with positive outcomes for women in organisations, but also for women's lives in society.

In the study, we collected the data by means of a survey that was filled out by 66 social enterprises. The study was performed in collaboration with PwC Netherlands (PwC NL) and the Dutch network organisation for social enterprises, Social Enterprise NL. We analysed the empirical data in view of the goal of this chapter and will discuss them in light of scholarly theory on entrepreneurship and governance with respect to the following research questions: (1) Do the examined social enterprises in the Netherlands facilitate the role and position of women as compared to men in the structure and functioning of the organisation?[1] (2) To what

---

[1] Although it is not usual to use closed-ended questions in academic literature, we formulated question (1) as a close-ended question because it is tested in the empirical part of the

extent do the results of the examined social enterprises suggest not only a change in the role and position of women in organisations, but also an improvement of women's lives in the Netherlands?

The chapter is structured as follows: Section 8.2 defines 'social enterprises' for the purpose of this chapter. The same section also discusses the manner in which social enterprises in the Netherlands may contribute to sustainable outcomes in organisations and in society. Section 8.3 elaborates on the relationship of gender and social enterprise to empower women's position and role in organisations. Section 8.4 discusses how female-driven social enterprises may be actors of change in women's lives in society. Section 8.5 begins with presenting the methodology of the survey and then the gender-related results. The section goes on to discuss the gender-related results in light of the extant literature discussed in Sections 8.3 and 8.4 and in response to the research questions. Conclusions are drawn in Section 8.6.

8.2   Social Enterprises in the Netherlands and their Contribution to Sustainability

A great number of EU countries have introduced the concept of social enterprises in their national legislation. By means of tailor-made legal forms and/or conducive legislation, social enterprises are promoted as economic agents which contribute to 'sustainable growth' and development.[2] According to the European Commission's definition, a social enterprise is:

---

research and because an open-ended question would provide results too broad to commence a meaningful discussion.

[2] A. Argyrou and T. Lambooy, 'An introduction to tailor-made legislation for social enterprises in Europe: A comparison of legal regimes in Belgium, Greece and the UK', (2017) 12 *International and Comparative Corporate Law Journal*, 3, pp. 47–107; T. E. Lambooy and A. Argyrou, 'Improving the legal environment for social entrepreneurship' (2014) 11 *European Company Law*, 2, 71–76; A. Argyrou, T. Lambooy, R. J. Blomme and H. Kievit, 'Unravelling the participation of stakeholders in the governance models of social enterprises in Greece' (2017) 17 *Corporate Governance: The International Journal of Business in Society*, 4, 661–677; A. Argyrou, T. Lambooy, R .J. Blomme, H. Kievit, G. Kruseman and D. H. Siccama, 'An empirical investigation of supportive legal frameworks for social enterprises in Belgium: A cross-sectoral comparison of case studies for social enterprises from the social housing, finance and energy sector perspective', in V. Mauerhofer (ed.), *Legal Aspects of Sustainable Development: Horizontal and Sectorial Policy Issues* (Vienna: Springer International Publishing, 2016). European Commission, *Communication from the Commission to the European Parliament, the Council, the European Economic and Social Committee and the Committee of the Regions, Social*

an operator in the social economy whose main objective is to have a social impact rather than make a profit for their owners or shareholders. It operates by providing goods and services for the market in an entrepreneurial and innovative fashion and uses its profits primarily to achieve social objectives. It is managed in an open and responsible manner and, in particular, involve[s] employees, consumers and stakeholders affected by its commercial activities.[3]

Social enterprises according to the Commission's definition are hybrid market organisations pursuing primarily social but also other types of sustainable objectives (i.e., environmental) while demonstrating participatory, transparent and socially responsible attributes in their structure and practice. Although the notion of sustainability is not reflected in the Commission's definition, scholarly literature establishes a direct link between sustainability and social enterprises' objectives.[4] Social enterprises are organisations driven by entrepreneurs who 'find new and efficient ways to create products, services or structures that either directly cater to social needs or that enable others to cater to social needs that must be satisfied in order to achieve sustainable development'.[5] However, social enterprises address the essence of sustainability in a way that does not refer only to the social dimension of sustainability but includes also the 'inextricable interrelatedness of the environmental, social, and economic facets of sustainability'.[6] They provide solutions for societal problems and needs with a focus in their goal and mission on 'environmental,

---

Business Initiative: Creating a favourable climate for social enterprises, key stakeholders in the social economy and innovation (Social Business Initiative Communication), COM (2011) 682 final, p. 2. 'Sustainable growth' has been embedded in the EU strategy and policy goals for 2020, see http://ec.europa.eu/europe2020/europe-2020-in-a-nutshell/pri orities/sustainable-growth/index_en.htm.

[3] Social Business Initiative Communication, pp. 2–3.

[4] A. Picciotti, 'Towards sustainability: The innovation paths of social enterprise' (2017) 88 Annals of Public and Cooperative Economics, 2, 233–256 at 235. A. Rahdari, S. Sepasi and M. Moradi, 'Achieving sustainability through Schumpeterian social entrepreneurship: The role of social enterprises' (2016) 137 Journal of Cleaner Production, 347–360 at 352; Argyrou et al., 'An empirical investigation of supportive legal frameworks for social enterprises in Belgium', pp. 181–182.

[5] Picciotti, 'Towards sustainability', p. 235. Picciotti citing C. Seelos and J. Mair, 'Social Entrepreneurship: The contribution of individual entrepreneurs to sustainable development' IESE Working Paper No. 553 (2004), p. 8. See also the distinction of the two types of social entrepreneurs in Ch. 9.

[6] B. Sjåfjell and B. J. Richardson, 'The future of company law and sustainability', in B. Sjåfjell and B. J. Richardson, Company Law and Sustainability: Legal Barriers and Opportunities (Cambridge: Cambridge University Press, 2015), p. 313.

social and economic sustainability'.[7] Picciotti notes that 'due to the emergence of new needs, such as environmental protection, the creation of new jobs for young people and the regeneration of social ties in local communities, projects and activities aimed at sustainable development are being considered with increasing frequency, and taking on the role of innovation strategies for the social enterprise'.[8] Goyal and Sergi argue that sustainability is an important factor for social enterprises, because the way social enterprises behave is determined by their social goal, 'the need for sustainability and the prevailing environmental dynamics'.[9]

There are also scholars with diverging opinions on this topic. Hall et al. argue that social entrepreneurship differs from sustainable entrepreneurship, as according to these authors sustainable entrepreneurs focus more on the natural environment aspect, whereas social entrepreneurs mainly target a social issue.[10] They state that on the basis of literature it appears that solving social problems drives both social and sustainable entrepreneurs; however, the sustainable entrepreneur would focus more on environmental problems, which may not be a priority for the social entrepreneur.[11] There could be an overlap between sustainable and social entrepreneurship, as 'the issue of sustainability is however, in the macro sense, a social issue as it impacts societal level concerns'.[12] This is confirmed by Kury, who argues that 'environmental problems are social problems as the impact that the choices made regarding sustainability have far reaching implications for society'.[13]

Additionally, social enterprises may be said to be organisations demonstrating participatory, transparent and socially responsible practices in managing the interests and the demands of multiple stakeholders to which they are accountable.[14] In the literature, it is noticed that social

---

[7] Picciotti, 'Towards sustainability', p. 234.   [8] Ibid.

[9] S. Goyal and B. S. Sergi, 'Social entrepreneurship and sustainability – Understanding the context and key characteristics' (2015) 4 *Journal of Security and Sustainability Issues*, 3, 269–278 at 270.

[10] J. K. Hall, G. A. Daneke and M. J. Lenox, 'Sustainable Development and Entrepreneurship: Past Contributions and Future Directions' (2010) 25 *Journal of Business Venturing* 5, 439–448; Also citing Hall et al. is K. W. Kury, 'Sustainability meets social entrepreneurship: A path to social change through institutional entrepreneurship' (2012) 4 *International Journal of Business Insights and Transformation*, 3, 64–71 at 64.

[11] Kury, 'Sustainability meets social entrepreneurship', p. 66.   [12] Ibid, p. 64.

[13] Ibid, p. 66.

[14] B. Doherty, H. Haugh and F. Lyon, 'Social enterprises as hybrid organizations: A review and research agenda' (2014) 16 *International Journal of Management Reviews*, 4, 417–436 at 422 and 426. Argyrou et al., 'Unravelling the participation of stakeholders in the

entrepreneurs carefully select their legal and organisational structures in order to effectively realise their social and other sustainable objectives while maintaining accountability to various stakeholder groups.[15] The development of stakeholder participatory governance structures by social enterprises, and their adherence to socially responsible reporting obligations facilitate accountability to stakeholders. Additionally, it stimulates the participation of stakeholders in the decision-making processes and internalisation of social and environmental externalities.[16]

Although in the scholarly discussion in the Netherlands much weight is placed on the definition of social enterprises as well as on the development of legal and organisational forms to accommodate social enterprises, the Netherlands is still among the few EU countries which has not yet developed a uniform definition nor a tailor-made legal form for social enterprises in its national legal system.[17] The Dutch Social and Economic Council (SER), upon request of the Dutch Government, identified the development of social enterprise organisations emerging in the Netherlands.[18] The SER accumulated particular characteristics of the Dutch social enterprises which can be used to describe these organisations operating in the Netherlands. According to this, a Dutch social enterprise: (1) is primarily an enterprise (as opposed to non-entrepreneurial actors); (2) prioritises the pursuit of its social objectives as opposed to the pursuit of financial objectives; (3) is independent from the government in terms of financing by employing an income-generating business model without relying on public grants, gifts and subsidies; (4) pursues

---

governance of social enterprises', p. 665; Argyrou et al., 'Supportive legal frameworks for social enterprises in Belgium', pp. 154–156. For the purpose of this chapter, the term 'stakeholder' comprises broadly any individual, group or system which affects or is affected by the social and entrepreneurial activity of the social enterprise, e.g., employees, volunteers, users, clients, beneficiaries, local community groups, social investors and/or society at large.

[15] Doherty et al., 'Social enterprises as hybrid organizations'.   [16] Ibid. See also Ch. 9.

[17] European Commission, 'A map of social enterprises and their eco-systems in Europe: Synthesis Report' (Publications Office of the European Union, 2015), see http://ec.europa .eu/social/main.jsp?langId=en&catId=89&newsId=2149; See also www.seforis.eu. A. Argyrou, P. A. Anthoni and T. Lambooy, 'Legal forms for social enterprises in the Dutch legal framework: An empirical analysis of social entrepreneurs' attitudes on the needs of social enterprises in the Netherlands' (2017) 12 International and Comparative Corporate Law Journal, 3, pp. 1–46.

[18] The Dutch Social and Economic Council (SER), 'Summary of Council advisory report on social enterprises' (2015), see www.ser.nl/~/media/files/internet/talen/engels/2015/2015-social-enterprises.ashx.

mainstream market activities which are independent from government policies.[19] In this way, the SER formulated the most common characteristics of Dutch social enterprises instead of formulating a uniform definition.

Contrary to the normative and political levels, in which the social enterprise concept is still underdeveloped in the Netherlands, in mainstream social entrepreneurial practice, the term 'social enterprise', in a converging way, is understood to comprise the cumulative elements introduced by the Commission's uniform definition concerning the social enterprise.[20] The Commission's definition of the social enterprise has been adopted by the largest platform organisation for social enterprises in the Netherlands, Social Enterprise NL,[21] as well as by professional organisations assisting the business development of social enterprises in the Netherlands.[22] The cumulative criteria for the social enterprise presented in the Commission's definition differ from the thin description of the Dutch social enterprise provided by the SER. As such, the Commission's definition regarding the social enterprise is the one adopted by the authors in the context of this chapter.

Additionally, in contrast to other European legal systems which offer a tailor-made legal form and framework particularly suited to social enterprises, social entrepreneurs in the Netherlands have to choose between various available legal forms provided in the Dutch legal system in order to initiate and incorporate their business activities. They can select to employ the partnership structure (VOF, *vennootschap onder firma*), the private limited liability company (BV, *besloten vennootschap*), the limited liability public company (NV, *naamloze vennootschap*), the cooperative (*coöperatie*), the foundation (*stichting*) or the association (*vereniging*), or

---

[19] Ibid, pp. 1–2.

[20] Social Business Initiative Communication 2011, p. 2. See also concerning the Social Business Initiative at the European Commission, social entrepreneurship at http://ec .europa.eu/internal_market/social_business/index_en.htm.

[21] Social Enterprise NL, see www.social-enterprise.nl/english.

[22] PwC NL, '*What is a social enterprise*', see www.pwc.nl/en/onze-organisatie/social-impact-lab/what-is-a-social-enterprise.html; EY, '*Social entrepreneurship: Emerging business opportunities creating value for society*' (Amsterdam, 2014) at 3, see www.ey.com/Publica tion/vwLUAssets/EY-social-entrepreneurship/$FILE/EY-social-entrepreneurship.pdf; Mckinsey & Company, '*Scaling the impact of the social enterprise sector* ' (Amsterdam, 2016) at 5, see www.mckinsey.com/industries/social-sector/our-insights/scaling-the-impact-of-the-social-enterprise-sector.

combine any two of these. For example, various Dutch social enterprises use a combination of the BV and the foundation.[23]

The lack of a tailor-made legal form and of a uniform definition has resulted in less visibility for social enterprises in the Netherlands. For years, Dutch social enterprises were to a great extent untraced, and they could not be recognised as such. Currently, membership organisations, platforms and networks (e.g., Social Enterprise NL) provide more visibility. Furthermore, less visibility has led to difficulty in acquiring accurate and credible statistical data concerning the types and the number of active Dutch social enterprises. Several attempts were made by scholarly academics and business professionals to categorise types and identify the number of social enterprises in the Netherlands. For instance, the Social Entrepreneurship GEM study in 2009 showed the existence of a variety of social enterprises in the Netherlands, such as 'hybrid social enterprises', 'NGO organisations', and 'socially committed regular enterprise'.[24] McKinsey reported in 2011 and subsequently in 2016 the size of the 'social enterprise sector', elaborating on data retrieved by the Dutch Chamber of Commerce.[25] According to these McKinsey reports, the Netherlands had approximately 4,000–5,000 social enterprises in 2011 and 5,000–6,000 in 2016. However, two completely different definitions were employed concerning the social enterprises in the two McKinsey reports, such that the results might not be considered reliable.

In 2015, the Commission published the findings of a large mapping study that examined the ecosystems (i.e., the network of legal frameworks, social impact investment markets, impact measurement and reporting systems, network and support organisations, business development services and support, certification systems and labels) of social enterprises in Europe.[26] A country report on the Netherlands provided

[23] Argyrou et al., 'Legal forms for social enterprises in the Dutch legal framework', p. 18; Argyrou and Lambooy, 'An introduction to tailor-made legislation for social enterprises in Europe', p. 48.

[24] S. Terjesen, J. Lepoutre, R. Justo and N. Bosma, *'Global Entrepreneurship Monitor (GEM): 2009 Report on social entrepreneurship'* (2012) at 19, see www.gemconsortium.org/report/48437.

[25] Mckinsey & Company, *'Opportunities for the Dutch social enterprise sector'* (Amsterdam, November 2011) at 10–13, see https://www.social-enterprise.nl/files/6714/4181/6376/Opportunities.pdf and https://www.social-enterprise.nl/files/9314/7809/5072/Scaling-the-impact-of-the-social-enterprise-sector.pdf Mckinsey & Company, *'Scaling the impact of the social enterprise sector'*, p. 5.

[26] European Commission, *'A map of social enterprises and their eco-systems in Europe: Synthesis Report'* (Publications Office of the European Union, 2015), see http://ec.europa.eu/social/main.jsp?langId=en&catId=89&newsId=2149.

relevant information regarding the ecosystem of Dutch social enterprises, their spectrum and the legal forms that social enterprises in the Netherlands use.[27] The study also provided a numeric overview which illustrated an estimated number of the Dutch social enterprises which might fulfil the uniform criteria of the definition for social enterprises provided by the Commission in 2011.[28] According to this report, up to 7,000 organisations belong to the social enterprises sector in the Netherlands.

Finally, the most recent development is a synthesis of a multi-stakeholder group comprising social entrepreneurs, consultants, experts and academics in 2016 under the initiative of Social Enterprise NL. The goal was to elaborate on a proposal for a Dutch *Code Sociale Ondernemingen* (i.e., to develop a text of a Code of Conduct for Dutch social enterprises).[29] The final text, published in June 2017, introduces the concept that social enterprises which adhere to this code can be registered in a to-be-formed Social Enterprise Register with the purpose of being more easily identifiable as a social enterprise for stakeholders.[30]

8.3 Social Enterprises as Agents of Change to Empower Women's Position in Organisations

Several studies indicate that worldwide, but also in the Western world, there are notably fewer women than men involved in entrepreneurship.[31]

---

[27] European Commission, '*A map of social enterprises and their eco-systems in Europe: Country Report: the Netherlands*' (Publications Office of the European Union, 2014), see http://ec.europa.eu/social/keyDocuments.jsp?pager.offset=10&&langId=en&mode=advancedSubmit&advSearchKey=socentcntryrepts.

[28] Ibid, p. 21.

[29] Social Enterprises NL, *Commissie Code Sociale Ondernemingen*, see www.social-enterprise.nl/actueel/nieuws/commissie-code-sociale-ondernemingen-is-van-start-699.

[30] Ibid. The Code Sociale Ondernemingen, see www.social-enterprise.nl/actueel/code-sociale-ondernemingen/reageren-op-de-code-als-geheel-738.

[31] Minniti examined in her study 34 countries from the five continents including: Argentina, Australia, Belgium, Brazil, Canada, Croatia, Denmark, Ecuador, Finland, France, Germany, Greece, Hong Kong, Hungary, Iceland, Ireland, Israel, Italy, Japan, Jordan, New Zealand, Norway, Peru, Poland, Portugal, Singapore, Slovenia, South Africa, Spain, Sweden, the Netherlands, Uganda, the United Kingdom and the United States. M. Minniti, 'Female entrepreneurship and economic activity' (2010) 22 *European Journal of Development Research*, 3, 294–312 at 295 and 299–300; See Minniti at 295 citing the studies of Y. Georgellis, and H. Wall, 'Gender differences in self-employment' (2005) 19 *International Review of Applied Economics*, 3, 321–342 and G. Kim, 'The analysis of self-employment levels over the life-cycle' (2007) 47 *Quarterly Review of Economics and Finance*, 3, 397–410.

The lower participation and involvement of women in entrepreneurship may be attributed to the existence of gender stereotypes and perceptions which influence not only the willingness of women to start an enterprise (i.e., their entrepreneurial intentions), but also their employment or operational position in enterprises.[32] Scholarship claims that gender stereotypes may have shaped labour and entrepreneurship on the basis of the dominant gender characteristics of men.[33] These stereotypes may have influenced widely held perceptions concerning the qualities and the roles that women and men could bring into a job.[34] Additionally, there are societies, even in the Western world, which – regardless of women having daily full-time employment or being involved in entrepreneurial attempts – due to patriarchal attitudes still assign to women the main role of carer of the family.[35] In these societies, women's responsibility to take care of the household, raise children and care for elderly or dependent relatives is a determinant of their choices regarding their profession and ability to start an enterprise.[36]

However, although entrepreneurship has been predominantly viewed as an economic activity in which the low participation of women is noticed, this concept is being challenged primarily by upcoming social enterprise business ventures and also most fundamentally by the theory of entrepreneurship as a social change activity with positive outcomes.[37] Calás et al. reframe 'for-profit entrepreneurship' to 'entrepreneurship as part of society and fundamentally a process of social change – which can be understood without attention to economic and managerial logic'.[38]

---

[32] V. K. Gupta, D. B. Turban, S. Arzu Wasti and A. Sikdar, 'The role of gender stereotypes in perceptions of entrepreneurs and intentions to become an entrepreneur' (2009) 33 *Entrepreneurship Theory and Practice*, 2, 397–417 at 409.

[33] Ibid, p. 398. See Ch. 11.   [34] Ibid Ch. 11.

[35] For instance, in Greece, see A. Argyrou and S. Charitakis, 'Gender equality in employment utilizing female social entrepreneurship in Greece' (2017) 12 *International and Comparative Corporate Law Journal*, 2, 36–60.

[36] C. Christopher Baughn, B. L. Chua and K. E. Neupert, 'The Normative context for women's participation in entrepreneurship: A multicountry study' 30 *Entrepreneurship Theory and Practice*, 5, 687–708 at 689–690. See Ch. 11.

[37] M. B. Calás, L. Smircich and K. A. Bourne, 'Extending the boundaries: Reframing "entrepreneurship as social change" through Feminist Perspectives' (2009) 34 *Academy of Management Review*, 3, 552–569. K. D. Hughes, J. E. Jennings, C. Brush, S. Carter and F. Welter, 'Extending women's entrepreneurship research in new directions' (2012) 36 *Entrepreneurship Theory and Practice*, 3, 429–442.

[38] Calás et al., 'Extending the boundaries', p. 553; D. M. Hechavarria, A. Ingram, R. Justo and S. Terjesen, 'Are women more likely to pursue social and environmental entrepreneurship?' in K. D. Hughes and J. E. Jennings (eds.), *Global Women's Entrepreneurship*

Additionally, feminist theories would contribute to reframing entrepreneurship as social change. As Calás et al. mention, 'all feminist theorizing is about social change. It is premised on the assumption that gender is fundamental in the structuring of society, with women being historically disadvantaged, and it seeks to end this condition. Feminist theorizing critically analyses social change agendas on these terms'.[39]

Entrepreneurship may contribute to the social change pointed out by Calás et al. if more equal opportunities are created for women in entrepreneurial organisations. In this vein, barriers that impede women from becoming an entrepreneur should be removed, and instead, opportunities for women should be implemented, such as the possibility of flexible working hours and better work-life balance. Other opportunities could be provided in the form of 'equal access to resources and/or enhancing human and social capital', meaning that if more women are engaged in entrepreneurial activities, this social change may happen.[40]

The extant literature describes that entrepreneurship in general is, amongst other things, about opportunities and recognising these opportunities. According to De Bruin et al., self-perceptions influence the way in which opportunities are recognised.[41] Due to stereotyped, gender-role-influenced self-perceptions in the current societal environment, women often become blind to business opportunities. As a result, women may feel that they do not have the right knowledge and opportunities to set up, lead or manage their own business. Therefore, they may not choose to either initiate or evolve an entrepreneurial career path.[42] However, these self-perceptions are also influenced by how society thinks about female entrepreneurs. If society does not support female entrepreneurs, this may influence their number negatively. Consequently, if society and societal values regarding gender roles and capacities support female

---

Research (Cheltenham, UK and Northampton, MA: Edward Elgar Publishing, 2012), pp. 135–151 at 135.

[39] Calás et al., 'Extending the boundaries', p. 554.

[40] Ibid., p. 555. See also Gupta et al., 'The Role of gender stereotypes in perceptions of entrepreneurs', p. 398.

[41] A. de Bruin, C. G. Brush and F. Welter, 'Advancing a framework for coherent research on women's entrepreneurship' (2007) 31 *Entrepreneurship Theory and Practice*, 3, 323–339 at 330.

[42] Ibid, p. 330; M. D. Griffiths, L. K. Gundry and J. R. Kickul, 'The socio-political, economic, and cultural determinants of social entrepreneurship activity: An empirical examination' (2013) 30 *Journal of Small Business and Enterprise Development*, 2, 341–357 at 350.

entrepreneurs, their number is likely to increase,[43] as women will perceive opportunities differently.[44]

Social enterprises could bring about a social change with respect to the roles and capacities of women as female entrepreneurs but also in their lives in society. This is confirmed by Lyon and Humbert, who claim that social enterprises, in particular, are more egalitarian organisations and could therefore contribute to eliminating inequality in the workforce for women.[45] This could be done in terms of creating opportunities for employment, opportunities for education, opportunities for leadership, and convenient work settings to facilitate a better work-life balance for women in social enterprises. For instance, social entrepreneurship could bring women's issues into prominence, such as child care, women's health or violence against women, as well as opportunities for their re-entry to the labour force or building up their skills.[46]

However, this chapter does not suggest that social enterprises are suitable for women just because they 'align their interests with the roles that have been attributed to them culturally, closely linked to altruism, care and protection of disadvantaged groups',[47] as this stance might perpetuate stereotypically established perceptions concerning the role and position of women. On the contrary, we suggest that social enterprises, with their sustainable objectives and responsible and participatory character, may strategically be used by women to change their position in organisations and their lives in society in general, and through that to contribute to a necessary societal change.

Griffiths et al. observe in an empirical study the social change which was mentioned by Calás et al.: 'as more women enter and participate in the workforce [of social enterprises], they may have greater access to

---

[43] Griffiths et al., 'The socio-political, economic, and cultural determinants of social entrepreneurship activity', p. 350.

[44] De Bruin, 'Advancing a framework for coherent research on women's entrepreneurship', p. 331.

[45] F. Lyon and A. Humbert, 'Gender balance in the governance of social enterprises' (2013) Third Sector Research Centre, Working Paper 107, pp. 1–18 at 14. See also Argyrou and Charitakis, 'Gender equality in employment utilizing female social entrepreneurship in Greece', pp. 56–59.

[46] A. L. Humbert, 'Women as social entrepreneurs' (2012) Third Sector Research Centre, Working Paper 72, pp. 1–14 at 8; Argyrou and Charitakis, 'Gender equality in employment utilizing female social entrepreneurship in Greece', pp. 56–59.

[47] C. Nicolás and A. Rubio, 'Social enterprise: Gender gap and economic development' (2016) 25 *European Journal of Management and Business Economics*, 2, 56–62 at 56. See the criticism regarding this type of gendered construction of values in Chs. 11 and 12.

funding resources and support networks and training that may, in the future, determine their entrepreneurial behaviour (either social or commercial)'.[48] Other empirical findings indicate a better representation of women on the boards of social enterprises as opposed to commercial enterprises.[49] As such, female social entrepreneurs may also be able to challenge the stereotypical hierarchical patterns predominantly viewed in mainstream organisations and to generate this type of 'more egalitarian' organisation.[50] Lyon and Humbert's study provides an insight into the gender balance in the governance of social enterprises. These scholars found that women are particularly active on boards of social enterprises operating in specific sectors, particularly those sectors in which women are stereotypically working, such as youth and childcare, health and social care, arts, culture and sports and education.[51]

Other scholars note in that respect that the features of social entrepreneurship may 'align ideologically' with women's 'feminine' characteristics, such as with 'altruism', 'caring' and 'relational values' influencing their intention to start an enterprise. On the contrary, commercial entrepreneurship would be historically linked to the dominant male ideology.[52] Bruni et al. assert main features of commercial entrepreneurship which are assigned to leaders, such as 'initiative-taking', 'accomplishment' and 'risk-taking' and which stereotypically reside 'in the symbolic domain of the male', but when assigned to women 'they become uncertain'.[53] In the empirical study conducted by Hechavarria and Ingram, men were found to be more interested in entrepreneurial opportunities related to commercial business than social business.[54]

---

[48] Griffiths et al., 'The socio-political, economic, and cultural determinants of social entrepreneurship activity', p. 351.

[49] Lyon and Humbert, 'Gender balance in the governance of social enterprises', p. 14.

[50] Calás et al., 'Extending the boundaries', p. 557. See also the need for structural reforms in the corporate sector in Ch. 11.

[51] Lyon and Humbert, 'Gender balance in the governance of social enterprises', pp. 8–9.

[52] D. M. Hechavarria and A. E. Ingram, 'The entrepreneurial gender divide: Hegemonic masculinity, emphasized femininity and organizational forms' (2016) 8 *International Journal of Gender and Entrepreneurship*, 3, 242–281 at 247–248. D. Urbano, E. Ferri and M. Noguera, 'Female social entrepreneurship and socio-cultural context: An international analysis' (2014) 2 *Revista de studio sempre sariales. Segunda Época*, 2, 26–40 at 35. See the criticism regarding this type of gendered construction of values in Chs. 11 and 12.

[53] A. Bruni, S. Gherardi and B. Poggio, 'Doing gender, Doing entrepreneurship: An ethnographic account of intertwined practices gender' (2004) 11 *Work and Organization*, 4, 406–429 at 408–409.

[54] Hechavarria and Ingram, 'The entrepreneurial gender divide', p. 250.

8.4   Female Social Enterprises as Actors of Change for Women's Lives in Society

Calás et al. point out that it is not easy to bring about the social change in a world where men are still dominating all the structures of society.[55] In literature, however, a direct link is established between social entrepreneurship and social change towards 'social wealth'.[56] One of the key elements of the social enterprise is that it creates social value – intrinsically tied to its mission – for its various stakeholders and beneficiaries and for society at large (as a beneficiary of the social purpose that the social enterprise pursues) rather than creating financial value for the business only.[57] This is done in a process of internalising the stakeholders' (social and/or environmental) interests through participatory decision-making processes which are 'open to diverse stakeholder influences' while these organisations are also 'embedded in local communities' and 'relational in [their] approach by shaping networks across sectors (commercial, non-profit, and government) to stimulate social change as well as to leverage resources'.[58] Their primary mission is to generate 'the social change and development of their client group'.[59]

The role of social entrepreneurs as change agents is significantly embedded in the definition of the social entrepreneur as noted by Nicholls and outlined by Hubert.[60] Nicholls mentions that 'social entrepreneurs play

---

[55] Calás et al., 'Extending the boundaries', p. 554.

[56] S. Estrin, T. Mickiewicz and U. Stephan, 'Entrepreneurship, social capital and institutions: Social and commercial entrepreneurship across nations' (2013) 37 *Entrepreneurship Theory and Practice*, 3, 479–504 at 481. S. Estrin, T. Mickiewicz and U. Stephan, 'Human capital in social and commercial entrepreneurship' (2016) 31 *Journal of Business Venturing*, 4, 449–467 at 450–452. Bruni et al., 'Doing gender, doing entrepreneurship', p. 408.

[57] Estrin et al., 'Human capital in social and commercial entrepreneurship', p. 452. Nicolás and Rubio, 'Social enterprise', p. 56.

[58] Estrin et al., 'Human capital in social and commercial entrepreneurship', p. 452, citing U. Stephan, M. Patterson, C. Kelly and J. Mair, 'Organizations driving positive social change: A review and an integrative framework of change processes' (2016) 42 *Journal of Management*, 5, 1250–1281.

[59] J. Levie and M. Hart, 'What distinguishes social entrepreneurs from business entrepreneurs? Insights from GEM', p. 2, unpublished paper, see http://strathprints.strath.ac.uk/32357. The official article was published as J. Levie and M. Hart, 'Business and social entrepreneurs in the UK: Gender, context and commitment' (2011) 3 *International Journal of Gender and Entrepreneurship*, 3, 200–217.

[60] A. Nicholls, 'Social entrepreneurship', in S. Carter, and D. Jones-Evans (eds.), *Enterprise and Small Business: Principles, Practice and Policy* (Harlow: Financial Times Prentice Hall, 2006), pp. 220–242.

the role of change agents in the social sector'.[61] Brouard and Larivet designed their own definition of social entrepreneurs and define them as 'any individuals who with their entrepreneurial spirit and personality will act as change agents and leaders to tackle social problems by recognising new opportunities and finding innovative solutions, and are more concerned with creating social value than financial value'.[62] Accordingly, women as social entrepreneurs could serve as a paradigm to change hierarchical patterns and stereotypical positions in organisations and in society not only for themselves but also for others. This paradigm may allow women to 'influence change and to make a difference in the lives of other women and the community in general'.[63] In this way, female social enterprises may lead to a social change in organisations in a more sustainable direction, but also the lives of other women in society. As such, female social enterprises may be actors of change that would not only promote gender equality and diversity in the (entrepreneurial) workforce and organisation, but 'also play a fundamental role in improving society' and in improving the lives of women in it.[64]

8.5   Women in the Dutch Social Enterprises' Structure and Functioning

8.5.1   Methodology Employed in the Survey

As explained in Section 8.1, our empirical analysis is based on data collected in 2015 by means of a survey that was sent to 366 and responded to by 66 social enterprises in the Netherlands, in collaboration with Social Enterprise NL[65] and PwC NL.[66] The aim of this survey was to

---

[61] Humbert, 'Women as social entrepreneurs', p. 4, citing Nicholls, 'Social entrepreneurship', p. 224.

[62] Kury, 'Sustainability meets social entrepreneurship', p. 64, citing F. Brouard and S. Larivet, 'Essay of clarifications and definitions of the related concepts of social enterprise, social entrepreneur and social entrepreneurship' in A. Fayolle and H. Matlay (eds.), *Handbook of Research on Social Entrepreneurship* (Cheltenham: Edward Elgar Publishing Limited, 2010), pp. 29–56.

[63] Griffiths et al., 'The socio-political, economic, and cultural determinants of social entrepreneurship activity', p. 351; Nicolás and Rubio, 'Social enterprise', p. 61.

[64] Hechavarria et al., 'Are women more likely to pursue social and environmental entrepreneurship?', p. 147; Estrin et al., 'Human capital in social and commercial entrepreneurship', p. 465.

[65] Social enterprises NL, see www.social-enterprise.nl.

[66] Among the 366 selected social enterprises, 242 were registered at the time of the survey as members of the Social Enterprise NL, whereas 124 additional social enterprise organisations were selected from the direct client network of PwC NL.

identify the needs and perceived barriers of social enterprises in the Netherlands in relation to the Dutch legal system, as well as success factors of social enterprises in terms of their business-operating model. The survey included gender and gender-related questions. The response rate for the survey was approximately 18 per cent, a low response rate with which to provide generalizable and representative statistical results with certainty with respect to the entire population evaluated. However, the survey results are adequate to provide preliminary information which can be used for exploratory purposes, such as shedding light on this emerging sector and its characteristics, as well as the role of female social entrepreneurs in the Netherlands.[67]

Although the survey was predominantly elaborating on questions regarding the success factors of Dutch social enterprises in relation to their operating models and legal-institutional environment, a number of demographic questions were also posed. These were dichotomous, close-ended, and multiple choice questions requiring information concerning gender-related and other characteristics of the respondents. For instance, there were questions asking the respondent's gender, position and working experience, and educational and professional background, as well as the organization's name, mission, size, number of employees, legal form and means of financing.

The collected data were processed by an explorative analysis with the use of descriptive statistics (i.e., an analysis of the responses by means of multivariate data displays).[68] The statistical analysis of data was supported by an analysis of digressions provided via open text boxes following the dichotomous, close-ended, and multiple-choice questions included in the survey. Those text boxes allowed the respondents to provide clarifications, explanatory descriptions and/or elaborate on their responses. The digressions comprised the perceptions, thoughts and personal opinions of the survey respondents. To analyse and shorten the qualitative data collected from the open text boxes, a method of coding was applied.[69] By means of coding, patterns were identified in

---

[67] Among those responding social enterprises, 42 organisations were members of the Social Enterprises NL platform, whereas 14 organisations were members of the PwC client network. The survey results on the other topics, as well as further details concerning its methodology can be found in Argyrou et al., 'Legal forms for social enterprises in the Dutch legal framework', pp. 12-34.

[68] The multivariate pivot function in Excel was used to short, analyse, visualise and filter the collected data. By means of the pivot functions, the percentages were compared.

[69] J. Saldana, *The Coding Manual for Qualitative Researchers* (Los Angeles, CA: Sage, 2009).

the data on the basis of periodically repeated and routine responses by which commonly occurring thematic categories were developed.

8.5.2   Female Involvement, Role and Position

Although the number of male respondents to the survey was higher than the number of female respondents, the survey data revealed that women are notably involved in the sixty-six Dutch social enterprises which participated. As a matter of fact, out of the sixty-six respondents to the survey, 59.09 per cent were men, whereas 40.91 per cent were women. This is in line with scholarly literature in entrepreneurship which shows that the percentage of women involved in entrepreneurship worldwide is in general lower than that of men, but there may be a shift in social entrepreneurial practice.[70] It was also previously noted that women generally are less involved in enterprises than men, and that men are more likely to become commercial entrepreneurs than women.

However, literature on social enterprises indicates that women – in comparison with men – are more likely to become social entrepreneurs and engage in social and environmental entrepreneurial activity rather than becoming commercial entrepreneurs.[71] One possible reason suggested in the literature is that women are more likely driven in their entrepreneurial careers by societal rather than economic motives, whereas for men it is the other way around.[72] This aligns well with social enterprises because their main goal is to tackle sustainability and social challenges and to contribute to solving these issues.[73] However, these interlinkages are not directly reflected in the examined data from Dutch social enterprises.

---

[70] Minniti, 'Female entrepreneurship and economic activity', p. 298; T. J. Devine, 'Changes in wage-and-salary returns to skill and the recent rise in female self-employment' (1994) 84 *The American Economic Review*, 2, 108–112; Georgellis and Wall, 'Gender differences in self-employment', pp. 321–342; Kim, 'The analysis of self-employment levels over the life-cycle', pp. 397–410.

[71] Estrin et al., 'Entrepreneurship, social capital and institutions: Social and commercial entrepreneurship across nations', p. 496. Estrin et al., 'Human capital in social and commercial entrepreneurship', pp. 458, 462 and 464; Hechavarria et al., 'Are women more likely to pursue social and environmental entrepreneurship?', p. 144; Levie and Hart, 'What distinguishes social entrepreneurs from business entrepreneurs? Insights from GEM', p. 6.

[72] Griffiths et al., 'The socio-political, economic, and cultural determinants of social entrepreneurship activity', p. 346. Urbano, Ferri and Noguera, 'Female social entrepreneurship and socio-cultural context', p. 35.

[73] S. Teasdale, S. McKay, J. Phillimore and N. Teasdale, 'Exploring gender and social entrepreneurship: Women's leadership, employment and participation in the third sector and social enterprises', pp. 3–37 at 19, unpublished. The official publication was published as S. Teasdale, S. McKay, J. Phillimore and N. Teasdale, 'Exploring gender and

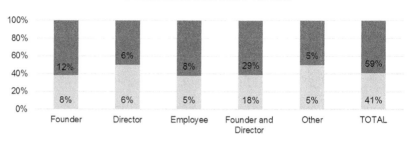

Female   ■ Male

Figure 8.1   Role of female respondents as opposed to male respondents in the Dutch social enterprises. In this figure the numeric values are displayed as percentages of the grand total of respondents. E.g. 8% of respondents were female founders, while 12% of total respondents were male founders. Participation in the particular role can also be estimated as a percentage by reference to the percentage scale on the left so that less than 40% of founders are women and more than 60% of founders are men.

Women in the examined Dutch social enterprises were found to have various roles and positions in their organisations' functioning. They participate in the higher echelons of their organisations, such as in the position of 'director and founder', but also in the human capital of their organisations, such as in the position of the 'employee'. The survey responses revealed that female respondents comprise predominantly managerial positions in the social enterprises (i.e., as founders and directors). The results can be found in Figure 8.1.

Most of the female respondents (approximately 78 per cent, or 32 per cent of the 41 per cent; see Figure 8.1) reported that they hold a high position in the organisational structure of the social enterprise, such as 'founder', 'founder and director', or 'director', whereas only 11.11 per cent of female respondents (Figure 8.1) belong to the category 'employee', and 11.11 per cent to the category 'other'. Other positions held by female respondents include 'treasurer' and 'advisor'. These results suggest a lower gender bias in the higher managerial positions and roles in Dutch social enterprises than what generally is reported in the literature concerning commercial companies. Please note that in small and medium-sized social enterprises, the roles of 'founder', 'founder and director', 'director' and 'employee' often overlap. For the survey, respondents were only able to select one position, because this question was multiple-choice.

social entrepreneurship: women's leadership, employment and participation in the third sector and social enterprises' (2011) 2 *Voluntary Sector Review*, 1, 57–76.

Nonetheless, when comparing the data concerning the responses of female survey participants with those of male respondents, women's participation was found to be significantly lower than men's in almost all the higher organisational positions in the examined Dutch social enterprises, particularly in the positions of 'founder and director' and 'founder' (i.e., respectively, 18 per cent female versus 29 per cent male and 8 per cent female versus 12 per cent male in Figure 8.1). However, in regard to the category 'director', female respondents were found to have equal standing with male respondents (i.e., 6 per cent for both female and male). That is interesting, as Lyon and Humbert point out that despite the fact that women are in general more often participating in social enterprises rather than in commercial enterprises, women are still under-represented in social enterprises.[74]

In their study on Dutch listed companies, Diepeveen et al. also refer to the undermined role of women in the Dutch economy in general – women are underrepresented in senior-management and decision-making positions, in the government, in universities, and in particular in large Dutch companies. Moreover, these scholars point at the inequality in wages and in opportunities for women in the Dutch labour market.[75]

Furthermore, the survey results reveal that although the participation of women and men is equal in the role of director, it appeared that in the position of CEO (or 'president' or any other applicable term to express the position of the chief executive officer or equivalent), the male gender prevails (70.83 per cent) over the female (29.17 per cent) in the participating social enterprises. This result shows that the examined Dutch social enterprises may not facilitate women into leadership and authority as much as theory would claim. Nonetheless, scholarship reflects that the career and leadership experiences of women and men are still regarded as being more equal in social entrepreneurship than in commercial entrepreneurship.[76] As we have argued on the basis of the literature review, this phenomenon might be attributed to the societal goal, type, structure

---

[74] Lyon and Humbert, 'Gender balance in the governance of social enterprises', pp. 13–14.

[75] R. A. Diepeveen, T. E. Lambooy and R. M. Renes, 'The Two-pronged approach of the (semi-) legal norms on gender diversity: Exploratory empirical research on corporate boards of Dutch listed companies', 12 *International and Comparative Corporate Law Journal*, 2, 103–139 at 110–113.

[76] K. Addicott, 'There may be trouble ahead: exploring the changing shape of non-profit entrepreneurship in third sector organizations' (2017) 37 *Public Money & Management*, 2, 81–88 at 81.

and size of the enterprise (for instance, the possibilities and opportunities to build relationships in a career path).[77]

A lower score was also revealed in the survey results concerning the prevalence of women as 'founder' in comparison to men. This might suggest that generally women have lower intentions to initiate a social enterprise and/or lower opportunities, which is in line with the findings in literature that women have lesser appetite to initiate a business or an enterprise.[78] However, the age-related results indicate that women aged 30–40 prevail over men in the category 'founder and director' (16.67 per cent female respondents as opposed to 11.11 per cent male respondents), hence a finding which suggests that young women more often take the lead in social enterprises.[79] Women also exceed men in the position 'director' in the age category of 40–50 (11.11 per cent female respondents as opposed to 5.56 per cent male respondents); this shows that older women might be preferred in more responsible positions in social enterprises.

8.5.3   Flexible Working Hours and the Possibility of Working at Home

Levie and Hart,[80] who particularly assess the characteristics of social entrepreneurs and their businesses, indicate that female social entrepreneurs are more likely to work part-time than women in purely commercial enterprises. Levie and Hart indicate that almost 74 per cent of the social entrepreneurs devoted less than 10 hours a week to their business; this was only the case for 22 per cent of business (commercial) entrepreneurs.[81] The flexibility in social enterprises in terms of working time and ability to work from home might also be a reason for women in the Netherlands to prefer social entrepreneurial positions in order to maintain a better work-life balance. Many Dutch women work part-time

---

[77] Ibid.

[78] Gupta et al., 'The Role of gender stereotypes in perceptions of entrepreneurs and intentions to become an entrepreneur', p. 409.

[79] Griffiths et al., 'The socio-political, economic, and cultural determinants of social entrepreneurship activity', p. 346.

[80] Levie and Hart, 'What distinguishes social entrepreneurs from business entrepreneurs? Insights from GEM', pp. 6 and 8.

[81] Ibid., p. 8.

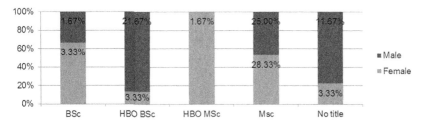

Figure 8.2 Educational background of female respondents as opposed to male respondents. The numeric values are displayed as percentages of the grand total of respondents.

for this reason. Part-time work by women in the Netherlands reaches the highest percentage of all European countries.[82]

8.5.4 Level of Education

The women involved in the examined social enterprises were found to have a high educational background, although variations were observed. The results can be found in Figure 8.2. The majority of female respondents (28.33 per cent) hold an academic master's (MSc) degree. Only 3.33 per cent of female respondents have no educational title, as opposed to 11.67 per cent of male respondents in this category. Scholarship indeed indicates that social entrepreneurship not only is likely to attract more women than men, but particularly, more highly educated women.[83] Other empirical studies show that in developed countries women entrepreneurs generally attain a higher education level than male entrepreneurs and that they mainly undertake entrepreneurial activities around the age of 35–44.[84] This can be explained by the fact that in richer countries women may spend more time on their education.[85] This proposition finds ground in the survey's findings, which reveal that in the survey sample, more women than men are highly educated with a master's degree, and more men than women have no educational title.

---

[82] OECD, *Part-time employment rate for women 2016*, see https://data.oecd.org/emp/part-time-employment-rate.htm.

[83] Estrin et al., 'Entrepreneurship, social capital and institutions', p. 498.

[84] E. Allen, N. Langowitz and M. Minniti, 'The 2006 Global Entrepreneurship Monitor Special Topic Report: Women in Entrepreneurship' (2007) Center for Women Leadership, Babson College, Babson Park, MA; M. Cowling and M. Taylor, 'Entrepreneurial women and men: Two different species?' (2001) 16 *Small Business Economics*, 3, 167–176.

[85] Minniti, 'Female entrepreneurship and economic activity', p. 298.

8.5.5   Types of Social Enterprises Involving Women

The survey digressions indicate that female respondents are predominantly involved in Dutch social enterprises whose purpose relates to women's improvement of life. Particularly, the results demonstrate that women are predominantly involved in social enterprises with the objective to improve women's lives (24 per cent) in terms of: (1) offering education to women; (2) addressing work integration considering women's inferior position in the labour market; and (3) stimulating women in gaining financial independence and empowerment in society considering the existence of a gender pay gap and their undermined role in society. Other categories were also identified which align with the sectors in which women stereotypically are working in, such as: (4) children's education, assistance and access to culture (20 per cent); (5) support and work integration of people with disabilities (8 per cent); and (6) elderly care (4 per cent). Finally, other types of Dutch social enterprises with broader sustainability-oriented objectives were identified to involve women such as: (7) sustainable and ecological market activities (12 per cent); (8) sustainable financing of organisations and access to capital (8 per cent); (9) improving social interaction and recreation (20 per cent); and (10) social impact measuring (4 per cent). The results can be found in Figure 8.3. These findings suggest that indeed female social entrepreneurship can contribute to sustainability but also to changing women's lives – that is, not only the life of the female social entrepreneur herself, but also the lives of other women and their role in society. The identified categories of social objectives of the social enterprises involving particularly women also confirm that female entrepreneurs are likely to focus on social and environmental value creation.[86] As such, they would be found to participate in social enterprises which promote sustainable and ecological market activities and sustainable financing, with improving social interaction and/or the care of the vulnerable parts of society (i.e., children, the elderly and the disabled) as a goal.

The survey also indicated that the BV is the most common legal form used by the participating social enterprises (42.42 per cent).[87] Few enterprises indicated that they use the legal form of a foundation (22.72 per cent) and even fewer indicated that they use a complex

---

[86] Hechavarria et al., 'Are women more likely to pursue social and environmental entrepreneurship?', pp. 135–136, 144.

[87] Argyrou et al., 'Legal forms for social enterprises in the Dutch legal framework', p. 18.

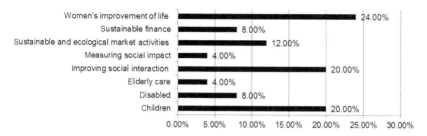

Figure 8.3 Mission of social enterprises in which female respondents are involved

combination of the legal forms of BV and foundation (12.12 per cent).[88] The remainder of the respondents indicated that their business was either performed in the form of sole trader (3.03 per cent), or that they employed the legal forms of partnership (1.52 per cent) or association (3.03 per cent).

The female respondents were predominantly found to participate in the legal forms of foundation and association and had a weaker presence in the BV and/or in the combination BV-foundation legal form as compared to men, whose participation was dominant in the legal forms of BV, partnership, and sole trader. As such, the results of this survey indicate that women are often involved in enterprises which are organised in not-for-profit legal forms such as the foundation and the association, rather than in organisations employing for-profit legal forms such as the BV and the combination BV-foundation. These findings from the survey also align with scholarship which shows that in private sector enterprises, the number of female entrepreneurs remains low in comparison to men, whereas in third (voluntary) sector organisations, the number of male and female entrepreneurs are nearly equal.[89] In relation to the legal form, scholarly findings also point out that when comparing female-owned businesses and male-owned businesses, female entrepreneurs are more likely to set up their businesses with a lower start-up capital and to finance with equity instead of debt – attributed to legal forms with such characteristics – than male entrepreneurs, who were found to have a higher ratio of debt finance.[90]

[88] Ibid.
[89] Teasdale et al., 'Exploring gender and social entrepreneurship', pp. 5–6, 24; Humbert, 'Women as social entrepreneurs', p. 9. Argyrou et al., 'Legal forms for social enterprises in the Dutch legal framework', p. 17.
[90] De Bruin et al., 'Advancing a framework for coherent research on women's entrepreneurship', p. 325.

8.6 Conclusions

The undermined position of women in economic activities in general can be evidenced from gender gaps in entrepreneurship and a lack of opportunities for women to thrive in economic activities. Existing stereotypes, patriarchal attitudes and the perceived (female) duty of care in various countries predominantly determine women's choices regarding employment or intention to start an enterprise. Gender stereotypes also dominate the entrepreneurial world, undermining women's skills and talents. Empirical evidence shows that women's participation in entrepreneurship is lower than men's. In general, women's participation in entrepreneurship is a way to access opportunities and improve life in economic terms. Accordingly, we emphasise the reframing of entrepreneurship as an actor towards social change and the concept of social entrepreneurship as a type of economic activity that may also lead to the changing of women's role in organisations and the improvement of women's lives as well as to changing the dominant perception of women's capacities in society. This type of social change can be achieved if more women are engaged in social entrepreneurship and if more opportunities are provided to them in terms of human capital, education and promotion in leadership. Female social entrepreneurship might result in reducing inequality in employment for women, in providing a better representation of women in higher organisational positions and in providing access to opportunities with respect to education and a better balance in work and life. Female social entrepreneurs may challenge structural inequalities and hierarchical patterns based on stereotypes while changing society's dominant perception concerning the role of women. Social entrepreneurship may also gradually contribute to a change through introducing women's issues into organisational aspects and social entrepreneurial objectives. As such, social change and social value may be created by female social entrepreneurship. Social enterprises may be change agents, and thus women in social enterprises could contribute to that change. Accordingly, social enterprises might be women's vehicle to social change.

In the Netherlands, the social enterprises sector is young and evolving. However, the discussion concerning women's role in Dutch social enterprises has not previously been addressed by academic scholarship. This chapter introduces the discussion and presents empirical evidence which demonstrates that women have taken up various roles in Dutch social enterprises. They can be found in the higher as well as in managerial and employee positions of the examined Dutch social enterprises. However, we have shown that their overall participation in higher organisational positions is lower than men in the majority of the organisational positions identified in the examined organisations. At the same time, the empirical results reveal that women in the participating Dutch social enterprises were found to be more highly educated than men.

Additionally, women in the examined Dutch social enterprises are more involved in social enterprises that employ a non-profit rather than a for-profit organisation legal form. Most importantly, women in Dutch social enterprises are predominantly involved in social enterprises which have adopted sustainability objectives and that promote the improvement of women's lives. As such, they could constitute agents for change in their lives and in the lives of other women, consequently effecting broader social change as well.

9

How Change Happens

The Benefit Corporation in the United States and Considerations for Australia

VICTORIA SCHNURE BAUMFIELD

9.1 Introduction

A quiet revolution has been taking place in corporate law in recent years. Alongside the growing interest in so-called dual mission social enterprises that seek to advance one or more social or environmental goals while simultaneously producing profits, since the mid-2000s numerous jurisdictions have created new hybrid corporate forms that combine traditional for-profit corporations'[1] ability to seek profits with not-for-profits' obligation to pursue social objectives. These forms include benefit corporations and low-profit limited liability companies (L3Cs) in the United States, and community interest companies (CICs) in the United Kingdom. Yet other forms have been created in Canada and continental Europe, and a movement is currently on foot to introduce benefit corporations in Australia.

These hybrid forms are intended to facilitate social enterprise by eliminating the greatest inadequacies of the traditional forms. Unlike not-for-profits, the hybrids may issue shares to raise funds. Unlike traditional corporations, the hybrids may pursue social objectives[2] at the expense of profit maximisation without risking managerial liability.[3] Many scholars and practitioners have lauded the new hybrids as facilitating the ability of socially minded entrepreneurs to accomplish their social objectives.[4] This chapter queries, however, whether these new

---

[1] Referred to herein as 'traditional corporations'.

[2] Including objectives that further corporate sustainability.

[3] Keeping in mind that, as this chapter argues, the perceived risk is in fact almost non-existent.

[4] See, eg, W. H. Clark, Jr and L. Vranka, 'The Need and Rationale for the Benefit Corporation: Why It Is the Legal Form that Best Addresses the Needs of Social Entrepreneurs,

structures are ultimately just a sideshow to distract from the failure to reform traditional corporations, which are still too often presented as inadequate to support socially responsible business practices. Even if these new hybrid forms really serve their intended social benefit objective, might the spread of these structures inadvertently serve to ghettoise expectations for socially beneficial and sustainable corporate behaviour to entities specifically incorporated as a hybrid?[5]

The remainder of this chapter is structured as follows: Section 9.2 will briefly describe a selection of the new structures that have emerged in recent years, while simultaneously examining who or what has been the agent for change regarding the adoption of the new hybrid forms. Section 9.3 presents two central arguments focusing on how directors' duties owed to the traditional corporation do not preclude the consideration of other stakeholders and how presenting alternative, more socially responsible corporate hybrids skews our understanding of the traditional corporation and indeed might have the perverse effect of slowing acceptance of the need for socially responsible conduct on the part of traditional corporations. The chapter then, in Section 9.4, considers the case for adopting a corporate structure of this sort in Australia. The Australian experience resonates with experience in the United States as it relates to the traditional corporation, demonstrating how the traditional corporation can be understood. The chapter closes by concluding that traditional corporations can be socially responsible and sustainable, and encourages the change agents who have been pushing the new hybrid

Investors, and, Ultimately, the Public', White Paper, (18 January 2013), see www.benefitcorp.org; M. Vargas, 'The Next Stage of Social Entrepreneurship: Benefit Corporations and the Companies Using this Innovative Form' (July 2016) *Bus Law Today* 1; R. Gaffney, 'Hype and Hostility for Hybrid Companies: A Fourth Sector Case Study' (2012) 5 *J Bus Entrepreneurship & L* 329; H. Rose, 'The Social Business: The Viability of a New Business Entity Type' (2007) 44 *Willamette L Rev* 131; R. Esposito, 'The Social Enterprise Revolution in Corporate Law: A Primer on Emerging Corporate Entities in Europe and the United States and the Case for the Benefit Corporation' (2013) 4 *William and Mary Business L Rev* 639.

[5] See, e.g., M. Underberg, 'Benefit Corporations vs "Regular" Corporations: A Harmful Dichotomy', Harvard Law School Forum on Corp Governance and Financial Regulation (2012), see https://corpgov.law.harvard.edu/2012/05/13/benefit-corporations-vs-regular-corporations-a-harmful-dichotomy; J. Blount and O-D. Kwabena, 'The Benefit Corporation: A Questionable Solution to a Non-Existent Problem' (2013) 44 *St Mary's Law Journal* 617, 659; A. S. Ball, 'Social Enterprise Governance' (2016) 18 *University of Pennsylvania Journal of Business Law* 919, 943; J. W. Yockey, 'Does Social Enterprise Law Matter?' (2015) 66 *Alabama Law Review* 767, 800.

forms – not exclusively or even primarily women – to re-focus on the possibilities inherent in the traditional corporation.

9.2   The New Structures: What, Why and How

9.2.1   Type A Businesses: Quasi-Non-Profits

The new hybrid forms are said to rectify inadequacies in the traditional for-profit and not-for-profit structures for two types of entrepreneur, which this chapter will refer to as Type A and Type B entrepreneurs. Type A entrepreneurs are 'social activists'.[6] Their primary motivation is to solve social problems, but they see a commercial business operation as an effective tool to do so. A prototypical example is a bakery formed explicitly to provide job training and employment opportunities to a disadvantaged population, such as high school drop-outs or the long-term unemployed.[7] Type A entrepreneurs might hope to generate a profit for themselves and their investors in the process – for example, as a way to induce investors to fund the business, and simply to keep the business running – but their primary motivation is mitigating the particular social problem that is the subject of the organisation's focus. Hybrids may offer superior benefits in terms of scalability and efficiency in comparison with traditional charities.[8] They also may offer commercially focused charitable organisations a superior fundraising model through the ability to issue shares, rather than being forced to rely on donations or grants.

Two of the new hybrid forms – US Low Profit Limited Liability Companies (L3Cs), currently available in eleven US jurisdictions since first introduced in 2008,[9] and British Community Interest Companies (CICs), available since 2005[10] – are mainly appropriate for Type A – entrepreneurs because both contain features that make them effectively quasi-non-profits. For example, once assets are committed to British

---

[6] Vargas, 'The Next Stage of Social Entrepreneurship'.

[7] See, e.g., D. B. Reiser, 'Theorizing Forms for Social Enterprise' (2013) 62 *Emory Law Journal* 681–682; Yockey, 'Does Social Enterprise Law Matter?', 775–776.

[8] D. B. Reiser, 'Regulating Social Enterprise' (2014) 14 *UC Davis Business Law Journal* 231.

[9] M. J. Dulac, 'Sustaining the Sustainable Corporation: Benefit Corporations and the Viability of Going Public' (2015) 104 *Georgetown Law Journal* 171, 173–174.

[10] Department for Business Innovation & Skills, *Office of the Regulator of Community Interest Companies: Information and Guidance Notes* (May 2016), see www.gov.uk/government/publications/community-interest-companies-how-to-form-a-cic, Ch. 1: Introduction, p. 3.

CICs, those assets must stay in the charitable stream even if the CIC winds up.[11] There is also a cap on the profits that CICs may distribute via dividends.[12] L3Cs, meanwhile, were specifically designed to satisfy US Internal Revenue Service (IRS) rules regarding eligibility to receive charitable foundations' program-related investments. If they could not organize as L3Cs, the target organizations would otherwise likely organize as non-profits.[13] Although there is no limitation on the distribution of profits by L3Cs,[14] the primary motivating factor behind these businesses must be a charitable rather than profit-making objective as required by IRS rules.[15]

Their legal requirement to have a primarily charitable or socially beneficial purpose and restricted ability to seek or distribute profits make L3Cs and CICs fundamentally different from Type B businesses, which could and often do function as traditional corporations. This distinction removes the L3C and CIC forms from my critique: that the expansion of the more profit-oriented hybrid forms will strengthen the false perception that the traditional corporation is not suitable for socially responsible business practices.

9.2.2   Type B Businesses: The Classic Double or Triple Bottom Line Business

Unlike Type A entrepreneurs, for whom profitability appears more of an afterthought, Type B entrepreneurs always intended to operate a profitable business, but one operated under sustainable or socially responsible business principles. These are the classic 'mission driven companies'.[16] Examples of Type B businesses (not necessarily incorporated using a hybrid form) include Ben & Jerry's ice cream,[17] the recreational clothing

---

[11] Ibid, Ch. 6: The Asset Lock, p. 3.   [12] Ibid, Ch. 6, pp. 7–8.

[13] R. Cohen, 'Social Responsibility or Marketing Ploy? The Branding of L3Cs' (2014) *Nonprofit Quarterly*, see https://nonprofitquarterly.org/2014/05/27/social-responsibility-or-marketing-ploy-the-branding-of-l3cs.

[14] D. B. Reiser, 'Blended Enterprise and the Dual Mission Dilemma' (2010) 35 *Vermont Law Review* 105, 108–109.

[15] Intersector Partners, L3C, *L3C Home*, see www.intersectorl3c.com. See, e.g., 11 Vermont Statutes Annotated § 4162.

[16] Vargas, 'The Next Stage of Social Entrepreneurship'.

[17] A. Plerhoples, 'Can an Old Dog Learn New Tricks? Applying Traditional Corporate Law Principles to New Social Enterprise Legislation' (2012) 13 *Transactions: The Tennessee Journal of Business Law* 221; D. Gelles, 'How the Social Mission of Ben & Jerry's Survived Being Gobbled Up' (21 August 2015) *The New York Times*,

manufacturer Patagonia,[18] the cleaning products company Method Products, the eyeglass brand Warby Parker, and the internet microbusiness marketplace Etsy.

Many Type B social enterprises are organised as traditional corporations. For example, while Patagonia and Method are benefit corporations, Etsy and Warby Parker are traditional corporations with Certified B Corp status. This demonstrates my point that it is not necessary to use a hybrid form to run a social enterprise. However, hybrids are purported to offer benefits including:[19]

. decreased risk of liability for breaches of directors' duties where directors prioritise the social mission over profits (i.e., solving the 'Dodge v Ford problem');
. branding/marketing benefits;[20]
. eligibility for otherwise restricted sources of investment capital such as specialist funds operated by social investors;[21] and
. a greater ability to 'lock in' the social objective, so that the entity may maintain its social mission even following a change of control.[22]

The forms most relevant to Type B entrepreneurs are the benefit corporation and the Certified B Corp, discussed in greater detail in Sections 9.2.4 and 9.2.5, because those forms limit neither profit seeking nor profit taking. This chapter's critique of the hybrid form will be directed at its

---

see www.nytimes.com/2015/08/23/business/how-ben-jerrys-social-mission-survived-being-gobbled-up.html?_r=0>16.

[18] J. H. Murray, 'Defending Patagonia: Mergers & Acquisitions with Benefit Corporations' (2013) 9 *Hastings Business Law Journal* 485.

[19] See, e.g., B Lab, *Why is Benefit Corp Right for Me?*, see http://benefitcorp.net/businesses/why-become-benefit-corp.

[20] As the hybrid forms become better known, proponents suggest that the forms' commitment to social objectives will add marketing cachet similar to labels such as the 'Fair Trade' designation. Proponents claim that this cachet will be attractive to both retail consumers and socially conscious investors.

[21] Also known as ethical or impact investors.

[22] The legacy problem refers to the risk that an entity will stray from its social mission after its founders depart. For a discussion in the context of the sale of Ben & Jerry's, see, e.g., A. Page and R. A. Katz, 'The Truth about Ben and Jerry's' (2012) *Standford Social Innovation Review,* see http://www.ssireview.org/articles/entry/the_truth_about_ben_and_jerrys; A. Page and R. A. Katz, 'Freezing Out Ben & Jerry: Corporate Law and the Sale of a Social Enterprise Icon' (2010) 35 *Vermont Law Review* 211; Plerhoples, 'Can an Old Dog Learn New Tricks?'; Gelles, 'How the Social Mission of Ben & Jerry's Survived Being Gobbled Up'; Wharton School of the University of Pennsylvania, 'How Ben & Jerry's Got Bought Out without Selling Out' (2016) Knowledge@Wharton, see http://knowledge.wharton.upenn.edu/article/ben-jerrys-got-bought-without-selling.

use by Type B entrepreneurs and the marketing of the hybrid form to this market. The central thrust of the critique is that the use of the hybrid form by Type B social enterprises is founded on the misconception that the traditional corporate form does not allow for or adequately support sustainable business practices. By propagating this premise, those selling hybrid forms to Type B entrepreneurs (including proponents who profess to support sustainable and socially responsible business practices) are also helping to reinforce the mistaken notion that socially responsible business practices are not appropriate for the wider business community.[23]

9.2.3   The Social Enterprise as Implementer of Feminist Values and B Lab as an Agent for Change

In light of this book's focus on gender as an agent of change, it is interesting to consider the role – or lack thereof – of gender in the social enterprise movement, in particular considering the extent to which social enterprise implements the feminist ethic of care.[24] The ethic of care focuses on 'the needs of *all* members of the community' and the need to make decisions 'based on those collective considerations' such that our 'individual actions should be guided by their impact on others'.[25] Feminist theorists were arguing at least a decade before the development of any hybrid forms that corporations must be viewed not just as business enterprises but as social organizations.[26] As Cohen argued, 'a feminist theory of corporations would, by definition, be a theory of corporate social responsibility'.[27]

Feminist writers have argued that what is needed is a change to the core philosophy driving corporations.[28] All forms of social enterprise embody this view: their defining feature is a realignment from a purely

---

[23] See, e.g., L. Johnson, 'Pluralism in Corporate Form: Corporate Law and Benefit Corps' (2012–2013) 25 *Regent University Law Review* 269, 295–296.

[24] See, e.g., Ch. 10. See also B. A. White, 'Feminist Foundations for the Law of Business: One Law and Economics Scholar's Survey and (Re)View' (1999) 10 *UCLA Women's Law Journal* 39, 48; R. Cohen, 'Feminist Thought and Corporate Law: It's Time to Find Our Way Up from the Bottom (Line)' (1994) 2 *Journal of Gender & the Law* 1, 11. As to the extent to which social enterprises do not necessarily facilitate the advancement of women – and vice versa – see Ch. 8.

[25] White, 'Feminist Foundations for the Law of Business', p. 48 (emphasis in original).

[26] Cohen, 'Feminist Thought and Corporate Law', p. 16.   [27] Ibid, p. 24.

[28] See, e.g., K. Y. Testy, 'Capitalism and Freedom: For Whom?: Feminist Legal Theory and Progressive Corporate Law' (2004) 67 *Law and Contemporary Problems* 87, 97, citing

individualistic, profit-seeking objective to a legally enforceable implementation of the feminist ethic of care. Yet it has been men who have
driven much of the innovation in the social enterprise space. For
example, CICs were first dreamed up by lawyer Stephen Lloyd and social
entrepreneur Roger Warren-Evans during a conversation in which they
bemoaned the lack of options for British businesses with social
objectives.[29] Benefit corporations and Certified B Corp status were
developed by B Lab, a US-based non-profit company founded by three
businessmen, Jay Coen Gilbert, Bart Houlahan, and Andrew Kassoy, who
'share passion for creating a better world through business'.[30] B Lab
professes to have the goal of 'build[ing] an infrastructure for capitalism
that incorporates stakeholder values'.[31] Arguably, what B Lab is effectively saying is that it seeks to incorporate the feminist ethic of care into
business.[32]

It is not clear why it took men to effect these changes to the corporate
system when women had been arguing for conceptually similar developments.[33] Perhaps women did not have the political power or connections
that these men had.[34] Perhaps the feminist theorists, like so many other
theorists, were too focused on high-level, conceptual theorizing and
criticism to get their hands dirty with the pragmatic need to flesh out
exactly how to create the change advocated. Or perhaps feminist corporate law theorists would not be as willing to accept the compromise, the
halfway house of these new corporate forms while leaving what many

---

K. A. Lahey and S. W. Salter, 'Corporate Law in Legal Theory and Legal Scholarship: from
Classicism to Feminism' (1985) 23 *Osgoode Hall Law Journal* 543.

[29] S. Lloyd, 'Transcript: Creating the CIC' (2010) 35 (Fall) *Vermont Law Review* 31.

[30] B Lab, *About B Lab*, see www.bcorporation.net/what-are-b-corps/about-b-lab.

[31] F. Alexander, 'Delaware Public Benefit Corporations: Widening the Fiduciary Aperture to
Broaden the Corporate Mission', New York City Bar (29 September 2016). For more
about B Lab, see ibid.

[32] Although, ironically, if that ethic extends to paying women as much as men, B Lab
appears to have an uphill battle. According to Part VII of its 2015 US federal income tax
return, of the ten officers, directors, or highly paid employees listed as earning compensation in 2015 (the directors worked for free), seven were men, and six of those men
earned more than all three of the women. B Lab's financial information is available at
Guidestar.org. Its 2015 tax return is located at www.guidestar.org/FinDocuments/2015/
205/958/2015-205958773-0d10187c-9.pdf.

[33] Of course, similar arguments have existed since at least the famous Berle-Dodd debate of
the 1930s and the conclusion of Berle and Means's 1932 classic, *The Modern Corporation
and Private Property*. Interest in the social obligations of corporations and the public
interest clearly extends far past the confines of the feminist literature.

[34] As explored in Ch. 13.

consider to be the conventional understanding of the traditional corporation unchanged – or, worse, now portrayed as an institution in opposition to the socially responsible and sustainable hybrids. That said, B Lab seems to have attracted a largely female workforce, indicating the extent to which B Lab's aims and values resonate with women. For example, of forty-six 'team members' listed on B Lab's website, thirty are women. While B Lab's board of directors contains more men than women (5:3) as of May 2017, its several advisory boards each appear to contain over 50 per cent women.

The professional affiliations of B Lab's advisers are also perhaps surprising. The members of B Lab's various boards are affiliated with major corporations, professional services firms, investment funds, and academic institutions including Danone, Prudential, Campbell's Soup Co, Linklaters, Morgan Stanley, and Harvard Business School.[35] Several of these institutions are also funders of B Lab. As a non-profit organization under s 501(c)(3) of the US Internal Revenue Code, B Lab has no shareholders. It receives much of its funding from major foundations and other entities, including multimillion-dollar donations from the Rockefeller Foundation, B Lab's co-founders, the accounting firm Deloitte LLP, the Inter-American Development Bank, and even the United States Agency for International Development.[36] (B Lab also earns income from the certification fees that it charges companies to receive the 'Certified B Corp' designation. According to its tax return for the 2015 financial year, it earned approximately $3.7 million from program revenue as opposed to approximately $3.1 million in donations.[37]) One may query why such dominant members of the business community are supporting an initiative seemingly at odds with the traditional corporate values of competition and individual gain. A cynic might assume that B Lab's corporate funders understand that the development of hybrid forms might take pressure off traditional corporations to become more sustainable and socially responsible. Funder testimonials on B Lab's website indicate institutional recognition of the economic importance of efforts to 'address social and environmental issues' and inculcate sustainability.[38] Supporting B Lab also, of course, helps burnish those institutions' own social credentials.

---

[35] B Lab, *About B Lab*.
[36] B Lab, *Our Funders*, see www.bcorporation.net/what-are-b-corps/the-non-profit-behind-b-corps/our-funders.
[37] B Lab 2015 tax return.   [38] B Lab, *Our Funders*.

B Lab amassed the power and influence to effect an incredible amount of change in the corporate law space in a relatively short period of time. Its two main contributions to the universe of hybrid forms are described in the following two sections.[39]

9.2.4   B Corp Certification

B Lab created the 'Certified B Corporation' (also known as 'B Corp'[40]) designation in 2006–2007.[41] The certification is available to businesses anywhere in the world that establish that they are a bona fide social enterprise to the satisfaction of B Lab.[42] B Lab aspires for the designation to become as ubiquitous and well-known as the Fair Trade certification, symbolizing social and environmental responsibility, accountability, and transparency.[43] As its website explains,

> Government and the non-profit sector are necessary but insufficient to address society's greatest challenges. Business, the most powerful man-made force on the planet, must create value for society, not just share-holders. Systemic challenges require systemic solutions and the B Corp movement offers a concrete, market-based and scalable solution.[44]

It is not clear why a private licencing regime to use a marketing designation is a better solution to the need for greater corporate sustainability than a program to encourage all businesses to take a more long-term and holistic view of corporate success. Nevertheless, B Corp certification is available to any for-profit corporation meeting B Lab's criteria, which include achieving a minimum required score on its 'B Impact

---

[39] In addition, B Lab has created tools to facilitate investment in social enterprises, including analytics tools such as the Global Impact Investing Rating System (GIIRS). A discussion of these tools is outside the scope of this chapter.

[40] Despite some confusion in the literature, B Lab asserts that a B Corp is not equivalent to a benefit corporation and it is not correct to refer to a benefit corporation as a B Corp (B Lab, *Why Is Benefit Corp Right for Me?*).

[41] B Lab, *Our History*, see www.bcorporation.net/what-are-b-corps/the-non-profit-behind-b-corps/our-history.

[42] B Lab, *Why Is Benefit Corp Right for Me?*.

[43] B Lab, *What Are B Corps?*, see www.bcorporation.net/what-are-b-corps. Interestingly, older versions of the bcorporation.net website did not emphasise that B Corps are for-profit companies.

[44] B Lab, *Why B Corps Matter*, see www.bcorporation.net/what-are-b-corps/why-b-corps-matter.

Assessment' measuring the business's environmental and social performance.[45] Interestingly, while corporations in states (and foreign jurisdictions) that do not provide for the benefit corporation form may acquire Certified B Corp status without changing their corporate form, the contractual scheme governing the B Corp system requires B Corps incorporated in states that provide for the benefit corporation form to reorganise under that form within a limited time period after attaining the certification.[46] This requirement would appear to be at odds with B Lab's stated purpose of facilitating the inclusion of stakeholder values in business because it effectively discourages traditional corporations in benefit corporation states that do not wish to reorganize as benefit corporations from committing to a measurable, 'concrete' (to use B Lab's own language) sustainability program at all.

In addition, although this requirement is basically redundant for Certified B Corps that must reorganize as benefit corporations, many Certified B Corps are contractually required by B Lab's rules to modify their articles of incorporation to recognize stakeholders' interests. Most significantly, Certified B Corp candidates must insert a clause in their articles making clear that the directors 'shall not be required to regard any interest, or the interests of any particular group affected by such action, including the shareholders, as a dominant or controlling interest or factor'.[47] This final clause effectively nullifies any argument that those directors are bound by any perceived norms of shareholder primacy or shareholder wealth maximisation. Moreover, the fact that traditional for-profit corporations may put such language in their articles illustrates that any corporation that was concerned about liability for considering stakeholders could similarly do so, even without formally certifying as a

---

[45] B Lab, *Benefit Corporations and Certified B Corps*, see http://benefitcorp.net/businesses/benefit-corporations-and-certified-b-corps; B Lab, *What Are B Corps?*. B Corp certification also requires the payment of a fee to B Lab. Fees range from $500 for a company with sales up to $149,999 to $50,000+ for companies with annual sales of $1 billion or more: B Lab, *Make It Official*, see www.bcorporation.net/become-a-b-corp/how-to-become-a-b-corp/make-it-official-2.

[46] Furthermore, as of 1 January 2017, corporations in nineteen of the states with benefit corporation statutes are required to become a benefit corporation or Social Purpose Corporation (a benefit corporation variant) *before* they may receive B Corp certification. See B Lab, *Corporation Legal Roadmap*, see www.bcorporation.net/become-a-b-corp/how-to-become-a-b-corp/legal-roadmap/corporation-legal-roadmap.

[47] Ibid.

B Corp or converting to a hybrid form.[48] This point negates one of B Lab's main arguments about why benefit corporations are supposedly necessary.

Unlike the new hybrid forms, which provide legally enforceable obligations to further the organisation's social goals, B Corp certification is enforced by audit (called a 'Certification Evaluation'). Ten per cent of Certified B Corps (down from 20 per cent[49]) are audited each year.[50] Certified B Corps that fail their audit lose their Certified B Corp status. In this sense, B Corporation certification can be characterised as a voluntary regime under which B Lab acts as an independent, private regulator.

As part of the certification process, B Lab requires B Corp directors to sign a Declaration of Interdependence affirming their belief, inter alia, that 'all business ought to be conducted as if people and place mattered', and 'that, through their products, practices, and profits, businesses should aspire to do no harm and benefit all.'[51] While B Lab's stated motivations are admirable, the contents of their Declaration of Interdependence, asserting that *all* business ought to be conducted in a socially responsible manner while at the same time lauding the creation of a new type of business to do just that, illustrates the contradiction with which this chapter is concerned. B Lab's emphasis on singling out socially responsible businesses as distinctive signals that other businesses are *not* expected to act this way. The Declaration of Interdependence itself illustrates the contradiction. Its preface lauds the creation of a 'new sector of the economy' whose corporations will act for all stakeholders, *unlike* traditional corporations. Yet a few lines later, the Declaration contains a 'list of truths' averring that all corporations should attempt to benefit all stakeholders. Which is it? If the latter 'truth' was impossible, the simultaneous promotion of a separate 'new sector' would not be inconsistent

---

[48] If the response is that the corporation is incorporated in Delaware, where it is not clear that such an amendment could validly be made to a traditional corporation's articles in light of *eBay v Newmark* (discussed in Section 9.3), keep in mind that the company could always reincorporate in a state with a corporate constituency statute.

[49] See D. B. Reiser, 'Benefit Corporations – A Sustainable Form of Organization?' (2011) 46 *Wake Forest Law Review* 591, 602.

[50] B Lab, *Make It Official*.

[51] B Lab, *The B Corp Declaration*, see www.bcorporation.net/what-are-b-corps/the-b-corp-declaration. Note that directors must affirm not their *commitment* to the social enterprise movement but their *belief* in its ideals, as set forth by B Lab. It appears that the thought police are alive and well in the social enterprise movement.

with the latter aspiration. But, despite the scare tactics that B Lab uses to sell its new products – in particular its use of the extremely limited *eBay Holdings v Newmark*[52] decision (discussed in Section 9.3) as a bogeyman[53] – the reality is that most if not all Anglo-American jurisdictions, including, of course, the many jurisdictions that have corporate constituency statutes, now recognise that traditional corporations may consider the impact of corporate conduct on stakeholders in their decision making.[54] As such, the underlying assumptions in the two halves of the Declaration (that a 'new sector' is either necessary, or not) are fundamentally incompatible. The more one argues for the 'new sector', the more one strengthens the argument that we should not expect social responsibility from traditional corporations.[55] That seems perverse in light of B Lab's 'self-evident truth' that all companies should be socially responsible. The same contradiction seen on a small scale in the case of Certified B Corps presents on an even bigger scale when applied to the burgeoning sector of benefit corporations.

9.2.5   Benefit Corporations

The benefit corporation is a bona fide new corporate form that has existed since 2010, when it was legalized in the US state of Maryland. As of June 2017, benefit corporations are available in thirty-three US jurisdictions, and six more are 'working on it'.[56]

---

[52] *eBay Domestic Holdings, Inc v Newmark*, 16 A.3d 1 (Del. Ch. 2010).

[53] See, e.g., Clark and Vranka, 'The Need and Rationale for the Benefit Corporation'; A. Kassoy, B. Houlahan and J. C. Gilbert, 'Impact Governance and Management: Fulfilling the Promise of Capitalism to Achieve a Shared and Durable Prosperity', Brookings Institution Center for Effective Public Management (July 2016), see https://www.brookings.edu/research/impact-governance-and-management-fulfilling-the-promise-of-capitalism-to-achieve-a-shared-and-durable-prosperity/, pp. 6–7.

[54] V. S. Baumfield, 'Stakeholder Theory from a Management Perspective: Bridging the Shareholder/Stakeholder Divide' (2016) 31 *Australian Journal of Corporate Law* 187, 196–199; 200–202; E. Elhauge, 'Sacrificing Corporate Profits in the Public Interest' (2005) 80 *New York University Law Review* 733; L. E. Paterno, 'Irresponsible Corporate-Responsibility Rules' (2016) 77 *University of Pittsburgh Law Review* 499, 526–532 ('Benefit-corporation statutes address a problem that does not exist'). This point is discussed in greater detail in Sections 9.3 and 9.4.

[55] Underberg, 'Benefit Corporations vs "Regular" Corporations'.

[56] B Lab, *State by State Status of Legislation*, see http://benefitcorp.net/policymakers/state-by-state-status.

Benefit corporations are characterized by the following features[57] that distinguish them from traditional corporations:

- Purpose: a requirement to create some sort of public benefit.
- Accountability/fiduciary duties: directors owe enforceable duties to consider stakeholder interests and the corporation's public benefit purposes in corporate decision making.
- Transparency: a requirement to publish a 'benefit report' reporting the benefit corporation's impact on stakeholders as assessed against a third-party standard.
- Right of action: allows the corporation itself or its shareholders, derivatively, to enforce the corporation's social objectives.
- Change of control: to lock in the social objective even upon a change of control, a supermajority shareholder vote is required to change the corporate purpose or structure (e.g., back to a traditional corporation).

Although individual states' legislation varies, the general model for standard benefit corporations is the Model Benefit Corporation Legislation (the Model Legislation), which was drafted by corporate lawyers working pro bono for B Lab. The leading alternative to the standard model is Delaware's Public Benefit Corporation (PBC) model.[58]

Like other hybrids, the benefit corporation form requires managers to focus on both profit and social benefit. Oddly, B Lab claims that it is a 'misconception' to call benefit corporations a 'hybrid entity'.[59] It is unclear why B Lab is so sensitive about the use of the term 'hybrid' considering that the whole raison d'être of benefit corporations is that they have greater obligations to non-shareholder stakeholders than traditional corporations. In fact, that difference is B Lab's main marketing angle, which it uses to promote this form to the corporate marketplace and legislators both in the United States and overseas. B Lab asserts that traditional corporations may not be socially responsible without risking suit for breach of fiduciary duty.[60] While that argument may be a useful

---

[57] The precise details vary by state or other jurisdiction that has adopted benefit corporation legislation.

[58] A. E. Plerhoples, 'Social Enterprise as Commitment: A Roadmap' (2015) 48 *Washington University Journal of Law & Policy* 89, 106; Delaware Code tit. 8, §§ 361–368.

[59] B Lab, *Benefit Corporations and Certified B Corps* (scroll down to 'Common Misconceptions'); Kassoy, Houlahan and Gilbert, 'Impact Governance and Management', pp. 6–7.

[60] Compare, e.g., B Lab, *Why We Need Benefit Companies*, see http://bcorporation.com.au/blog/why-we-need-benefit-companies and Kassoy et al., 'Impact Governance and Management', pp. 6–7 with Baumfield, 'Stakeholder Theory'; Elhauge, 'Sacrificing Corporate

way to expand the ranks of businesses using hybrid forms, it is not, as described in Sections 9.3 and 9.4, entirely accurate.[61] Nor is it an especially useful way to achieve B Lab's stated ultimate objective of seeing all corporations act in a sustainable, socially responsible manner because it may well dissuade risk-averse directors of traditional corporations from pursuing socially responsible business practices. Even experienced outside corporate counsel may be subtly influenced by B Lab's steady flow of negative statements about traditional corporations' ability to behave responsibly towards corporate stakeholders, despite the many reasons why it is more likely that directors of traditional corporations will face liability for harm to their company if they do *not* adequately take stakeholders into account.[62]

9.3   US Corporate Law Allows Socially Responsible Business Practices

B Lab is playing a counterproductive game in continuing to insist that traditional corporations may only pursue socially responsible business practices at their peril, as well as a hypocritical one given that B Lab has been marketing its Certified B Corp label to traditional corporations.

The question surrounding the need for new hybrid forms is effectively the latest salvo in the famous Berle/Dodd debate over the extent to which corporations have an obligation to fulfil social responsibilities.[63] The January 2013 White Paper on the Need and Rationale for the Benefit

---

Profits in the Public Interest'; Underberg, 'Benefit Corporations vs "Regular" Corporations'; Johnson, 'Pluralism in Corporate Form'; Blount and Kwabena, 'The Benefit Corporation'; and D. Groshoff, 'Contrepreneurship? Examining Social Enterprise Legislation's Feel-Good Governance Giveaways' (2013) 16 *University of Pennsylvania Journal of Business Law* 233.

[61] See also, e.g., B. Sjåfjell, A. Johnston, L. Anker-Sorensen, & D. Millon 'Shareholder Primacy: The Main Barrier to Sustainable Companies' in B. Sjåfjell & B. J. Richardson (eds.), *Company Law and Sustainability: Legal Barriers and Opportunities* (Cambridge: Cambridge University Press, 2015), pp. 79–147.

[62] See Baumfield, 'Stakeholder Theory from a Management Perspective'; T. Clarke, 'The Widening Scope of Directors' Duties: The Increasing Impact of Corporate Social and Environmental Responsibility' (2016) 39 *Seattle University Law Review* 531; S. Barker, 'Directors' Duties in the Anthropocene: Liability for Corporate Harm Due to Inaction on Climate Change', Corporate Law, Economics & Science Association (2013), see www.clesa.net.au/blog/2015/1/14/directors-duties-in-the-anthropocene-liability-for-cor porate-harm-due-to-inaction-on-climate-change.

[63] A. A. Berle, Jr, 'Corporate Powers as Powers in Trust' (1931) 44 *Harvard Law Review* 1049; E. Merrick Dodd, Jr, 'For Whom Are Corporate Managers Trustees?' (1932) 45

Corporation, prepared by B Lab's pro bono lawyers, emphasised the liability risk that directors of traditional corporations face for breach of fiduciary duty to the extent that they explicitly consider stakeholder interests. The authors claimed that all such directors faced such liability, particularly where making a decision that explicitly placed some other value ahead of profits, and noted that there was particular pressure when directors faced change of control and other major corporate events.[64] The authors took the view that there was somewhat less risk for directors of corporations located in one of the thirty-one US states whose corporations legislation contains 'corporate constituency statutes', which explicitly allow directors to consider the needs of corporate constituents (i.e., stakeholders) other than shareholders.[65] But the authors claim that constituency statutes provide little real protection because there is a dearth of case law interpreting 'the weight the directors should assign to shareholder and non-shareholder interests and what standards a court should use in reviewing directors' decisions to consider (or not consider) non-shareholder interests.'[66] Accordingly, the authors claim, courts confronted with constituency statutes 'often fall back on shareholder primacy'.[67] In support of this proposition, the White Paper cites only one case: *Baron v Strawbridge & Clothier*,[68] which concerned an attempted takeover of a Philadelphia department store company. In that case, however, the federal district court for the Eastern District of Pennsylvania sided with the directors *against* the complaining shareholder (the hostile bidder), stating 'It was proper for the company to consider the effects the Berry tender offer would have, if successful, on the Company's employees, customers and community.'[69] The case hardly supports the proposition that courts disregard constituency statutes in favour of

---

Harvard Law Review 1145; A. A. Berle, Jr, 'For Whom Corporate Managers *Are* Trustees: A Note' (1932) 45 *Harvard Law Review* 1365.

[64] Clark and Vranka, 'The Need and Rationale for the Benefit Corporation', pp. 7–14. As discussed in their paper, this pressure emanates from a line of Delaware case law emphasising the need to prioritise shareholder wealth maximisation in certain change of control scenarios (p. 13).

[65] Ibid. For additional discussion of constituency statutes, see J. D. Springer, 'Corporate Constituency Statutes: Hollow Hopes and False Fears' (1999) *Annual Survey of American Law* 85; Baumfield, 'Stakeholder Theory from a Management Perspective', pp. 196–197.

[66] Clark and Vranka, 'The Need and Rationale for the Benefit Corporation', p. 10. Note that this point seems to ignore the general understanding that the business judgment rule would normally apply.

[67] Ibid.   [68] *Baron v Strawbridge & Clothier*, 646 F Supp 690, 697 (E.D. Pa. 1986).

[69] Ibid.

shareholder primacy, even in the critical takeover context. Nor do the authors explain why the business judgment rule would not presumptively apply.

Moreover, benefit corporation proponents seem to suggest that, other than in states with constituency statutes, corporations have no ability to identify social objectives as within their corporate mission.[70] This proposition is incorrect. It also goes against the prevailing contractarian view that the participants in the corporate enterprise may tailor the corporation, as a nexus of contracts, to suit their objectives.[71] Before the introduction of constituency statutes, charter amendments were used to allow directors to consider other constituencies.[72] Therefore, the suggestion that legislation providing for constituency statutes or even hybrid forms is necessary to allow for consideration of social objectives is false. That is not to say that the creation of a standardized hybrid model with off-the-rack default rules may not be efficient – as well as a useful signalling device of state support for socially responsible business practices[73] – even if not technically necessary.

The best argument in favour of the need for a distinct hybrid form is the Delaware Chancery Court's 2010 *Newmark* decision.[74]

---

[70] For example, B Lab itself, in the context of B Corp certification, requires companies in states that have constituency statutes to amend their charters to effectively add the equivalent of a constituency statute into the corporate charter, but it does not require this of companies in states without a constituency statute. This implies that those constituency statutes are not operative until they have been effectively ratified by the company. With the exception of the three states that have opt-in constituency statutes (Georgia, Tennessee, and Pennsylvania), that is wrong: Springer, 'Corporate Constituency Statutes', p. 101. If anything, B Lab should require the companies in states *lacking* constituency statutes to amend their charters in this way. In states with constituency statutes, B Lab's required charter amendments are in large part superfluous.

[71] See F. H. Easterbrook and D. R. Fischel, *The Economic Structure of Corporate Law* (Cambridge, MA: Harvard University Press, 1991), pp. 35–36 (the corporate contract can include terms that privilege social objectives over profit maximisation, and investors should not be able to complain about non-profit maximising behaviour where on notice of those objectives or where the share price 'reflected the corporation's tempered commitment to a profit objective').

[72] Springer, 'Corporate Constituency Statutes', p. 94 ('charter amendments came first, authorizing directors to consider interests of non-shareholders in takeover situations', and referring to eighty such charter amendments). But see Reiser, 'Theorizing Forms for Social Enterprise', p. 687 (noting 'anecdotal reports' of the 'unwillingness of a secretary of state's office to accept articles of incorporation from for-profit corporations that evinced a blended mission').

[73] Cf. Yockey, 'Does Social Enterprise Law Matter?', pp. 812–813.

[74] *eBay Domestic Holdings, Inc v Newmark*, 16 A.3d 1 (Del. Ch. 2010).

Newmark concerned the internet auction site eBay's investment in the online classified ad service Craigslist.[75] Despite being incorporated in Delaware as a (closely held) for-profit corporation, Craigslist 'largely operates its business as a community service'.[76] eBay, which sought to acquire Craigslist, believed that Craigslist should be 'monetized'.[77] After eBay began competing with Craigslist in the online advertising market, Craigslist implemented 'defensive measures, including a poison pill rights plan',[78] to prevent eBay from acquiring Craigslist. The Chancery Court allowed certain other defensive measures as a reasonable response to eBay's attempt to use its minority shareholder position to gain valuable confidential information that would allow it to better compete with Craigslist. However, applying the leading case of *Unocal Corporation v Mesa Petroleum Company*[79] from Delaware's specialised body of corporate takeover case law, the Court invalidated the poison pill that Craigslist had adopted as one of its defensive measures on the basis that it was implemented to further the invalid corporate purpose of preventing the maximization of shareholder value:

> The corporate form in which craigslist operates ... is not an appropriate vehicle for purely philanthropic ends, at least not when there are other stockholders interested in realizing a return on their investment. Jim and Craig opted to form craigslist as a *for-profit Delaware corporation* and voluntarily accepted millions of dollars from eBay as part of a transaction whereby eBay became a stockholder. Having chosen a for-profit corporate form, the craigslist directors are bound by the fiduciary duties and standards that accompany that form. Those standards include acting to promote the value of the corporation for the benefit of its stockholders. The "Inc." after the company name has to mean at least that. Thus, I cannot accept as valid for the purposes of implementing the Rights Plan a corporate policy that specifically, clearly, and admittedly seeks *not* to maximize the economic value of a for-profit Delaware corporation for the benefit of its stockholders. ... Directors of

---

[75] Craigslist, Inc (whose formal name is not capitalized) owns an extremely popular American website, craigslist.org, which provides online classified ads that are, in most cases, free of charge. Certain categories, such as job listings and New York City apartments, attract fees. Craigslist also offers local websites for cities around the world, although it seems to be most popular in the United States.

[76] *eBay Domestic Holdings v Newmark* at 8.   [77] Ibid, pp. 8–9, 16.

[78] D. A. Wishnick, 'Corporate Purposes in a Free Enterprise System: A Comment on *eBay v Newmark*' (2012) 121 *Yale Law Journal* 2405, 2407.

[79] *Unocal Corporation v Mesa Petroleum Company*, 493 A.2d 946 (Del. 1985).

a for-profit Delaware corporation cannot deploy a rights plan to defend a business strategy that openly eschews stockholder wealth maximization – at least not consistently with the directors' fiduciary duties under Delaware law.[80]

It is interesting to note that even *Newmark*, while applying a legal requirement to maximize shareholder value over some unspecified time frame, does not impose the shareholder primacy social norm, 'which insists that the board of directors and senior managers … should maximize returns to shareholders as measured by the current share price'.[81] In any event, *Newmark*'s influence should be limited because: (1) it only applies in Delaware and elsewhere is persuasive authority at best, even considering the Delaware courts' significant prestige in the corporate law realm; (2) it clearly does not apply to jurisdictions with corporate constituency statutes since those states explicitly allow the consideration of interests other than stakeholders'; (3) it only applies in change of control scenarios;[82] (4) despite strongly asserting the fundamental importance of shareholder wealth maximization, the decision did not actually require Craigslist's managers to change a single aspect of how they do business in order to move from a social objective to a profit-maximising objective; and (5) the decision is in some respects at odds with the US Supreme Court's 2014 *Hobby Lobby* decision,[83] which affirmed that shareholders in (at a minimum) closely held corporations may choose to govern themselves in a way that places other objectives ahead of profit maximization.

Assuming that eBay was fully aware that Craigslist's majority owners were not running Craigslist as a profit-maximising business at the time it made its investment,[84] an investor like eBay would seem to be precluded from asserting a valid legal claim by the *Hobby Lobby* principle

---

[80] *eBay Domestic Holdings v Newmark* at 34 (emphasis in original).

[81] Sjåfjell et al., 'Shareholder Primacy'.

[82] It is, of course, not unusual to have different rules in change of control situations. Takeover-specific rules are also seen, for example, in the EU Takeover Directive. See, e.g., B. Sjåfjell, 'The Core of Corporate Governance: Implications of the Takeover Directive for Corporate Governance in Europe' (2011) 22 *European Business Law Review* 641.

[83] *Burwell v Hobby Lobby Stores Inc*, 573 US ___ (2014); 134 S Ct 2751.

[84] And query what this even means considering that by 2017 Craigslist was reported to be earning 'in upwards of $690 million in revenue, most of which is net profit': Ryan Mac, 'Craig Newmark Founded Craigslist to Give Back, Now He's a Billionaire' (3 May 2017) *Forbes*, see www.forbes.com/sites/ryanmac/2017/05/03/how-does-craigslist-make-money/#5e4afa6027b1.

(discussed later in this section).[85] Furthermore, *Newmark*, like *Dodge v Ford*,[86] is an idiosyncratic case because of the majority shareholders' purportedly complete disavowal of the profit incentive.[87] As in *Dodge v Ford Motor Co*, the majority shareholders effectively painted the court into a corner by refusing to acknowledge how the business benefitted from their supposedly philanthropic activities.[88] This gives rise to the question whether, if the majority shareholders in Craigslist had taken a more balanced approach by pointing out the great commercial success of their community-focused 'philanthropic' business, their defence might have been more persuasive. After all it was this commercial success that caused eBay to seek to acquire it in the first place. Unfortunately, instead of taking this more nuanced approach, which arguably would have been a better fit with corporate law principles, therefore finding favour with the court, the majority shareholders in Craigslist, like Henry Ford, almost aggressively thumbed their noses at the notion of making a profit for the benefit of all of the shareholders.[89] In any event, as B Lab emphasises on its website, benefit corporations, too, are for-profit business forms. Therefore, under *Newmark*'s reasoning, Craigslist might still have a problem even if it converts to benefit corporation status (and one can also query why a firm like Craigslist has not bothered to do so).[90]

Further, as stated previously, *Newmark* must be read in light of the Supreme Court's later decision in *Hobby Lobby* as to corporate purpose. *Hobby Lobby* confirmed that for-profit companies were entitled to prioritise values other than financial gain for the benefit of shareholders. In that case, the relevant value was the religious value of running the company according to perceived Christian values, but under *Hobby*

---

[85] See also Easterbrook and Fischel, 'The Economic Structure of Corporate Law', pp. 35–36 (the corporate contract can include terms that privilege social objectives over profit maximisation, and investors should not be able to complain about non-profit maximising behaviour where on notice of those objectives or where the share price 'reflected the corporation's tempered commitment to a profit objective').

[86] *Dodge v Ford Motor Co*, 170 NW 668 (Mich 1919).

[87] Compare the *eBay Domestic Holdings v Newmark* court's characterisation of Craigslist as 'purely philanthropic' with Henry Ford's assertion that his shareholders had made enough money in *Dodge v Ford*.

[88] Cf. Baumfield, 'Stakeholder Theory'.

[89] This point is also made in L. Johnson and D. Millon, 'Corporate Law after *Hobby Lobby*' (2015) 70 *The Business Lawyer* 1, 11.

[90] The counterargument is that Delaware's benefit corporation statute explicitly allows directors to balance shareholder, stakeholder, and community interests. But one could argue that if Craigslist is really being run on a 'purely philanthropic' basis, then it is not 'balancing' all three interests at all.

Lobby's reasoning, non-religious social objectives may be equally protected. There is no basis for distinguishing between the two. On the facts of that case, it was found that the shareholders had agreed to the company being run according to Christian values because explicit religious objectives were placed in the company's constitutional and other documents. So the Supreme Court has, at a minimum, effectively adopted Easterbook and Fischel's argument that a corporation, as a nexus of contracts, may pursue social objectives that detract from profit maximisation where there is agreement among the participants in the corporate contract (in particular, the founding members and others that later bought in to a company being run in this fashion) as to those objectives.[91] That is not to say, however, that the Supreme Court endorsed the contention that the corporate purpose is profit maximization for shareholders if such an agreement among shareholders is *not* in place. The Court stated no such thing. As Johnson and Millon note, 'the Court spoke to the question of corporate purpose without reliance on or reference to any modification of or "contracting around" some supposed background maximization rule'.[92]

It is in any event wrong to say that *Newmark* forbids traditional corporations from pursuing any social objective not tied to shareholder profits. The Chancery Court's concern in *Newmark* was clearly the apparent *total* disregard of profit-making,[93] not disapproval of a *dual* purpose, as the hybrid forms create. Indeed, if the opposing view were correct, then the non-profit-maximising religious objectives in *Hobby Lobby* would similarly breach the proper purpose doctrine as conceived by the Delaware Chancery Court. Yet far from invalidating those objectives, the Supreme Court enforced them. Under US federalism principles, Delaware is not bound to follow Supreme Court precedent on the interpretation of state-level corporate law (although it would have significant persuasive effect), but *Hobby Lobby* certainly calls alarmist interpretations of *Newmark* into doubt, not least for corporations registered outside of Delaware that have explicitly adopted a social mission.

---

[91] Easterbrook and Fischel, 'The Economic Structure of Corporate Law', p. 36. ('If a corporation is started with a promise to pay half of the profits to the employees rather than the equity investors, that too is simply a term of the contract').

[92] Johnson and Millon, 'Corporate Law after *Hobby Lobby*', p. 28.

[93] Note the Court's reference in the quoted material not only to 'purely philanthropic' activities but also to 'openly eschew[ing]' profit maximisation.

9.4   Australian Companies May Be Socially Responsible, Too

B Lab is currently lobbying to create a 'benefit company' form in Australia, which currently has no hybrid forms.[94] The form is no more necessary in Australia than it is in the United States.[95] The Australian situation illustrates how the US arguments may apply in other common law jurisdictions.

Australian corporate law requires directors to act in good faith in the best interests of the company[96] and provides no constituency statute. Moreover, Australia follows English jurisprudence establishing that stakeholders cannot be given preference over shareholders where there will be no opportunity for the company to receive the benefit of that largesse (i.e., through increased goodwill, employee loyalty, etc.) in the future.[97] On the other hand, there is no case law explicitly requiring directors to maximize shareholder wealth to the exclusion of other corporate objectives. The most explicit case law on point, rather, states that

> It does not follow that in determining the content of the duty to act in the interests of the company, the concerns of shareholders are the only ones to which attention need be directed or that the legitimate interests of other groups can safely be ignored.[98]

B Lab Australia and New Zealand claims that a 'benefit company' form is necessary in Australia because

> there is no case law or legal framework for directors to consider the interests of wider stakeholders including employees, customers,

---

[94] B Lab, *Why We Need Benefit Companies*.

[95] Carol Liao has made similar arguments with regard to Canada. See C. Liao, 'A Critical Canadian Perspective on the Benefit Corporation' (2017) 40 *Seattle University Law Review* 683. There are similar comparisons to be made with understandings of the corporate function in the Member States of the European Union, and reflected in EU legislation and policy documents. See further I. Lynch Fannon, *Working within Two Kinds of Capitalism* (Oxford and Portland, OR: Hart Publications, 2003).

[96] Corporations Act 2001 (Cth), s. 181(1)(a).

[97] E.g., *Hutton v West Cork Railway Co* (1883) 23 Ch D 654; *Parke v Daily News Ltd* [1962] Ch 927.

[98] *Bell Group Ltd (in liq) v Westpac Banking Corporation* (No 9) (2008) 39 WAR 1; [2008] WASC 239. See also *Darvall v North Sydney Brick & Tile Co Ltd [No 2]* (1987) 16 NSWLR 212, 239-240 (proper to take into account the interests of not only present shareholders but also future shareholders, creditors, and the company as a commercial entity).

> contractors and the community when making company decisions.
> Although directors can choose to take non-shareholder interests into
> account, directors face considerable legal uncertainty about their statutory
> and fiduciary duties should they favour non-shareholder interests.[99]

While it is true that an explicit 'framework' does not exist, the risk that
directors will be liable for breach of fiduciary duties if they 'choose to take
non-shareholder interests into account' is minimal at best. Similar to
Hobby Lobby, the Australian High Court has explicitly allowed a business
to engage in conduct seemingly at odds with shareholder wealth maximisation, although, unlike *Hobby Lobby*, that conduct was likely beneficial to the corporation in the long term.[100] In *Miles v Sydney Meat
Preserving Co*, a meat preserving company had come to an agreement
with cattle producers to limit the range of prices at which it would buy
meat so that low prices during times of glut would not make the vendors
destitute and high prices during times of scarcity would not put the
company out of business. The corporate constitution (a deed of settlement) authorized directors at their discretion to pay dividends out of
profits, or to set aside funds for the company's needs. A shareholder sued
on the grounds that the company, which had never paid a dividend, was
putting the needs of 'the pastoral industry in general' above the
shareholders.

The High Court dismissed his appeal.[101] First, the social objectives
did not conflict with the company's constitution. Second, the Court
seemed to tacitly acknowledge that it was in the company's long-term
interest to manage itself in a way that preserved both the company and
its customers, foreshadowing modern sustainability arguments. It also
applied the business judgment doctrine of not second-guessing management decisions. As in *Hobby Lobby*, the High Court found that the
directors were not limited to maximising profits, and certainly not to
distributing any such profits in the short term.[102] As Griffith CJ wrote
for the majority:

> His whole case is based upon the conduct of the Directors in not trying to
> earn a profit for the purpose of immediate distribution. He contends that

---

[99] B Lab, *Developing Model Legislation for Australian B Corps*, see http://bcorporation
.com.au/benefitcorp_au.

[100] *Miles v Sydney Meat-Preserving Co Ltd* (1912) 16 CLR 50; [1912] HCA 87.

[101] The decision was affirmed by the Privy Council at (1913) 17 CLR 639.

[102] *Miles v Sydney Meat-Preserving Co Ltd*, at 66.

in the case of every company which is established for gain, . . . an implied contractual duty is imposed upon the directors of endeavouring to earn profits so as to be able to distribute them. If this is so, the duty must surely extend to making the largest possible profits, and to distributing the profits when earned. . . . In my opinion, no such contractual duty is known to the law. In the case of a great many companies, the practical question arises whether they shall be carried on for the purpose of earning immediate profits or with the motive of indirectly achieving some ulterior object which the members may consider beneficial. Take, for instance, the case of a Company formed to establish communication by water or land with a new suburb or newly-settled locality. If the contention of the appellant is sound, the Company would be bound to charge such tolls and dues as would produce the largest immediate profit, without regard to the encouragement of settlement in the new locality. *Again, a trading Company which thought fit to expend part of its income upon providing good and wholesome residences for its employees, instead of distributing it in dividends, could be enjoined from doing so. In my judgment, such matters are entirely matters of internal management, with which the court has no authority to interfere.*

* * *

The law does not require the members of a company to divest themselves, in its management, of all altruistic motives, or to maintain the character of the company as a soulless and bowelless thing, or to exact'the last farthing in its commercial dealings, or forbid them to carry on its operations in a way which they think conducive to the best interests of the community as a whole, or a substantial part of it, rather than in a way which they think detrimental to such interests, though more beneficial (in a pecuniary sense) to themselves.[103]

In recent years, two government reviews have concluded that directors may legitimately consider social factors in their decision making without the need for explicit statutory (or shareholder) authorisation to that effect.[104] Moreover, companies listed on the Australian Securities Exchange (ASX) are subject to Principle 3 of the ASX Corporate Governance Principles and Recommendations, which explicitly directs companies to act 'ethically and responsibly', in a manner that is 'consistent

---

[103] Ibid., pp. 64–66 (emphasis added).

[104] Corporations and Markets Advisory Committee (CAMAC), *The Social Responsibility of Corporations* (December 2006); Parliamentary Joint Committee on Corporations and Financial Services, *Corporate Responsibility: Managing Risk and Creating Value* (Parliament of Australia, June 2006).

with the reasonable expectations of investors *and the broader commu-nity*'.[105] The commentary to Principle 3 suggests that companies should be 'good corporate citizens', including by acting fairly in their dealings with stakeholders such as employees, suppliers, customers and the broader community. ASX listed companies are required to comply with the ASX Corporate Governance Principles unless they publicly explain why they are not doing so.

It should be noted that Australia has had a statutory business judg-ment rule (BJR) since 2000,[106] although it is largely unused.[107] Unlike the US context, the rule is not useful to directors who seek to pursue social objectives because it only acts as a defence to claimed breaches of the statutory duty of care set forth in Corporations Act 2001, s. 180(1) and its common law analogue. It does not act as a defence to breaches of the duty to act in good faith in the best interest of the corporation, which is where the issue of the ability to consider stakeholders is usually situ-ated.[108] Moreover, unlike in the United States, where the BJR presump-tively applies, the (sparse) Australian case law has held that the onus is on defendant directors to establish that the elements of the statutory BJR have been satisfied before it will be found to apply, just like any other defence. (This approach has been criticized, however.) In any event, there is a complete absence of Australian case law finding directors liable for prioritising stakeholders over shareholders in the context of a going concern even without recourse to the BJR. Moreover, as illustrated by

---

[105] ASX Corporate Governance Council, *ASX Corporate Governance Principles and Recommendations* (Australian Securities Exchange, 3rd ed) (2014), p. 19 (emphasis added). See also S. Marshall and I. Ramsay, 'Stakeholders and Directors' Duties: Law, Theory and Evidence' (2012) 35(1) *University of New South Wales Law Journal* 291, 292 (discussing the 'widely held view ... that current Australian company law permits directors sufficient freedom to pursue stakeholder interests without requiring that they do so').

[106] Corporations Act 2001 (Cth), s. 180(2).

[107] Australia's business judgment rule has only been applied in a small handful of decisions where directors were held not to have breached their affirmative duty of care in any event: see the leading case of *Australian Securities and Investments Commission v Rich* [2009] NSWSC 1229, 2975–2996. See also *Australian Securities and Investments Com-mission v Mariner Corp* [2015] FCA 589 [483]–[495] (directors did not breach duty of care but would have satisfied the business judgment rule in any event).

[108] Under the question of 'who is "the corporation"?'. See, e.g., the reference to CAMAC's position, fn. 104.

the *Miles* case as well as more recent cases such as *Harlowe's Nominees*[109] and *Howard Smith v Ampol*[110], the common law business judgment doctrine will protect most good faith and informed exercises of management discretion even if the statutory BJR will be of less assistance.

The introduction of a hybrid form in Australia such as a benefit company might be useful from a branding perspective. It might also facilitate better reporting about social impact. But B Lab's scaremongering is clearly unwarranted. And introducing hybrids would ultimately cause more harm than good if it reduced pressure on traditional corporations to operate sustainably.

9.5   Conclusion

Perhaps the best argument in favour of the use of a hybrid form such as the benefit corporation is to appease risk-averse directors and lawyers even when the risk of litigation from pursuing socially responsible strategies is low to non-existent.[111] On the other hand, society would be better off in the long run if all companies were urged to return to a stewardship model, where corporate success is understood to relate to long-term value maximisation for all stakeholders, not short-term profits. That entails the concomitant success of all stakeholders in the corporate enterprise.

This chapter has established that traditional corporations can be socially responsible and sustainable without any real risk of liability. B Lab, which has proven to be a powerful change agent, asserts that it seeks to make *all* corporations more sustainable and socially responsible. To do this, rather than emphasizing initiatives which work against this goal, it should re-focus on the possibilities inherent in the traditional corporation. Reinforcing and emphasising that position is the key to ensuring *true* corporate sustainability.

---

[109] *Harlowe's Nominees Pty Ltd v Woodside (Lakes Entrance) Oil Co NL* (1968) 121 CLR 483, 493 (High Court of Australia).

[110] *Howard Smith Ltd v Ampol Petroleum Ltd* [1974] AC 821, 832 (Privy Council).

[111] K. Westaway, 'Beyond Black and White: The New Paradigm of Social Enterprise' (2013) 9 *NYU Journal of Law & Business* 439, 441.

PART III

Feminist Theories and Corporate Sustainability

10

Exploring Spatial Justice and the Ethic of Care in Corporations and Group Governance

YUE S. ANG

10.1 Introduction

The corporate group is an important legal construction enabling the parent company (hereafter referred to as the parent) to prosper on the global platform.[1] The corporate veil is, for example in the UK, the legacy left by *Salomon v. Salomon*,[2] and enables the parent to separate itself from its subsidiaries. This principle is widely cited and applied globally to limit the parent's liability in the corporate group. In this regard, the parent owes no obligations or responsibilities to third parties. A mix of case law and legislation deriving from Albania, the United Kingdom, Norway and the Netherlands will be used to emphasise the global reach of *Salomon*'s principle and also highlight an emerging global trend in creating better corporate group governance.

This chapter argues for placing emphasis on the parent's role in regulating corporate behaviour and for better corporate group governance. There is an emerging jurisprudence from a selection of jurisdictions in case law,[3] legislation,[4] and legal procedure[5] emphasising the parent's role. This chapter investigates whether or not the emerging jurisprudence can withstand the two legal doctrines in corporate law: the corporate veil and limited liability. The corporate veil argument still dominates the parent's role within the corporate group and it shields the parent from

---

[1] See A. Daehnert, 'Lifting the Corporate Veil: English and German Perspectives on Group Liability' (2007) 18 *International Company and Commercial Law Review* 393–403. See also J. Dine, *The Governance of Corporate Groups* (Cambridge: Cambridge University Press, 2006).
[2] *Salomon v. Salomon* [1897] AC 22.
[3] *Lubbe and others v. Cape PLC* [2000] 4 All ER 268; *Chandler v. Cape PLC* [2012] EWCA Civ 525; *Hempel AS v. the Norwegian State* [2013] LG-2013–210482; and *Hempel AS v. the Norwegian State* [2015] HR-2015-470-U.
[4] The Albania Law No. 9901 on Entrepreneurs and Companies 2008, and the UK Modern Slavery Act (2015 c30).
[5] 6.20 UK Civil Procedure Rule, and Art. 2 EU Brussels Convention 1968.

its subsidiaries' risks and liabilities.[6] This shield is also referred to as the corporate group's death of liability.[7]

This chapter begins in Section 10.2 by giving a brief account of the emerging jurisprudence's direction by taking examples from the UK, Albania and Norway which seems to circumvent the doctrine of corporate personality and its related idea of limited liability.[8] This circumvention creates a new type of robust parent-subsidiary relationship and is a sign of an evolving law. Section 10.3 briefly introduces the two feminist theories demonstrating a close alignment with the evolving law. Section 10.4 explores the corporate veil and the parent's justification for limited liability. It also discusses whether or not the emerging jurisprudence withstands the corporate veil argument. It is suggested that the parent-subsidiary relationship strengthens two things: its (1) structure and (2) substance. Section 10.5 shows that the feminist theory of spatial justice can create a more suitable structure for the parent-subsidiary relationship so that it can exist alongside the corporate veil. In the parent-subsidiary relationship, spatial justice pinpoints where the subsidiary's corporate autonomy ought to be respected, and where its interdependence with the parent is permitted. Section 10.5 also shows that the feminist theory of ethic of care adds substance to the parent's onus within the parent-subsidiary relationship in times of dependency.

In light of corporate scandals such as the British Home Store's (BHS) pension fund deficit,[9] Sports Direct's misuse of precarious employment,[10] the Panama Papers's tax evasion scandal[11] and Unioil's

---

[6] L. Anker-Sørensen, 'Parental Liability for Externalities of Subsidiaries: Domestic and Extraterritorial Approaches' (2014) *Dovenschmidt Quarterly* 102–118. See also J. Dine, 'Stopping Jurisdiction Arbitrage by Multinational Companies: A National Solution?' (2014) 11 *European Company Law* 77–80.

[7] See L. LoPucki, 'Death of Liability' (1996) 106 *The Yale Law Journal* 8, 20. See also J. Morgan, 'Vicarious Liability for Independent Contractors?' (2015) 31 *Personal Negligence* 235, 241.

[8] Created in *Salomon v. Salomon* [1897] AC 22, and affirmed in *Adams v. Cape PLC* [1990] BCLC 479.

[9] J. Edwards, 'How BHS Pension Fund Collapsed while Sir Philip Green made £307 Million' (26 July 2016) *UK Business Insider*.

[10] A. Armstrong, 'Sports Direct Board Agrees to External Review in Wake of Working Practices Row' (18 August 2016) *Telegraph*. See also M. Clarke, W. Lewchuk, A. de Wolff and A. King, 'This Just Isn't Sustainable: Precarious Employment, Stress, and Workers' Health' (2007) 30 *International Journal of Law and Psychiatry* 311–326.

[11] UK calls for a new tax legislation to prevent tax evasion after the Mossack Fonseca (aka Panama Papers) leak. See T. Magill, 'Analysis: Corporate Failure to Prevent Facilitation of Tax Evasion' (2016) *Tax Journal* 12–13.

bribes scandal,[12] this chapter emphasises a crucial need for group governance and a corporate duty of care obligating parent companies to acknowledge and monitor their subsidiaries' operations; their impact on the environment, health and safety; and the well-being of the workers within the corporate group. Both the feminist theories would have the parent engage in the responsible cultivation of human resources, natural resources, and corporate spaces. The parent company taking these responsibilities into consideration has the potential to facilitate its respect of the planetary boundaries.[13]

10.2   Corporate Group Governance: An Emerging Jurisprudence

This section briefly draws on examples of recent case law,[14] legislation[15] and legal procedure[16] from Albania, Norway and the United Kingdom that place emphasis on the parent's role in the corporate group. The examples drawn from various jurisdictions also emphasise that the emerging jurisprudence is not only from one specific jurisdiction. Arguably, the trend is an emerging global norm. The examples of cases demonstrate the courts' legal innovation which has imposed responsibility on the parent. The evolving law can also be seen, for example, in legislation in Albania and the United Kingdom. The purpose of these laws is to obligate the parent to govern corporate behaviour within its corporate group. The two legal procedures referred to place importance on due diligence, which serves to encourage the parent to act in the interest of its corporate group. Corporate group governance is the emerging jurisprudence. Therefore, the parent's role is to consider issues such as the corporate group's environmental impact and its workers' well-being. These considerations arguably should be the parent's responsibility.[17]

---

[12] In *World Bank v. Wallace* [2016] 1 SCR 207, the Canadian Supreme Court and the Multilateral Development Bank take on their role to fight global corruption. See J. Clark, 'Multilateral Development Bank Immunity in the Age of Anti-Corruption' (2016) 8 *Journal of International Banking and Financial Law* 481–482.

[13] See G. Whiteman, B. Walker, and P. Perego, 'Planetary Boundaries: Ecological Foundations for Corporate Sustainability' (2012) 50 *Journal of Management Studies* 307–336. There is a disconnect between corporate sustainability and ecology. As the former increases, the latter is decreasing. Through good practices in law, this chapter attempts to make a viable connection between the two. This connection is the corporate duty of care.

[14] See n. 3.   [15] See n. 4.   [16] See n. 5.

[17] Janet Dine highlighted the binary between autonomous entities in a corporate group or a group as a single economic unit. None of which establishes the parent's role. See J. Dine,

10.2.1   Case Law

10.2.1.1   Lubbe v. Cape plc[18]

The parent, Cape, was incorporated in the United Kingdom. It had subsidiaries operating several asbestos mines in South Africa. The claimants, most residing in South Africa, sought redress before the UK courts. Two legal issues arose in *Lubbe*. First, the House of Lords had to decide whether or not the claimants' choice was *forum conveniens*. Second, the House of Lords had to determine whether or not Cape owed a duty of care to its subsidiaries' workers. In relation to the first issue, it was found that there were no other suitable forums available 'for the trial of the action'.[19] It was decided that the UK courts were where 'the case may be tried more suitably for the interests of all parties and for the ends of justice'.[20] With the case being heard in a UK forum, the House of Lords approached the second legal issue with care. The establishment of a duty of care between Cape and its subsidiaries' workers needed substantial evidence, which *Lubbe*'s claimants were expected to provide to the court's satisfaction.[21]

Although *Lubbe* focused on the issue of *forum conveniens* and the UK forum's suitability for litigation, *Lubbe's* outcome also indicated that a parent may have an obligation to its subsidiaries' workers.[22] This obligation forms the duty of care's foundation, on which the following case expands.

10.2.1.2   Chandler v. Cape plc[23]

What is sometimes described as enterprise liability[24] was applied in *Chandler* whereby the same parent, Cape, was liable for the harm caused

---

The Governance of Corporate Groups (Cambridge: Cambridge University Press, 2006), p. 42.

[18] *Lubbe v. Cape plc* [2000] 4 All ER 268.   [19] Ibid, 274.

[20] Per *Sim v. Robinow* (1892) 19 R 665. And see *Spiliada Maritime Corporation v. Consulex Ltd* [1987] 1 AC 460.

[21] See n. 18.

[22] Finding the Cape responsible was not possible because the claimants had run out of money after the House of Lords' 2000 ruling. House of Lords' Opinion of the House of Lords of Appeal for Judgement, See www.publications.parliament.uk/pa/ld199900/ldjudgmt/jd000720/lubbe-1.htm

[23] *Chandler v. Cape* [2012] EWCA Civ. 525.

[24] D. Brodie, *Enterprise Liability and the Common Law* (Cambridge: Cambridge University Press, 2010), pp. 27–44. See also J. Dine, *The Governance of Corporate Groups* (Cambridge: Cambridge University Press, 2006).

by its English subsidiary, Cape Products. The underlying justification for this approach was based on the imposition of a duty of care between the parent and the employees of its subsidiary.[25] This approach defines *Chandler's* parent-subsidiary relationship. Owing to a non-delegable duty[26] being passed from Cape to Cape Products relating to health and safety precautions, Cape was found jointly liable in negligence with Cape Products to its employees. Liability for the asbestos exposure was for two reasons: (1) the health and safety precautions taken required Cape's superior and actual knowledge[27] and (2) Cape satisfied the doctrine of assumption of responsibility and the other requirements necessary to impose a duty of care following the decision in *Caparo Industries plc v Dickman*.[28]

The finding of Cape's liability does not affect the separate legal personality doctrine. The preceding case of *Adams v. Cape Industries plc*[29] suggested the parent should not be burdened with the subsidiary's negligence. The corporate veil can only be pierced or lifted under three exceptions: a subsidiary is used for committing illegal acts, concealing obligations or evading obligations.[30] None of these exceptions were present in *Chandler*, but *Chandler's* liability still left the corporate veil intact.

A parent's duty of care owed to its subsidiary by assumed responsibility might be a solution to the corporate group's 'death of liability' problem.[31] By creating this 'duty of care', *Chandler*'s corporate veil circumvention sits awkwardly both in company law and tort law. In company law, having a parent's assumed responsibility somehow presupposes that the parent owes its subsidiaries obligation or more specifically owes stakeholders of the subsidiaries such as employees some obligations. This raises issues as to whether or not the subsidiary's corporate autonomy and their parent's limited liability are infringed. In tort law, this circumvention does not follow the assurance, reliance and detriment formula when establishing an assumption of responsibility.[32] Therefore, *Chandler's* justification seems weak. Furthermore, *Chandler's*

---

[25] Brodie, *Enterprise Liability*, pp. 95–113.

[26] Ibid, p. 149. A duty that cannot be fully delegated to a third party. See P. Giliker, *Vicarious Liability in Tort* (Cambridge: Cambridge University Press, 2013), p. 116.

[27] *Chandler v. Cape* [2012] EWCA Civ 525, 659.   [28] [1990] 2 AC 605.   [29] Ibid.

[30] Ibid., 515–520.   [31] See n. 7.

[32] Per *Hedley Byrne v. Heller* [1964] AC 465. See C. Witting, 'Duty of Care: An Analytical Approach' (2005) 25 *Oxford Journal of Legal Studies* 33, 52–57.

parent-subsidiary relationship[33] is treated no differently from that of the employer-employee.[34] This treatment undermines the significance of the corporate veil and therefore it makes the enterprise liability justification unconvincing. These two relationships are fundamentally different; therefore, the application of these principles should not be conflated. With this conflation (the governing of parent-subsidiary in company law and employer-employee in tort law), *Chandler's* argument for the parent's liability is so weak that it may be difficult to replicate this liability in later cases.[35] Nevertheless, *Chandler's* liability outcome is evidence of an evolving law which can be seen in the recent *Hempel* cases.

10.2.1.3 *Hempel* Cases

The *Hempel* cases were two Norwegian environmental law cases. One was heard in 2013 before the Supreme Court,[36] and the other in 2015 before the Court of Appeals.[37] The nature of Hempel (the parent) and its corporate group's business was of the kind that one of its subsidiaries had polluted assets transferred into its possession from the previous owners. Two legal issues rose in *Hempel*: (1) whether *Hempel* should be responsible for the costs of investigating the extent of the pollution caused by the assets in its subsidiary's possession and (2) whether Hempel should also be responsible for the cost of cleaning up the pollution. In both cases, Hempel was found liable without fault for its subsidiary. As it was the previous owners who had caused the polluted assets, Hempel's subsidiary was also without fault. The courts in both cases affirmed that the Norwegian Pollution Control Act (PCA)[38] could hold the parent liable for these kinds of events.

The decisions of the *Hempel* cases go beyond *Lubbe* and *Chandler*. According to Anker-Sørensen's matrix,[39] *Lubbe* was extraterritorial, case-law-based and fault-based liability, and *Chandler* was domestic, case-law-based and fault-based liability. The *Hempel* cases were

---

[33] Born out of *Salomon*.

[34] For employer-employee relationship, see P. Giliker, *Vicarious Liability in Tort* (Cambridge: Cambridge University Press, 2013), pp. 55–80.

[35] As the discussion in Section 10.4.1 will demonstrate.

[36] *Hempel AS v. the Norwegian State* [2013] LG-2013–210482.

[37] *Hempel AS v. the Norwegian State* [2015] HR-2015–470-U.

[38] Pollution Control Act 1986 no. 6.

[39] As it is refereed in B. Sjåfjell, 'The Courts as Environmental Champions: The Norwegian *Hempel* Cases' (2016) 5 *European Company Law* 199, 205.

extraterritorial, a hybrid between case-law and legislative based and non-fault-based liability.[40]

The finding of non-fault-based liability was striking because it goes against the successful piercing of the veil argument which must require some legal form of fault-based justification.[41] The Norwegian courts have made an innovative and bold step towards a non-fault liability of a parent which might become a tool for the environmental piercing of the veil. Beate Sjåfjell cautioned that while *Hempel* 'did not fulfil the tentatively agreed upon conditions for a general piercing of the corporate veil in Norwegian company law, [she] argued that the courts, starting out and concluding with an interpretation of one provision in the Pollution Act, in reality pierced the veil'.[42]

For the lack of a legal basis to hold the parent liable in these environmental law issues, Sjåfjell pointed out that the *Hempel* cases also 'promote due diligence with greater focus on potential environmental liability'.[43] Perhaps this exercise of due diligence underpinned by the polluter pays principle *is* the foundation for the parent's duty of care to its corporate group.

There is a theme emerging from the *Lubbe, Chandler* and *Hempel* cases. In *Lubbe,* the parent's onus is by way of *forum conveniens.* In *Chandler,* the parent's onus is by way of a duty of care imposed alongside the parent-subsidiary relationship. In the *Hempel* cases, the non-fault-based liability creates a foundation for a duty of care through the parent's role in conducting the due diligence.

10.2.2   Legislation

10.2.2.1   Albania Law No. 9901 on Entrepreneurs and Companies 2008

The Albania Law on Entrepreneurs and Companies (ALEC) emphasises the parent's fiduciary duties in two specific corporate groups: the control group[44] and the equity group.[45] Janet Dine was one of ALEC's drafters

---

[40] Ibid.   [41] As it is in *Lubbe v. Cape, Adams v. Cape* and *Chandler v. Cape.*

[42] Sjåfjell, 'The Courts as Environmental Champions'.   [43] Ibid., p. 206.

[44] The Albania Law on Entrepreneurs and Companies, Art. 207(1), the control group describes subsidiaries which operate under the instruction of the parent. J. Dine, 'Jurisdictional Arbitrage by Multinational Companies: A National Law Solution?' (2012) 3 *Journal of Human Rights and Environment* 44, 62.

[45] The Albania Law on Entrepreneurs and Companies, Art. 207(2), the equity group describes the parent company having the controlling shares in its subsidiaries.

and she applied enterprise liability to ALEC's framework.[46] Unlike *Chandler*, the parent is held liable for the breach of its fiduciary duties. Dine's strategy in drafting ALEC circumvents the corporate veil better, as the Albanian parent owes a direct statutory duty to its corporate group, which makes piercing the veil an obsolete exercise.

Article 207 of ALEC upgrades the parent-subsidiary relationship as we saw in Chandler from having assumed responsibility to having fiduciary duties. Article 208 establishes the legal consequences of a parent-subsidiary relationship. The parent is accountable for the subsidiary's losses, as well as for any creditors' claims against that subsidiary. Article 209 imposes fiduciary duties on the parent controlling an equity group. It can be held accountable for any decision adversely affecting the corporate group *as a whole*. Article 210 lays down joint and severable liability in the corporate group. A negligent or criminal breach caused by any board member of any subsidiary could have the parent jointly liable. Joint and severable liability is designed to ensure that the parent is the main compensator for any damage caused by its subsidiary.

ALEC adds depth and substance to the Albanian parent's role. The parent's duties include conducting due diligence on its subsidiaries' operations, ensuring that they comply with health and safety and that they are also well-resourced financially. In doing so, full compensation will be given to its subsidiary's victims and creditors. As *Salomon*'s globally held principle does not allow the parent to indemnify liability incurred by its subsidiary, the poor decisions made by the parent will fall under ALEC's fiduciary breaches. The parent therefore does not compensate for its subsidiary's negligence or criminal activities; rather it compensates for the poor decisions it has made which adversely affect the corporate group. The separate personality doctrine remains intact. The parent's limited liability is also respected because it still has a decision-making role within the corporate group.

10.2.2.2   UK Modern Slavery Act 2015

The UK Modern Slavery Act (MSA)[47] adopts a human-rights-based approach focusing on prevention, prosecution and protection.[48] Modern slavery occurs when the perpetrator exploits the victim(s) by subjecting

---

[46] Ibid.   [47] The UK Modern Slavery Act 2015 c30.

[48] A. Weatherburn, 'Using an Integrated Human Rights-based Approach to address Modern Slavery: The UK Experience' (2016) 2 *European Human Rights Law Review* 184, 185.

them to slavery or servitude, or forcing them into compulsory labour.[49] This legislation aims to expose businesses practicing modern slavery and hold them accountable. It also aims to prevent businesses being complicit in modern slavery. The latter issue is the focal point for this discussion because it establishes the UK parent's role and its obligations towards UK and non-UK subsidiaries.

A UK parent falling under the MSA is defined as a commercial organisation with a turnover of £36 million or more.[50] This turnover is the accumulation of the parent and all its subsidiaries within the corporate group regardless of where they are based.[51] Transparency is promoted under Section 54(5) by producing an annual slavery and human trafficking statement. The corporate group produces this statement, which includes its structure, policies in relation to human trafficking, training programmes for workers, due diligence, and risk management conducted in the operating areas which are most vulnerable to human trafficking and slavery. If the statement is found not to be satisfactory, the Secretary of State holds the parent accountable.

The UK parent has an obligation to prevent and protect staff within its corporate group from modern slavery. This onus is akin to the Albanian parent's fiduciary duties. Legislation obligates the parent to conduct due diligence in its stakeholders' interests (i.e., workers and creditors). Such duties go beyond the assumed responsibility professed in *Chandler*. A new corporate duty of care has evolved from the two legislations.

10.2.3   Legal Procedure

10.2.3.1   *Forum Conveniens* for the Victims

Lubbe's forum conveniens doctrine is clear. When a case is brought to the UK court, it can stay proceedings if it finds that another forum is more suitable 'for the interests of all parties and for the ends of justice'.[52] Overseas subsidiaries of a UK-domiciled parent may have cases brought against them heard in UK courts. The UK legal system is therefore a point of redress for the corporate group's victims and creditors.

The United Kingdom is also *forum conveniens* when a UK-domiciled victim is injured whilst being overseas and using a third-party business

---

[49] S1 Modern Slavery Act.
[50] K. Sartin and C. Justesen, 'Employment Compliance Update: Modern Slavery, Gender Pay Equality, and Employee Privacy' (2016) 5 *Compliance and Risk* 2.
[51] Ibid.   [52] See n. 18.

with UK-domiciled company ties. *Owusu v. Jackson*[53] involved a UK-domiciled victim who was injured when on holiday in Jamaica. He sued multiple companies and one of them was a UK-domiciled defendant company with which he had a holiday contract. Whilst in Jamaica, the victim was injured on the grounds owned by the non-UK domiciled co-defendant. The victim sued both defendants in the UK and the Court of Appeals decided that the UK was not the appropriate forum and as a result the proceedings were stayed.[54] *Owusu*'s case was later referred to the European Court of Justice where it was confirmed that the Court of Appeals had *forum conveniens*. Citing both the Brussels Convention and a UK legislation, Article 2 of the Brussels Convention precludes the UK courts from staying proceedings like *Owusu's*,[55] and UK Civil Procedure Rules 6.20 also stipulates that companies residing outside the United Kingdom or European Economic Area (EEA) can be served with litigation procedures if they have ties with a UK-domiciled defendant. These two rules also apply to parent companies and their overseas subsidiaries.

Procedurally, UK-domiciled parents are potentially open to litigation from two kinds of victims: (1) those residing overseas who have been injured by subsidiaries operating overseas and (2) those who are UK domiciled who have been injured by overseas companies with UK parent ties. With the trinity of case law, legislation and legal procedure, a strong foundation is formed for increasing the parent's onus for the corporate group's activities. A parent would have to prove that it has dutifully discharged its onus through conducting due diligence.

10.2.3.2   The Importance of Due Diligence

The concept of due diligence is not new. Businesses perform routine risk management exercises through due diligence. Due diligence is also enshrined in the United Nations Guidelines for Business and Human Rights.[56] The evolving law defines the parent's obligations towards its subsidiaries. In the aforementioned case law and legislation, a rough idea of the parent's due diligence emerges. This idea is centred around its subsidiaries' financial stability, workers' well-being, premises' health and safety, low-pollution business activities, and disassociation with modern slavery.[57]

---

[53] *Owusu v. Jackson* [2005] QB. 801.   [54] Ibid., 806.   [55] Ibid., 810.
[56] See n. 38, 206.
[57] In addition to due diligence already established in areas such as in supply chains, see P. Henty and S. Holdsworth, 'Big Businesses and Modern Slavery: What Your

At first sight, the parent's role in conducting due diligence seems very wide, which might infringe upon its corporate personality and its limited liability. The two feminist theories can help reconcile this by providing a tailor-made structure for a parent's corporate duty of care. In refining the corporate duty of care's structure and substance, the parent's management of due diligence will be well within its legal capacity.

10.3   Towards a Feminist Direction?

The two feminist theories drawn on in this chapter are Andreas Philippopoulos-Mihalopoulos's spatial justice,[58] and Eva Kittay's ethic of care.[59] Both theories challenge the law's purpose and its function in society.[60] The reason for picking these out of the rich tapestry of feminist theories is their close alignment with the case law, legislation and legal procedure discussed in the previous section.

Philippopoulos-Mihalopoulos's spatial justice urges law to move beyond legal rules.[61] In this discussion, the examination of corporate behaviour in a corporate group has to move beyond the corporate veil argument. The decisions in *Lubbe* and *Chandler* circumvent the corporate veil argument by imposing direct responsibility on the parent. The courts in the *Hempel* cases imposed a non-fault-based liability on the parent. Spatial justice is manifested when law breaks away from its surrounding rules.[62] Philippopoulos-Mihalopoulos suggests that law is made to recoil into the legal spaces because of the legal boundaries, for

---

Organisation Should Be Doing' (2015) 4 *Compliance and Risk* 11–13. In Merger & Acquisitions, see D. Boyd and W. Sharpe, 'Trends in Legal Due Diligence in Acquisition Finance' (2007) 11 *Journal of Banking and Financial Law* 658. In project finance, see M. Torrance, 'Equator Principles III: New Sustainability Rules Requiring Legal Strategy Rethink' (2013) 8 *Journal of Banking and Financial Law* 503.

[58] A. Philippopoulos-Mihalopoulos, *Spatial Justice: Body, Landscape, Atmosphere* (London: Routledge, 2015).

[59] E. Kittay, *Love's Labor* (London: Routledge, 1999).

[60] A. Hunt, 'The Critique of Law: What is 'Critical' about Critical Legal Theory?' (1987) 14 *Journal of Law and Society* 5–19. See also D. Rhode, 'Feminist Critical Theories' (1990) 42 *Stanford Law Review* 617–638.

[61] Philippopoulos-Mihalopoulos, *Spatial Justice*, pp. 174–175. The present concepts such as distributive justice or social justice cannot be relied upon as they cannot apply to the corporate group. The corporate duty of care requires a structure beyond the current foundations of law.

[62] Ibid., p. 186. Within the debate around piercing the corporate veil or not, spatial justice withdraws from these types of conflict. Like in the Albanian and UK legislation, law withdraws from the exercise of piercing the veil.

example the corporate veil, restricting law within its borders.[63] With legal boundaries and borders being drawn, spaces are demarcated and divided, and this results in law being fragmented. Fragmented laws take attention away from the atmosphere,[64] which is the interconnectedness of the living species, societies, businesses, resources and the environment. The corporate group has a corporate atmosphere which includes its subsidiaries' financial stability, workers' well-being, premises' health and safety, low-pollution business activities, and disassociation with modern slavery.[65] When the corporate atmosphere is disregarded, the corporate pressure on the finite planetary boundaries may similarly be ignored. Therefore, the fragmented law serves the interests of those who reside within those legal boundaries. Within a corporate group, the fragmented law promotes the parent's interests.

There are some circumstances where the theory of spatial justice challenges the boundaries of law so that it becomes impossible to recoil into its legal confines. Spatial justice is seen in *Lubbe*,[66] *Chandler*[67] and *Hempel*[68] where the corporate veil argument cannot triumph over the need to protect the corporate atmosphere. If it can be argued that the finite natural resources and the vulnerable human resources are the main components to the corporate atmosphere, then it must be argued that all corporate group activities must recognise the planetary boundaries. Spatial justice prioritises the planetary boundaries through creating the parent-subsidiary relationship. This relationship enables the law to evolve[69] and adapt to the current need for a more responsible parent.

Where spatial justice provides structure, Kittay's ethic of care adds substance to the parent-subsidiary relationship. Because the traditional legal parent-subsidiary relationship does not recognise the corporate atmosphere, the parent's awkward duty of care by way of assumed

---

[63] A. Philippopoulos-Mihalopoulos, 'Spatial Justice: Law and the Geography of Withdrawal' (2010) 6 *International Journal of Law in Context* 207–208.

[64] Philippopoulos-Mihalopoulos, Spatial Justice, p. 122.

[65] In addition to due diligence already established in areas such as in supply chains, see Henty and Holdsworth, 'Big Businesses and Modern Slavery'. In Merger & Acquisitions, see Boyd and Sharpe, 'Trends in Legal Due Diligence'. In project finance, see Torrance, 'Equator Principles III'.

[66] The parent residence can be *forum conveniens*.

[67] The creation of parent-subsidiary relationship.

[68] The importance of due diligence in the parent's non-fault-based liability. See n. 38.

[69] 'Law evolving' meaning law's spatial turn into a new justice. A. Philippopoulos-Mihalopoulos, 'Law's Spatial Turn: Geography, Justice and a Certain Fear of Space' (2010) 7 *Law, Culture and the Humanities* 188–189.

responsibility is highlighted in *Chandler*.[70] This legal relationship is traditionally known to preserve the autonomy between the incorporator and the incorporated.[71] Fully autonomous entities like subsidiaries must abide by the principles of equality where each subsidiary is an equal to its parent. Equality leaves no room for an interdependent parent-subsidiary relationship.

This traditional legal concept is arguably being ousted by the emerging jurisprudence. The structure and substance of the corporate duty of care shifts the focus away from the fragmented corporate spaces. As a result, the group's atmosphere is acknowledged. The parent's obligation to re-invest into the corporate group may be said to be discernible in the case law, legislation and legal procedure discussed in Section 10.2. The incorporation of theory into law allows the opportunity for better case law, legislation and legal procedure, in turn facilitating future legal principles. These legal principles can then help change the process of achieving business sustainability and eco-profitability. Before each theory is fully explored, it is important to investigate whether or not this emerging parent-subsidiary relationship withstands the corporate veil argument. The next section explores the corporate veil's purpose.

10.4 The Corporate Veil's Purpose

In this chapter, the corporate veil has three purposes: (1) demarcating corporate spaces, (2) preserving corporate autonomy and (3) establishing equality amongst corporations. In a corporate group, the corporate veil can be useful in benefiting a subsidiary, for example in praising a subsidiary for its good governance. The veil is also useful in holding a subsidiary responsible – for example, finding a subsidiary liable for wilfully defaulting on its creditors. Crucially, the corporate veil is mostly used in shielding the parent from its subsidiaries' liabilities and risks.[72] This chapter suggests that the corporate veil's purpose does not preclude the argument for an interdependent parent-subsidiary relationship. Therefore, its purpose does not preclude the parent's role of conducting due diligence on the corporate group and in that regard the possible liability arising from being negligent. The interdependent parent-subsidiary and the corporate veil can exist side-by-side.

---

[70] Per *Adams v. Cape*.   [71] Per *Salomon v. Salomon*.   [72] See n. 6.

10.4.1   Demarcating Corporate Spaces

With incorporation, the demarcation of corporate spaces enables the
parent to do two things: (1) gain global presence by operating through
subsidiaries across the world[73] and (2) gain leverage by forming value
chains.[74] A subsidiary is an agent which situates the parent higher in the
value chain so that the parent can perform a number of tasks. It achieves
a lean organisation, levers risks, and externalises liabilities to its subsidiaries.[75] Law operates within the value chain; however, it rarely crosses
the legal boundaries between parent and subsidiary.[76] Within the articles
of association, law preserves a strict relationship between the corporation
and its incorporators. It is imagined that each corporation is like a silo
being filled with a legal space. A corporate group is imagined to be like
several silos laying next to one another (A Ltd., B Ltd. and C Ltd.). The
walls of each silo (the corporate veil) are in contact with each other, but
the legal spaces do not mix. When law encounters the silo's walls, it
recoils into its respective corporate spaces.[77] Nothing flows through the
walls or the corporate veil. The atmosphere in the corporate group is
fragmented. This legal concept is critiqued for its poor reflection of the
interconnectedness within business. Although the parent's profits and
markets flow freely within the corporate group, law still recoils within the
legal boundaries of each respective corporation.

With law recoiling into its legal boundaries, *Chandler's* fault-based
liability approach is futile in holding a parent responsible for its subsidiary's negligence or criminal activities. The Dutch case *Akpan v. Royal
Dutch Shell*[78] is a perfect example. The case involved a victim whose land
in Nigeria was damaged by a subsidiary operating in the vicinity. The
subsidiary extracted oil from the land and transported the oil via pipelines. On two specific occasions, the pipelines were sabotaged by third
parties, which resulted in crude oil contaminating the victim's land. It

---

[73] See n. 7.

[74] For value chains, see G. Gereffi, J. Humphrey and T. Sturgeon, 'The Governance of Global
Value Chains' (2005) 12 *Review of International Political Economy* 78, 79. For leverage in
the apparel supply chain, see G. Gereffi and S. Frederick, 'The Global Apparel Value
Chain, Trade and the Crisis' (2010) *The World Bank's Policy Research Working Paper* 11.
In agriculture, see J. Clapp, 'ABCD and Beyond from Grain Merchants to Agricultural
Value Chain Managers' (2015) 2 *Canadian Food Studies* 126.

[75] F. Contractor, V. Kumar, S. Kundu and T. Pedersen, 'Global Outsourcing and Offshoring'
in F. Contractor, V. Kumar, S. Kundu and T. Pedersen, *Global Outsourcing and Offshoring* (Cambridge: Cambridge University Press, 2011) 3.

[76] See n. 62.   [77] Ibid.   [78] *Akpan v. Royal Dutch Shell* [2013] HA ZA 09–1580.

transpired that both the Dutch-domiciled parent and its Nigerian subsidiary were aware of the pipelines being prone to sabotage. Measures had been put in place, but those two incidences of sabotage affecting the victim were not prevented. The victim filed a case against the corporate group arguing joint and severable liability of the parent and subsidiary.

The court in The Hague decided that the subsidiary was liable in tort for the victim's harm, and it was ordered to compensate the victim.[79] The court, however, was not convinced that the parent should be held jointly or severally liable.[80] Although the parent was aware of the likelihood of the sabotage, it did not commit the tort against the victim.[81] The parent-subsidiary legal relationship was found not proximate enough to have the parent assume responsibility.[82] The reasons being: (1) the locations of the companies, in the Netherlands and Nigeria, were not proximate; (2) both of their businesses were so different that the parent's superior knowledge could not be shared and (3) the victim did not fall within a 'limited group of people' identified for compensation.

Owing to these reasons, the legal spaces between the parent and subsidiary were kept strictly separate. The corporate veil in *Akpan* prevented the subsidiary's responsibility from turning into the parent's responsibility. Law does not flow through the veil in the case of this corporate group. Instead, the law found one body corporate responsible and recoils within the space of that body corporate. Here, the corporate group's atmosphere resembles a jigsaw puzzle. On the one hand, the pieces match and mirror the interconnectedness within business. On the other hand, liability detaches the corporate pieces, isolating the parent from its subsidiaries. The legal puzzle which is the corporate veil shields the parent and leaves the tortious subsidiary to absorb costs and the victim without any recourse if the subsidiary cannot pay.

In *Akpan,* the demarcation of the corporate spaces was the court's focal point. *Akpan's* decision has bad implications for corporate behaviour within the corporate group. With the artificial legal boundaries, corporations tend to operate in isolation, and that dilutes governance within the corporate group. Law being cornered in the parent's corporate spaces only serves its interests. Maximising the parent's profit without taking into consideration the well-being of others contributes to the transgression of planetary boundaries. Furthermore, the parent benefits from accessing the subsidiary's resources. These could be in the form of

---

[79] Ibid., para. 4.45.   [80] Ibid., para. 4.34.   [81] Ibid.   [82] Ibid., para. 4.29–4.32.

geographical locality, its infrastructure and security, workforce accessibility and so forth. Yet in the same vein, the parent can utilise the veil to sever itself from the interconnected group. A subsidiary might have high-risk business operations and it might also lack financial resources. Therefore, holding a subsidiary solely responsible for its obligations exonerates its parent from incurring potential liabilities with great practical importance.[83]

Chandler's reasoning and its application was noted in *Akpan*, but *Chandler's* spirit was not followed. The fault-based liability approach through assumed responsibility is henceforth ineffective. Holding the parent and subsidiary jointly and severally liable seems ill-focused. The emerging jurisprudence, however, shifts the focus and places onus on the parent. Thus, the focus is not about the parent absorbing the subsidiary's liability; rather, it is about the parent's obligations in preventing the subsidiary's negligence or criminal activity. Fault-based liability in the form of the parent's non-fulfilment of its obligations arguably serves justice better. Law stemming from these kinds of obligations cannot recoil into either the parent's or the subsidiary's corporate spaces. Law in this form belongs to the corporate atmosphere where it governs the interdependence between parent and subsidiaries.

10.4.2 Preserving Corporate Autonomy

Demarcating corporate spaces is essential for autonomy. A subsidiary is a fully functional legal person and it can undertake most things its parent can. It can purchase or rent premises, enter into contracts, sue and/or be sued, employ and fire its workers, raise debts, takeover or merge, and manage risks. *Lubbe* and *Chandler* did not fall under *Adams's* exceptions and therefore the subsidiary's autonomy was recognised. The parents in *Chandler* and *Hempel* were not asked to indemnify their subsidiary's negligence or criminal activities and therefore *Salomon's* global legacy was not infringed. Rather, the parents were liable for their failure to conduct ample due diligence on the corporate group. The emerging jurisprudence therefore withstands the corporate veil argument. It respects the separate legal spaces and preserves the subsidiary's autonomy.

---

[83] See n. 6. Utilising corporate groups in this way breeds injustices. H. Collin, 'Ascription of Legal Responsibility to Groups in Complex Patterns of Economic Integration' (1990) 53 *Modern Law Review* 731, 738. But, it facilitates limited liability. Also see n. 7.

10.4.3   Establishing Equality Amongst Corporations

Subsidiaries function as fully fledged legal persons to give them equal status on par with their parent. They undertake risks, raise debts and trade on their own. Because their parent cannot indemnify on their behalf, *Salomon* makes sure that the subsidiaries handle their own debts and liabilities.[84] Having equality in a corporate group is akin to treating every corporation like a prudent flourishing adult. A flourishing adult exhibits social independence, emotional independence and financial independence. Similarly, an autonomous subsidiary is expected to generate its own income by extrapolating resources from its environment to make a profit. Autonomy and demarcated legal spaces are essential for a subsidiary's existence within the corporate group. Equality makes a subsidiary invulnerable to weaknesses.

Equality in this manner creates inequity within the corporate group.[85] It is noted that costs, risks and resources flow freely in the group instead of liabilities. With the diluted governance in the group, subsidiaries like in *Lubbe, Chandler* and *Hempel* find themselves operating in unfavourable conditions and environments.[86] These high-risk conditions expose potential harm to the workers' well-being, their local communities, creditors and the environment. The emerging jurisprudence outlines the interdependence between parent and subsidiary. The parent's duty of care is an acknowledgement that the subsidiary can at times access its support. This underlying concept is based on equity,[87] as opposed to equality. Equity is sensitive to the power imbalances in the corporate group. In gaining the best leverage, the parent is the most resourceful and the most resilient; it must therefore be the onerous entity in the group. Duties to ensure sustainability of subsidiaries in the group must be vested in the parent.

10.4.4   Conclusion

It is argued here that the corporate veil argument does not defeat the emerging new parent-subsidiary relationship. This interdependent relationship respects the corporate spaces where subsidiaries are still liable for their own liabilities and debts. So, the parent's limited liability is also

---

[84] *Salomon v. Salomon* [1865–99] All ER Rep 33, 36.   [85] See n. 58, p. 87.
[86] The parents decide over subsidiaries.
[87] See n. 58, p. 53. Equity underpinned by an ethic of care.

respected. This relationship also preserves the subsidiaries' autonomy where they can conduct business independently. Therefore, the corporate veil's sanctity is respected. With the veil's sanctity intact, the interdependent relationship and the corporate veil argument can exist side-by-side. An interdependent spatial layer can also be added to the corporate group's legal sphere. The parent's obligations created by the case law, legislation and legal procedure discussed in Section 10.2 add changes to the dynamics of the group. Equality gives way for equity where equity acknowledges each subsidiary's position in the value chain. Equity highlights each subsidiary's vulnerability, which is a very important step towards creating the parent's obligations within the parent-subsidiary relationship.

The following section explores the corporate duty of care's structure and substance in the interdependent parent-subsidiary relationship.

10.5   The Parent-Subsidiary Relationship

10.5.1   Structure: Spatial Justice in the Atmosphere

As mentioned in Section 10.4, law disregards the atmosphere by recoiling into the legal boundaries. The parent having the best leverage maximises its interests through utilising the fragmented corporate spaces in the corporate group. Spatial justice disrupts this traditional legal principle.[88] The breaking away from tradition in case law, legislation and legal procedure (discussed in Section 10.2) shows that attention has shifted to the corporate atmosphere. The corporate group is recognised as an interconnected web of entities as opposed to an aggregation of autonomous legal persons. A structure is required for this shift. The case law, legislation and legal procedure indicate placing onus on the parent. This can be done in two ways: (1) legislate on the parent's fiduciary duties or (2) make judicial changes in fault-based liability in a corporate group. As mentioned previously, neither proposal infringes upon the legal doctrines of the corporate veil and the parent's limited liability. Both proposals also prioritise the corporate atmosphere over the parent's interests. Maintenance of the corporate atmosphere requires prioritising the well-being of the subsidiaries. In essence, the agendas for profitability and business sustainability are not mutually exclusive.

---

[88] See n. 57, p. 186.

The expansion of the parent's onus establishes the corporate duty of care in the corporate group, and it is also to encourage stewardship over the corporate group. A parent discharges this duty through conducting due diligence. The parent-subsidiary relationship can be assessed by accounting the differences in leverage power between all corporations in the group. Vulnerabilities in some corporations can be detected. The standard of care for due diligence is the measurable amount of re-investments placed into the vulnerable corporation. Re-investments can be of any kind of assistance other than money. The main consideration is to nurture resilience in a vulnerable corporation.

The parent's obligation to conduct due diligence on the corporate group in relation to corporate spatial justice is the structure for the parent-subsidiary relationship. The substance in this relationship is the method by which due diligence is exercised.

10.5.2   Substance: The Ethic of Care

Kittay's ethic of care is a critique of equality, especially in the areas of society's personal development and human flourishing.[89] According to John Rawls,[90] society's rules should be created from the original position composed of individuals with equal stature with the disregard of talents and non-talents.[91] In this way, the rules created neither benefit the talented nor disadvantage the non-talented. With an equal amount of resources and opportunities afforded to them, every individual is expected to flourish. That said, Rawls expects the society's flourishing individuals are adults, autonomous, fully independent and able-bodied.[92] Kittay argues that individuals with leverage (as Rawls considers them, the talented) flourish better than others.[93] Rawls's difference principle restores an equilibrium between the talented and the non-talented.[94] Societal institutions are the main agents for the exercise of the difference principle. This principle centres on distributive justice where a fraction of the talented individual's profits are distributed to the less fortunate in the society.[95]

---

[89] See n. 57, p 87.
[90] J. Rawls, *A Theory of Justice* (Cambridge, MA: Harvard University Press, 1999).
[91] Ibid., pp. 119–121. The original position set behind Rawls's 'veil of ignorance'.
[92] Ibid., p. 452. Those acting within the boundaries of a good society.   [93] See n. 57, p. 87.
[94] See n. 89, pp. 65–70. An egalitarian concept where the talented will be rewarded for being successful, but that does not mean that the non-talented will be worse off as they will also benefit from the rewards.
[95] Ibid., pp. 242–251.

The difference principle's soft-touch version is practiced by some talented individuals. Celebrities and successful business entrepreneurs voluntarily participate in charitable giving. These practices are unfortunately less ingrained in global business practices. Since the 2007–2008 financial crisis, the gap between the leveraged individuals (talented) and the non-leveraged ones (non-talented) is widening.[96] Furthermore, the flourishing in an equal society causes disadvantages to the non-leveraged individuals.[97] Kittay makes a poignant case for the non-leveraged individuals who are carers. Carers look after dependants, and the clear examples are infants. Dependants do not fit into Rawls's description of the autonomous, fully independent and able-bodied.[98] A carer is someone whose day-to-day undertakings must take their dependant's interests into account. For the flourishing of both the carer and the dependant, sacrifices needed to be made[99] – for example, a single mother bringing up her children without a recourse to extra resources.

Carers are nevertheless autonomous, fully independent and able-bodied.[100] However, the dependant's burden results in the quick depletion of the equal resources afforded to the carer. Individuals without caring duties could flourish with that same amount. Flourishing for the carer becomes more cumbersome. Kittay concludes that the carer (without leverage) is the vulnerable individual in society. Kittay notes that equality is inequitable. It breeds hardships for the individuals with no leverage.[101] It also rejects an interdependent society. Kittay's critique resonates with the inequity appearing in a corporate group. Subsidiaries might be starved of resources, and they are more prone to bad business practices. They might disregard their workers' well-being, engage in modern slavery, make wasteful business decisions, create high risk leverage and/or pollute the environment.

---

[96] Urban poverty and poor mental health suffered by those without leverage. See C. Tacoli, G. McGranahan and D. Satterthwite, 'Urbanisation, Rural-Urban Migration and Urban Poverty', IIED Working Paper 27 (2015). For poor housing affecting physical health and mental health, see M. Egan, L. Lawson, A. Kearns, E. Conway and J. Neary, 'Neighbourhood Demolition, Relocation and Health' (2015) *Health and Place* 101, 106–107. Fuel poverty contributes to poor physical health and mental health, see D. Roberts, E. Vera-Toscano and E. Phimister, 'Fuel Poverty in the UK' (2015) 87 *Energy Policy* 216, 221.

[97] Ibid.   [98] See n. 57, p. 86.   [99] See n. 57, p. 99.   [100] Ibid.

[101] Furthermore, it is recently reported that UK young carers who fit Rawls's description of able-bodied flourishing individuals are less likely to qualify for government support. P. Butler, 'Four out of Five Young Carers Receive No Council Support' (26 December 2016) *The Guardian*.

A corporate group based on an ethic of care re-conceptualises autonomy and independence. Like a growing individual, a person gaining autonomy and independence is a process. A subsidiary's incorporation therefore should not guarantee full autonomy or independence. An ethic of care shows that corporations are not completely immune to hardships. The parent's support should to be at hand when hardships strike. Kittay also makes a very important point where she states that every carer is 'some mother's child'[102] and because of that obligations should be owed to them. Similar to Rawls, Kittay highlights that societal institutions such as the State should provide welfare and support to the carers facing hardship.[103] In a corporate group, each subsidiary can be considered to be 'some mother's child'. A subsidiary has stewardship over its well-being and also the well-being of its workers and creditors. With a subsidiary facing hardships, the parent is the appropriate societal institution in the corporate group to provide support.

Due diligence is the measure for the ethic of care. The parent's onus should take into account the corporate group's financial stability, health and safety regulations, environmental protection and the workers' well-being. The parent's leverage in the corporate group justifies having this onus. Due diligence conducted effectively would see both profitability and sustainability agendas embedded into the corporate day-to-day activities. With this level of group governance, the parent would be well-informed in relation to whether or not the incorporation of new subsidiaries is necessary, and subsidiaries' operations would be better monitored with their financial capacities and assets well-scrutinised. This could be an essential element in ensuring that the corporate group would become a closely knit, interdependent web of businesses working within planetary boundaries.

10.6   Conclusion

The experience of headlined corporate scandals seems to drive the evolution of law in very significant ways. At the same time a general awareness of ongoing issues which have proved problematic – such as encouraging corporations to act sustainably, imposing accountability on multinational groups for actions of subsidiaries, corporate crime and human rights abuses – is heightened every time a new scandal breaks.

---

[102] See n. 58, p. 115.   [103] See n. 58, p. 54.

The case law, legislation and legal processes discussed in this chapter are examples of this phenomenon. The chapter connects the evolving law with two feminist theories, the theory of spatial justice and the ethic of care theory. This analysis shows us how law evolves and breaks away from the boundaries encasing it and provides us with a theoretical framework in which to understand the particular evolution of corporate law discussed in this chapter. The chapter demonstrates how there is a limitation in the legal parent-subsidiary relationship within the corporate group. Legal autonomy and equality of each entity in the corporate group promote only the parent's interests. Both feminist theories highlight the importance of due diligence. These theories, together with the examples of 'law in action' illustrate that the parent's role is ever evolving in the corporate group. It must take on proper stewardship by conducting due diligence. The interests surrounding the corporate atmosphere should replace the parent's corporate spaces. The ethic of care addresses the vulnerabilities of subsidiaries in the group. Equity ensures that resources are re-invested into the corporate group. Resilience is an important feature in this economically uncertain climate. Having an interdependent parent-subsidiary relationship reduces legal autonomy and increases equity in the corporate group as a whole, providing new possibilities for the control and mitigation of emerging scandals and, perhaps even more importantly, proactive resolution of the concerns discussed here and elsewhere in this collection. The theories discussed provide us with an intellectual map which makes sense of evolving legal principles.

The Uneasy Relationship between Corporations and Gender Equality

A Critique of the 'Transnational Business Feminism' Project

ROSEANNE RUSSELL

11.1 Introduction

The relationship between women and the paid labour market has long been a complex and contested one. The strict 'dichotomy' between the market and the family, particularly in developed western capitalist economies, is premised on the assumption that 'the market structures our productive lives and the family structures our affective lives'.[1] Maintaining the distinctiveness of these two spheres has typically led to women's exclusion from economic life, or more limited advancement and segregation into feminised roles for those women who do work in paid employment. Although working-class women have long been engaged in paid employment,[2] it is in the post–World War II period that the image of the 'ideal worker' arguably became dominated by a particular kind of masculinity. Women who had taken on masculinised work roles during the war were encouraged, post-war, to return to care-giving and create opportunities for the men returning home. Meanwhile, the growth in technology and service work in lieu of traditional blue-collar occupations led to new definitions of masculinity such as working long hours and excessive displays of stamina.[3] This adjustment in the labour market

---

[1] F. E. Olsen, 'The Family and the Market: A Study of Ideology and Legal Reform' (1983) 96 (7) *Harvard Law Review* 1497 at 1498.

[2] See, for example, the female workers' strike at the Bryant and May match factory in 1888, which led to the UK Trades Union Congress passing a resolution that year in favour of men and women receiving equal pay for equal work.

[3] J. C. Williams, *Reshaping the Work-Family Debate: Why Men and Class Matter* (Cambridge, MA: Harvard University Press, 2010), pp. 86–87.

has resulted in the shaping of a masculine image of an 'ideal worker' based on the assumption of the presumed natural separation of life into distinct areas, with the result that women continue to bear primary responsibility for the necessary but unpaid labour of social reproduction.[4] As Pateman has observed,

> the construction of the 'worker' presupposes that he is a man who has a woman, a (house)wife, to take care of his daily needs. The private and public spheres of civil society are separate, reflecting the natural order of sexual difference, and inseparable, incapable of being understood in isolation from each other.[5]

Despite the traditional separation of many women's lives into these distinct market and domestic spheres, those boundaries have gradually become eroded over preceding decades as women have entered into the paid labour market in significant numbers. Yet, notwithstanding women's clear presence in the paid labour market, there remain substantial obstacles to their progression and inclusion in corporate life. What is more intriguing is that these barriers persist despite an arguable intensification in corporate interest about the contribution that women can make to economic life. The start of the current wave of corporate interest arose before the 2008 financial crisis[6] but appears to have deepened since then.

This chapter takes Roberts's theoretical framework of transnational business feminism (explored in more detail in Section 11.3) as a point of departure to explore how companies are complicit in assisting one aspect of the transnational business feminism agenda: women as post-crisis saviours. The central claim advanced is that despite the apparently neutral effects of bringing gender into discussions of corporate behaviour, the current vogue for transnational business feminism risks reproducing and valorising existing corporate power hierarchies. The chapter focuses on the Anglo-American model of the corporation and is particularly concerned with the operations of multi-national and transnational

---

[4] J. C. Williams, 'Beyond the Glass Ceiling: The Maternal Wall as a Barrier to Gender Equality' (2003) 26 (1) *Thomas Jefferson Law Review* 1.

[5] C. Pateman, *The Sexual Contract* (Bristol: Polity Press, 1988), p. 131.

[6] For example, in the UK, interest in boardroom diversity has been evident since at least 2004: Department of Trade and Industry, *Building Better Boards* (London: DTI, 2004). See also J. Elias, 'Gendering Liberalisation and Labour Reform in Malaysia: Fostering "Competitiveness" in the Productive and Reproductive Economies' (2009) 30 (3) *Third World Quarterly* 469 at 477 where she describes discussion in 2007 around 'drawing "unproductive" groups of people into the global capitalist workplace'.

companies whose impact extends beyond jurisdictional boundaries. Those hierarchies are confirmed in three key ways: (1) by an underpinning rationale promoted by the women-as-saviours idea that the appropriate goal for these companies is to maximise profit; (2) by adopting a narrow, liberal-feminist agenda that leaves much of the workplace structural barriers to women's progress in place; and (3) by creating a falsely gendered view of values in which women are portrayed as ethical business persons and companies as inherently masculine and unethical. Women are presented in stereotyped ways, which merely emphasises that they are a 'new Other of man'.[7] Little attention is paid to the fact that 'the very structures of organisations are based on masculinised assumptions – about the timing of work, the structure of tasks and ways of doing things, schemes of appraisal and promotion'.[8] Instead, women are simply encouraged to 'lean in' to a man's world.[9] The chapter concludes by arguing that masculinised work practices fuelled by an acceptance that shareholder value is often the only appropriate corporate goal are unsustainable. It suggests that existing corporate hierarchies should be challenged rather than accepting the current business preoccupation with 'getting a smattering of individual women into positions of power and privilege within existing social hierarchies'.[10]

11.2   Review of Feminist Theory

For decades a significant body of feminist literature has drawn attention to the ways in which women have been excluded from, and subordinated within, hierarchical organisations such as corporations. A spectrum of feminist theories exists, which is mirrored in the variety of reform strategies suggested by feminist scholars. These strategies have typically centred on either helping women to advance in traditionally male-dominated domains or by arguing that typically feminised traits and roles should be valued.[11] The liberal-feminist model of equality of treatment between men and women has led to important reforms such as

---

[7] E. Prügl, '"If Lehman Brothers Had Been Lehman Sisters...": Gender and Myth in the Aftermath of the Financial Crisis' (2012) 6 *International Political Sociology* 21.

[8] L. McDowell, *Capital Culture: Gender at Work in the City* (Oxford: Blackwell, 1997), p. 137.

[9] S. Sandberg, *Lean In: Women, Work, and the Will to Lead* (New York: WH Allen, 2013).

[10] G. Gutting and N. Fraser, 'A Feminism Where "Lean In" Means Leaning on Others' (15 October 2015) *The New York Times*.

[11] Williams, 'Beyond the Glass Ceiling', 12.

prohibiting discriminatory treatment of women in recruitment and progression, but requires that women assimilate with existing organisational structures. This model stands accused of arguably putting the onus on women to conform to masculine patterns of behaviour,[12] and institutions (including companies) are mistakenly presumed to be gender-neutral entities.[13] These tensions are felt acutely in large public companies built upon 'gladiatorial' working cultures, which sit uncomfortably with the reality of many women's lives.[14] The second reform strategy – of valuing feminised traits or characteristics – is no less problematic. This strategy finds its roots in the difference school of feminist thought, which emphasises women's shared distinctive characteristics. As Gilligan observed, 'women not only define themselves in a context of human relationship but also judge themselves in terms of their ability to care'.[15] Underpinning this school of thought is the capacity of women to bear children and their continued caring responsibilities, which have been determinative of their roles within the family and have shaped a highly gendered paid labour market.[16] By focussing on women's apparent differences from men, women risk being treated as an essentialised, homogenous and stereotyped group. This strategy risks a 'conflation of *women* with *conventional femininity*'.[17] Other important characteristics that shape our experiences of the world (such as class or race) are overlooked.[18] A third school of feminism, which acknowledges some of the limitations of the 'sameness-difference' debate is MacKinnon's influential dominance theory, which views women as subordinated to or dominated by men in law, institutions, and society more generally.[19]

[12] I. Young, *Justice and the Politics of Difference* (Princeton, NJ: Princeton University Press, 1990).

[13] P. Cain, 'Feminism and the Limits of Equality' (1990) 24 *Georgia Law Review* 803.

[14] M. O'Connor, 'Women Executives in Gladiatorial Corporate Cultures: The Behavioural Dynamics of Gender, Ego, and Power' (2006) 65 *Maryland Law Review* 465. See also Ch. 12.

[15] C. Gilligan, *In a Different Voice: Psychological Theory and Women's Development* (Cambridge, MA: Harvard University Press, 1982), p. 17.

[16] N. Chodorow, *The Reproduction of Mothering: Psychoanalysis and the Sociology of Gender* (Berkeley: California University Press, 1978).

[17] J. Williams, '*Reshaping the Work-Family Debate*', p. 135. Emphasis retained. See also Chodorow, *The Reproduction of Mothering*.

[18] A. Harris, 'Race and Essentialism in Feminist Legal Theory' (1990) 42 *Stanford Law Review* 581.

[19] Of MacKinnon's extensive literature see C. A. MacKinnon, *Women's Lives: Men's Laws* (Cambridge, MA: Belknap, 2005); *Feminism Unmodified: Discourses on Life and Law* (Cambridge, MA: Harvard University Press, 1987); and *Toward a Feminist Theory of the*

The 'ferocity' of the debates and tensions between different schools of feminist thought has been noted by Munro.[20] To help inform the arguments in this chapter, the theory of 'reconstructive feminism' advanced by Joan Williams will be used. Williams argues that women in the workplace

> tend to adopt two broadly differing strategies. Some act the 'tomboy', adapting to the roles and behaviors conventionally associated with masculinity. Others act the 'femme', following more traditionally feminine roles.[21]

Although Williams makes clear that she is generalising between two arguably reductive viewpoints, she argues that all women 'in different ways and to different degrees' experience

> four basic patterns of workplace gender bias rooted in masculine norms: the maternal wall, double standards, double binds, and gender wars among women.[22]

For Williams, it is essential that women break out of 'these gender wars' by, she argues, changing or removing the gendered structural barriers that hold women back and then, once these have been addressed, calling for equal treatment of men and women.[23] Her idea of reconstructive feminism

> defines equality as treating men and women the same but only after deconstructing the existing norms defined by and around men and masculinity, and reconstructing existing institutions in ways that include the bodies and traditional life patterns of women.[24]

Despite the important contributions of various feminist schools of thought to seeking gender equality in the workplace, it remains elusive. The post-crisis 'intensified casualisation of employment' has affected

---

State (Cambridge, MA: Harvard University Press, 1989). Another important contribution to feminist scholarship is that of post-modern feminist thought: J. Butler, *Gender Trouble: Feminism and the Subversion of Identity* (London and New York: Routledge, 1990).

[20] V. Munro, *Law and Politics at the Perimeter: Re-evaluating Key Debates in Feminist Theory* (Oxford: Hart Publishing, 2007), p. 1.

[21] Williams, '*Reshaping the Work-Family Debate*', p. 5.   [22] Ibid.

[23] J. Williams, '"It's Snowing Down South": How to Help Mothers and Avoid Recycling the Sameness/Difference Debate' (2002) 102 *Columbia Law Review* 812 at 817. See also J. Williams, 'Dissolving the Sameness/Difference Debate: A Post-Modern Path Beyond Essentialism in Feminist and Critical Race Theory' (1991) *Duke Law Journal* 296.

[24] J. Williams, 'Jumpstarting the Stalled Gender Revolution: Justice Ginsburg and Reconstructive Feminism' (2012) 63 *Hastings Law Journal* 1267 at 1280.

women more negatively than men,[25] the gender pay gap remains high[26] and 'women continue to face staggering levels of discrimination in the workplace on grounds of pregnancy or maternity leave'.[27] In sum, the strict separation between the productive paid labour of the market and the unpaid care of family life persists to the detriment of many women.[28]

11.3   Renewed Interest in the Contribution of Women to Corporate Life

Against this intractably problematic background, there is renewed interest in helping women maintain their presence or progress in corporate life. Notably, this 'turn' has been driven by the corporate and wider economic sector. Interest in the contribution that women can make to economic life appears to have intensified in the post-2008 crisis period as momentum has gathered around the idea that 'prudent women' may have helped avert the crisis and can contribute to post-crisis economic recovery.[29] For Roberts, the coalescing of a variety of economic and corporate actors around encouraging women's contribution to economic life has given rise to the 'politico-economic project' of transnational business feminism (TBF):

> an increasingly large coalition of feminist organizations, capitalist states, regional and international funding institutions, non-governmental organizations (NGOs) and transnational corporations (TNCs) that converge on the need to promote women's equality, particularly in the Global South. This coalition finds its ideological basis in what has been termed 'the business case for gender equality'.[30]

[25]   D. McCann, 'Equality through Precarious Work Regulation: Lessons from the Domestic Work Debates in Defence of the Standard Employment Relationship' (2014) 10 (4) *International Journal of Law in Context* 507.

[26]   J. Rubery and D. Grimshaw, 'The 40-Year Pursuit of Equal Pay: A Case of Constantly Moving Goalposts' (2015) 39 *Cambridge Journal of Economics* 319.

[27]   S. Fredman, 'Reversing Roles: Bringing Men into the Frame' (2014) 10 (4) *International Journal of Law in Context* 442 at 444.

[28]   M. A. Fineman, 'Feminist Legal Theory', (2005) 13 (1) *Journal of Gender, Social Policy & The Law* 13.

[29]   E. Prügl, '"If Lehman Brothers Had Been Lehman Sisters...": Gender and Myth in the Aftermath of the Financial Crisis' (2012) 6 *International Political Sociology* 21.

[30]   A. Roberts, 'Financial Crisis, Financial Firms...and Financial Feminism? The Rise of "Transnational Business Feminism' and the Necessity of Marxist-Feminist IPE" (2012) 8 (2) *Socialist Studies* 85 at 87.

Roberts argues that there exist three related ideas which are central to transnational business feminism.[31] First, there is a concern to promote financial empowerment, notably via female entrepreneurship. This is particularly the case insofar as companies are engaging with communities in the global South. As Elias has observed, 'the corporate sector has come to play an ever more significant role in the governance of gender and development issues'.[32] The second idea adopts the image of women as metaphorical 'saviours' of the financial world, which highlights their perceived differences to men and champions the distinctive advantages that women can purportedly bring to organisations and economic markets. The third strand is captured by the term 'womenomics'. This speaks directly to women as consumers and producers.[33] It is the confluence of these different strands of economic interest in women (as entrepreneurs, creditors, consumers and leaders) and from different economic actors (transnational companies, global governance actors, banks and NGOs) that Roberts has termed 'transnational business feminism'.[34] This chapter aims only to analyse the second strand of TBF; that of portraying women as post-crisis saviours.

A plethora of initiatives have been developed with the 'saviours' ideology apparently in mind. In the United Kingdom, Lord Davies's report *Women on Boards* highlighted the business case for companies engaging more female directors[35] and advocated doing so on a voluntary basis. In October 2012, the UK Financial Reporting Council amended its Corporate Governance Code, which applies to all listed companies, to include a revised principle that 'the search for board candidates should be conducted, and appointments made, on merit, against objective criteria and *with due regard for the benefits of diversity on the board, including gender*'.[36] In November 2012 the EU proposed a directive on gender

---

[31] A. Roberts, 'Gender, Financial Deepening and the Production of Embodied Finance: Towards a Critical Feminist Analysis' (2015) 29 (1) *Global Society* 107 at 108.

[32] J. Elias, 'Davos Woman to the Rescue of Global Capitalism: Postfeminist Politics and Competitiveness Promotion at the World Economic Forum' (2013) 7 *International Political Sociology* 152.

[33] Roberts, 'Gender, Financial Deepening and the Production of Embodied Finance', p. 108.

[34] Roberts, 'Financial Crisis, Financial Firms. . .and Financial Feminism?' For a further discussion of Roberts's concept of transnational business feminism see R. Russell and C. Villiers, 'Gender justice in financial markets' in L. Herzog (ed.) *Just Financial Markets: Finance in a Just Society* (Oxford: Oxford University Press, 2017) 271 at 274.

[35] Lord Davies of Abersoch, *Women on Boards* (UK Government, February 2011).

[36] Financial Reporting Council, *Feedback Statement: Gender Diversity on Boards* (London: FRC, October 2011). Emphasis added. See also Ch. 6.

balance amongst non-executive board directors[37] and in fifteen jurisdictions across the globe, firm quota targets have been adopted to increase the number of women directors.[38]

Within companies, the women as saviours claim has been particularly pronounced. It is this trope that lies behind topical debates on the composition of corporate boardrooms following concerns about the robustness of corporate governance structures. Implicit in this is a growing consensus that increasing the number of women directors will bring benefits to business by challenging 'groupthink', making the most of the available talent pool and enhancing a company's reputation on matters such as 'diversity'.[39] Despite these so-called benefits being contested, 'boardroom diversity' has increasingly become a matter of legislative and policy attention across a number of jurisdictions.[40] Leadership is, however, just one facet of a noticeable corporate interest in gender but is emblematic of the increasingly central role played by corporations in a range of regulatory and policy concerns that historically were matters for the state. Prügl and True argue that 'we are witnessing new roles of business as power has increasingly shifted away from legislatures towards a range of technocratic and private actors'.[41] Companies now wield significant political influence in a globalised corporate environment.[42] As companies adopt more state-like behaviours, a corporate interest in gender equality can be detected not just with regards to *internal* matters such as directorships but in *external* matters such as engaging with women as consumers, in the supply chain or as creditors/entrepreneurs. In this way companies are 'building corporate patriotism, emphasizing "soft issues" such as their value to society, causes such as poverty

---

[37] European Commission, *Proposal for a DIRECTIVE OF THE EUROPEAN PARLIAMENT AND OF THE COUNCIL on improving gender balance among non-executive directors of companies listed on stock exchanges and related measures*, COM (2012) 614 final.

[38] S. Terjesen and R. Sealy, 'Board Gender Quotas: Exploring Ethical Tensions from a Multi-Theoretical Perspective' (2016) 26 (1) *Business Ethics Quarterly* 23 at 24.

[39] C. Villiers, 'Achieving Gender Balance in the Boardroom: Is It Time for Legislative Action in the UK?' (2010) 30 (4) *Legal Studies* 533.

[40] M. McCann and S. Wheeler, 'Gender Diversity in the FTSE100: The Business Case Claim Explored' (2011) 38 (4) *Journal of Law and Society* 542.

[41] E. Prügl and J. True, 'Equality Means Business? Governing Gender through Transnational Public-Private Partnerships' (2014) 21 (6) *Review of International Political Economy* 1137 at 1138.

[42] A. S. Scherer and G. Palazzo, 'The New Political Role of Business in a Globalized World – A Review of a New Perspective on CSR and Its Implications for the Firm, Governance, and Democracy' (2011) 48 (4) *Journal of Management Studies* 899.

eradication, labor standards...gender equality'.[43] Examples include gender 'empowerment' projects (these include Goldman Sachs's 10,000 Women Global Initiative and the Unilever Shakti project) allowing them to benefit from 'women's business acumen ... stabilise supply chains ... and develop a reputation as good corporate citizens in a globalised economy'.[44]

The interest of transnational companies in gender equality is reflected by the discourse of other international organisations such as the UN, the World Bank and the World Economic Forum (WEF). Women post-crisis are regarded as 'the world's most under-utilized resource' and transformed into productive contributors to global economic recovery.[45] Elias's analysis of the WEF's Gender Gap Reports found that all 'contain an important section in which the supposed link between gender and economic competitiveness is explained', while another strand of WEF's work has been to highlight the positive 'investment' states can make in girls and women.[46] In the context of the global South, gender empowerment projects have simultaneously created 'new opportunities for businesses and investment firms' in the years post-crisis.[47]

On one view, the current corporate interest in women is welcome. It helps draw attention to the obstacles women face in navigating the paid labour market and, particularly in the case of boardroom diversity, has had results in securing a greater percentage of women directors.[48] In the case of gender empowerment projects in the global South, participants do comment positively on feeling 'empowered' and the relative independence that small-scale entrepreneurialism can offer.[49] Stressing the business benefits of gender equality may also be a deliberately strategic tactic to overcome ambivalent, resistant or even hostile corporate cultures.[50] As a 'rhetorical strategy', focussing on the business benefits of engaging with

---

[43] Prügl and True, 'Equality Means Business?'.

[44] E. Prügl, 'Neoliberalising Feminism' (2015) 20 (4) *New Political Economy* 614 at 626.

[45] Roberts, 'Financial Crisis, Financial Firms...and Financial Feminism?', p. 88.

[46] Elias, 'Davos Woman to the Rescue of Global Capitalism', p. 163.

[47] Roberts, 'Gender, Financial Deepening and the Production of Embodied Finance', p. 108.

[48] S. Vinnicombe, E. Doldor, R. Sealy, P. Pryce and C. Turner, *The Female FTSE Board Report 2015: Putting the UK Progress into a Global Perspective* (Bedford: Cranfield School of Management, 2015).

[49] See for example C. Dolan and L. Scott, 'Lipstick Evangelism: Avon Trading Circles and Gender Empowerment in South Africa' (2009) 17 (2) *Gender & Development* 203 at 211.

[50] T. W. Joo, 'Race, Corporate Law, and Shareholder Value' (2004) 54 (3) *Journal of Legal Education* 351 at 351–352.

gender equality is appealing, and even well-intentioned feminist advocates speak of the need for 'establishing an effective business case'.[51] However, as Joo observes, 'it has limitations and costs. Diversity and improved corporate performance may not always go hand in hand'.[52]

There is, however, a less benign explanation for the current corporate and wider economic interest in women. Elias posits that WEF's interest in gender equality is 'reflective of broader trends relating to how international organizations championing neoliberal policy solutions employ legitimacy-enhancing techniques that serve to underscore their relevance in the face of wider societal criticism'.[53] Women are portrayed as a (stereotyped) panacea 'for the risk-taking, testosterone-driven masculinity associated with the excessive speculation leading to the global financial crisis', while the drawing-in of women as creditors and entrepreneurs in the global South ensures the 'ongoing expansion' of capitalist markets and Western neo-liberal economic policy.[54] Transnational business feminism offers up capitalism as 'the best, if not the only, way of organizing society' and 'frames empowerment in terms of the right to participate in the market economy'.[55] For Roberts, this is regressive and 'empties' gender of 'its meanings of politics, power and history'.[56]

At the theoretical level, the underlying foundations of transnational business feminism are also confused. Arguments for greater participation of women in economic life echo in part the liberal feminist strategy of encouraging women to assimilate with existing organisational cultures, take their rightful place on corporate boards, or start their own businesses. Women are, on this account, equal to men. Simultaneously and paradoxically, transnational business feminism promotes distinct, feminised values and behaviour. Its conceptualisation of the 'prudent woman' is, argues Prügl forcefully, 'a matter of pure ideology, a deceptive story to hide capitalist doings after its embarrassing excesses were revealed'.[57]

Overall, while the impression is given of sincere engagement with feminist values, the reality is that corporations and surrounding social and economic structures remain untouched. Society continues to be

---

[51] Fawcett Society, *Equal Pay: Where Next?* (London: Fawcett Society, 2010), pp. 5–6.
[52] Joo, 'Race, Corporate Law, and Shareholder Value', p. 352.
[53] Elias, 'Davos Woman to the Rescue of Global Capitalism', p. 154.
[54] Prügl and True, 'Equality Means Business?', p. 1142.
[55] Roberts, 'Financial Crisis, Financial Firms...and Financial Feminism?', p. 101.
[56] Ibid. at 87.   [57] Prügl, 'If Lehman Brothers Had Been Lehman Sisters', p. 31.

shaped largely around the outdated male breadwinner/female caregiver model.[58] For multi-national companies, it is 'business as usual'.

11.4 'Business as Usual': How Transnational Business Feminism Entrenches Existing Corporate Hierarchies

Although it is 'difficult to find support within company law for the notion of shareholder primacy',[59] 'shareholder value' (as 'shareholder primacy' is sometimes loosely referred to) has arguably become the central organising principle of the modern public company.[60] As Sjåfjell notes, the legal norm of shareholder value has become so confused with the social norm of shareholder primacy that the latter has become a legal myth.[61] This has resulted in an unquestioned assumption that 'shareholder primacy' – the privileging of shareholder interests above all others – is the required corporate legal objective. The dominant Anglo-American corporate governance model confers 'owner-like rights in the shareholders to appoint, monitor, and replace the most senior tier of management and to make certain other fundamental decisions'.[62] The shareholder ownership model has remained influential and has been used to both justify and condemn shareholder behaviour in recent years. Post-crisis criticisms of institutional shareholders for a lack of monitoring were voiced in the language of 'ownerless corporations.'[63] As Talbot notes, 'neoliberalism has enabled shareholder irresponsibility and absenteeism to an unprecedented level and on a global scale while at the same

---

[58] D. Perrons, '"Global" Financial Crisis, Earnings Inequalities and Gender: Towards a More Sustainable Model of Development' (2012) 11 *Comparative Sociology* 202 at 221; S. Fredman, 'Reversing Roles: Bringing Men into the Frame' (2014) 10 (4) *International Journal of Law in Context* 442.

[59] S. Deakin, 'The Coming Transformation of Shareholder Value' (2005) 13 (1) *Corporate Governance* 11.

[60] L. Stout, *The Shareholder Value Myth: How Putting Shareholders First Harms Investors, Corporations and the Public* (San Francisco: Berrett-Koehler, 2012).

[61] B. Sjåfjell, 'Dismantling the Legal Myth of Shareholder Primacy: The Corporation as a Sustainable Market Actor' (6 February 2017) University of Oslo Faculty of Law Research Paper No. 2017–03; Nordic & European Company Law Working Paper No. 16–20, see https://ssrn.com/abstract=2912141.

[62] J. E. Parkinson, *Corporate Power and Responsibility: Issues in the Theory of Company Law* (Oxford: Clarendon, 1993), p. 53.

[63] House of Commons Treasury Committee, *Banking Crisis: Reforming Corporate Governance and Pay in the City* (London: The Stationery Office, May 2009); on the monitoring strategies available to shareholders see A. Keay, 'Company Directors Behaving Poorly: Disciplining Options for Shareholders' (2007) *Journal of Business Law* 656.

time shareholders continue to enjoy the promotion of their interests in law and in governance'.[64] Strategies to re-engage shareholders and empower them with enhanced stewardship responsibilities may be misguided. Talbot is more critical and argues that they are 'a political project to concretise the claims of investors against those of labour'.[65]

If, as Talbot argues, shareholder empowerment initiatives 'are ultimately designed to reinvigorate shareholder entitlements in the context of financial crisis and austerity',[66] the TBF project and its insistence on emphasising the business case for gender equality might similarly be interpreted as an exercise in reinforcing a primary corporate focus on shareholder wealth maximisation. While it may be too simplistic to say that a focus on shareholders is per se detrimental for other corporate constituents,[67] employee interests are, more often than not, subordinated within this paradigm.[68] A particular type of worker is moulded and favoured by the pursuit of shareholder value. This is arguably a 'self oriented to the short term, focused on potential ability, willing to abandon past experience . . . an unusual sort of human being'.[69] Labour can never 'be on the same footing as capital' as it cannot replicate its 'risk management capacities'.[70] The inability to absorb risk is especially prevalent in the global South where multinational companies operate in reliance of cheap, disposable labour.[71] It is also evident in the global North

---

[64] L. Talbot, 'Why Shareholders Shouldn't Vote: A Marxist-progressive Critique of Shareholder Empowerment' (2013) 76 (5) *The Modern Law Review* 791 at 797.

[65] Ibid., p. 793.   [66] Ibid., p. 812.

[67] Wanjiru Njoya argues, for example, that it is 'increasingly unreliable to presume a classic labor-capital divide in the modern publicly held firm': W. Njoya, 'Job Security in a Flexible Labor Market: Challenges and Possibilities for Worker Voice' (2011–2012) 33 *Comparative Labor Law and Policy Journal* 459 at 477.

[68] C. Villiers, 'Why Employee Protection Legislation Is Still Necessary' (2012) 33 (3) *Comparative Labor Law and Policy Journal* 481. Other essential considerations in respect of sustainable companies, such as the impact of companies on the environment, are also subordinated by this model. See, for example, C. Bradshaw, 'The Environmental Business Case and Unenlightened Shareholder Value' (2013) 33 (1) *Legal Studies* 141.

[69] R. Sennett, *The Culture of the New Capitalism* (New Haven, CT: Yale University Press, 2006), p. 5.

[70] D. Bryan, R. Martin and M. Rafferty, 'Financialization and Marx: Giving Labor and Capital a Financial Makeover' (2009) 41 (4) *Review of Radical Political Economics* 458 at 469.

[71] S. J. Lim and J. Phillips, 'Embedding CSR Values: The Global Footwear Industry's Evolving Governance Structure' (2008) 81 *Journal of Business Ethics* 143.

where the precarious nature of employment has been particularly marked post-crisis.[72] For Bradley et al.

> the Conservative government sought to re-educate the workforce into a new mindset, where the emphasis is on flexibility, individualism and entrepreneurialism, rather than collectivism and rigidity. Moreover, this message has penetrated, as many workers have come to see their employment as more precarious than that enjoyed by previous generations.[73]

The current corporate interest in gender equality might best be read as a form of corporate social responsibility (CSR).[74] In the same way that CSR has been criticised for becoming 'an ideological movement designed to consolidate the power of large corporations',[75] transnational business feminism encourages the instrumental use of women to allow companies to 'sustain a competitive advantage'.[76] In its very instrumentalism and focus on 'the business case', it provides a fresh endorsement of shareholder value.

11.5 How Transnational Business Feminism Endorses Gender Hierarchies

Persons act in 'gendered' ways; that is, they 'bring their beliefs about gender into social relations ... thus gendered performance becomes pervasive and taken for granted'.[77] As men are often in positions of power and superiority in organisations, it is their behaviour that informs cultural dynamics.[78] In the workplace 'the institutional bases of men's power'[79] converge. Men are numerically well-represented in management

---

[72] On the gendered effects of the financial crisis on matters including employment, health, poverty and welfare see S. Walby, 'Gender and the Financial Crisis', Paper for UNESCO Project on 'Gender and the Financial Crisis', 9 April 2009.

[73] H. Bradley, M. Erickson. C. Stephenson and S. Williams *Myths at Work* (Cambridge, MA: Polity Press, 2000), p. 58.

[74] K. Grosser, 'Corporate Social Responsibility and Gender Equality: Women as Stakeholders and the European Union Sustainability Strategy' (2009) 18 *Business Ethics: A European Review* 290.

[75] S. B. Banerjee, 'Corporate Social Responsibility: The Good, the Bad and the Ugly' (2008) 34 *Critical Sociology* 51 at 59.

[76] Ibid., p. 61.

[77] P. Y. Martin, '"Mobilizing Maculinities": Women's Experiences of Men at Work' (2001) 8 (4) *Organization* 587–618 at 587.

[78] Ibid., p. 588.

[79] R. W. Connell, *Gender & Power: Society, the Person and Sexual Politics* (Cambridge, MA: Polity Press, 1987), p. 244.

and supervisory positions, and working life is typically structured around the masculinist 'ideal worker' who can work full time (or more) in a fixed pattern of regular hours.[80] In the corporate workplace, this 'ideal worker' embodies a further set of behaviours which are associated with minimising transaction costs and enhancing returns to shareholders. Risk-taking, uncompromising toughness and a pre-occupation with profit maximisation are characteristically associated with large corporations, particularly those operating in the financial services sector. These are also characteristics associated with hegemonic ideas of masculinity. For McDowell, 'the City is a gendered arena where a particular masculinized set of performances is more highly valorized than other ways of being in the workplace'.[81] The statesman-like leader of a city institution is still invariably male, while traders commonly continue to display 'exaggerated forms of masculinized language and behaviour'.[82]

Even in industries operating outside the financial services sector, gendered hierarchies are prevalent. Indeed, Elias argues that the multinational corporation can be 'a site for the active construction of gendered identities across globalizing production lines'.[83] Multinationals are 'presented as rational economic actors, spreading the benefits of an economically liberal globalization worldwide ... one that is "socially disembedded" from the social, cultural, and economic context that it either comes from or invests into'.[84] Far from being progressive, with their promises of benefits to local communities, multinationals reflect deeply held, ideological commitments to a particular form of market economy:

> this progressive firm perspective is ideological in character – exhibiting entrenched (neo)liberal values concerning the priority of the market over society. Within this context, we find that the firm is constructed as a gender-neutral market actor that has the potential to actually undermine gender inequalities in 'backward' host economies.[85]

---

[80] J. C. Williams, 'Reconstructive Feminism: Changing the Way We Talk About Gender and Work Thirty Years after the PDA' (2009–10) 21 *Yale Journal of Law and Feminism* 79.

[81] L. McDowell, 'Capital Culture Revisited: Sex, Testosterone and the City' (2010) 34 (3) *International Journal of Urban and Regional Research* 652 at 653.

[82] Ibid.

[83] J. Elias, 'Stitching-up the Labour Market' (2005) 7(1) *International Feminist Journal of Politics* 90 at 91; 'Hegemonic Masculinities, the Multinational Corporation, and the Development State' (2008) 10 (4) *Men and Masculinities* 405.

[84] Elias, 'Hegemonic Masculinities, the Multinational Corporation, and the Development State', p. 407.

[85] Ibid., p. 408.

In its promulgation of a particularly narrow and market-oriented conception of gender equality, TBF endorses current organisational gender hierarchies by compelling women to fit within dominant masculinist corporate practices. These are 'practices that glorify the competitive and aggressive capitalist spirit yet are, at the same time, infused with notions of rational business practice'.[86] At the organisational level, women are invited to progress and aspire to directorships but working practices and cultures that have inhibited many women for decades, such as the assumption that women will bear primary responsibility for child care, often remain unchanged. For example, the United Kingdom's recently introduced model of shared parental leave, where fifty-two weeks' maternity leave can, should the couple wish, be shared with the father is, argues Mitchell, unlikely to lead to genuinely 'shared parenting' as 'the legislation continues to prioritise the caring role of mothers'.[87] Indeed, Mitchell points to the UK Government's own estimate that only 2–8 per cent of fathers are likely to participate in the scheme.[88]

Far from providing a critical counterpoint to the status quo, the diluted form of feminism espoused in TBF arguably masks the reality of persistent and deep gender inequalities. Instead of critiquing capitalism and suggesting an alternative economic and societal vision, the distinct focus on the business case for equality suggests that this form of feminism 'appears to have gone to bed with capitalism'.[89] Women are portrayed as free to engage in the opportunities the market offers, and actively empowered to do so by corporate campaigns. Yet, in the corporate context, when women do enter the workplace, there remain barriers in place that hinder their progression, such as expectations around the length of working hours and responsiveness of employees. Moreover, criticisms have been directed at the efforts of some women who have attempted to more explicitly put the female voice on the business agenda. On one view, it is admirable that women who do have a highly influential voice (such as Christine Lagarde) have done much to raise the profile of women. Yet, as Elias has noted, 'Davos woman' (so-called after the WEF's annual meeting in Davos and which is directly engaged with the 'woman as saviours' agenda) is 'a distinctly postfeminist manifestation'.[90]

---

[86] Ibid., p. 409.
[87] G. Mitchell, 'Encouraging Fathers to Care: The Children and Families Act 2014 and Shared Parental Leave' (2015) 44 (1) *Industrial Law Journal* 123 at 124.
[88] Ibid., p. 128.   [89] Prügl, 'Neoliberalising Feminism', p. 614.
[90] Elias, 'Davos Woman to the Rescue of Global Capitalism', p. 164.

In WEF's pursuance of a distinctly pro-business gender equality agenda, Elias suggests that there is an uncomfortable side-effect: 'the implication is that Davos women, despite their privileged class status, are able to speak for their underprivileged sisters on the basis of a deep and unproblematized gender essentialism'.[91]

As corporations and other economic actors continue to think of innovative new ways to engage women in market life, there is little reflection on the social fact that 'work/family conflict' continues to remain 'an inherent feature of capitalism',[92] which impacts on gender equality within the corporate environment.[93] This is problematic for men and women. Women may be more present in the labour market, but they continue to be segregated and marginalised as masculine power structures persist.

11.6   The Need for Structural Reform in the Corporate Sector

If companies are to engage sincerely with gender equality, it is not enough to 'be content with leaving all structure in place and tinkering only with questions such as board composition'.[94] While many companies appear to be making attempts to address gender inequality with widespread initiatives, they are often hampered by barriers such as few board-ready women in the pipeline or the lack of women entering particular sectors such as engineering.[95] More fundamental reform of corporate cultures, structures and institutions is arguably needed. In an attempt to move the debate forward in a more progressive direction, utilising a range of feminist methods to expose the gendered nature of companies and broader economic architecture will help establish a fruitful agenda for reform. 'Asking the woman question' to highlight women's absence or subordination from organisations has long been recognised as

---

[91]   Ibid., p. 165.
[92]   K. Abrams cited in J. Williams, 'The Evolution of "FReD": Family Responsibilities Discrimination and Developments in the Law of Stereotyping and Implicit Bias' (2008) 59 *Hastings Law Journal* 1311 at 1316.
[93]   M. C. Still, 'Family Responsibilities Discrimination and the New Institutionalism: The Interactive Process Through Which Legal and Social Factors Produce Institutional Change' (2008) 59 *Hastings Law Journal* 1491 at 1504.
[94]   K. Y. Testy, 'Capitalism and Freedom – For Whom? Feminist Legal Theory and Progressive Corporate Law' (2004) 67 *Law and Contemporary Problems* 87 at 105.
[95]   R. Russell, 'How Do FTSE100 Companies Frame Gender Equality?' (2017) 12 (2) *International and Comparative Corporate Law Journal* 80.

one important feminist method.[96] It is 'designed to identify the gender implications of rules and practices which might otherwise appear to be neutral or objective'.[97] Using this method reveals, for example, the gendered nature of the corporate 'ideal worker' norm. This is because, 'while the law regulating work in the marketplace has pretended that the body of the worker is unsexed, it has subtly constructed this body as male, by treating the female body as only one for sex, not for work'.[98] To help unsettle this norm, its detrimental effect and pressure on *both men and women* to adopt intensely masculinist behaviours might be emphasised.[99] As Martin and Collinson have observed, companies are

> systems of power relations that are embedded in gender ... Indeed, the workplace is a, if not the, prime arena where men in developed countries construct their masculine identities and relations with each other and, as the privileged and dominant gender, significantly shape femininities and women.[100]

Both men and women therefore 'need to be liberated from a rapacious economic system that both degrades the environment and does not value the necessary work that goes into maintaining social life'.[101] Masculinity in the corporate context is particularly prevalent. Whereas the masculinity performed in traditional blue-collar male occupations is often concerned with displays of physical prowess, white collar jobs are equally capable of being performed by women. This, argues Williams, creates a tension for men in white collar occupations which 'leaves [them] eager to shift the definition of manliness'.[102] Masculinity is then performed as long hours at work, beating targets and displaying exhaustion.[103]

There are, however, strong barriers inhibiting men from reacting against the 'ideal worker' norm, particularly if this involves (as it

---

[96] K. T. Bartlett, 'Feminist Legal Methods' (1990) 103(4) *Harvard Law Review* 829.
[97] Ibid., p. 837.
[98] N. Naffine and R. Owens 'Sexing law' in N. Naffine and R. Owens (eds.) *Sexing the Subject of Law* (Sydney: LBC, 1997), p. 13 discussing R. Owens 'Working in the sex market', pp. 119–148 of that collection.
[99] Williams, '"It's Snowing Down South", p. 813.
[100] P. Y. Martin and D. Collinson, '"Over the Pond and Across the Water": Developing the Field of "Gendered Organizations"' (2002) 9(3) *Gender, Work and Organization* 244 at 258.
[101] C. Albertyn, S. Fredman and J. Fudge, 'Introduction: Elusive Equalities – Sex, Gender and Women' (2014) 10 (4) *International Journal of Law in Context* 421 at 425.
[102] J. Williams 'Jumpstarting the Stalled Gender Revolution: Justice Ginsburg and Reconstructive Feminism' (2012) 63 *Hastings Law Journal* 1267 at 1285.
[103] Williams, *Reshaping the Work-Family Debate*.

inevitably would if we are to overcome the market/family dichotomy)
implying to any conception of a worker that he/she has care-giving
responsibilities.[104] Some men may be reluctant to 'giv[e] up the psychological and economic wages of maleness that they currently have in the
workplace'.[105] In the same way as race scholars have suggested that
whiteness may be construed as 'property' and thus of value,[106] self-
interest and intense pressure to comply with masculinist workplace
norms may prevent men from readily disturbing what it means to be
an 'ideal worker'.[107] The focus, then, is not on asking men to change but
on compelling companies to take seriously the gendered implications of
their insistence on shaping the workplace to maximise shareholder value.
The corporate ideal worker with low transaction costs and who is well-
placed to create surplus value is not a gender-neutral norm.

   Attention also needs to be turned on the broader economic and
financial architecture within which companies are situated. To achieve
genuinely transformative change requires going beyond introducing a
range of gender equality policies to companies and other economic actors
'while still maintaining a focus on market-based criteria, price stability
and privatization'.[108] Leaving the broader institutional and structural
contexts untouched necessarily limits the potential for genuine transformation towards gender equality. TBF's confusing theoretical foundation – of emphasising both women's sameness with and difference to
men – fails to tackle these deeper, structural concerns of 'gender privilege'.[109] As Williams has observed, both the 'sameness' and 'difference'
schools of feminist thought

> ultimately concede the legitimacy of such structural disadvantage by
> arguing that outsiders can do as well as 'anyone else' if only given the
> chance (the sameness position), or that they should be given special
> treatment because they can't live up to societal standards designed with-
> out them in mind (the difference position).[110]

---

[104] Williams, 'The Evolution of "FReD"', p.1318.

[105] R. S. Chang, 'Joan Williams, Coalitions, and Getting Beyond the Wages of Whiteness
and the Wages of Maleness' (2011) 34 *Seattle University Law Review* 825 at 833.

[106] C. Harris, 'Whiteness as Property' (1993) 106 *Harvard Law Review* 1709 at 1713.

[107] Chang, 'Joan Williams, Coalitions, and Getting Beyond the Wages of Whiteness and the
Wages of Maleness', p. 833.

[108] B. Muchhala, 'Barricades to Gender Equity in the International Financial Architecture'
(2012) 55 (3) *Development* 283 at 284.

[109] Williams, 'Dissolving the Sameness/Difference Debate', pp. 303–304.

[110] Ibid., p. 305.

TBF's greatest failing is that it promises greater emancipation for women but, in reality, risks reinforcing existing structural disadvantages.

An increasing sense that inequalities have increased post-crisis has, argues Brodie, opened up a space 'to reignite equality claims-making in an expanding field of opposition to the dominant governing paradigm'.[111] Progressive corporate scholars are well-placed to help fill this space. Although Gabaldon has remarked that addressing feminism to corporate scholars may be 'an exercise akin to observing an embroidery demonstration at a board meeting',[112] some have already begun the important work of showing how shareholder value is normatively biased[113] and revealing the gendered nature of the corporation.[114]

11.7   Conclusion

The purpose of this chapter has been to demonstrate how companies are complicit, perhaps unintentionally, in the politico-economic project of transnational business feminism, and how this complicity risks reproducing and valorising existing corporate power hierarchies.

While the current business interest in gender equality is superficially appealing, it obscures the need for sincere and fundamental reform of those corporate structures and practices that perpetuate women's subordination in a market economy. By maintaining a concentrated focus on making 'the business case' for women's involvement in corporate life, TBF provides fresh valorisation of shareholder primacy at a time when absentee shareholders have been criticised as being implicated in the global financial crisis. In so doing, it entrenches the dominance of

---

[111] J. Brodie, 'Elusive Equalities and the Great Recession: Restoration, Retrenchment and Redistribution' (2014) 10 (4) *International Journal of Law in Context* 427 at 428. See also Russell and Villiers, 'Gender justice in financial markets', p. 273.

[112] T. A. Gabaldon, 'The Lemonade Stand: Feminist and Other Reflections on the Limited Liability of Corporate Shareholders' (1992) 45 (6) *Vanderbilt Law Review* 1387 at 1415.

[113] J. Sarra, 'The Gender Implications of Corporate Governance Change' (2002–2003) 1 *Seattle Journal for Social Justice* 457 at 472–473.

[114] R. Cohen, 'Feminist Thought and Corporate Law: It's Time to Find Our Way Up from the Bottom (Line)' (1994) 2 *Journal of Gender and the Law* 1; Gabaldon, 'The Lemonade Stand'; K. A. Lahey and S. W. Salter, 'Corporate Law in Legal Theory and Legal Scholarship: From Classicism to Feminism' (1985) 23 (4) *Osgoode Hall Law Journal* 543; Testy, 'Capitalism and Freedom – For Whom?'; R. Russell, 'Implicating Public Companies in the Equal Pay Debate' (2012) 12 (2) *International Journal of Discrimination and the Law* 81.

shareholders within the corporate context. Meanwhile, existing gendered hierarchies remain largely uncontested. Corporate equality initiatives are incorporated into institutions where masculinised assumptions of the ideal worker continue to inform recruitment and progression decisions. At the macro-level, financial empowerment projects promise gender equality, but they also show how 'companies use a version of feminism to gain an advantage over competitors . . . and to earn legitimacy as they counter the critiques of social forces that challenge them on the public impact of their operations'.[115]

The question of how we might begin to divorce companies from their adherence to the business case for equality and framing of women to suit the needs of capitalism must be the next step in shaping a business environment where gender equality is meaningful. This is no easy task, in part because of the paradoxical and often contradictory claims made by the TBF movement. This chapter has suggested that we might make a start on this task by reflecting on the unspoken yet gendered norms behind how companies conceptualise the 'ideal worker' and by more explicitly drawing attention to the ways in which the market benefits from the often strict separation of life into domestic and economic activity.

As a way forward, an 'ecosystem' approach to gender within companies has been suggested. This may include giving serious consideration to adopting quotas for women directors, 'supported by other mechanisms such as reporting requirements and mentoring and networking support for women as they climb the career ladder'.[116] To this may be added initiatives such as greater protection for those engaged on zero hours contracts (often used in caring and hospitality sectors in which women are prevalent); affordable, decent childcare provision; encouragement by companies for fathers to share in parental leave; and greater openness in considering how flexible working patterns need not come at the expense of the quality of work.

These suggestions will also go some way towards fostering a more sustainable model not just of working practices within companies but in other areas too. Promotion of agile and home working at all levels of the corporation, for example, has a number of advantages, including less environmental impact with reduced commutes, greater ability to

[115] Prügl, 'Neoliberalising Feminism', p. 626.
[116] Russell and Villiers, 'Gender justice in financial markets', p. 286.

participate in community initiatives due to an increased presence at home, and perhaps mundanely (yet importantly) likely less reliance on processed, transported food commodities.

TBF may be commended for having raised awareness of women's contribution in the economic context and given (some) women a voice. A critique of this trend has, however, revealed how it, as currently formulated, risks upholding shareholder primacy and continuing to promote practices which are ultimately detrimental to men and women and which have wider ramifications for the sustainability of the corporate status quo.

The Gendered Corporation

The Role of Masculinities in Shaping Corporate Culture

CATHERINE O'SULLIVAN

12.1 Introduction

In the wake of the most recent economic crash, popular analysts looked at the gender of those involved in corporate governance and asked whether the recession would have happened if there were more women involved in senior corporate and banking management roles.[1] The press blamed 'macho masculinity' and testosterone-fuelled recklessness for the financial collapse. On one level this response was positive as it recognised that there is something about the way in which men as a group dominate high-finance that is problematic. It also represented a shift away from the traditional focus on bad apples that tends to predominate when the media looks at corporate malfeasance and crime.[2] Unfortunately rather than pursuing this line of inquiry and considering what it is about companies (bad barrels) or the structuring of capitalism (bad orchards) that encourages the group performance of 'macho masculinity', testosterone as an explanation prevailed. This allowed for recourse to the old trope of innate differences between men and women with the concomitant reinforcement of traditional gender roles where women's inherently

---

[1] For analysis of the press reporting, see E. Prügl, '"If Lehman Brothers Had Been Lehman Sisters . . .": Gender and Myth in the Aftermath of the Financial Crisis' (2010) 6 *International Political Sociology* 21; M. Fisher, 'Wall Street Women: Professional Saviors of the Global Economy' (2015) 11(2) *Critical Perspectives on International Business* 137.

[2] D. Machin & A. Mayr, 'Corporate Crime and the Discursive Deletion of Responsibility: A Case Study of the Paddington Rail Crash' (2012) 9(1) *Crime Media Culture* 63. This is not to say that individual men were not denounced, rather that in addition to the behaviours of individual men being highlighted, attention was also given to men working in groups.

risk-averse and caring natures ('benevolent motherhood'[3]) render them suitable to solve market woes.

In this chapter I will add to Russell's critique of the simplistic and essentialising 'add women and stir' solution to corporate governance issues[4] by focusing on the enactment of gender by corporate actors. In Section 12.2 I will introduce the concept of hegemonic masculinities which has influenced the sociological and criminological literature that I will discuss in Section 12.3. The former considers how gendered hierarchies within corporations foster an environment conducive to unethical, unsustainable and sometimes criminal conduct, while the latter shows that corporate offenders enact masculinities and femininities concordant with broader cultural understandings of appropriate gendered ways of behaving. The implication of this literature is that it is not the sex of those involved in corporate governance that matters in preventing unethical and unsustainable corporate practice but what gender performances are valourised within the specific corporate environment(s) that the corporate actor finds him/herself and the degree to which those performances accord with societal gender expectations. Rather than testosterone-fuelled recklessness being the appropriate focal point of blame for the recent crash, it is the performance of a particular form of masculinity (in which specific gendered forms of recklessness are socially sanctioned) that is the better target of opprobrium. This means that if more women are added to corporate governance structures without changes being made to the underlying gendered business culture that incentivises unethical, unsustainable and sometimes criminal business practices, then women may attempt to adopt those masculine-coded (rather than inherently male) behaviours in order to succeed[5] or will exit those structures when the sexist practices normalised by them become intolerable.[6] As such, I will conclude in Section 12.4 that creating true

---

[3] A. Kwolek-Folland, *Engendering Business: Men and Women in the Corporate Office, 1870–1930* (Baltimore, MD: Johns Hopkins Press, 1994) at 136, quoted in Fisher, 'Wall Street Women' at 147.

[4] See Ch. 11.

[5] Such adoptions are not necessarily effective, see, e.g., A. H. Eagly, M. G. Makhijani & B. G. Klonsky, 'Gender and the Evaluation of Leaders: A Meta-Analysis' (1992) *Psychol. Bull.* 3; J. L. Pierce, *Gender Trials: Emotional Lives in Contemporary Law Firms* (Oakland: University of California Press, 1996); Catalyst, *The Double-Bind Dilemma for Women in Leadership: Damned if You Do, Doomed if You Don't* (New York: Catalyst, 2007).

[6] For example, women leave jobs in the tech sector at more than twice the rate of men; L. Mundy, 'Why Is Silicon Valley so Awful to Women?' (April 2017) *The Atlantic* 60 at 65. In a survey that was conducted with 210 women who had at least 10 years' experience in

corporate sustainability requires making visible the gendered nature of the problematic practices and reshaping them, with the ultimate result of more women in meaningfully reformed corporate governance structures.

12.2   Hegemonic Masculinities: Understanding Gendered Behaviour

The concept of hegemonic masculinity appeared in a series of articles in the early 1980s, receiving its first clear articulation in six pages of the first edition of Connell's influential *Gender and Power*.[7] As originally formulated, hegemonic masculinity was understood to be the normative ideal of masculinity[8] established through physical prowess, strong sexual impulses towards women, work and success in the paid market (enabling the gendered division of labour), competitive individualism, the pursuit of independence, and the capacity for violence. It 'embodied the currently most honored way of being a man, it required all other men to position themselves in relation to it, and it ideologically legitimated the global subordination of women to men'.[9] Connell's work belongs to the social constructionist tradition where the various forms of masculinity are 'configurations of practice structured by gender relations',[10] in particular the patriarchal gender system which prioritises masculinities over femininities. She argues that masculinities are defined with reference to other masculinities (complicit, subordinated and marginalised[11]) and in opposition to the various forms of femininity. Their relational nature

---

the tech sector in 2015, it was found that 60 per cent had experienced unwanted sexual advances and 1 in 3 had feared for their personal safety; T. Vassalo, E. Levy, M. Madansky, H. Mickell, B. Porter & M. Leas, *Elephant in the Valley*, see www.elephantinthevalley.com.

[7] R. W. Connell, *Gender and Power* (Sydney: Allen & Unwin, 1987).

[8] More recent research has emphasized its normative status. For example, Tannenbaum and Frank have looked at the emotional costs of suppressing emotions that is part of the masculine ideal; C. Tannenbaum & B. Frank, 'Masculinity and Health in Late Life Men' (2011) 5(3) *American Journal of Men's Health* 243. See too R. W. Connell & J. W. Messerschmidt, 'Hegemonic Masculinity: Rethinking the Concept' (2005) 19 *Gender and Society* 829 at 846, 852.

[9] Connell & Messerschmidt, 'Hegemonic Masculinity' at 832.

[10] R. W. Connell, *Masculinities* (Cambridge: Polity Press, 1995) at 44.

[11] Complicit masculinities are enacted by men who do not meet the normative standards of hegemonic masculinity but do not challenge it and therefore obtain a patriarchal dividend by virtue of their status as men in a system where men are positioned as superior to women. Subordinated masculinities are forms of masculinity that do not conform to the norms promoted, e.g., homosexual masculinities. Marginalised masculinities are those

means that masculinities and femininities are not simply imposed on individuals but can be resisted by them and are subject to change. According to Connell then, 'gender is "done" to subjects but they also "do" gender'.[12]

In their reformulation of the concept in 2005, Connell and Messerschmidt emphasised hegemony does not necessarily require active oppression at all times. Various forms of non-hegemonic masculinity can and do inform the content of what is hegemonic, and women are often central in the process of constructing masculinities.[13] Indeed it would be contrary to the concept of hegemony, 'an idea that embeds certain notions of consent and participation by subaltern groups',[14] if it operated only in an oppressive fashion. However hegemonic masculinities are not self-reproducing, which is why the boundaries of the masculinities that are deemed hegemonic at a particular place in a given time require the continual policing of men and the exclusion of women.[15]

Connell and Messerschmidt's 2005 article is also important for its acknowledgment that hegemonic masculinity is not a singular concept. Instead hegemonic masculinities exist at local (families, communities and organisations), regional (societies, cultures and States) and global (transnational businesses, media and politics) levels and there are links between them.[16] Messerschmidt explains their relationship thus: 'global hegemonic masculinities pressure regional and local hegemonic masculinities, and regional hegemonic masculinities provide cultural materials adopted or reworked in global arenas and utilized in local gender dynamics'.[17] This recognition of a multiplicity of masculinities is important for two reasons. First their plurality challenges binary essentialist reasoning when discussing women and men.[18] Second the focus on the relational nature of the performances is what has been termed 'the element of optimism in an otherwise rather bleak theory'.[19] Connell writes: 'multiple

---

who are disqualified from attaining hegemonic status because of their race, ethnicity or class. Connell, ibid. at 78–80.

[12] C. Beasley, 'Problematizing Contemporary Men/Masculinities Theorizing: The Contribution of Raewyn Connell and Conceptual-Terminological Tensions Today' (2012) 63(4) *Brit. J. of Sociology* 747 at 755.

[13] Connell & Messerschmidt, 'Hegemonic Masculinity' at 848.   [14] Ibid. at 840.

[15] Ibid. at 844.   [16] Ibid. at 849.

[17] J. W. Messerschmidt, 'Engendering Gendered Knowledge: Assessing the Academic Appropriation of Hegemonic Masculinity' (2012) 15 *Men and Masculinities* 56 at 59.

[18] R. W. Connell, 'Margin Becoming Centre: For a World-Centred Rethinking of Masculinities' (2014) 9(4) *NORMA* 217 at 219.

[19] Connell and Messerschmidt, 'Hegemonic Masculinity' at 833.

masculinities represent [a] complexity of interests and purposes which open possibilities for change'.[20] Evidence of this change has been found in more gender-equality based masculinities identified in various Scandinavian studies and in research in Mozambique.[21] Crucially these shifts have been facilitated by, among other factors, State interest in the promotion of women's rights. However, changes to hegemonic masculinities do not always move unidirectionally towards egalitarianism. An example is transnational business masculinity, a new iteration of corporate masculinity engaged in by those who work for multinational corporations. Connell and Wood note that while transnational business masculinity does not adhere to the homophobic and gendered views of traditional corporate masculinities,[22] it nonetheless remains a power-orientated rather than egalitarian masculinity.[23]

Unfortunately there has been a tendency within some masculinities work to equate hegemonic masculinity with character traits possessed by particular groups of dominant or dominating men, an issue that Connell and Messerschmidt have acknowledged.[24] This is problematic because the collapse of hegemonic masculinity to particular groups of men fails to acknowledge that individual men can assume different performances of masculinity depending on the social context,[25] the time of day,[26] or indeed engage in interactional styles more associated with feminine norms for strategic reasons.[27] It also deflects attention away from the legitimating function that hegemonic masculinity performs in stabilising

---

[20] R. W. Connell, *The Men and the Boys* (Cambridge: Polity Press, 2000) at 226.

[21] For a summary of such studies, see A. D. Christensen & S. Q. Jensen, 'Combining Hegemonic Masculinity and Intersectionality' (2014) 9(1) *NORMA* 60 at 65.

[22] R. W. Connell & J. Wood, 'Globalization and Business Masculinities' (2005) 7(4) *Men and Masculinities* 347 at 358–361. However, they note that while gender equality may be endorsed, it is not necessarily practiced (359).

[23] Connell, 'Margin Becoming Centre' at 227.

[24] Connell & Messerschmidt, 'Hegemonic Masculinity' at 847. See also J. W. Messerschmidt, 'And Now, the Rest of the Story ... A Commentary on Christine Beasley's "Rethinking Hegemonic Masculinity in a Globalizing World"' (2008) 11(1) *Men and Masculinities* 104 and Messerschmidt (2012), above n. 17.

[25] R. Collier, 'Rethinking Men and Masculinities in the Contemporary Legal Profession: The Example of Fatherhood, Transnational Business Masculinities, and Work-Life Balance in Large Law Firms' (2013) 12 *Nev. L.J.* 410 at 430.

[26] P. Levin, 'Gendering the Market: Temporality, Work, and Gender on a National Futures Exchange' (2001) 28(1) *Work and Occupations* 112.

[27] J. Angouri, '"We are in a Masculine Profession...": Constructing Gender Identities in a Consortium of Two Multinational Engineering Companies' (2011) 5(2) *Gender and Language* 373 at 389, 392, 394.

hierarchal and unequal patriarchal relationships through the subordination of women, femininities and non-hegemonic masculinities.[28]
Accordingly, a dominant or dominating masculinity is only also hegemonic if it legitimates patriarchal relations.[29] To illustrate the difference
between hegemonic and dominant masculinities, it is useful to consider
Beasley's contrast of accountants and working-class men:

> a senior manager in a major accounting firm ... may represent a domin-
> ant masculinity in that he wields a widely accepted institutional power ...
> but ... [a]ccountants ... are scarcely deemed the mobilizing model of
> manliness to which all men should aspire. They may exercise power, but
> they are not able to legitimate it ...
>
> By the same token ... while actual working-class men may not wield
> institutional power, muscular working-class manhood *is* commonly
> employed as a highly significant mobilizing cultural ideal intended to
> invoke cross-class recognition and solidarity regarding what counts as a
> man.[30]

Jefferson's focus on men who batter women is useful regarding the
distinction between dominating and hegemonic masculinities. He notes
that while such men clearly subordinate women, they do not boast about
their violence because it is not seen as 'the currently most honored way of
being a man'[31] but rather as a 'failure of manhood'.[32] As such it is not a
hegemonic form of masculinity.

It is important to note that Connell's work, although pre-eminent in
the field of masculinities studies for thirty years, has also been criticised
for being too constrained by its modernist origins. It has been argued that

---

[28] J. Elias & C. Beasley, 'Hegemonic Masculinity and Globalization: "Transnational Business
Masculinities" and Beyond' (2009) 6(2) *Globalizations* 281 at 288; C. Beasley, 'Rethinking
Hegemonic Masculinity in a Globalizing World' (2008) 11(1) *Men and Masculinities* 86
at 94.

[29] Messerschmidt, 'Engendering Gendered Knowledge' at 73.

[30] Beasley, 'Rethinking Hegemonic Masculinity' at 90. Emphasis in original.

[31] Connell & Messerschmidt, 'Hegemonic Masculinity' at 832.

[32] T. Jefferson, 'Subordinating Hegemonic Masculinity' (2002) 6(1) *Theoretical Criminology*
63 at 71. In her response to this article, Connell accepts the point but complicates it, noting
the extent to which men in a variety of social contexts are expected to keep 'their' women
under control and that their failure to do so is seen to negatively reflect on their manhood.
R. W. Connell, 'On Hegemonic Masculinity and Violence: Response to Jefferson and Hall'
(2002) 6(1) *Theoretical Criminology* 89 at 93–94. It should also be noted that Jefferson's
article pre-dates the reformulation of the concept in 2005 where dominant and hegemonic
were distinguished, and Messerschmidt's subsequent recognition of the distinction between
hegemonic, dominant and dominating masculinities; J. Messerschmidt, *Hegemonic Masculinities and Camouflaged Politics* (Boulder, CO: Paradigm, 2010).

it should pay more attention to post-modern theory, specifically the problematising of the sex-gender dichotomy and the understanding of subjects as discursive assemblages rather than formed in dialectical interaction with material structures.[33] Apart from the fact that such critiques neglect Connell's recognition of the discursive dimension in the construction of various masculinities,[34] I would agree with Connell that gender is not just discursive but is also 'a system of material practices resulting in material inequalities'.[35] As Connell notes:

> One is not free to adopt any gender position in interaction simply as a discursive or reflexive move. The possibilities are constrained massively by embodiment, by institutional histories, by economic forces, and by personal and family relationships. The costs of making certain discursive choices can be extremely high . . . .[36]

Accordingly, I subscribe to the views of Connell and others who appreciate the insights postmodernism has generated in relation to the discursive, but who are concerned that the proposition that everything is discourse ignores the reality of structural systemic inequalities and thereby negates the possibility of making substantive and positive change to the material conditions of women and men.[37] Finally, even those who are critical of the concept of hegemonic masculinity acknowledge its continued value although they suggest different reformulations. Christensen and Jensen write that 'the concept of hegemonic masculinity is so deeply anchored in the theoretical history of masculinity research that "throwing the baby out with the bathwater" is both undesirable and impossible'.[38] Similarly Hearn does not entirely reject Connell's approach; he integrates it into his new proposition that it is men rather

---

[33] For a very helpful and critical discussion of the differences between Connell's work and postmodernism, see Beasley, 'Problematizing Contemporary Men/Masculinities'.

[34] Connell and Messerschmidt write '"masculinity" represents not a certain type of man but, rather, a way that men position themselves through discursive practices'. ('Hegemonic Masculinity' at 841).

[35] Connell, 'On Hegemonic Masculinity and Violence' at 94.

[36] Connell & Messerschmidt, 'Hegemonic Masculinity' at 843.

[37] Connell writes: 'Deconstructionist gender analysis tends to individualize politics, representing opposition to hierarchy mainly as acts of rejection or subversion, rather than group mobilization'; R. W. Connell, 'A Thousand Miles from Kind: Men, Masculinities and Modern Institutions' (2008) 16(3) *Journal of Men's Studies* 237 at 245. See also M. Nussbaum, 'The Professor of Parody' (2003) 4 *Raisons Politiques* 124; A. Howe, *Sex, Violence and Crime: Foucault and the 'Man' Question* (London: Routledge, 2009) at 138–142.

[38] Christensen & Jensen, 'Combining hegemonic masculinity', above n. 21 at 72.

than masculinities that are hegemonic.[39] As such, hegemonic masculinity and its correlates remain an important conceptual tool in theorising gendered behaviour in local, regional and global locations.

12.3 Using Masculinities Research to Understand the Conduct of Corporate Actors

The concept of hegemonic masculinities has informed sociological and criminological research on the behaviour engaged in by corporate actors. In this chapter I will highlight literature that examines how corporate actors perform masculinity through discursive practices, either through enforcing gendered hierarchies by means of aggressive and masculinised language or in the gendered ways they attempt to justify their wrong-doing. My focus on language is in part a response to the unwarranted critique that masculinities research fails to attend to the discursive, but it is also simply because 'Language is the primary means by which individuals construct and negotiate their identities ... "Identity talk" can be used to present oneself as a certain type of person, explain nonnormative or otherwise unexpected behavior, and manage impressions'.[40]

12.3.1 Masculinities and Corporations

One of Connell's important contributions to the study of men and masculinities has been her insight that corporations are gendered male, reflecting the masculinised public realm from which they originated.[41] Connell writes:

> gender discrimination [in corporations] is not an accidental feature of bureaucracy[] which can be fixed by changing a few attitudes. Gender is a structural feature of corporate life, linked to gender relations in other sectors of society. Gender shapes job definitions, understandings of 'merit' and promotion, management techniques, marketing and a whole lot more.[42]

---

[39] J. Hearn, 'From Hegemonic Masculinity to the Hegemony of Men' (2004) 5(1) *Feminist Theory* 49 at 59; J. Hearn, 'Men, Masculinities and the Material(-)Discursive' (2014) 9(1) *NORMA* 5 at 10.

[40] M. J. Gathings & K. Parrotta, 'The Use of Gendered Narratives in the Courtroom: Constructing an Identity Worthy of Leniency' (2013) 42(6) *Journal of Contemporary Ethnography* 668 at 670.

[41] R. W. Connell & R. Pearse, *Gender in World Perspective*, 3rd ed. (Cambridge: Polity Press, 2015) at 131–134.

[42] Ibid. at 132.

In this she draws from and feeds into the work of various feminist scholars, including Acker, who have similarly exposed the false gender-neutrality of organisations and their structures.[43] Acker notes that the ideal worker assumes 'a particular gendered organization of domestic life and social production'[44]; specifically, he is a male who is able to devote his time to work because he has a wife who looks after him and any children. In his study of the American Commodities Exchange (ACE), Levin found that traits traditionally associated with masculinity – such as being aggressive and physical – implicitly informed the understanding of what it was to be a competent trader during busy periods in the day.[45] This masculine coding became apparent when high-performing women were discussed. They are regarded as competent, but not women, or they are described in non-flattering gendered terms (e.g., bitch).[46] The implicit gendering of work as male means that even when men are not engaging in work – for example, partaking in self-aggrandising and homosocial-bonding talk at meetings – they regard themselves as working.[47] This conflation of masculinity performances with work is possible, Martin explains, because men 'predominate in the powerful positions and because men and masculinity have more legitimacy . . . in work contexts'.[48]

Yet because gender is an on-going accomplishment which requires men to assert their status as men, in addition to paid work being implicitly gendered male, the practice of work becomes explicitly so through physical or discursive means. It is obviously easier for blue-collar men to physically 'do gender' than white-collar men because of the nature of blue-collar work. Absent the proof of manliness that physical labour provides, white-collar men 'shift the definition'[49] of what it means to be male by working long hours which demonstrates their 'commitment,

---

[43] J. Acker, 'Hierarchies, Jobs, Bodies: A Theory of Gendered Organizations' (1990) 4(2) *Gender & Society* 139.

[44] Ibid. at 149.

[45] Levin, 'Gendering the Market' at 122. Levin also found ACE to be explicitly gendered in its sexualisation and commodification of women's bodies during the mid-day lull.

[46] Ibid. at 121–122.

[47] P. Y. Martin, '"Mobilizing Masculinities": Women's Experiences of Men at Work' (2001) 8(4) *Organization* 587 at 605.

[48] Ibid.

[49] J. Williams, 'Jumpstarting the Stalled Gender Revolution: Justice Ginsburg and Reconstructive Feminism' (2011) 63 *Hastings L.J.* 1267 at 1285.

stamina, and virility'.[50] Discursively, masculinity is performed in blue- and white-collar work environments through the use of masculinised aggressive language. Indeed, it has been suggested that linguistic displays of dominance are more important to white-collar workers precisely because of their jobs' lack of physicality.[51] As well as using profanities, studies have found that white-collar workers use strongly masculinised linguistic imagery when describing themselves or those they admire. For example, the language lawyers use to describe those they regard as effective trial lawyers is 'not only intimidating but strongly masculine' (e.g., Rambo litigator, hired guns, barbarians of the bar).[52] They also use aggressive and often sexualised linguistic imagery in describing their work. Cross-examination is a 'mental duel' where the object is to 'destroy[] witnesses' or 'rape' them.[53] Those who are dominated are frequently described in feminised terms. They are described as 'having no balls', as 'sissies' and 'wimps'.[54] The same is true of the ACE futures traders observed by Levin. They described their work as 'war', as a 'battle', and one trader memorably stated, 'You have to want to cut someone's balls off'.[55]

The metaphors that corporate actors use to express success and failure are also masculine-coded. In addition to military metaphors such as those just noted, the two most commonly discussed in the literature are work as sports or sexual prowess/violence.[56] Writing in the context of large corporations who pit employees against each other in promotion and retention contests, O'Connor notes that military and sports metaphors 'inculcate both competitiveness and loyalty', features valued by employers, even though they may be at the expense of ethical conduct.[57] Sexual prowess/violence metaphors perform a similar function by facilitating homosocial bonding between the (appropriately heterosexual) male employees and excluding the feminine/feminised Other. Lawyers

---

[50] M. Cooper, 'Being the "Go-To Guy": Fatherhood, Masculinity, and the Organization of Work in Silicon Valley' in N. Gerstel et al. (eds.), *Families at Work: Expanding the Bounds* (Nashville, TN: Vanderbilt University Press, 2002), quoted in Williams, 'Jumpstarting the Stalled Gender Revolution' at 1286.

[51] J. Pierce, 'Rambo Litigators: Emotional Labor in a Male-Dominated Occupation' in C. Cheng (ed.), *Masculinities in Organizations* (London: Sage, 1996) 1 at 3.

[52] Ibid. at 8–9.   [53] Ibid. at 9, 11.   [54] Ibid.

[55] Levin, 'Gendering the Market' at 122.

[56] L. McDowell, *Capital Culture: Gender at Work in the City* (Oxford: Blackwell Publishers, 1997) at 148; Angouri, '"We are in a Masculine Profession …"' at 385–386.

[57] M. A. O'Connor, 'Women Executives in Gladiator Corporate Cultures: The Behavioral Dynamics of Gender, Ego, and Power' (2006) 65 *Maryland L.R.* 465 at 489.

are told to seduce juries ('getting in bed with the jury'[58]), while ACE traders 'often spoke … about getting "fucked" by the market or accidentally "screwing" a customer'.[59] In the merchant banks in London, successful traders were 'big swinging dicks', while a 'hard on' was a rising market, 'lift your skirts' meant to reveal your position, deals were 'consummated' and to exaggerate one's expense claims was 'to rape the cards'.[60] In a recent case, the Libyan Investment Authority (LIA) unsuccessfully sued Goldman Sachs for abuse of trust in trades executed between January and April 2008.[61] The plaintiffs presented in evidence an email from a Goldman executive who described LIA as 'unsophisticated' clients whom 'anyone could "rape"'.[62]

Sexual violence is also expressed in jokes that serve to create and maintain group solidarity through the exclusion of women and non-hegemonic men. McDowell found that

> sexualised language was used to objectify and humiliate women – 'I'd like to screw her/nail her if I got the chance' – as well as references to women colleagues as 'skirts', 'slags', 'brasses' and 'tarts', synonyms for prostitutes. … A range of practical jokes revolving around, variously, sexy computer passwords, smutty messages and faxes, underwear and blow-up dolls were reported.[63]

The male workers stopped when their female colleagues told them to, but resumed when the women left. This, McDowell observed, 'was another mechanism of exclusion'.[64] Revisiting that study in 2010, McDowell noted that little had changed: 'Horseplay, sexualized banter, loud and aggressive talk, as well as forms of sexual harassment are tolerated and women are often forced either into the position of unwilling arbiters of boundaries or less than willing participants in the sexualized banter'.[65] Levin similarly found that the use of heterosexist jokes and jokes about sexual violence 'facilitate[d] the identification of the ACE as a man's world' and operated to exclude women, and by necessary implication homosexual men, from the social community

---

[58] Pierce, 'Rambo Litigators' at 20.   [59] Levin, 'Gendering the Market' at 123.

[60] McDowell, *Capital Culture* at 148, 179.

[61] C. Bray, 'Goldman Sachs didn't Trick Libyan Fund, Judge Says' (14 October 2016) *New York Times*.

[62] R. Allen-Mills, 'Watch out, world: Goldman's "vampire squid" is back from the depths' (19 June 2016) *Sunday Times* News Review 2.

[63] McDowell, *Captial Culture* at 141.   [64] Ibid. at 144.

[65] L. McDowell, 'Capital Culture Revisited: Sex, Testosterone and the City' (2010) 34(3) *International Journal of Urban and Regional Research* 652 at 653.

being solidified.[66] Stories about being fellated by girlfriends/one-night stands and of hiring female prostitutes also served 'to communicate [the traders' heterosexual] manliness to each other'.[67] Women who tried to participate in such 'banter' were regarded negatively, revealing its homo-social and sexist nature. Women could not be sexual subjects, just objects.[68]

This exclusionary language co-exists with, and possibly legitimates, exclusionary practice. A report into London's financial institutions in 2008 described a 'lap dance ethos' that undermined women who worked in those firms.[69] A 2014 survey undertaken by the *Financial Times* found that sexism was particularly prevalent in fund management, with a fifth of female fund staff having been sexually harassed at work, and a third reporting that sexist behaviour was directed at them on a weekly or monthly basis.[70] The repeated awarding of damages to women in corporate sex discrimination lawsuits is testimony to the scale of the problem. On Wall Street, Citigroup's Smith Barney, Merrill Lynch and Morgan Stanley each paid more than $100 million between 1990 and 2006. Morgan Stanley settled another lawsuit for $54 million in 2008.[71] More recently there have been high-profile examples of women in key corporate roles in the technology sector making sex discrimination allegations against their employers.[72]

In line with Connell's theory that masculinities are not self-reproducing, men who fail to live up to the socially constructed masculine norms being policed also face negative repercussions. This can often take the form of physical and/or verbal abuse. The latter is often in the form of name-calling where the man who is or is assumed to belong to a marginalised masculinity is equated with women/the feminine.[73] Connell describes this discursive strategy as a symbolic blurring which re-inscribes the superiority of men/masculinities over women/femininities[74]

---

[66] Levin, 'Gendering the Market' at 124.   [67] Ibid. at 125–126.   [68] Ibid. at 125.

[69] Fawsett Society, *Sexism and the City: What's Rotten in the Workplace and What We Can Do About It* (London: Fawsett Society, 2008).

[70] C. Newlands & M. Marriage, 'Women in asset management: Battling a culture of "subtle sexism"' (30 November 2014) *Financial Times Financial Management Supplement.*

[71] Prügl, '"If Lehman Brothers Had Been Lehman Sisters"' at 25.

[72] For an account of the accusations against Google, Facebook, Uber and Tesla, refer to A. Simon-Lewis, 'Facebook becomes latest tech giant to face claims of sexism. What is Silicon Valley's problem?' (4 May 2017) *Wired,* see www.wired.co.uk/article/tesla-sexism-lawsuit-harassment-uber.

[73] S. R. Bird, 'Welcome to the Men's Club: Homosociality and the Maintenance of Hegemonic Masculinity' (1996) 10 *Gender & Soc.* 120.

[74] Connell, *Masculinities* at 79.

The bullying behaviour that gender non-conforming men experience is the flip-side to the camaraderie of the men's club and shows that the enactment of this form of corporate masculinity is a way that men seek to position themselves discursively and through social practice as hierarchically superior to other lesser men and to women. This negative reinforcement of aggressive and reckless masculinity also has implications from a corporate sustainability perspective in that the kinds of considerations that underlie sustainable practice, such as prudence or concern for social justice and environmental issues, are coded feminine and thus become unspeakable for those seeking to present themselves as conforming to the hegemonic norm.

Finally, the relational and shifting nature of masculinities is evident in research on corporations. In addition to the homosocial bonding aspect of the performance of masculinity in workplaces, McDowell's seminal work on investment banking in London noted the shift in the hegemonic form of masculinity within that arena in the 1980s from the measured, rational calm of the disembodied patriarch to the youthful, masculine energy of the modern, brash trader. Collier has noted a similar change in large law firms, where the hegemonic form has moved 'away from the model of the male "lawyer as gentleman" ... to the more fragmented, entrepreneurial, hyper-competitive, and increasingly commercial profession of today'.[75] This shift, Collier suggests, fits well with the model of transnational business masculinity proposed by Connell.

12.3.2   Masculinities and Corporate Crime

Connell did not focus on the relationship between masculinities and crime, although she suggested that through committing crime men are, in part, 'doing masculinity' by asserting what they believe is 'their essential nature' when other legitimate routes are blocked. She regards this as 'protest masculinity', an often Pyrrhic means of reclaiming lost power.[76] This insight was taken up by Messerschmidt. He argued that 'Crime is a resource that may be summoned when men lack other resources to accomplish gender'.[77] For example, he noted that boys/

---

[75] Collier, 'Rethinking Men and Masculinities' at 432–433.
[76] Connell, *Masculinities* at 111–118.
[77] J. W. Messerschmidt, *Masculinities and Crime* (Lanham, MD: Rowman & Littlefield Publishers, 1993) at 85.

men who are members of lower-class and/or minority groups have fewer legitimate routes to demonstrate their 'essential nature' as men. This can lead to the creation of 'a physically violent opposition masculinity' because physical strength expressed through violence is one of the few 'hegemonic masculine ideals that remain available'.[78] Pursuant to this theory, crime is not committed because it is just the way boys/men are, it is a choice to undertake a gendered strategy of action that is enabled and circumscribed by gendered social structures.

In the ensuing criminological engagement with masculinities, research has tended to focus on male violence against men (particularly in working-class areas), male sexual violence against women and domestic violence. However, it is also useful in understanding corporate culture, of which corporate crime is a facet, particularly its valorisation of recklessness:

> risk-taking and defying social convention are qualities more admired in men than in women. . . . [M]en find it easier than women to justify illegal wrongdoing because law-violating behaviour, especially for status-seeking or financial reasons, is more compatible with male focal concerns. Stereo-typically masculine qualities align not only with committing business fraud, but also with actions that might precipitate fraud, such as engaging in risky financial ventures or bad business deals and gambling, drinking, or sexual affairs.[79]

Men have three focal concerns ascribed to them: maintaining domin-ance/control, attaining status in the public sphere (with attendant pro-vider/protector roles in the private) and heterosexual sexual success.[80] The status and financial rewards attendant on (il)licit masculine risk-taking behaviour in parts of the corporate sector certainly meet these concerns, enabling 'a sort of playboy dream life which included holidays in exotic locations, often on board yachts, participation in extreme sports, the collection of classic cars, and the use of private planes'.[81] This visible rewarding of individuals who take reckless risks in turn creates or reinforces a culture of recklessness. As such, the practice of individuals

---

[78] Ibid. at 104–105.
[79] D. J. Steffensmeier, J. Schwartz & M. Roche, 'Gender and Twenty-First-Century Corpor-ate Crime: Female Involvement and the Gender Gap in Enron-Era Corporate Frauds' (2013) 78(3) *American Sociological Review* 448 at 452.
[80] Ibid. at 451–452.
[81] L. McDowell, 'Making a Drama Out of a Crisis: Representing Financial Failure, or a Tragedy in Five Acts' (2011) 36 *Transactions of the Institute of British Geographers* 193 at 197.

becomes the culture of the institution becomes the practice of individuals – an unvirtuous circle.[82]

For some, as Steffensmeier et al. noted, living the high-life associated with masculine success leads to criminality. Cressey similarly found that embezzlers lived beyond their means for quite some time before they 'borrowed' money to solve the problem they had created.[83] For others, it is the previously noted survival-of-the-fittest style promotion tournaments that create an environment where 'the winners must continuously produce profits'.[84] In such a context, when legitimate means of obtaining profits or promotions are blocked, 'corporate executives are positioned to engage in specific illegitimate practices that seek to ensure not only their own, but corporate success as well'.[85] Accordingly, corporate crime is as much a resource for some men to accomplish gender as physical violence is for others.

In light of the behaviour described in the previous section that was documented in non-criminal corporate environments, it is unsurprising that the same behaviour is present in those organisations that are actively engaging in criminal wrongdoing. Indeed, what is striking when looking at retrospective analyses of the behaviour in firms such as Enron,[86] at various (auto)biographies of reformed corporate offenders including that of Jordan Belfort which was adapted into the commercially and critically successful movie *The Wolf of Wall Street*,[87] or at thinly veiled fictionalised accounts of such,[88] are the commonalties of the masculinised behaviour engaged in by (non-)criminal corporate actors. It is sometimes only a matter of the degree to which particular harmful activities are practiced

---

[82] In contrast to Ayers and Braithwaite's virtuous circle; I. Ayers & J. Braithwaite, *Responsive Regulation: Transcending the Deregulation Debate* (New York: Oxford University Press, 1992) at 82.

[83] D. R. Cressey, *Other People's Money: A Study in the Social Psychology of Embezzlement* (New York: Free Press, 1953).

[84] O'Connor, 'Women Executives' at 488.

[85] Messerschmidt, *Masculinities and Crime* at 135.

[86] R. Bryce, *Pipe Dreams: Greed, Ego, and the Death of Enron* (New York: Public Affairs, 2002) at 146.

[87] *Wolf of Wall Street* (Paramount, 2014). In addition to being nominated for 133 awards, including five Oscars, it is said to be the highest grossing film of Martin Scorsese's career, earning $392 million worldwide. See www.imdb.com/title/tt0993846/?ref_=nv_sr_1.

[88] G. Anderson, *Cityboy* (London: Headline Book Publishing, 2009). For an analysis of this book, see R. Smith, 'Masculinity, *doxa* and the institutionalisation of entrepreneurial identity in the novel *Cityboy*' (2010) 2(1) *International Journal of Gender and Entrepreneurship* 27.

and condoned that distinguishes a criminal from a non-criminal corporate environment and the various shades of grey in between. Accordingly, a more interesting angle to look at is criminological research on how convicted corporate offenders have sought to explain and neutralise their criminal wrongdoing. This will show the links between the local (within the corporation) and the regional (on a societal level) in terms of comprehensible gender performances. The primary focus in this section will be Klenowski et al.'s study of twenty male and twenty female convicted white-collar offenders because it brings together neutralisation techniques and hegemonic masculinity.[89]

Sykes and Matza introduced the influential concept of techniques of neutralisation in 1957, based in part on previous research by Sutherland[90] and Cressey,[91] to explain how delinquents can share society's values and respect for the law and yet justify breaking it.[92] They identified five main neutralisation techniques: denial of responsibility, denial of injury, denial of the victim, condemnation of the condemners and an appeal to higher loyalties. Although the concept was initially devised with reference to juvenile delinquency, Sykes and Matza hinted that these techniques could be useful in understanding white-collar offenders given the latter's commitment to conventional values.[93] Subsequent research into white-collar offenders has identified three further neutralisation techniques. Corporate criminals have claimed that their behaviour was normal, that they were entitled to act as they did and/or that it was necessary for them to break the law.[94]

Originally, neutralisation techniques were theorised as linguistic devices that allowed offenders to rationalise and legitimate their criminal wrongdoing before they committed the crime. However, partly due to difficulties in determining the causal order of the neutralisations and the offending (as research is typically conducted with convicts), it has now

---

[89] P. M. Klenowski, H. Copes & C.W. Mullins, 'Gender, Identity, and Accounts: How White Collar Offenders Do Gender When Making Sense of Their Crimes' (2011) 28(1) *Justice Quarterly* 46.

[90] E. H. Sutherland, *White Collar Crime* (Rome: Italiana Tecnico-Economica del Cemento, 1949).

[91] Cressey, *Other People's Money*.

[92] G. Sykes & D. Matza, 'Techniques of Neutralization: A Theory of Delinquency' (1957) 22 *American Sociological Review* 664 and 'Juvenile Delinquency and Subterranean Values' (1961) 26 *American Sociological Review* 712.

[93] Sykes & Matza, 'Techniques of Neutralization' at 479.

[94] See Klenowski et al., 'Gender, Identity, and Accounts' at 49.

been recognised that they can also operate as post-act rationalisations.[95] As such, neutralisation techniques function on two levels. On an internal level they permit and/or excuse the commission of crime, allowing the offender to maintain a favourable self-impression; on an external level they allow offenders to present a socially acceptable narrative of their behaviour and so justify it to others. On both of these levels, local and regional gender expectations are important because they frame our understandings of our own behaviour and the receptiveness of others to the explanations offered. There has been regrettably little research on the role of gender and neutralisation, but the research that has been done explains why, when white-collar criminals attempt to justify their offending, they do so in gender-appropriate ways.[96] This research also shows us that these gendered neutralisations derive not just from society more generally but also from the perpetrator's work environment. This is because the rationalisations relied upon by the offender could not have been called upon or been comprehensible if they were not already present in the corporate environment in which s/he was inculcated.[97]

Klenowski et al. found that the most common technique relied upon was that of an appeal to higher loyalties. In men, this manifested itself in the breadwinner/provider motif. Male offenders pointed not only to family breadwinning responsibilities but also to a wider category of dependents for whom they felt responsible, such as the need to save the company and thereby save the jobs of other employees.[98] That they personally profited from their illegal activities was incidental. By way of contrast, women highlighted their caregiving role and focused on familial relationships. Women also implicitly blamed the men in their lives for being ineffective breadwinners (even where this was due to illness on the part of the male partner). If men had fulfilled their duties as providers,

---

[95] Ibid.

[96] Cressey, *Other People's Money*; D. Zietz, *Women Who Embezzle or Defraud: A Study of Convicted Felons* (New York: Praeger Pub, 1981); K. Daly, 'Gender and Varieties of White Collar Crime' (1989) 27 *Criminology* 769; H. Copes & L. M. Vieraitis, *Identity Thieves: Motives and Methods* (Boston, MA: Northeastern University Press, 2012); L. M. Vieraitis, N. L. Piquero, A. R. Piquero, S. G. Tibbetts & M. Blankenship, 'Do Women and Men Differ in their Neutralizations of Corporate Crime?' (2012) 37(4) *Criminal Justice Review* 478; P. Klenowski, '"Learning the Good with the Bad": Are Occupational White-Collar Offenders Taught How to Neutralize Their Crimes?' (2012) 37(4) *Criminal Justice Review* 461; Klenowski et al., 'Gender, Identity, and Accounts'.

[97] Cressey, *Other People's Money* at 137; Klenowski, 'Gender, Identity, and Accounts'.

[98] F. S. Perri, 'White-Collar Criminals: The "Kinder, Gentler" Offender?' (2011) 8 *J. Invetig. Psych. Offender Profil*. 217 at 223. Klenowski et al., 'Gender, Identity, and Accounts' at 55.

then they would not have been forced into the active 'male' roles of breadwinner and offender.[99] As a side note, the male worker/breadwinner role and female caretaker/economic dependency roles have also been found to be significant in terms of accessing sentencing leniency in more traditional street crime cases.[100] This ties in with research undertaken by Stadler and Benson that white-collar offenders engage in similar neutralisation processes to other offenders, despite demographic differences between the groups.[101]

In keeping with Levin's insight that competence is not a gender-neutral word, but one infused with masculine-coded traits, Klenowski et al. also found that it was easier for women to deny responsibility for their actions, often blaming their bosses, than it was for men. Referencing Connell, they explained:

> In part, these women were trading on the acceptability of women not being in control or fully knowledgeable about the details and particulars of their work tasks. While men would be expected to have as much information within an organization as possible to present an image of competence and justify promotion, women's historical experiences of limited advancement provide a socially validated shield for their lack of knowledge and competence.[102]

They also found that the few men who accessed the technique claimed their lack of responsibility was due to ill-health, 'one of the few acceptable ways for men attempting a hegemonic presentation of self to deny responsibility'.[103] This insight may explain Stadler and Benson's finding that the male white-collar offenders they studied were more willing to take responsibility for their actions than were the ordinary offenders interviewed.[104] Klenowski et al. also found that men were less likely than women to try to access the claim of necessity because doing so would signify that they were unable to compete with other men without resorting to crime which would threaten their masculine identity.[105]

[99] Klenowski, 'Gender, Identity, and Accounts' at 60; Klenowski, '"Learning the Good with the Bad"' at 467–468.

[100] Gathings & Parrotta, 'Gendered Narratives in the Courtroom' at 673.

[101] White-collar offenders tend to be older, married, have higher socio-economic status and better levels of education, and are less likely to have prior convictions; W. A. Stadler & M. L. Benson, 'Revisiting the Guilty Mind: The Neutralization of White-Collar Crime' (2012) 37(4) *Criminal Justice Review* 494 at 500.

[102] Klenowski et al., 'Gender, Identity, and Accounts' at 62.   [103] Ibid.

[104] Stadler & Benson, 'Revisiting the Guilty Mind' at 505.

[105] Klenowski et al., 'Gender, Identity, and Accounts' at 66.

Corroborating Cressey's 1953 research on embezzlers,[106] Klenowski et al. found that denial of injury was commonly used by males, typically by reframing their fraudulent acts as borrowing.[107] While women also invoked this neutralisation device, they did so less frequently than men. Again relying on Connell, the authors postulate that 'the demands of emphasised femininity ... direct women to be attentive to the consequences of their behaviors on the lives and experiences of others. ... It is likely that denying injury has less cultural credibility when done by someone who is expected to be hyper-attuned to unjust injuries'.[108] A point not noticed by the authors is that representing their crime as borrowing also becomes a denial that the law was broken at all. Research on convicted white-collar offenders has found that many of them do not regard what they did as criminal. They do not regard their actions as equivalent to those of 'real' criminals,[109] and are correspondingly less likely than ordinary offenders to express guilt for their offences or to accept the application of the criminal label.[110] The impact of gender expectations was also evident in the frequency with which men condemned the condemners as compared to women. This is because 'Males are expected to challenge hierarchies to advance within them. Women have historically been expected to accede to authority, legitimate or not'.[111]

The claim of normality supports corporate offenders' attempts to deny criminality. As Benson perceptively notes, it allows them to distinguish themselves from street offenders whose crimes often involve conduct which is out of the ordinary.[112] It also reflects the misanthropic view of society that is held by white-collar offenders, where everyone is dishonest and self-interested and those who do not engage in legally questionable practices are naïve.[113] For the antitrust convicts in Benson's study, if all avenues towards obtaining profit were not pursued, then 'one is not really

---

[106] Cressey, *Other People's Money*.

[107] Klenowski et al., 'Gender, Identity, and Accounts' at 55.   [108] Ibid. at 64.

[109] Perri, 'White-Collar Criminals' at 223; M. L. Benson, 'Denying the Guilty Mind: Accounting for Involvement in White-Collar Crime' (1985) 23(4) *Criminology* 583 at 592–593, 594, 595–596 (looking at anti-trust violators, tax offenders and embezzlers).

[110] Stadler & Benson, 'Revisiting the Guilty Mind' at 505–506. See too Sutherland, *White Collar Crime* at 222–225.

[111] Klenowski et al., 'Gender, Identity, and Accounts' at 65.

[112] Benson, 'Denying the Guilty Mind' at 599.

[113] Perri, 'White-Collar Criminals' at 224; J. W. Coleman, *The Criminal Elite: Understanding White-Collar Crime*, 6th ed. (New York: Worth, 2006) at 207.

"in business"'.[114] This belief that corruption is endemic and necessary in business is not confined to corporate offenders. A 2013 survey of the Wall Street financial services sector undertaken by Labaton Sucharow, a New York-based law firm, found that 52 per cent of those surveyed believed that their competitors engaged in unethical or unlawful behaviour in order to gain a competitive edge and 29 per cent believed that it was necessary to do so in order to be successful in the industry. Indeed, 26 per cent believed that bonus structures within the industry incentivised such behaviour.[115] A subsequent survey of the US and UK financial services industries found that 47 per cent believed that their competitors engaged in unethical or illegal activity (increasing to 51 per cent where the respondent earned $500,000 or more per annum) and 33 per cent believed that bonus structures encouraged such behaviour.[116] A number of the participants in Klenowski et al.'s study spoke about learning the tricks of the trade from others when they began to work and that this entailed pushing the law to its limits and beyond.[117] Finally, Levi suggests that a sense of masculine entitlement may lie behind some corporate crime: 'they cannot face the inability to maintain a comfortable lifestyle following their anticipated bankruptcy'.[118] Klenowski et al. similarly found a strong sense of entitlement expressed by the men they interviewed.[119] From Connell's perspective, this sense of entitlement would be one of the side-effects of the patriarchal system, where men's status as men is sufficient merit for reward.

12.4 Conclusion

In this chapter I introduced the concept of hegemonic masculinity and considered its application in sociological and criminological literature. This was done to contest popular analysis after the recent crash that proposed the insertion of women into corporate governance structures

---

[114] Benson, 'Denying the Guilty Mind' at 593.

[115] Labaton Sucharow U.S. Financial Services Industry Survey, *Wall Street in Crisis: A Perfect Storm Looming* (July 2013) at 6.

[116] Labaton Sucharow & University of Notre Dame, *The Street, The Bull and The Crisis: A Survey of the US & UK Financial Services Industry* (May 2015) at 3.

[117] Klenowski, '"Learning the Good with the Bad"' at 471–472.

[118] M. Levi, 'Masculinities and white-collar crime' in T. Newburn & A. Stanko (eds.), *Just Boys Doing Business? Men Masculinities and Crime* (London: Routledge, 1996) 234 at 247.

[119] Klenowski et al., 'Gender, Identity, and Accounts' at 57.

as the prophylactic against future recklessness in high finance. The socio-logical literature shows that it is not men, per se, who were responsible for the behaviour that enabled the crash. Instead it was the performance of particular forms of socially constructed and enforced masculinity that predominate in corporate environments. The criminological literature on neutralisation techniques illustrated not only that convicted offenders drew from cultural understandings of appropriate masculine and feminine behaviours but also that they drew from beliefs prevalent within their particular local subculture, namely their workplaces and the corporate sector. It also shows us that women can and do engage in corporate crime[120] and so are not immune to the temptations of the corporate sector simply by virtue of their sex. Taken together, this literature tells us that it is insufficient to 'add women and stir' and expect that corporate governance issues will be resolved. As O'Connor notes, 'rather than women changing corporations . . . corporations are more likely to change women' as 'occu-pational experiences will override socialized gender roles'.[121]

Accordingly, it is necessary to make visible the gendered nature of the problematic individual, group and corporate practices and reshape them at local, regional and ultimately global levels. This is because the gen-dered recklessness that was implicated in the recent recession was not unique to it or to individual bad apples. Gendered behaviour within corporations has played and continues to play a role in other ongoing economic, social and environmental harms. As Collinson and Hearn note (albeit with a focus on men rather than masculinities),

> it is . . . important to examine the *consequences* of men's continued dominance of organizational processes . . . [such as] the lack of long-term vision in policy, strategy or investment decisions, low employee morale, poor communication and negative working relationships, the absence of research and design initiatives (e.g. regarding ecological issues), the increasingly large salaries of senior managers and board members and even the proliferation of white collar crime.[122]

---

[120] As with crime more generally, men disproportionately represent the majority of corpor-ate offenders and when women are involved in corporate crime they tend to profit less. For an interesting discussion see Steffensmeier et al., 'Gender and Twenty-First-Century Corporate Crime'.

[121] O'Connor, 'Women Executives' at 475. See also Ch. 7, Section 7.5 on the importance of moving away from the mere symbolic representation of women on boards to a changed model where women are active participants at board level.

[122] D. Collinson & J. Hearn, 'Naming Men as Men: Implications for Work, Organization and Management' (1994) 1(1) *Gender, Work and Organization* 2 at 17. Emphasis in original.

In order to address the behaviours identified in this chapter, which are but one manifestation of the problematic gendering of corporate culture, it is necessary to focus on the specific environment in which these behaviours are enacted and change the conditions that foster them. Gobert and Punch's promotion of the socially responsible company, conceived of with a view to reducing corporate crime, may provide a model for doing so.

Gobert and Punch propose individual self-regulation, where companies are responsible for monitoring themselves, subject to oversight by professional or statutory reviewing bodies.[123] This may not seem like a radical reform because internal compliance officers and other safeguards are common in companies, yet unsustainable, unethical and sometimes illegal practices persist. There are many reasons for this, including the fact that the benefits of breaching laws often outweigh the costs of being caught[124] and that compliance officers often lack clout within organisations or are beholden to them.[125] However, if compliance officers were able to draw external support from 'representatives of non-governmental organisations ... public interest groups, worker associations and other "stakeholders"'[126] whose interests are not solely focused on short-term goals like profit-generation, then they would be more effective at identifying and stopping unethical and unsustainable business practices at individual, group and corporate levels. Gobert and Punch also suggest that stakeholders could be appointed to boards of directors or given powers to institute legal proceedings 'as representatives of the public interest to hold directors to their fiduciary obligations, including those to society'.[127] Such an interference in corporate governance structures is warranted, they believe, because companies are given various rights and privileges by the State, in exchange for which they should be obligated to conduct business in a socially responsible manner.[128]

---

[123] J. Gobert & M. Punch, *Rethinking Corporate Crime* (London: Lexis Nexis, 2003) at 325.

[124] See, e.g., T. Newburn, *Criminology*, 3rd ed. (Abingdon, Oxon: Routledge, 2017) at 425; N. Groombridge, 'Masculinities and Crimes against the Environment' (1998) 2(2) *Theoretical Criminology* 249 at 249–250.

[125] Gobert & Punch, *Rethinking Corporate Crime* at 329–330.   [126] Ibid. at 331.

[127] Ibid. at 345.

[128] Ibid. at 342. In order to protect public interest directors from the possible effects of groupthink, where the search for consensus in small groups can override independence, I would recommend that they be appointed for one-off time-limited terms. For a useful summary of the literature on groupthink see O'Connor, 'Women Executives' at 495–497.

This externally supported pressure on companies to act responsibly, in addition to encouraging more socially and environmentally sustainable corporate practice at the regional and possibly global level if the companies operate multinationally, would also push corporations towards more ethical behaviour in their daily internal operations through the adoption of positive (codes of ethics and best practice) and negative (anti-sexism, anti-racism and anti-bullying policies) self-governance mechanisms. On a practical level, the enforcement of these codes would be particularly effective if bonuses and promotions were linked to them[129] rather than primarily to the ability to generate profits, which, as approximately a quarter to a third of respondents to the Labaton Sucharow surveys believe, is conducive to illegality.[130] If the prioritisation of profits does this, it is also likely to promote other practices that are less illegal but no less serious in terms of their social or environmental consequences. To further encourage compliance, the outcomes of disciplinary proceedings, including a summary of the facts that led to them, should be published to show that the company takes violations seriously.[131] A more ethical work environment will necessarily result in better working conditions for all employees, but particularly for women. This is because the problematic masculine-coded performances that have been considered in this chapter would no longer be tolerated, thus reducing or removing gendered barriers to women's advancement and ultimately leading to more women in corporate governance roles. This is an egalitarian good in and of itself independent of any financial benefit to the company or the economy[132] that is problematically assumed to derive from essentialist conceptions of feminine reasoning or from a gendering of the concept of corporate responsibility (and the consequent ghettoising of female executives in such roles[133]).

Obviously a self-regulatory approach is not the panacea to corporate governance issues; as noted previously, various forms of corporate malfeasance continue despite the existence of compliance mechanisms. Nonetheless, there are good reasons to be optimistic about the usefulness of a self-regulatory approach as one of the means by which greater

---

[129] Gobert & Punch, *Rethinking Corporate Crime* at 324.
[130] See text accompanying fn. 114 and fn. 115.
[131] Gobert & Punch, *Rethinking Corporate Crime* at 333.
[132] See Ch. 6, Section 6.3.3. Indeed, as Lynch-Fannon notes, the economic and social justice benefits of equality are stronger arguments in favour of more women on boards than the benefits to the company itself. (Sections 6.2 and 6.3.1–6.3.2).
[133] O'Connor, 'Women Executives' at 470.

corporate sustainability can be achieved.[134] The literature reviewed in this chapter shows us that corporate actors are part of corporate and societal culture rather than autonomous individuals who stand apart from it, and as such they will respond to norm-setting cues in their social environment. Indeed, as professionals who have frequently invested time and effort in order to position themselves to attain success through respectable means – employment in the corporate sector – corporate actors are ideal candidates for normative measures designed to nudge them towards socially, economically and environmentally sustainable behaviour. To return to Connell, hegemonies are not immutable. Masculinities and femininities are relational and shifting, which means that corporate culture can be changed for the better if there is sufficient will to do so. At some point, the increasing economic, social and environmental costs of conducting business as usual will make such change imperative.

---

[134] Others could include the establishment of more publicly funded regulatory agencies to ensure that the self-regulation is effective, or increasing the funding to existing agencies, such as the Office of Corporate Enforcement. The recent collapse of a high-profile criminal case in Ireland, which has been blamed in part on inadequate resourcing, is evidence of the importance of not only having such offices but also of ensuring that they are able to properly pursue prosecutions. For a history of the case and its faults see C. Kenna, '"Get Seánie": The Prosecution of Seán Fitzpatrick' (27 May 2017) *Irish Times*.

Power and the Gender Imperative in Corporate Law

CAROL LIAO

13.1 Introduction

Business and power are intertwined concepts. Identifying a correlation between the two, however, requires an intervening variable of capital. Within our capitalist system, a reasonable presumption can be made that greater success in business generally correlates to a greater accumulation of capital, which tends to correlate to greater power, and vice versa. This is the case whether one's starting point is significant capital (translating to more power and likelihood of business success) or power (greater access to capital and entrepreneurial success). Thus an advantage lies in one's starting point, and it is important to remember the male-dominated history that belies the storied rise of big business, pooling of capital, and concentration of power in the world.[1] In the last few decades, women have made 'unprecedented gains in rights, education, health, and access to jobs and livelihoods', but there are significant gaps that remain.[2] Among other things, the World Bank notes that women represent 40 percent of the world's labour force but hold just 1 percent of the world's wealth.[3] If women constitute over 50 percent of the world's population, what does holding 1 percent of the world's capital signify in terms of power? And the more pressing question: Will the allocation of power meaningfully diffuse across gender lines in the foreseeable future?

In his 1954 book *The 20th Century Capitalist Revolution*, Adolf Berle observed how the corporation has become the chief centre of power outside of government. Include in that pervasive corporate lobbying,

---

[1] P. Stearns, *Gender in World History*, 2nd ed. (New York: Routledge, 2000), p. 8, noting 'men's characteristic superiority in power throughout world history, at least in terms of cultural standards, law and economic position, and very often in personal life as well'.

[2] World Bank, *2012 World development report on gender equality and development*, see www.worldbank.org.

[3] Stearns, 'Gender in World History', p. 10.

the privileged status of financial capital, the growth of multinational enterprises and global supply chains, and the expansion of cross-border technological innovations, and corporations can be said to 'rival the state, and certainly the church, in institutional power and influence'.[4] There are many legal concepts addressing different power dynamics within the corporation. Directors and officers hold certain powers, shareholders hold certain powers, creditors hold certain remedial powers, and other stakeholders may also hold powerful influences. Part and parcel with these doctrinal divisions of power are other notions of power that have a pervasive impact on human ordering. Berle remarked on how in practice, corporations are guided by 'tiny self-perpetuating oligarchies' that are only indirectly judged by public consensus and state regulation, noting that:

> Change of management by contesting for stockholders' votes is extremely rare, and increasingly difficult and expensive to the point of impossibility. The legal presumption in favor of management, and the natural unwillingness of courts to control or reverse management action save in cases of the more elementary types of dishonesty or fraud, leaves management with substantially absolute power. Thus the only real control which guides or limits their economic and social action is the real, though undefined and tacit, philosophy of the men who compose them.[5]

The 'philosophy of the men' in power is reflected in the normative underpinnings that guide the trajectory of regulatory development. This 'normative muscle'[6] affects the decisions that corporations make every day, directly and indirectly influencing the ways in which issues are identified as problems, how such problems are solved, and whose interests are protected.[7]

A growing number of corporations worldwide have made pointed efforts to increase the number of women on boards and in management

---

[4] K. Testy, 'Linking Progressive Corporate Law and Progressive Social Movements' (2002) 76 *Tulane Law Review* 1228.

[5] A. Berle, *The 20th Century Capitalist Revolution* (New York: Harcourt, 1954), p. 180.

[6] J. Sarra, 'Oversight, hindsight, and foresight: Canadian corporate governance through the lens of global capital markets' in J. Sarra (ed.), *Corporate Governance in Global Capital Markets* (Vancouver: UBC Press, 2003), p. 42.

[7] Institutional law and economics and new institutional economics may be useful to consider how dialogues and institutions are shaped. Significance rests on the issue of whose rights are enabled through law, as well as on the subsequent structures that perpetuate those rights. N. Mercuro & S. Medema, *Economics and the Law: From Posner to Post-Modernism and Beyond*, 2nd ed. (Princeton, NJ: Princeton University Press, 2004), p. 225.

positions but the numbers indicate there is still a significant way to go.[8] The level of gender diversity in public company boardrooms in countries without quotas has only grown incrementally.[9] While there may be some comfort in seeing the steady albeit slow rise of women up the corporate ranks, it is noteworthy that progress in the past decade has remained stubbornly low. For S&P 1500 companies, the share of board seats held by women has only grown from 11 percent in 2006 to 14 percent in 2012, and women are also underrepresented as chairs of compensation, audit, and nominating committees, which are among the most influential board positions.[10] At these rates of change, 'it would take almost 70 years before women's representation on corporate boards reached parity with that of men'.[11]

When contemplating the future diffusion of power, it is critical to consider how gender plays a role in the construction of our corporate institutions and the regulatory infrastructure that governs them. The lack of women in executive positions and corporate boardrooms is a direct consequence of our male-dominated history, and so are the laws and norms guiding the institutions that hold these positions. This chapter aims to tackle some difficult questions related to business and power through the lens of feminist legal theory, and provide an unapologetic and ambitious call to redesign existing power structures and internal power dynamics that are leading our world into environmental crises.

There is a long and complex history on the social construction of gender, issues in intersectionality, and national and jurisdiction-specific problems, and of course presumptions are always vulnerable to anecdotal counterexamples. As a visible minority cisgender female, focusing solely on gender at the expense of race, class, and other power dynamics can be a bitter pill to swallow, although at times necessarily strategic. For example, many regulators have chosen to address diversity in the business world by focusing solely on gender, citing manageability as the main reason,[12] and for proponents of diversity, a gendered focus is an

---

[8] S. Devillard, S. Sancier-Sultan & C. Werner, *Moving mind-sets on gender diversity: McKinsey global survey results* (McKinsey & Company, January 2014) see http://mckinsey.com.

[9] Catalyst, *2014 Catalyst census: Women Board Directors*, see www.catalyst.org; D. Rhode & A. Packel, 'Diversity on Corporate Boards: How Much Difference Does It Make?' (2014) 39 (2) *Delaware Journal of Corporate Law* 381.

[10] Rhode & Packel, 'Diversity on Corporate Boards'.   [11] Ibid.

[12] See, e.g., Canadian Coalition for Good Governance, *CCGG Policy on board gender diversity* (October 2015), see www.ccgg.ca, which states 'CCGG's adoption of a board

acceptable first step, and far better than nothing. Other challenges include the fact that priorities differ when addressing gender from a business perspective versus a sociological one. The theoretical foundations, context, sources, and terminology are different. One must navigate through these differences and essentially contested concepts carefully in order to preserve the value of one's analysis across different readerships and backgrounds.

This chapter begins in Section 13.2 with a short primer on the social construction of gender, and how society continuously reinforces different behaviour from men and women. Section 13.3 then identifies some entrenched ideological beliefs in corporate law and highlights the gendered predispositions imbued in them. Next, building upon the work of Kellye Testy, Section 13.4 draws upon feminist legal theory to emphasize the critical partnership that must be forged between it and corporate sustainability to overcome the formidable challenges in attaining a greener future. Section 13.5 then emphasizes the pervasiveness of gendered norms by highlighting how invisible implicit biases also prevent or slow the rise of women in the corporate world. These invisible power imbalances within the corporation need to be widely recognized as they subvert the ability of women to attain meaningful positions of power that instigate change. Section 13.6 concludes.

13.2   Gender as a Social Construct

Gender is a social construction that assigns behaviours and values based on biological facts.[13] At birth people are subjected to socialised notions of what constitutes 'masculine' and 'feminine' characteristics and behaviours, which are reinforced throughout their lives. If one is male, there are societal expectations as to how a male is to look, dress, and behave. The same is true for a female, but with a different set of expectations. Studies have shown the impact environment has on gendered behaviour,

---

gender diversity policy should not be interpreted as a sign that the lack of other forms of diversity is less deserving of remediation. Since women comprise half the population and remain persistently under-represented on boards, however, gender is an appropriate focus'.

[13] J. Lorber, *Paradoxes of Gender* (New Haven, CT: Yale University Press, 1994), p. 13.

from the way babies are held,[14] to the types of toys marketed for children,[15] to sports,[16] education,[17] careers,[18] parenting,[19] etc. Gender roles can be defined as the 'behaviors and ways of thinking and feeling that the culture teaches are appropriate for the two genders'[20] which informs one how to function within society in order to belong. Penelope Eckert and Sally McConnell-Ginet note how 'the world swarms with ideas about gender – and these ideas are so commonplace that we take it for granted that they are true, accepting common adage as scientific fact'.[21] As Judith Lorber describes, 'Gender is so pervasive that in our society we assume it is bred into our genes'.[22]

As a social institution, gender 'is a process of creating distinguishable social statuses for the assignment of rights and responsibilities'.[23] Although gender roles have varied somewhat among differing cultures at different points in history, there has been a historic division between the two binary options of male and female.[24] Gender is one of the major ways that human beings organize their lives: 'Human society depends on a predictable division of labor, a designated allocation of scarce goods, assigned responsibility for children and others who cannot care for themselves, common values and their systematic transmission to new members, legitimate leadership, music, art, stories, games, and other symbolic productions'.[25] Our learned responses to gender cover a wide range of interactions, and 'are re-enforced by

---

[14] C. R. Beal, *Boys and Girls: The Development of Gender Roles* (New York: McGraw-Hill, 1994), identifying several sociological influences from the moment of birth.

[15] See, e.g., C. Auster & C. Mansbach, 'The Gender Marketing of Toys: An Analysis of Color and Type of Toy on the Disney Store website' (October 2012) 67 *Sex Roles* 375–388.

[16] See, e.g., M. Messner, M. Duncan & K. Jensen, 'Separating the Men from the Girls: The Gendered Language of Televised Sports' (1993) 7 *Gender & Society* 121–137.

[17] See, e.g., R. Bigler, 'The Role of Classification Skill in Moderating Environmental Influences on Children's Genderstereotyping: A Study of the Functional Use of Gender in the Classroom' (1995) 66 *Child Development* 1072–1087.

[18] See, e.g., E. Reuben, P. Sapienza & L. Zingales, 'How Stereotypes Impair Women's Careers in Science' (2014) 111 *Proceedings of the National Academy of Sciences* 4403–4408.

[19] See, e.g., H. Lytton & D. Romney, 'Parents' Differential Socialization of Boys and Girls: A Meta-analysis' (1991) 109 *Psychological Bulletin* 267.

[20] L. Girshwick, *Transgender Voices: Beyond Women and Men* (Hanover, NH: University Press of New England, 2008).

[21] P. Eckert & S. McConnell-Ginet, *Language and Gender*, 2nd ed. (Cambridge, MA: Cambridge University Press, 2013), p. 1.

[22] Lorber, 'Paradoxes', p. 13.   [23] Ibid., p. 56.

[24] Stearns, 'Gender and World History'.   [25] Lorber, 'Paradoxes', p. 60.

the government, legal system, schools, religious groups, family, social groups, and other systems'.[26] Lori Girshwick notes how 'what we believe – how we think about ourselves, our relationships, our social world – has less to do with scientific or biological "facts" and more to do with profound familial, cultural, and social training that reinforces what is considered "normal"'.[27] There is a cultural learning loop, in that we are subjected to constant images and messages about gender from the moment of birth, and then, in turn, we contribute to the construction of the gendered system and its power.[28] Society continuously reinforces and rewards different types of behaviour from men and women.[29] Gender roles can evolve, and in some cultures there has been a general acceptance of some blending of roles.[30] Nevertheless, the pervasiveness of norms maintains 'hierarchical political structures, economic systems, and social conventions that benefit those at the top of the pyramid',[31] and these existing power inequities are deeply entrenched.

The relevance of gender in social ordering is apparent when considering the norms that belie the construction of corporate legal theory and accompanying institutions. Section 13.3 considers embedded ideological beliefs and norms that echo from history, which developed largely absent of female voices. Berle's observation that it is the philosophy of men in power evokes not only the customary language of that generation but also the predominance of the male gender in the corporate world. Testy points out:

> For feminism, theory built without context is at best hollow and at worst dangerous, because the hollowness is likely to be filled by norms of privilege. For example, when no race is specified, that silence codes as white; when no sex is specified, that silence codes as male. Thus, contractarianism's hypothetical bargainer, with no race, no gender, no class, no sexual orientation—in short no social location—fails to address the power disparities that flow from structural societal inequalities.[32]

---

[26] Ibid.   [27] Girshwick, 'Transgender Voices', p. 5.   [28] Lorber, 'Paradoxes', p. 13.

[29] A. Eagly, *Sex Differences in Social Behavior: A Social-Role Interpretation* (Hillsdale: Lawrence Erlbaum Associates, 1987).

[30] K. Steinmetz, 'Beyond he or she: how a new generation is redefining the meaning of gender' (2017) *Time Magazine*.

[31] Lorber, 'Paradoxes', p. 61.

[32] K. Testy, 'Capitalism and Freedom – For Whom?: Feminist Legal Theory and Progressive Corporate Law' (2004) 67 *Law and Contemporary Problems* 87 at 108.

Testy's analysis on the default nature of particular norms of privilege needs to be kept close at hand when reflecting upon entrenched beliefs in corporate law, as discussed in the next section.

13.3   Embedded Norms in Corporate Law

In their well-known 2001 article 'The End of History for Corporate Law', Henry Hansmann and Reinier Kraakman held that 'the triumph of the shareholder-oriented model of the corporation over its principal competitors is now assured', as the basic law of corporate governance had already achieved a high degree of uniformity to the shareholder primacy model and 'continued convergence towards [this] single, standard model is likely'.[33] They noted:

> Logic alone did not establish the superiority of this standard model or of the prescriptive rules that it implies, which establish a strong corporate management with duties to serve the interests of shareholders alone, and strong minority shareholder protections. Rather, the standard model earned its position as the dominant model of the large corporation the hard way, by out-competing during the post-World-War-II period the three alternative models of corporate governance: the managerialist model, the labor-oriented model, and the state-oriented model.[34]

Hansmann and Kraakman's article reverberated in corporate legal scholarship, both positively and negatively. It is one of the most cited articles of all time,[35] and has led to a number of responses from prominent scholars around the world,[36] including those challenging Hansmann and Kraakman's base observations on likely convergence,[37] and follow-up

---

[33] H. Hansmann & R. Kraakman, 'The End of History for Corporate Law' (2001) 89 *Georgetown Law Journal* 439 at 439.

[34] Ibid., p. 468.

[35] F. Shapiro & M. Pearse, 'The Most-Cited Law Review Articles of All Time', (2012) 110 *Michigan Law Review* 8 at 1495.

[36] See generally, e.g., M. A. Welsh, P. Spender, I. Lynch Fannon & K. Hall, 'The End of the "End of History for Corporate Law"?', (2014) 29 *Australian Journal of Corporate Law* 147; K. Greenfield, *The Failure of Corporate Law* (University of Chicago Press, 2007).

[37] For example, Irene Lynch Fannon has argued extensively that the European model of corporate governance has proven to be much more robust than Hansmann and Kraakmann's prediction. See I. Lynch Fannon, *Working within Two Kinds of Capitalism*, (Oxford: Hart Publications, 2003); I. Lynch Fannon, 'Employees as Corporate Stakeholders: Theory and Reality in a Transatlantic Context' (2004) 27 *Journal of Corporate Law Studies* 155. See further I. Lynch Fannon, 'The European Social Model of Corporate Governance: Prospects for Success in an Enlarged Europe' in P. Ali and G. Gregoriou

articles from Hansmann and Kraakman themselves.[38] Regardless of the validity of one's theoretical arguments for or against shareholder primacy, pervasive norms perpetuate the continued domination of this mainstream model and act as formidable barriers to true transformational change. These normative beliefs permeated the psyche of corporate governance practices in global capital markets.[39]

The first entrenched belief is that the purpose of the corporation should be to maximise the wealth of its shareholders only, which in turn will increase the wealth of society.[40] Many regard the singular pursuit of shareholder wealth maximisation as necessary for the efficient management of the corporation. Michael Jensen declares that 'it is logically impossible to maximise in more than one dimension at the same time ... The result will be confusion and a lack of purpose that will handicap the firm in its competition for survival'.[41] He echoes Adam Smith's concept of the invisible hand, insisting that '200 years' worth of work in economics and finance indicate that social welfare is maximised when all firms in an economy attempt to maximise their own total firm value'.[42] The convenience of calculating efficiency based on the normative view of shareholder wealth vis-à-vis share price is that it 'frequently

---

(eds.), *International Corporate Governance after Sarbanes-Oxley* (Hoboken, NJ: John Wiley & Sons, 2006), ch. 20; I. Lynch Fannon, 'From Workers to Global Politics: How the Way We Work Provides Answers to Corporate Governance Questions' in J. O'Brien (ed.), *Governing the Corporation, Regulation and Corporate Governance in an Age of Scandal and Global Markets* (London: Wiley Publications, 2005); I. Lynch Fannon, 'Corporate Responsibility and European Corporate Governance: The View from Now' in A. Beck and P. Sheehy Skeffington (eds.), *The Impact of European Law on the Corporate World* (Dublin: Irish Centre for European Law, 2009).

[38] H. Hansmann & R. Kraakman, 'Reflections on the End of History for Corporate Law' in A. Rasheed & T. Yoshikawa (eds.), *Convergence of Corporate Governance: Promise and Prospects* (London: Palgrave-Macmillan, Yale Law & Economics Research Paper no. 449, 2012); H. Hansmann, 'How Close Is the End of History?', (2006) 31 *Journal of Corporate Law* 8, pp. 745–752.

[39] Section 13.2 borrows liberally from select portions of Section 2.1 on entrenched ideological beliefs in C. Liao, 'Limits to Corporate Reform and Alternative Legal Structures' in B. Sjåfjell & B. Richardson (eds.), *Company Law and Sustainability: Legal Barriers and Opportunities* (Cambridge: Cambridge University Press, 2015), p. 274.

[40] This dogma has been at the core of modern economics since A. Smith, 'An Inquiry into the Nature and Causes of the Wealth of Nations' (1776) 1 *Eighteenth Century Collections Online* 1.1.2.

[41] M. Jensen, 'Value Maximization, Stakeholder Theory, and the Corporate Objective Function' (2001) 14 *Journal of Applied Corporate Finance* 8, pp. 10–11.

[42] Ibid., p. 11.

externalizes particular costs of corporate activity such as environmental or consumer harms'.[43] Thus, corporations may choose to be unhampered by externalities such as social and environmental consequences, and allow others to bear external costs that are not reflected in share or bond prices. Corporations are then only beholden to externalities that are regarded as serious enough to be protected (and adequately enforced) by external regulatory means, without having to comprehend the negative impact their collective actions have on the environment beyond those regulations. The ability for corporations to ignore these negative effects simplifies questions of accountability, perpetuating power inequities in the model.

The second belief, which builds upon the first, is that stakeholder interests are adequately protected through separate public regulation, such as pollution control legislation, labour regulation, and human rights standards, rather than through corporations that supposedly tend to lack the expertise, resources, or legitimacy to address such problems. As more studies show how long-term economic benefits are often realised from corporate social responsibility (CSR) practices, CSR advocates are motivated to trumpet those economic benefits over environmental concerns in order to garner the attention of profit-focused managers. Since CSR is able to co-exist alongside shareholder primacy – despite significant temporal challenges that heavily favour short-termism[44] – there tends to be little desire to reform the model in order to incorporate stakeholder interests beyond what companies are already driven to do from the market.

Finally, the third belief is that shareholder primacy is superior to alternative models. As noted previously, Hansmann and Kraakman contend that shareholder primacy has 'earned its position as the dominant model' as alternative models have already been tried and have failed.[45] Despite strenuous counterarguments from scholars around the world that other models have not failed,[46] that shareholder primacy is not

---

[43] J. Sarra, 'Oversight, hindsight, and foresight', p. 41.

[44] See, e.g., F. Brochet, G. Serafeim & M. Loumioti, 'Short-termism: Don't Blame the Investors' (June 2012) *Harvard Business Review* 1 (citing empirical research that suggests short-termism is rooted in corporate culture).

[45] Hansmann & Kraakman, 'End of History', pp. 443–447.

[46] See, e.g., I. Lynch Fannon, *Working within Two Kinds*, 'The European Social Model' and 'From Workers to Global Politics'; see also William T. Allen, 'Contracts and Communities in Corporation Law' (1993) 50 *Washington and Lee Law Review* 1 (addressing how philosophical differences create different views of the corporation).

reflected in corporate laws,[47] and other compelling counterarguments,[48] the lack of strong oppositional consensus on what consists of a better alternative to the shareholder primacy model only bolsters the belief that the existing model is superior. Other than modest countervailing pressures, there is little to no collective contrary support pushing for the adoption of another nation's model. Alternative discourse has been classified in an assortment of approaches and models, such as the communitarian approach,[49] the team production theory,[50] systems theory (or 'enterprise corporatism'),[51] the director primacy model,[52] and as later discussed, progressive corporate law.[53] Each theoretical model carries its own views on what corporate rules and structures should prevail, how value is measured, and whose rights should be protected. The shareholder primacy model will endure if there continues to be a lack of consensus for an alternative course.

Using the lens provided by Testy, there are legitimate concerns that arise from the observation of these pervasive norms within the business world. How are the 'power disparities that flow from structural societal inequalities' addressed?[54] It seems not at all. Power, in fact, is tacitly regarded as something earned, and the dominance of the shareholder primacy model itself is due to its competitive 'superiority' over other alternative models. Beyond state regulations, corporations are to focus solely on shareholder interests, which disregards the significant influence

---

[47] See, e.g., C. Liao, 'A Canadian Model of Corporate Governance' (2014) 37 (2) *Dalhousie Law Journal* 559. The multijurisdictional research of the Sustainable Companies Project highlights how, despite normative assumptions, shareholder primacy is not the law in any of the investigated countries. University of Oslo, Faculty of Law, Sustainable Companies, see jus.uio.no/companies under Projects, Concluded; B. Sjåfjell, A. Johnston, L. Anker-Sørensen and D. Millon, 'Shareholder Primacy: The Main Barrier to Sustainable Companies', in B. Sjåfjell & B. Richardson (eds.), *Company Law and Sustainability: Legal Barriers and Opportunities* (Cambridge: Cambridge University Press, 2015), pp. 79–147.

[48] See, e.g., L. R. Rotman, 'Debunking the "End of History" Thesis for Corporate Law' (2010) 33 *Boston College International & Comparative Law Review*.

[49] See, e.g., D. Millon, 'Communitarianism in corporate law: foundations and law reform strategies' in L. E. Mitchell (eds.), *Progressive Corporate Law: New Perspectives on Law, Culture and Society* (Boulder, CO: Westview Press, 1995).

[50] M. Blair & L. Stout, 'A Team Production Theory of Corporate Law' (1999) 85 *Virginia Law Review* 248.

[51] G. Teubner, 'Enterprise Corporatism: New Industrial Policy and the "Essence" of the Legal Person' (1988) 36 *American Journal of Comparative Law*.

[52] S. Bainbridge, 'Director Primacy: The Means and Ends of Corporate Governance' (2003) 97 *Northwestern University Law Review* 547.

[53] Mitchell, 'Progressive Corporate Law'.   [54] Testy, 'Capitalism and Freedom', p. 108.

of corporate lobbying on legislative rollbacks, the paucity of environmental regulation, the disadvantage to marginalised voices and lack of
access to justice in cases when non-shareholder stakeholders' rights are
encroached by corporate behaviour, among other power imbalances.
Janis Sarra also notes how

> most theoretical approaches to corporate governance are modelled on
> strong historical notions of property and thus on a particular distribution
> of economic power that is highly gendered within the marketplace. They
> generally fail to articulate and value the experience and contributions of
> women to the economic and social life of corporations, and thus the
> distributive effects of various governance models.[55]

How, then, do reformers champion progressive ideals when gendered
beliefs supporting the mainstream model are so ingrained in the psyche
of corporate power? In the next section, connections between feminist
legal theory and corporate law are drawn which may provide a more
cohesive and powerful critique against these embedded norms, and in
Section 13.5, practical ways to dismantle invisible power imbalances
within the corporation are raised.

13.4   Feminist Legal Theory and Corporate Sustainability

Feminist legal theory is a diverse area of scholarship, spanning several
fields of law, and within those fields various approaches have emerged.[56]
This section will not attempt to demarcate the broad landscape of
feminist legal theory across disciplines. Instead, building on the work of
Testy and others, this section will highlight connections between feminist
legal theory, corporate law, and corporate sustainability. Testy suggests
there are important linkages between key feminist values and 'progressive' corporate law: nurturing connectedness, attending to context, and
furthering equality and human flourishing.[57] This section provides a
refresher on progressive corporate law, which has a somewhat fragmented history, and the term has petered out as of late. It identifies

---

[55] J. Sarra, 'The Gender Implications of Corporate Governance Change', (2002) 1 *Seattle Journal for Social Justice* 457 at 460.
[56] See, e.g., F. Olsen, *Feminist Legal Theory*, new ed., 2 vols. (New York: New York University Press, 1995); S. James & S. Palmer, *Visible Women: Essays on Feminist Legal Theory* (London: Hart Publishing, 2002); M. Chamallas, *Introduction to Feminist Legal Theory*, 2nd ed., (Gaithersburg, MD: Aspen Law & Business, 2003).
[57] Testy, 'Capitalism and Freedom', p. 100.

how the concepts in progressive corporate law are revived in modern-day concepts of corporate sustainability, and as suggested by Testy, these counter-hegemonic discourses are supported by, and require the support of, feminist legal principles.

A unifying concept in feminist legal theory is that it 'centers on an analysis of the use and distribution of power, seeking to articulate both a normative vision of equality and human flourishing for society as well as a critique of structures of subordination, particularly for women, that impede those values'.[58] 'Consciousness-raising' is a necessary component of feminist legal theory; diverse voices are encouraged.[59] Intersectionality[60] has gained in prominence as feminist scholars have promoted a more interconnected and multidimensional understanding of lived experiences; different social categorisations (including gender, race, class, sexual orientation, age, religion, disability/ability) are highly relevant in the context of power structures and different forms of privilege and oppression.[61] Testy notes how in the evolution of feminist legal theory 'it has increasingly focused on power relationships, group-based oppression, and systemic subordination'.[62]

The output of scholarship in feminist legal theory and its connections to corporate law in the past could be described as 'sparse'[63] relative to other fields,[64] but it is growing. A number of scholars have considered the relevance and impact of gender in corporate governance frameworks.[65] Gender diversity in corporate boardrooms has garnered considerable attention from several scholars.[66] Many feminist legal scholars have built upon the work of psychologist Carol Gilligan on

[58] Ibid., p 94.   [59] Ibid., p. 95.
[60] Term coined in K. Crenshaw, 'Demarginalizing the Intersection of Race and Sex: A Black Feminist Critique of Antidiscrimination Doctrine, Feminist Theory and Antiracist Policy' (1989) 139 *University of Chicago Legal Forum*; see also A. P. Harris, 'Race and Essentialism in Feminist Legal Theory' (1990) 42 *Stanford Law Review* 581.
[61] O. Hankivsky, 'Intersectionality 101' (2014) *The Institute for Intersectionality Research & Policy, SFU*, see http://vawforum-cwr.ca/sites/default/files/attachments/intersectionallity_101.pdf at 2.
[62] Testy, 'Capitalism and Freedom', p. 95.   [63] Ibid., p. 56.
[64] See, e.g., C. Chinkin, S. Wright & H. Charlesworth, 'Feminist Approaches to International Law: Reflections from Another Century' in D. Buss & A. Manji (eds.), *International Law: Modern Feminist Approaches* (Oxford: Hart, 2005).
[65] See, e.g., J. Sarra, 'Gender Implications'; C. L. Wade 'Transforming Discriminatory Corporate Cultures: This Is Not Just Women's Work' (2006) 65 *Maryland Law Review* 2.
[66] A. Anand & V. Jog, 'Diversity on Boards', (2016) 58 *Canadian Business Law Journal* 2; I. Boulouta, 'Hidden Connections: The Link between Board Gender Diversity and Corporate Social Performance' (2013) 113 *Journal of Business Ethics* 2.

moral reasoning,[67] using an 'ethic of care' to challenge the design of corporate laws,[68] including Yue Ang on corporate groups in this book.[69] This book itself adds an important collection of voices on the topic of gender and corporate law to date.

Testy notes how feminist legal theory has put forth important challenges to core tenets of corporate law:

(1) ... a challenge to shareholder primacy and an argument that corporate decision-making should consider a wider array of constituents without the hierarchy of the shareholder primacy model;

(2) ... a critique of the shortcomings of existing fiduciary duty law, and an argument that feminist insights into concepts of care and connection can and should give increased substantive content to director and officer duties; and

(3) ... a critique of concentrations of undemocratic corporate power together with an argument that to the extent that power works hardships on individuals in society, those hardships fall disproportionately on women (especially third-world women).[70]

Testy observed in 2004 how the progressive corporate law movement–which had been gaining momentum in the prior decade as a growing critique of the dominant paradigm of corporate law – had no values consensus behind its reform efforts.[71] Testy argued that those values are found in feminism, which provides commitments to equality and human flourishing.[72] Progressive corporate law gained prominence in 1995 with the edited collection *Progressive Corporate Law (New Perspectives on Law, Culture and Society)*.[73] The book supported a more communitarian view of corporations in society, including a focus on a corporation's moral obligations to society as a whole, with several contributors considering how corporate law could be better designed to emphasize 'responsibility, altruism, and unity within the corporate form and between the corporation and broader society'.[74]

---

[67] C. Gilligan, *In A Different Voice: Psychological Theory and Women's Development*, (Cambridge, MA: Harvard University Press, 1993).

[68] M. J. Larrabee, *An Ethic of Care: Feminist and Interdisciplinary Perspectives*, (New York: Routledge, 1993); V. Held, *Feminist Morality: Transforming Culture, Society, and Politics* (Chicago: University of Chicago Press, 1993). Chamallas, 'Introduction to Feminist Legal Theory'.

[69] See Ch. 11.   [70] Testy, 'Capitalism and Freedom', p. 98.   [71] Ibid., p. 92.

[72] Ibid., p. 105.   [73] Mitchell, 'Progressive Corporate Law'.   [74] Ibid, p. xiv.

Mitchell identified the common premise of progressive corporate law being the belief that 'it was no longer reasonable (if it ever was) to treat the corporation as a purely private mechanism' and 'to disregard the actual public character of the modern corporation simply is wilfully to disregard reality'.[75] Quoting sociologist Alan Wolfe, Mitchell contended that progressive corporate law served to improve or redesign the corporate form to account for the fact that 'corporations really are both private and public simultaneously . . . . They are institutions that sometimes act as quasi-governments and, even when they do not, they take actions that affect every aspect of people's lives, including people who have no formal contractual relationship with them'.[76]

Testy noted in 2004 that 'in the realm of corporate law, unlike perhaps other legal systems of ordering, a progressive vision is at an embryonic stage'.[77] The term 'progressive' is normatively vague, and its usage in a corporate law context required clarification from the movement. The lack of a mutually accepted terminology, a collective voice, and common goals within progressive corporate law amounted to disagreements on what constitutes success in corporate practice. While scholars such as Testy attributed many counter-hegemonic discourses in corporate legal scholarship as progressive,[78] others describing similar progressive discourses bifurcated their research from a progressive approach, implying that their positions should stand alone as separate work.[79] The conflicting descriptions created a puzzle as to how to categorically place progressive corporate law in the context of alternative approaches. Still others critiquing progressive corporate law found the term 'progressive' contentious.[80]

---

[75] Ibid.

[76] A. Wolfe, 'The Modern Corporation: Private Agent or Public Actor?', (1993) 50 *Washington and Lee Law Review* 1673 at 1692.

[77] Testy, 'Capitalism and Freedom', p. 89.

[78] See, e.g., Testy, 'Linking Progressive Corporate Law', hinting several discourses fall under the purview of progressive corporate law.

[79] See R. Columbo, 'Ownership, Limited: Reconciling Traditional and Progressive Corporate Law via an Aristotelian Understanding of Ownership' (2008) 34 *Journal of Corporation Law* 1; see also Blair & Stout, 'Team production theory'.

[80] See, e.g., S. Bainbridge, 'Community and Statism: A Conservative Contractarian Critique of Progressive Corporate Law Scholarship', (1997) 82 *Cornell Law Review* 856 at 857–858. (attributing it as 'simply a code word used by the left to take advantage of the positive connotations associated by most Americans with the idea of progress').

Further prescriptive parameters within progressive corporate law were suggested by other scholars, such as Kent Greenfield, but continued to be initial-stage ideas in the movement. Greenfield described five progressive principles: (1) the ultimate purpose of corporations should be to serve the interests of society as a whole; (2) corporations are distinctively able to contribute to the societal good by creating financial prosperity; (3) corporate law should further principles (1) and (2); (4) a corporation's wealth should be shared fairly among those who contribute to its creation; and (5) participatory, democratic corporate governance is the best way to ensure the sustainable creation and equitable distribution of corporate wealth.[81] Along a similar vein, Testy contended that a progressive corporate law project should: (1) seek an increased dispersion of wealth in society; (2) seek measures that reduce all forms of subordination and discrimination; (3) be consistent with environmental justice movements; and (4) seek to enhance social democracy.[82]

The challenge of progressive corporate legal scholarship continued to be the struggle toward agreed upon normative goals, and concentrated efforts in reaching those goals. Voices advocating seemingly progressive projects tend to be disparate and, other than a few exceptions within *Progressive Corporate Law*, fairly individual. Progressive corporate law may be appropriately described as a field-focused structural reform where, 'instead of regulating the uses to which the tool is put, [progressive corporate law scholars] look to redesign the tool itself'.[83] Rather than insisting there are ways in which corporate behaviour can be improved without disturbing the focus on shareholder wealth, this approach challenges the fundamental core of the shareholder primacy model. Nevertheless, with a few exceptions,[84] there has been little developed under the flag of 'progressive corporate law' for some time now. The inability to find common terminology and consensus created a significant stumbling block to internal organisation and cohesion. Other positions, such as more advanced versions of progressive corporate law theory emanating from a pragmatic European perspective on corporate function,[85] or the

---

[81] K. Greenfield, 'New Principles for Corporate Law' (2005) 1 *Hastings Business Law Journal* 87.

[82] Testy, 'Linking Progressive Corporate Law', p. 1244.

[83] Mitchell, 'Progressive Corporate Law', p. xiv.

[84] Such as L. Talbot, *Progressive Corporate Governance for the 21st Century* (London: Routledge, 2014).

[85] Such as I. Lynch Fannon, 'Working with Two Kinds'.

fact that nations have adopted more stakeholder-based models of governance,[86] have not been recognised sufficiently in academic scholarship and have struggled to gain the necessary traction in popular discourse to overtake these entrenched normative beliefs.

The corporate sustainability movement may be the new reiteration of progressive corporate law, comfortably stepping into the place of Testy's unfinished work with the necessity of alternative discourse to link with feminist legal theory. The corporate sustainability movement itself is beginning to take hold globally. Initially gaining momentum from the CSR movement, it attempts to shed much of the baggage from critics of the movement[87] and redirect its goals toward the pointed goal of sustainability.[88] Led by scholars such as Beate Sjåfjell, some international undertakings in recent years include The Sustainable Companies Project,[89] made up of a global consortium of scholars[90] aiming to mitigate climate change by integrating environmental concerns into the decision making of companies, and its second broader reiteration in the Sustainable Market Actors for Responsible Trade (SMART) Project, with over sixty scholars worldwide and an end date of 2020,[91] and organisations such as Frank Bold and The Purpose of the Corporation

---

[86] See, e.g., C. Liao, 'A Canadian Model'; Cynthia Williams & John Conley, 'An Emerging Third Way? The Erosion of the Anglo-American Shareholder Value Construct' (2005) 38 *Cornell Int'l L J* 493; V. H. Ho, "Enlightened Shareholder Value": Corporate Governance Beyond the Shareholder-Stakeholder Divide' (2010) 36 *J Corp L* 59.

[87] See, e.g., P. Sethi, 'Dimensions of Corporate Social Performance: An Analytical Framework for Measurement and Analysis' 17 (3) *California Management Rev* 58; see also J. M. Conley and C. Williams, 'Engage, Embed, and Embellish: Theory Versus Practice in the Corporate Social Responsibility Movement' (2005) 38 *Journal of Corporation Law* 1.

[88] B. Sjåfjell has defined corporate sustainability as '[W]hen business in aggregate creates value in a manner that is (a) *environmentally* sustainable in that it ensures the long-term stability and resilience of the ecosystems that support human life, (b) *socially* sustainable in that it facilitates the respect and promotion of human rights and of good governance, and (c) *economically* sustainable in that it satisfies the economic needs necessary for stable and resilient societies'. B. Sjåfjell, 'When the solution becomes the problem: the triple failure of corporate governance codes' in J. J. du Plessis & C. K. Low (eds.), *Corporate Governance Codes for the 21st Century*, (Geneva: Springer, 2017), p. 28.

[89] University of Oslo, Faculty of Law, *The Sustainable Companies Project* (2010), see www.jus.uio.no/ifp/english/research/projects/sustainable-companies.

[90] Including David Millon, an original contributor in Mitchell, 'Progressive Corporate Law'.

[91] University of Oslo, Faculty of Law, *Sustainable Market Actors for Responsible Trade Project* (2016), see http://smart.uio.no.

Project,[92] and Cass Business School and the Modern Corporation Project.[93] In combination with growing movements in social finance – which scholars such as Tessa Hebb and those in the Academic Network of the United Nations Principles of Responsible Investment have championed –the rapid spread of responsible and socially responsible investment, impact investment, etc. suggests a growing chorus for more sustainable practices in the private sector. Sustainability is an 'emerging megatrend' that may soon 'force fundamental and persistent shifts in how companies compete'.[94]

Like progressive corporate law in 1995, the corporate sustainability movement is in its nascent years, but far more global in nature, and growing at a formidable pace. The next few decades mark a critical period in domestic and international corporate reform as businesses begin to adapt to global pressures for greater sustainability and changing consumer demands. The movement seems to be picking up where progressive corporate law left off, but with substantial backing across disciplines and industries. This book adds critical feminist voices to that movement, something Testy strongly argued for in 2004 with progressive corporate law. Time will tell if long-held norms in corporate law that favour existing power structures can be substantially upended.

13.5   Implicit Bias Obstacles to Corporate Power

The destabilisation of power structures that have been erected within a male-dominated history requires, at a minimum, participation from women. It includes challenging long-held beliefs in corporate law, as seen in the previous section, but also challenging power structures from within existing corporate institutions, at executive and board levels of management. While it is important to consider how regulations can support increased gender diversity, there are very real gendered power dynamics within firms that also impede a woman's rise to the top. This section sheds light onto implicit biases which are subversive power obstacles for women in the corporate world. This layered look at both

---

[92] Frank Bold Law Firm, *The Purpose of the Corporation Project*, see www .purposeofcorporation.org/en.

[93] University of London, Cass Business School, *The Modern Corporation Project* (2016), see www.cass.city.ac.uk/news-and-events/news/2016/november/academics-endorse-new-vision-for-corporate-governance.

[94] D. Lubin & D. Esty, 'The Sustainability Imperative' (2010) 88 *Harvard Business Review* 5, see https://hbr.org/2010/05/the-sustainability-imperative.

the normative power imbalances in Sections 13.3 and 13.4 and the empirically-proven power dynamics within existing structures in this section is crucial in understanding the magnitude at which change must occur.

The social constructions of gender have significant implications that reverberate in the business world, as more and more women join traditionally male-dominated industries holding much of the capital and power dictating human ordering. Discourse has developed regarding the systemic disadvantages women face up the corporate ladder (such as the glass ceiling,[95] motherhood penalty,[96] and organisational culture,[97] to name a few), as well as discussions relating to gender diversity in the boardroom specifically, such as board interlocks[98] and tokenism.[99] Moreover, and even more pernicious, are the implicit biases that pervade business culture, which this section highlights. These hidden biases greatly disadvantage women from obtaining valuable executive positions, positions that are often necessary to attain meaningful directorships on boards. Implicit biases are reflections of the embedded norms in corporate law that prioritize gendered notions of corporate practice in the private sector. Furthermore, implicit biases persist across gender lines – men and women alike judge women more harshly than men, exposing internalized forms of misogyny.[100]

Implicit bias can be defined as 'the attitudes or stereotypes that affect our understanding, actions, and decisions in an unconscious manner'.[101] The involuntariness of implicit bias is important to understand, as that aspect differs from explicit biases people are unwilling to forego, and 'are activated involuntarily and without an individual's awareness or intentional control ... [they] are not accessible through

---

[95] See, e.g., L. Aguilar, Commissioner of the U.S. Securities and Exchange Commission, Speech: 'Merely cracking the glass ceiling is not enough: Corporate America needs more than a just a few women in leadership' (22 May 2013) see www.sec.gov.

[96] S. Correll, S. Benard & I. Paik, 'Getting a Job: Is there a Motherhood Penalty?' (2007) 112 *American Journal of Sociology* 1297–1338.

[97] L. Chenier & E. Wohlbold, 'Women in senior management: where are they?' (2011) Conference Board of Canada, see www.conferenceboard.ca.

[98] Lu, 'Gender Diversity, Board Interlocks'.

[99] Tokenism theory began with R. M. Kanter, *Men and Women of the Corporation* (New York: Basic Books, 1977).

[100] L. MacNeill, A. Driscoll & A. Hunt, 'What's in a Name?: Exposing Gender Bias in Student Ratings of Teaching' (2015) 40 *Innovation of Higher Education* 291.

[101] Kirwan Institute for the Study of Race and Ethnicity, *Understanding implicit bias*, see http://kirwaninstitute.osu.edu/research/understanding-implicit-bias.

introspection'.[102] People's behaviours are shaped by implicit biases, stemming from repeated exposure to cultural stereotypes that 'portray women as less competent but simultaneously emphasize their warmth and likeability compared with men'.[103] These unconscious biases mean white males are more likely to be hired, promoted, and compensated better than women of comparable standing, and exist across sectors.[104] These biases are often difficult to detect without the aid of scientific research.

Project Implicit, a non-profit organisation founded by a consortium of international scholars, has sought to bring awareness and education to the public on implicit biases.[105] The project's virtual laboratory allows participants to undergo a series of different Implicit Association Tests (IATs) to reveal participants' hidden biases. A significant majority of participants that have taken the Gender-Career IAT are found to have a strong or moderate gender-bias correlation of 'Male' with 'Career' and 'Female' with 'Family' (including this author who received a strong correlation result).[106] The traditional characteristics of a leader are unconsciously regarded as incongruent with our socialized notions of the female gender, and numerous studies have shown that people hold an implicit bias against women holding leadership roles.[107] Women who attempt to assert themselves in ways that are traditionally attributed to the male gender, such as the propensity to negotiate for better salaries, could do more harm than good for their careers and are

---

[102] Ibid.

[103] C. Moss-Racusin et al., 'Science Faculty's Subtle Gender Biases Favor Male Students' (2012) 109 *PNAS* 16474.

[104] See, e.g., A. Eagly & A. Mladinic, 'Are People Prejudiced Against women? Some Answers from Research on Attitudes, Gender Stereotypes, and Judgments of Competence' (1994) 5 *European Review of Social Psychology* 1; R. E. Steinpreis, D. Ritzke & K. Anders, 'The Impact of Gender on the Review of the Curricula Vitae of Job Applicants and Tenure Candidates: A National Empirical Study' (1999) 41 *Sex Roles* 509; E. Reuben, P. Sapienze & L. Zingales, 'How Stereotypes Impair Women's Careers in Science' (2014) 111 *PNAS* 4403; M. Krawczyk & M. Smyk, 'Author's Gender Affects Rating of Academic Articles: Evidence from an Incentivized, Deception-Free Laboratory Experiment' (2016) 90 *European Economic Review* 326; C. Goldin & C. Rouse, 'Orchestrating Impartiality: The Impact of "Blind" Auditions on Female Musicians' (2000) 90 *American Economic Review* 715, 738.

[105] Project Implicit, see www.projectimplicit.net.   [106] Ibid.

[107] See, e.g., A. Eagly & L. Carly, *Through the Labyrinth: The Truth about How Women Become Leaders* (Boston, MA: Harvard Business School Press, 2007); K. Scott & D. Brown, 'Female First, Leader Second? Gender Bias in the Encoding of Leadership Behavior' (2006) 101 *Organizational Behavior and Human Decision Processes* 230.

more likely to be penalised for their actions.[108] Women are subjected to a 'prove-it-again' pattern in the workplace, where women and visible minorities have to repeatedly prove their skills and the value they add to the workplace as compared to white men.[109] They are also assigned more 'office housework' – necessary but undervalued and underappreciated tasks.[110]

How, then, can a corporation address these implicit biases? Although the number of women populating the business world has increased relative to the past, it is important to remember that 'mere increased presence is not evidence of the absence of bias'.[111] The belief that time will eventually solve gendered inequalities is foolhardy. The lack of gender parity in corporate leadership ranks lends credence to the argument that existing diversity efforts are not enough. In fact, some studies have shown that diversity training programs may backfire. Avivah Wittenberg-Cox argues that most diversity policies are designed to treat men and women the same, when they are not, and 'as long as men and women are treated exactly the same by organisations, most women will continue to be shut out of senior roles'.[112] Corinne Moss-Racusin et al. note that existing efforts to create more flexible work settings 'may not fully alleviate a critical underlying problem' but 'policies and mentoring' could contribute to reducing the gender disparity, although future research on the efficacy of such methods is needed.[113] To combat implicit gender biases directly, Joan C. Williams has promoted the development of 'bias interrupters' in the workplace, to be used on a day-to-day basis by individuals and colleagues intervening on behalf of individuals, and also in the form of institutional solutions.[114] Companies identify key metrics

---

[108] Ibid. See, e.g., H. Bowles, L. Babcock & L. Lai, 'Social Incentives for Gender Differences in the Propensity to Initiate Negotiations: Sometimes It Does Hurt to Ask' (2007) 103 *Organizational Behavior and Human Decision Processes* 84.

[109] J. Williams, K. Phillips & E. Hall, 'Double Jeopardy? Gender Bias against Women of Color in Science' (2014) Tools for Change WorkLifeLaw UC Hastings College of Law, pp. 11–17.

[110] See, e.g., J. Williams & R. Dempsey, *What Works for Women at Work* (New York: New York University Press, 2014).

[111] Moss-Racusin et al., 'Science Faculty's Subtle Gender Biases', p. 16478.

[112] A. Wittenberg-Cox, 'To Hold Back Women, Keep Treating Them Like Men' (2015) *Harvard Business Review*.

[113] Moss-Racusin et al., 'Science Faculty's Subtle Gender Biases', p. 16478.

[114] J. Williams, 'Hacking Tech's Diversity Problem' (October 2014) 92 *Harvard Business Review* 96; J. Williams, '*What Works for Women at Work: Individual Strategies and Bias Interrupters*' (11 April 2016) Center for WorkLife Law at UC Hastings College of Law, see: http://facultyexcellence.ucsd.edu.

for tracking the results of bias interventions, then make a change that will curb the effects on an ongoing basis, and continue to experiment and measure the effective of their interventions. Of course, implementing effective bias interrupters may be difficult depending on the organizational culture of a firm.

Katya Hosking and Roseanne Russell have noted that, in the context of discrimination laws, challenging implicit bias on an individual basis has the risk of 'downplay[ing] the extent to which systematic and structural disadvantage can undermine autonomy'.[115] In particular, they agree with treating implicit bias more as a public health concern, which would free the need for a blameworthy agent in the case of discrimination laws, and be more effective in combating the problem at its source, stating that 'to counter the group harm of implicit bias it is the dimensions of substantive equality ... redistribution, recognition, structural transformation, and participation—that are needed'.[116] While making legislative recommendations to shift the burden of proof in discrimination laws to better address implicit biases, they do not shy away from noting that while recommendations like theirs are relatively easy to achieve, that is not to say that 'persuasive arguments might well be advanced for more radical changes' particularly 'on wholesale structural displacement of current social and economic systems'.[117]

13.6   Conclusion

In order to obtain a position as a director at one of the Fortune 500 companies, an individual would need to hold at least one of three things: success in business, significant capital, or power via networks generating social and political influence. The question of how gender plays a role in the equation of business and capital, and in the future diffusion of power, is a question that historically has been ignored. Now, the role of gender in business and corporate law is becoming a complex and potentially evolving issue as more industry leaders and scholars weigh in. There seems to be growing global consensus in favour of increasing the number of women on corporate boards. Yet the path to obtaining corporate leadership roles remains rife with implicit bias obstacles for women.

[115] K. Hosking & R. Russell, 'Discrimination law, equality law, and implicit bias' in M. Brownstein & J. Saul, *Implicit Bias and Philosophy, Vol. 2: Moral Responsibility, Structural Injustice, and Ethics* (Oxford: Oxford University Press, 2016), p. 272.
[116] Ibid., p. 273.   [117] Ibid., p. 276.

Many proponents tout the 'business case' for gender diversity, in hopes that it will gain the ear of those that are only economically focused.[118] However, solely justifying the inclusion of women on the basis that it equates to more profits only perpetuates the shareholder primacy model of governance. More effort is needed to recognize and continually address the pervasive gendered norms that are inherent within the structure of corporate law. These norms perpetuate the implicit biases that subvert women from reaching positions of power.

The core tenets of feminist legal theory offer both incremental and radical approaches to redesigning corporate law to bring about social change from private sector organizations, and foster an environment where sustainable companies become the norm. Putting businesses on a more sustainable path will require the participation of all factions of society, not just one gender. Particularly in relation to women, the World Bank notes how 'countries that create better opportunities and conditions for women and girls can raise productivity, improve outcomes for children, make institutions more representative, and advance development prospects for all'.[119] Moss-Racusin et al. note that 'the dearth of women within academic science reflects a significant wasted opportunity to benefit from the capabilities of our best potential scientists, whether male or female' – equally so in all fields. Human beings all play a role in attributing certain social, behavioural, and cultural values, expectations, and norms within the binary options of male or female.

The business world has been male for quite some time, and that will not change without significant ideological destabilization. Consciousness-raising of power imbalances and the gender imperative in corporate law, in the legislature, academia, the boardroom, and in the day-to-day functioning of corporate activities, is an early step in attaining transformational change, but more is needed to disrupt embedded gendered norms within our legal institutions. More is needed to ensure corporations contribute to systems of equality and societal flourishing, rather than working against it. The term 'progressive corporate law' may no longer be in vogue, but its concepts thrive within feminist legal theory and

---

[118] See, e.g., N. M. Carter and H. M. Wagner, *The Bottom Line: Corporate Performance and Women's Representation on Boards (2004–2008)* (New York: Catalyst, 2011); Credit Suisse Research Institute, *Gender Diversity and Corporate Performance* (Zurich, 2012); McKinsey & Company, *Women Matter: Gender Diversity, a Corporate Performance Driver* (Paris, 2007).

[119] World Bank, '2012 World development report'.

provide a roadmap for the corporate sustainability movement. Building upon the words of Testy, we will see if Hansmann and Kraakman's declaration in 2001 of the end of history may have simply signalled 'The Beginning of Herstory in Corporate Law'.[120]

---

[120] K. Testy, 'The Beginning of Herstory for Corporate Law' (2002) 1 *Seattle Journal for Social Justice* 2.

14

Corporate Sustainability

Gender as an Agent for Change?

BEATE SJÅFJELL AND IRENE LYNCH FANNON

14.1 The Sustainability Imperative

There is an overwhelmingly clear imperative for a shift of business and finance away from 'business as usual', which is becoming a very certain path towards a very uncertain and unsustainable future. Sustainability is the grand challenge of our time, and finding out how to secure the social foundation for people now and in the future while staying within planetary boundaries[1] is arguably the greatest challenge humanity has ever faced. Business and finance are a necessary part of this shift. Although there are some indications that the shift may be beginning, it is still on the fringe of mainstream business and finance, and there are forces that serve to entrench and even exacerbate the exploitation of nature and of people and the undermining of the financial and economic stability of our societies. Positive change accordingly still appears to be incremental at best.

As we outlined in the introductory chapter to this volume,[2] while our concern is with business (law and finance, because of their interconnected nature) generally, we as editors chose the corporation as our focal point. The corporate form remains the dominant form and we have taken the view that while other legal forms may present very interesting alternative ways of organising business (as discussed by Aikaterini Argyrou et al. and Victoria Baumfield in their contributions),[3] we must not let them act as deflection devices. The corporation, this 'chief centre

---

[1] M. Leach, K. Raworth and J. Rockström, 'Between social and planetary boundaries: Navigating pathways in the safe and just pathway for humanity' in *World Social Science Report 2013: Changing Global Environments* (OECD, 2013), pp. 84–90, see www.worldsocialscience.org/activities/world-social-science-report/the-2013-report.

[2] Ch. 1.   [3] Ch. 8; Ch. 9.

of power outside of government' as Adolf Berle called it already in 1954,[4] must be the focus of a real shift towards sustainability – indeed, that is why we speak about 'corporate sustainability' as a concept encompassing sustainable business and finance.

The corporation (as shaped by law, economics, finance and politics) has a broader and more benevolent history and current purpose than the drive for maximisation of returns for shareholders/investors that we see today (and which has been identified as the main barrier to corporate sustainability).[5] While we use 'shareholder primacy' as a short form to indicate most of what has gone wrong in the current use of the corporate form, we recognise that this is merely one, albeit crucial, aspect of a broader economic system, indeed of organising our societies,[6] that appears to be fundamentally on an unsustainable and increasingly risky path.

The question that this volume discusses, and which this concluding chapter summarises and reflects upon, is whether gender can be an agent for changing how we view corporations and how we make progress towards sustainability. There is a potential for such an influence of gender on several levels and in various ways, as this volume has demonstrated.

Discussing gender as an agent for change gives rise to a number of questions. A fundamental one is whether the values and traits that we see reflected in the unsustainable 'business as usual' approach are specifically male values and traits. We do know that we have a concurrence of male

---

[4] A. Berle, *The 20th Century Capitalist Revolution* (New York: Harcourt, 1954), as quoted by C. Liao in Ch. 13.

[5] B. Sjåfjell, A. Johnston, L. Anker-Sorensen & D. Millon, 'Shareholder primacy: The main barrier to sustainable companies', in B. Sjåfjell and B. J. Richardson (eds.), *Company Law and Sustainability* (Cambridge: Cambridge University Press, 2015), pp. 79–147; see also the substantive contributions in the progressive corporate law scholarship from the 1990s onwards, pushing back against the shareholder primacy domination of the Chicago School, including D. Millon, 'Theories of the Corporation' (1990) *Duke L. J*, 201; L. E. Mitchell (ed.), *Progressive Corporate Law: New Perspectives on Law, Culture and Society* (Boulder, CO: Westview Press, 1995); I. Lynch Fannon, *Working Within Two Kinds of Capitalism* (Oxford and Portland, OR: Hart, 2003); K. Greenfield, 'New Principles for Corporate Law' (2005) *1 Hastings Business Law Journal* 87; C. Mayer, *Firm Commitment: Why the Corporation is Failing Us and How to Restore Trust in It* (Oxford University Press, 2013); and M. A. Welsh, P. Spender, I. Lynch Fannon and K. Hall, 'The End of the End of History for Corporate Law' (2014) 29 *AJCL*, 147–168.

[6] Lynch Fannon, *Working Within Two Kinds of Capitalism*, illustrates how different political structures, different legislative systems yield different understandings of corporate function; see in particular chapter 4: 'The Same Questions, Different Answers'.

domination and an unsustainable mainstream business and finance model within what appears to be a systemically flawed economic system. The restricted and fragmented economic theories that have been allowed to dominate our understanding of corporations (and of the economy, of society and even of individual humans[7]) also express a de facto male dominance over public debate.[8] As Carol Liao points out, just as the lack of women in executive positions and corporate boardrooms are a direct consequence of our male-dominated history, so are the laws and norms guiding these institutions.[9] As Catherine O'Sullivan shows in her contribution to this volume, there are values and traits in business and finance that cannot be concluded as being (biologically) male but that are evidentially (culturally) masculine. These are intrinsically a part of unsustainable behaviour and performance. These negative aspects have broader implications, ranging from the macro political-economic sphere through business and finance and to the micro level of our individual lives. O'Sullivan introduces the concept of hegemonic masculinity to contest popular analysis after the recent crash that proposed the insertion of women into corporate governance structures as 'the prophylactic against future recklessness in high finance'.[10]

In this context, an alternative approach and outsider perspective is the female perspective. The question of what a female perspective can bring into this debate is therefore of interest. Firstly, as indicated in Chapter 1, a female approach in a male-dominated area may bring in new perspectives and different values – and a basis for challenging underlying assumptions of status quo. Secondly, drawing on gender organisational studies helps recognise the extent to which organisations are gendered, and how typical masculine values dominate, as discussed in several contributions in this volume.[11] Thirdly, drawing on feminist organisational change strategies, we present a tentative basis for a deeper discussion of whether gender can be an agent for change, to mitigate shareholder primacy, or more positively phrased, to create or facilitate corporate sustainability. The latter resonates with the title of our volume:

---

[7] K. Raworth, *Doughnut Economics: Seven Ways to Think Like a 21st-Century Economist* (London: Cornerstone, 2017).

[8] See, e.g., E. Prügl, '"If Lehman Brothers Had Been Lehman Sisters..." Gender and Myth in the Aftermath of the Financial Crisis', *International Political Sociology*, 6, no. 1 (March 2012), pp. 21–35, referring to a study that suggests that the 'virtual male monopoly on financial policymaking produces gender-biased policies, including the groupthink that facilitated the financial crisis of 2008–09'.

[9] Ch. 13.   [10] Ch. 12.   [11] Ch. 10, 12 and 13.

Creating Corporate Sustainability: Gender as an Agent for Change, and is a much-needed analysis. Feminist theory has, together with critical theory, with which it has much in common, often been 'better at critiquing the status quo than changing it'.[12]

Accordingly, and in recognition of the sustainability imperative for change, this concluding chapter reflects on the contributions to this volume through the lens of organisational change strategies. We do this inspired by Kate Grosser's compilation of such strategies from a feminist-theoretical perspective,[13] which in turn is based on a literature review that focuses on action-based strategies for change (as opposed to, for example, epistemological analyses).[14] Thereafter, in the concluding section of this last chapter, we return to the grand challenge of our time and how we can begin to go about dealing with it.

14.2   Gender and Organisational Change

14.2.1   Liberal Individualism and Valuing the Feminine

A first strategy to achieve gender equality in and/or to change business and finance, on the individual level, is that which is denoted as *fixing individual women* or *liberal individualism*. The idea is here to help

---

[12] J. Martin, 'Feminist Theory and Critical Theory: Unexplored Synergies', in M. Alvesson, M. & H. Willmott (eds.), *Studying Management Critically* (London: Sage Publications, 2003), chapter 4, p. 67.

[13] This includes well-established feminist research streams that take an action-oriented approach to system change, as well as two strategies: 'hypocrisy as a resource' and external agents as change-makers, which Grosser identifies based on her literature review of gender organisational studies and CSR literature; K. Grosser, 'Corporate social responsibility, gender equality and organizational change: a feminist perspective', PhD thesis, University of Nottingham (2011), see http://eprints.nottingham.ac.uk/12138/2/KateGrosserPhDThesis2011._Corporate_Social_Responsibility%2C_Gender_Equality_and_Organizational_Change.pdf, ch. 2.3.4 'Feminist strategies for organizational change', drawing on P. Y. Martin, '"Said and Done" versus "saying and doing". Gendering Practices and Practicing Gender at Work' (2003) *Gender and Society*, 17, 342–366; D. E. Meyerson and D. M. Kolb, '"Moving out of the `Armchair": Developing a Framework to Bridge the Gap between Feminist Theory and Practice' (2000) *Organisation* 7 (4), 553–571; G. Coleman and A. Rippin, 'Putting Feminist Theory to Work: Collaboration as a Means towards Organizational Change' (2000) *Organisation* 7 (4) 573–587; and R. J. Ely and D. E. Meyerson, 'Theories of Gender in Organizations: A New Approach to Organizational Analysis and Change', *Research in Organizational Behavior* (2000) 22, 103–151.

[14] Our emphasis is somewhat different than Grosser's as ours is on corporate sustainability with gender as an agent for change and not gender equality as a goal in itself, while Grosser's work is an iterative analysis of literature on gender equality and CSR literature.

women succeed by changing them, and arguably empowering them, as we see reflected today in Sheryl Sandberg's 'Lean In' campaign.[15] Although it is arguably helpful for the individual woman to be encouraged to go into a male-dominated area and to succeed there (and indeed a network like Daughters of Themis also has a role in informally mentoring younger female scholars and supporting each other), as a strategy to achieve organisational change towards sustainability, it is clearly insufficient and inadequate. It could only be sufficient if liberal individualism led to a critical mass of women in business and if that in itself led to corporate sustainability.

This is of course also relevant for us as female business scholars – if the prerequisite for academic success were to behave like a male academic (for example, based on assumptions of assertiveness being a male rather than a female attribute), what challenge if any to the male-dominated status quo would more female business scholars make? Making 'leaning in' an individual responsibility risks conveying the message the female business academics should choose between conforming to succeed and leaving academia. On the other hand, understanding both the male-dominated thinking which informs the unsustainable status quo as well as gender inequality in academia (and more broadly in society) as systemic issues may better pave the way for nonconformist female (and progressive male) business scholars to challenge unsustainable aspects of the current dominant systems.

Liberal individualism has a limited effect on gendered organisations,[16] and as several of the contributions in our volume highlight, gendered organisations are part of the problem.[17] Liberal individualism also leaves men constrained by accepted norms of masculinity, as O'Sullivan shows in her contribution. As Roseanne Russell emphasises, both men and women 'need to be liberated from a rapacious economic system that both degrades the environment and does not value the necessary work that goes into maintaining social life'.[18]

---

[15] See, e.g., K. Bellstrom, 'Sheryl Sandberg, These Are the Biggest Obstacles For Women Trying to "Lean In"',; (27 September 2016) *Fortune*, which also contains Sandberg's suggestions about what businesses should do to facilitate gender equality to mitigate the tendency of 'pushing back'; and Ch. 11.

[16] The 'how to succeed' perspective may tend to be uncritical (or ignorant of) gendered organisations; K. Grosser and J. Moon, 'CSR and Feminist Organization Studies: Towards an Integrated Theorization for the Analysis of Gender Issues' (23 March 2017) *Journal of Business Ethics*.

[17] Chs. 11–13.   [18] Ch. 11.

The second strategy, related to liberal individualism, is that which may be denoted as *valuing the feminine*. This strategy identifies certain traits as 'feminine' and attempts to revalue them as equal to, or superior to, perceived masculine characteristics. The strategy tends to reify differences and reinforce gendered stereotypes. This strategy also gives primacy to instrumental organisational goals. As we will see in the next section, this is reflected in initiatives aimed to facilitate improved gender balance on corporate boards.

14.2.2   Liberal Structuralism

A third and broader but interconnected strategy is that of *liberal structuralism*, an appropriate label for much of what is currently in place of insufficient and inadequate legislative strategies to affect changes in business and finance. Liberal structuralism denotes minimal structural change, such as, notably, rules to promote greater gender balance on corporate boards; the trend with corporate reporting requirements concerning environmental, social and governance issues; and the stewardship rules.[19] These rules have the aim of affecting changes in corporations and in investor behaviour, which in turn will affect corporations. However, these rules operate in a restrained manner as they generally operate on a 'comply or explain' basis.

While promoting more women on corporate boards may be informed by three interlinked legislative objectives – gender equality, improved corporate governance, and corporate sustainability – we see that the business case argument is frequently used whatever the starting point, reflecting the *valuing the feminine* strategy.[20] Whether gender-balanced corporate boards could facilitate corporate sustainability is a very broad and contested issue,[21] and is in itself limited by the business case argument. Indeed, liberal structuralism leaving deeper systemic issues untouched gives us the double limitation of instrumentality: gender equality in business is seen as relevant only if it is good for business,

---

[19] Gender balance on boards and the reporting rules are discussed here, and the stewardship briefly in Section 14.2.5.

[20] Ch. 6. Much CSR research that has interacted with gender issues has also taken this business case perspective; Grosser and Moon, 'CSR and Feminist Organization Studies'.

[21] Discussed in B. Sjåfjell, 'Gender Diversity in the Boardroom and Its Impacts: Is the Example of Norway a Way Forward?' (2014) 19 *Deakin Law Review* 25. See also Ch. 7.

and corporate sustainability is only seen as a goal to strive for to the extent that it leads to better long-term returns to investors.

The Norwegian legislative reform, which may be said to have sparked an international discourse and inspired numerous legislative initiatives, remains one of the few (if not the only) example of mandatory legislation to this effect, with dissolution of the corporation as the ultimate consequence in case of non-compliance.[22] Conversely, a number of the other legislative initiatives remain tentative in their approach, an aspect they have in common with legislative reforms concerning reporting.[23]

On the EU level, as Irene Lynch Fannon shows us, even a proposal for a Directive with such a limited approach has become surprisingly divisive,[24] in stark contrast to the EU's earlier significant achievements in the field of gender equality.[25] Voluntarism as a defence to legislative interference is the currently preferred approach to these issues.[26] Idoya Ferrero-Ferrero et al. challenge this approach in their empirical study of gender initiatives in a panel of European listed corporations.[27] Their study shows that corporations may also tend to adopt gender policies in a symbolic manner only, reflecting the liberal structuralism that we see on the legislative level. They posit that this may explain the mixed findings in previous research about the relationship between gender diversity and corporate sustainability (as many of these analyses use

---

[22] Also in one of the most egalitarian countries in the world, the idea of a gender equality rule for corporate boards led to very strong opposition, with a 'business case' argument combined with a 'coup by tabloids' necessary to see the rule adopted; Sjåfjell, 'Gender Diversity in the Boardroom and Its Impacts'.

[23] Ch. 5.

[24] Adopted by the European Parliament, Members of the European Parliament urge the Council and EU Member States to move forward with this Directive, 'which has been on hold in the Council since 2013', see 'EU is stuck half way to achieving gender equality, MEPs say' (14 March 2017) *European Parliament News*, see www.europarl.europa.eu/news/en/press-room/20170308IPR65678/eu-is-stuck-half-way-to-achieving-gender-equality-meps-say.

[25] Ch. 6.

[26] That was also an argument against the Norwegian rule, leading the Norwegian legislators to give business a two-year grace period before the rule entered into force – if business had achieved a 40% female board membership on average, the rule would not have entered into force (Sjåfjell, 'Gender Diversity in the Boardroom and Its Impacts'). CSR is often misappropriated in this way, by those seeking voluntary change as a path to resisting legislative interference; I. Lynch Fannon, 'The Corporate Social Responsibility Movement and Law's Empire: Is there a Conflict?' (2007) 58(1) *Northern Ireland Legal Quarterly*, 1–21.

[27] Ch. 7.

percentage of women on the board as a proxy of effective gender diversity).[28] This is also interesting in light of the Norwegian debate, where criticism against the corporate law reform has shifted from criticising the rule itself to criticising the rule for not improving gender balance on management level.[29] This may serve to illustrate that when male domination is deeply entrenched, legal reform in one area may change that specific area but not the rest of business. Further, this supports the argument that increased gender diversity on boards most likely is insufficient to achieve corporate sustainability in itself, even if one presupposes that mitigating groupthink on corporate boards could be a small contribution to this.[30]

The compromise solution of reporting requirements is also illustrative of liberal structuralism, in that they aim to nudge corporations in the right direction, without addressing the systemic issues that have rendered so much of business and finance unsustainable. Informed by reflexive law theory, the idea is that having to report annually on issues will lead to increased consciousness of these issues amongst corporate decision-makers (notably the board), and thereby facilitate corporate sustainability. The problem is, of course, that this does not have much of an opportunity to function in practice because of the lax regulatory approaches which generally are not enforced and where the information that is reported is not verified.[31] As Gill North emphasises, despite increased corporate recognition of the need for corporate sustainability, numerous interconnected issues are compounded into a significant barrier to achieving high-quality sustainability-relevant information, with the much-lauded EU reform of 2014 and other such reporting regimes lacking sufficient substance, specificity and supervisory teeth to disrupt the entrenched power and information imbalances between corporations, investors and members of society.[32] The EU Directive is also illustrative through the language it uses – by denoting environmental impacts, human rights and other fundamental social issues, and other governance issues as 'non-financial', it is unintentionally

---

[28] Ibid.   [29] Sjåfjell, 'Gender Diversity in the Boardroom and Its Impacts'.   [30] Ibid.

[31] C. Villiers and J. Mähönen, 'Accounting, Auditing, and Reporting: Supporting or Obstructing the Sustainable Companies Objective?' in B. Sjåfjell and B. J. Richardson (eds.), *Company Law and Sustainability: Legal Barriers and Opportunities* (Cambridge University Press, 2015).

[32] Ch. 5, concerning Directive 2014/95/EU of the European Parliament and of the Council of 22 October 2014 amending Directive 2013/34/EU as regards disclosure of non-financial and diversity information by certain large undertakings and groups.

signalling that these issues are subordinated to and less important than the hard-core financial issues.[33]

14.2.3   From Dual Objectives to Separatism

A fourth organisational change strategy is that which is denoted *making small, deep cultural changes with dual objectives*. This strategy involves changing relatively small aspects with deeply embedded implications, and is in the literature used to describe what we may refer to as action-based case studies or pilot projects. The *dual objectives* aspect encompasses, for example, gender equality together with the aim of increasing efficiency.[34] The instrumental aim (i.e., the business case for change) may then tend to dominate. Indeed, in the one study, the researchers (Meyerson and Kolb) found that even for themselves the gender equality aim began slipping away because it was so often perceived as strategically advantageous not to mention it.[35] In our corporate sustainability context, action-based research and collaboration between business and academia arguably is a necessary contribution to achieving change, and may be highly successful in creating such 'pockets' of corporate sustainability; however, it may bring with it a risk of corporate capture. The dual goal of corporate sustainability and improvement of corporate economic performance may turn into a combination of objectives, with economic performance being the superior goal and corporate sustainability only being perceived as relevant insofar as it contributes to the superior objective. Waiting for incremental change and exceptional cases to become the norm is most likely insufficient.

Fifth, and a somewhat defensive organisational change strategy, turning away from dual objectives, is that of *separatism*, which we see reflected in the social entrepreneurship trend. While not inherently new (rather, the oldest business form arguably is the traditional social entrepreneurship of the cooperative),[36] there is a development of new forms of social entrepreneurship both through legislative initiatives, on an ad hoc

---

[33] B. Sjåfjell, 'Bridge Over Troubled Water: Corporate Law Reform for Life-Cycle Based Governance and Reporting' (2016) *University of Oslo Faculty of Law Research Paper* No 2016–23, see www.ssrn.com/abstract=2874270.
[34] Meyerson and Kolb, '"Moving out of the 'Armchair'", p. 555.   [35] Ibid., p. 569.
[36] And is lauded as the most sustainable business form by some, see, e.g., Andrew Bibby, 'Co-operatives are an inherently more sustainable form of business' (1 March 2014) *The Guardian*, see www.theguardian.com/social-enterprise-network/2014/mar/11/co-op-busi ness-sustainability.

business level and through business policy initiatives such as, notably, the B Corps described by Baumfield.[37]

Undoubtedly, there are positive implications of the social entrepreneurship trend, as Argyrou et al. show in their contribution, including that these can be real-life experiments on how to do business in a different way. Whilst we may find inspiration in these models for reform of the corporation, including stakeholder governance, we do not believe that this separate stream of business form will outcompete today's corporations thereby ensuring corporate sustainability. We see the potential for testing out new approaches, and together with microfinance, that social entrepreneurship (as a broad and general term) can bring new opportunities for bottom-up innovation. Nevertheless, as Baumfield indicates in her contribution, there is a risk that these new structures will be used 'ultimately just a sideshow to distract from the failure to reform traditional corporations'.[38]

14.2.4   Transforming Gendered Society: The Necessity of External Agents

The sixth organisational change strategy, *transforming gendered society*, situates corporations in society, and transcends institutional boundaries between the state, corporations, academia and civil society. The fundamental unsustainability of business today is so entrenched that such change is necessary, and understanding the implications our gendered society has on these issues is crucial. As O'Sullivan emphasises, when the kinds of considerations that inform corporate sustainability, such as concern for social justice and environmental issues, are 'coded feminine', they become 'unspeakable for those seeking to present themselves as conforming to the hegemonic norm'.[39] On the other hand, innovative approaches such as Yue Ang's analysis of emerging trends in corporate law through the lens of feminist theories (spatial justice and the ethic of care) indicate how it can be possible for law to evolve towards a legal infrastructure that promotes corporate sustainability.[40] To achieve transformational change, as Liao points out, power structures that have been erected within a male-dominated history need challenging, which will include critical analysis of long-held beliefs in corporate law as well as pushing back against male domination in business and finance.[41]

---

[37] Ch. 9.   [38] Ibid.   [39] Ch. 12.   [40] Ch. 10.   [41] Ch. 13.

This underlines the need for a systemic approach. Transforming a gendered – and unsustainable – society into a fair and sustainable society requires a whole jigsaw puzzle of sustainability. While Ragnhild Lunner's contribution highlights how negative corporate impact may be compounded with negative aspects of patriarchal society to render women doubly discriminated against,[42] Adaeze Okoye and Emmanuel Osuteye's contribution show how the bottom-up actions of women breaking out of their conventional roles may be a driver for corporate sustainability from below.[43] Indeed, Okoye and Osuteye demonstrate that this contribution 'from below' is a vital aspect, if we are to aim for a comprehensive shift towards corporate sustainability. Lorraine Talbot also makes the argument that it is necessary for women to act politically and in a coordinated manner for the women's own sake, and to contribute to corporate sustainability.[44] From different perspectives, Talbot and Lunner show how a broader and systemic approach is needed to understand both the impacts of corporate practice and what is necessary to achieve change from within the system.[45] The contribution of women as agents for corporate sustainability is necessary but not sufficient.

The seventh strategy, *external agents of organisational change*, is arguably necessary to achieve corporate sustainability and as such is a crucial organisational change strategy. Multijurisdictional comparative analysis of the barriers to environmental corporate sustainability has, together with other contributions to the area, shown that leaving corporate sustainability to market forces (whether from investors, consumers or procurers), or to business itself through CSR initiatives, is insufficient.[46] Shareholder primacy is so deeply entrenched that the competing social norms of corporate social responsibility and business and human rights appear unable to replace it. Liberal structuralist initiatives such as the reporting requirements remain inadequate. All this speaks to the necessity of a broader regulatory understanding and a comprehensive approach,[47] which could – and should – inform a deeper understanding of what makes effective law; that is, in our context, law that would

---

[42] Ch. 3.   [43] Ch. 4.   [44] Ch. 2.   [45] Chs. 1, 3.
[46] Sjåfjell et al., 'Shareholder Primacy'.
[47] See the regulatory ecology approach, which encompasses law, social norms, markets and 'architecture' as modalities of regulation, in B. Sjåfjell and M. B. Taylor, 'Planetary Boundaries and Company Law: Towards a Regulatory Ecology of Corporate Sustainability' (2015) University of Oslo Faculty of Law Research Paper No. 2015–11, see https://ssrn.com/abstract=2610583.

challenge the deep systemic reasons for corporate unsustainability and enable the shift to sustainability.[48]

14.2.5 Taking Sustainability Goals Seriously ('Hypocrisy as a Resource')

The eighth and last of the organisational change strategies we include here is the intriguingly formulated strategy of *hypocrisy as a resource*. It may be seen as an intermediate strategy – and an important and useful one – to achieving recognition for a more systemic change. In our context we see this as an inspiration to take sustainability goals seriously (and rephrase the strategy accordingly), with the aim of contributing to finding out how to operationalise them.

International law and policy shows that there is high-level support for sustainability as an overarching goal both in international treaties[49] and through the adoption of the UN Sustainable Development Goals (SDGs) in 2015.[50] On the EU Treaty level there has been an unprecedented development from the start of the European Economic Community where sustainability issues were barely recognised in the Treaty, to the current Treaties of the European Union. The Treaty on the European Union (TEU) now emphasises the position of sustainable development, in Europe and globally.[51] This is closely linked to a growing recognition in international law and politics of sustainable development as an all-important objective and as a general principle of international law.[52]

---

[48] A successful legal norm may have its origins in social or moral norms and may over time create social norms and even moral norms; J. Elster, *Explaining Social Behavior: More Nuts and Bolts for the Social Sciences* (Cambridge: Cambridge University Press, 2007), pp. 358–359.

[49] See, e.g., M.-C. Cordonier Segger, 'Sustainable Development in International Law' in H. C. Bugge and C. Voigt (eds.), *Sustainable Development in International and National Law* (Groningen: Europa Law Publishing, 2008), p. 117.

[50] United Nations General Assembly resolution 70/1, *Transforming Our World: The 2030 Agenda for Sustainable Development*, A/RES/70/1, (25 September 2015), see www.undocs.org/A/RES/70/1 and www.un.org/sustainabledevelopment/sustainable-development-goals.

[51] Articles 3(3) TEU and 3(5) TEU; see also Art. 21(2)(d) and (f) TEU.

[52] Cordonier Segger, 'Sustainable Development in International Law'; P. Birnie, A. Boyle and C. Redgwell (eds.), *International Law and the Environment*, 3rd edition (Oxford: Oxford University Press, 2009), pp. 125–127; C. Voigt, *Sustainable Development as a Principle of Integration in International Law. Resolving Potential Conflicts between Climate Measures and WTO Law* (Leiden: Martinus Nijhoff Publishers, 2009).

On the national level, a growing number of constitutions have been adopted or amended to include sustainability or aspects of sustainability, such as the right to a clean environment or the promotion of human rights as national goals.[53] On the international, European and national levels, the significance of business and finance contributing to the overarching goal of sustainability – environmentally, socially and economically – is recognised.[54] Notable international policy initiatives are the UN Guiding Principles for Business and Human Rights, the OECD Guidelines for Multinational Enterprises, and the UN Global Compact.[55] Indeed, business and investors also increasingly sign up to this recognition, as may be illustrated by the SDG Business Hub – a business response to the UN Sustainable Development Goals.[56]

Yet, in the face of continued unsustainable 'business as usual' by both business and finance, legislative initiatives are insufficiently coherent or co-ordinated to regulate business and finance to promote a shift to sustainability. It therefore remains an urgent issue for academia to take these sustainability goals seriously and spell out what is needed to achieve them.

The EU makes for an interesting case study here. Despite its tendency towards liberal structuralism over the last decade or so, the EU is still the trade block that appears to have the greatest potential for being a front-runner for sustainability. The EU is concerned with how to achieve policy coherence for sustainability, and indeed, how to achieve coherence poses itself as a crucial question, and as a main avenue for ongoing and future research.[57] As a regional and global actor, the EU presents itself as a being at the forefront regarding sustainability measures. The EU Treaties show that to achieve the EU's ultimate aim of promotion of peace, the

---

[53] See, e.g., D. R. Boyd, 'The Constitutional Right to a Healthy Environment' (2012) *Environment Magazine*, see www.environmentmagazine.org/Archives/Back%20Issues/2012/July-August%202012/constitutional-rights-full.html.

[54] See amongst numerous examples notably the SDGs, fn. 50.

[55] United Nations, *Guiding principles on business and human rights – implementing the United Nations 'Protect, Respect and Remedy' framework* (Office of the High Commissioner for Human Rights, 2011), see www.unglobalcompact.org/library/2; OECD, *Guidelines for multinational enterprises*, see www.oecd.org/corporate/mne; and the UN Global Compact, see www.unglobalcompact.org.

[56] The SDG Business Hub, see www.sdghub.com.

[57] The SMART Project is funded under the EU's Framework Programme, under the call for greater policy coherence for development (see smart.uio.no).

EU's values[58] and the well-being of its peoples,[59] sustainable development is a prerequisite. Sustainable development is an overarching objective and meant to be the guiding principle for the EU's policies and activities.[60] While progress has been made in some areas, this cross-sectorial principle has not been integrated fully in all sectors of the EU, with hardly any trace of discussion of these issues in corporate law and financial law until after the financial crisis of 2007–2008.[61]

The financial crisis naturally led to a reconsideration of the organisation of business and finance, including reflections on the problematic nature of short-termism, with the Internal Market and Services Commissioner Michel Barnier in 2014 stating that: 'The last years have shown time and time again how short-termism damages European companies and the economy. Sound corporate governance can help to change that'.[62] Nevertheless, the final compromise text of the recent reform of the Shareholder Rights Directive contents itself with gently encouraging institutional investors to be active, long-term and sustainability-oriented, through very tentative requirements asking institutional investors to present their policies or explain why they do not have any.[63]

---

[58] The European Union is according to Article 2 of the Treaty on the European Union (TEU) founded on the following values: 'respect for human dignity, freedom, democracy, equality, the rule of law and respect for human rights, including the rights of persons belonging to minorities'.

[59] Article 3(1) TEU.

[60] B. Sjåfjell, 'The Legal Significance of Article 11 TFEU for EU Institutions and Member States' in B. Sjåfjell and A. Wiesbrock (eds.), *The Greening of European Business under EU Law: Taking Article 11 TFEU Seriously* (London and New York: Routledge, 2015), see https://ssrn.com/abstract=2530006.

[61] Ibid. See also I. Lynch Fannon, 'Corporate Responsibility and European Corporate Governance, The View from Now' in A. Beck and S. Skeffington (eds), *The Impact of European Law on the Corporate World* (Dublin: The Irish Centre for European Law, 2010), www.icel.ie/userfiles/file/papers/ICEL%202008%20No.%204.pdf.

[62] European Commission Press Release, 9 April 2014, p. 1, see www.europa.eu/rapid/press-release_IP-14-396_en.htm and the focus in the EU on unrestricted short-termism as a problem in the *Green Paper on Corporate Governance*, COM (2011) 164 final.

[63] See DIRECTIVE (EU) 2017/828 OF THE EUROPEAN PARLIAMENT AND OF THE COUNCIL of 17 May 2017 amending Directive 2007/36/EC as regards the encouragement of long-term shareholder engagement. The reform of the EU Directive on Institutions for Occupational Retirement Provision (IORP) goes in the same direction, see Directive (EU) 2016/2341 of the European Parliament and of the Council of 14 December 2016 on the activities and supervision of institutions for occupational retirement provision (IORPs). See B. Sjåfjell, 'When the solution becomes the problem: the triple failure of

Much of what is relevant to corporate sustainability continues to be discussed not as corporate governance proper but rather under the umbrella of corporate social responsibility (CSR). The EU's efforts to promote social sustainability and labour standards in international trade, for example, took the form of encouraging 'companies to practice corporate social responsibility, while recognizing the voluntary nature of such initiatives'.[64] This is in line with the EU Commission's definition of CSR in 2001, as a concept 'whereby companies integrate social and environmental concerns in their business operations and in their interaction with their stakeholders *on a voluntary basis*'.[65] However, with the rising recognition of the significance of corporate sustainability, there has been a paradigm shift of the EU Commission's concept of CSR. In 2011 the concept was redefined as the *'the responsibility of enterprises for their impacts on society'* requiring an integration of 'social, environmental, ethical, human rights and consumer concerns into their business operations and core strategy'.[66] While the paradigm shift is laudable, this approach has achieved only very tentative and incremental progress, besides the 2014 reporting directive, which is insufficient unless followed strongly and clearly up by Member States. The EU has not yet adopted a new CSR strategy, in spite of the last one now being out of date.[67]

The EU's approach to promoting corporate sustainability arguably reflects how also relatively progressive legislators such as the EU continue to be influenced by mainstream economic postulates and their simplistic understanding of the relationship between shareholders, markets and corporations. This also reflects a lack of recognition of the deeper systemic issues that inform the unsustainable state we are in. Considering

---

corporate governance codes' in J. J. du Plessis & C. K. Low (eds.), *Corporate Governance Codes for the 21st Century* (Berlin: Springer, 2017), p. 28.

[64] European Commission, Communication from the Commission to the Council, the European Parliament and Social Committee and the Commission of the Regions on Promoting Core Labour Standards and improving social governance in the Context of Globalisation, COM (2001) 416.

[65] COM (2001) 366 final (emphasis added). Although the Communication went on to speak of 'not only fulfilling legal expectation, but also going beyond compliance and investing "more" into human capital, the environment and the relations with stakeholders' (paras 20–21), the definition of CSR as voluntary has been dominant.

[66] COM (2011) 681 final, Sect. 3.1 (emphasis added).

[67] The marginalisation of CSR in the renamed DG GROW, the European Commission's Directorate General for Internal Market, Industry, Entrepreneurship and SMEs, is also discouraging, with only two officers dedicated to CSR, see www.ec.europa.eu/growth/index_en.

the origins of the shareholder primacy drive in the Anglo-American understanding of corporations and corporate governance, this gives rise to the question of whether the EU Commission will reconsider these issues more closely now that the United Kingdom is set to leave the EU. It also remains to be seen whether and to what extent the Commission's initiative on Sustainable Finance will bring a deeper integration of corporate sustainability into the regulation of business and finance.[68]

14.3   Responding to the Sustainability Imperative

In considering the grand challenge that we face on a global scale, our contributors appropriately range from Africa, to Europe, to North America and Australia, and have interconnected with each other to provide shared insights into the many problems that are raised when we consider corporate action in the context of sustainability. Including also the role, position and perspective of women in lower-income countries (as we do in Part I), contributes to opening up the corporate sustainability debate beyond the traditional Western, top-down and masculine perspectives.[69]

To the forefront of this collection of essays are insights on the role of the corporation which pivot on problems that are at first presented as gender specific but provide insights into the resolution of the bigger challenge of sustainability. By providing insights into the oftentimes failed resolution of apparently easy problems, we shed light on the scale of the grander challenge of sustainability. If we need to be much more proactive regarding the resolution of simple problems of securing gender equality, how much more should be done to respond to complex or 'wicked' problems of creating corporate sustainability?

It is clear that the modern corporation needs to be rethought.[70] While the purpose of the corporation and its role in society was a topic of

---

[68] The High-Level Expert Group on Sustainable Finance appointed by the Commission will present its report by the end of 2017, intended to be a first step towards an EU sustainable finance strategy, see www.ec.europa.eu/info/business-economy-euro/banking-and-finance/sustainable-finance_en.

[69] As Grosser and Moon, 'CSR and Feminist Organization Studies', point out, these perspectives have been scarcely included in the CSR and business ethics literature, which an application of transnational feminist theory would have indicated.

[70] A recognition of this is expressed in recent publications such as B. Choudhury and M. Petrin (eds.), *Understanding the Company: Corporate Governance and Theory* (Cambridge: Cambridge University Press, 2017) and N. Boeger and C. Villiers, *Shaping the Corporate Landscape: Towards Corporate Reform and Enterprise Diversity* (Oxford and Portland, OR: Hart, 2018).

intellectually stimulating and heated discussions from the nineteenth century, recent decades have witnessed a narrowing of the debate, increasingly dominated by the law-and-economics inspired view of the corporation, first as the shareholders' property, and latterly as a 'nexus of contracts' in which only the shareholders require protection. Rather than witnessing an ever-evolving analysis and evaluation of assumptions, means and goals in this area, public debates about corporate law over the last few decades have been dominated by unsubstantiated axioms which have been very difficult to question, even in light of their apparent failure. Specifically, the rise to prominence in Anglo-American scholarship and public policy discourse of the social norm of shareholder primacy has dominated debates about corporate law reform across the world. This has sidelined the great tradition of lively debates in corporate law scholarship about the nature, purpose and interests of the corporation, which had taken place from the 1850s onwards, especially in Germany and in the United States.[71] As a reaction to this, from the 1990s onwards progressive corporate lawyers sought to respond to the increasingly hegemonic law and economics school (Chicago School) of corporate law theory. However, progressive corporate law scholarship was diverse, addressing different kinds of problems, and perhaps as indicated in our introduction did not deliver a 'big idea' that was sufficiently simple or coherent to gain traction.[72]

As a new reiteration of the progressive corporate law initiative, the corporate sustainability movement may stand a better chance of achieving the necessary change.[73] Firstly, because the context is different now than it was in the 1990s. After the financial crisis of 2007–2008, even many who wholeheartedly espoused a mainstream law and economics analysis can see that this theory of corporate function is limited. The issues of sustainability have become far more pressing. In terms of planetary boundaries, where four of the currently identified nine boundaries have been transgressed, climate change and biodiversity are the two most recognised yet still not properly dealt with.[74] And in terms of

---

[71] Including the famous Berle and Dodd debate in the 1930s, see, e.g., W. W. Bratton and M. L. Wachter, 'Shareholder Primacy's Corporatist Origins: A. Berle and 'the Modern Corporation' (2008) 34 *Journal of Corporation Law* 99.

[72] Ch. 1.   [73] Ch. 13.

[74] It is estimated that humanity has already transgressed or is at risk of transgressing at least four of the currently identified nine planetary Boundaries, including climate change, biosphere integrity, biogeochemical flows and land-system integrity. The other five being global freshwater use, ocean acidification, atmospheric aerosol loading, stratospheric

securing not only a safe but also a *just* operating space for humanity, income inequality within and between countries continues to emerge as a very serious issue of our time, threatening the stability of our societies.[75] Secondly, with a modern feminist agenda dovetailing with that of corporate sustainability, we are tapping into a new well of theoretical understanding, of compassion across genders and borders, and of a drive to contribute to a viable world. Thirdly, and interconnected, we share a common vision, the 'big idea', of business and finance that will contribute to a safe and just operating space for humanity.[76]

A new understanding of the corporation involves understanding the many different ways in which issues of gender and feminist theories interact with current conceptions of the corporation. It involves realising that in creating an ethical corporation for the future, the experience of women as outsiders, whether in developing countries in Africa or as putative ethical saviours of western corporations post crisis, has something to tell us about corporate sustainability. Policy makers, lawyers, economists and sociologists who are attempting to develop the corporation in responsive ways meet obstacles, the contours of which are described in part by our contributors.

Just as Kate Raworth has described the development of economics as a complex dynamic and ever-evolving discipline or mechanism,[77] so too the corporation is complex, dynamic and ever evolving. Understanding the corporation as the centre of a regulatory ecology which so far has kept it in on an unsustainable path can contribute to identifying how change can be brought about, and how the 'wicked' or complex issue of securing corporate sustainability can be dealt with.[78] This involves also understanding the connections between the corporation as a vital

---

ozone depletion and novel entities (e.g. nanomaterials and microbeads of plastic); W. Steffen, K. Richardson, J. Rockström, S. E. Cornell, I. Fetzer, E. M. Bennett, R. Biggs, S. R. Carpenter, W. de Vries, W. C. A. de Wit, C. Folke, D. Gerten, J. Heinke, G. M. Mace, L. M. Persson, V. Ramanathan, B. Reyers, S. Sorlin, 'Planetary Boundaries: Guiding Human Development on a Changing Planet' (2015) *Science*, 347.

[75] T. Piketty, *Capital in the Twenty-First Century* (Cambridge, MA: Harvard University Press, 2014).

[76] Leach, Raworth and Rockström, 'Between social and planetary boundaries: Navigating pathways in the safe and just pathway for humanity'.

[77] Raworth, 'Doughnut Economics: Seven Ways to Think Like a 21st-Century Economist'.

[78] B. Sjåfjell and M. B. Taylor, 'Planetary Boundaries and Company Law: Towards a Regulatory Ecology of Corporate Sustainability' (26 May 2015) University of Oslo Faculty of Law Research Paper No. 2015–11, see https://ssrn.com/abstract=2610583.

component of our economies and the broader macro-economic picture. The problem we encounter on the corporate theory level, with the domination of the Chicago School thinking, is reflected in the way mainstream economic theory is disconnected from the grand challenge of our time. As the Nobel prize-winning Elinor Ostrom said: 'We have never had to deal with problems of the scale facing today's globally interconnected society'.[79]

The recognition of the unsustainability of our current system appears still tentative, and high-level policy goals not sufficiently coherent. On the one hand, we see that there is an encouraging consensus internationally on sustainability as a goal. The UN SDGs contain all the elements that are necessary for a safe and just operating space for humanity, except for coherence and consistency. The SDGs do not address the pervasive question of whether sustained (indefinite) economic growth is compatible with planetary boundaries, which we are already putting increasingly under stress. On the EU level, the Seventh Environment Action Programme 'Living well, within the limits of our planet', clearly recognises that there are planetary limits, while indicating that it may possible to totally decouple growth from resource use, 'setting the pace for a safe and sustainable global society'.[80] The EU's Agenda 2020, with is goal of smart, sustainable and inclusive growth, does not explicitly discuss how this decoupling is to be achieved.[81] Tim Jackson convincingly argues that sufficient total decoupling is not possible,[82] while Raworth posits that we must become agnostic about growth, focusing rather on the important question of how we can ensure that humanity can thrive and prosper, independently of whether the economy grows, shrinks or levels out.[83] Given the current discussion amongst economists, the EU, to be ahead of the curve, needs to engage with this issue.

---

[79] Quoted by Kate Raworth, 'Old Economics is Based on the False Laws of Physics', *Guardian*, 6 April 2017.

[80] Environment Action Programme to 2020, Decision No 1386/2013/EU of the European Parliament and of the Council of 20 November 2013 on a General Union Environment Action Programme to 2020, *Living well, within the limits of our planet*, OJ L 354, 28.12.2013, pp. 171–200.

[81] European Commission, *EUROPE 2020 A strategy for smart, sustainable and inclusive growth*, COM/2010/2020 final.

[82] T. Jackson, *Prosperity without Growth: Economics for a Finite Planet*, 2nd ed. (London: Earthscan, 2017).

[83] For an alternative approach, placing economics firmly within planetary boundaries and with the aim of securing a safe and just operating space for humanity, see Raworth, *Doughnut Economics*.

The corporation is at the heart of this arguably unsustainable economic system. The mantra of maximisation of returns for shareholders is
the corporate version of the fixation on economic growth, and is exacerbated through the pressure for highest possible returns amongst institutional investors, and supported by the throw-away consumer society
encouraged by corporations (wishing to sell their goods) and politicians
(desiring to see their economy grow) alike. Redefining the corporation
may be key to reinventing a sustainable new economy, an essential piece
of the jigsaw puzzle of sustainability that we urgently need to get into
place.

This gives rise to a number of avenues for future research. Can
corporate sustainability be achieved within an arguably unsustainable
macro-economic system? Can corporate sustainability be a sufficient
driver for global sustainability, or will the macro-economic drivers for
unsustainability, for relentless continued economic growth, squash any
attempts at corporate sustainability? Is indeed capitalism itself the problem? We think that capitalism can be changed from within; indeed, it has
always been more than the mainstream Anglo-American version that we
see today.[84]

Future research will discuss how to operationalise planetary boundaries and the social foundation of a safe and just operating space on a
corporate level. Discussions may also involve how we can move from
concentrating on property and profit to focusing on commons and
community, as is eloquently outlined in Fritjof Capra and Ugo Mattei's
Ecology of Law,[85] and drawing on the rich possibilities depicted by Elinor
Ostrom in her groundbreaking work on commons.[86] We must aim to
understand the connections between the decision making in corporations, the workings of the financial markets and the macro-political
and economic drivers of our unsustainable state, as well as the natural
science insights into the ecological boundaries for humanity, and the
social and political aspects of the social foundation that we must secure.

---

[84] See generally, Lynch Fannon, *Working Within Two Kinds of Capitalism*. See further
I. Lynch Fannon, 'From workers to global politics: how the way we work provides
answers to corporate governance questions' in J. O'Brien (ed.), *Governing the Corporation, Regulation and Corporate Governance in an Age of Scandal and Global Markets*
(London: Wiley Publications, 2005).

[85] F. Capra and U. Mattei, *The Ecology of Law: Toward a Legal System in Tune with Nature
and Community* (Oakland, CA: Berrett-Koehler Publishers, 2015).

[86] E. Ostrom, 'Beyond Markets and States: Polycentric Governance of Complex Economic
Systems', (2010) *American Economic Review* 100 (3) 641–72.

To respond to the grand challenge of our time, unprecedented collaboration within and beyond academia is necessary. Interdisciplinary collaboration must gradually become the norm, not the exception.

Gender can be an agent for change, not on its own but as an important contribution, which also forms a basis for identifying important issues for future research. As a transdisciplinary group of female scholars, we contribute in this volume to positioning the problem in a larger theoretical, societal and value-based context. Insights into the gendered nature of organisations and indeed of society highlights that this affects all of us – regardless of sex, gender, nationality or social position. We see the significance of (gender) diversity and stakeholder engagement to achieving the necessary change of the combination of bottom-up and top-down initiatives within the complexity of multilayered regulatory structures, and the necessity of combining external regulation and enforcement and inside activism. We have a role in contributing to the public debate to stimulate the social mobilisation, where we can challenge the masculine hegemony of language in our field, which may contribute to explaining the fixation on growth and maximising returns, and the deeply entrenched societal tendency to monetise everything.[87] To propose solutions, to meet the grand challenge of our time, requires a systemic approach, and involves a discussion of values based on a vision. Our vision is business and finance contributing to a safe and just operating space for humanity. We look forward to continuing the discussion on how to get there.

---

[87] Ch. 11, and P. Cornelius and B. Kogut, 'Introduction' in P. Cornelius and B. Kogut (eds.), *Corporate Governance and Capital Flows in a Global Economy* (New York and Oxford: Oxford University Press, 2003), p. 21.

INDEX

Acker, J., 266
Ackerly, B., 22–23
Ahern, D., 131
Albania Law on Entrepreneurs and
    Companies (ALEC), 221–222
Anglo-American model, 69, 121–122,
    130–131, 247, 320–321
annual reports
    employee content, 94
    gender diversity reports, 94
    management discussion and analysis
        (MD&A), 93–94
    sustainability reporting, 93–94
Attansai, K., 22–23
Australia
    B Lab's 'benefit company' form in,
        208–209, 212
    Miles v *Sydney Meat Preserving Co*,
        209–210
    stakeholder vs shareholder interests
        in corporate law, 208–209
    statutory business judgment rule
        (BJR), 211

B Lab
    and the B Corp certification, 196–199
    'benefit company' form in Australia,
        208–209, 212
    benefit corporations, 200–201
    organisation, 194–196
    social responsibility/fiduciary duties
        tensions for traditional
        corporations, 200–203
Bangladesh
    child labour, 24–25
    demand dowries, 23
    economy, post-independence, 21–22

extraction of value from female
    workers in the global economy,
    28–29
garment industry, 21–24, 28
labour laws, 22–23, 36, 38–39
legal status of the female workforce,
    18, 25
maternity rights, 38
partial ratification of international
    human rights conventions, 39–41
Rana Plaza tragedy, 32–33
social norms/market norms dialectic,
    25–26
status of women in the workforce,
    17–18, 22–24, 28, 43–44
trade union organization, 36–37, 39,
    44
violence against women, 18, 23, 25–26
women and embedded cultural
    norms, 23–24, 37–39, 44
women's wider social positions,
    24–25
Bangladesh Accord 2013, 33–35, 44
Baumfield, V., 9, 12, 305, 314
Beasley, C., 263
benefit corporations, 191–194, 199–201
Benson, M. L., 275–276
Berle, A., 282–283, 287, 305–306
Bernier, Michael, 318
boards, women on *see also* Directive on
    Women on Boards (EU)
    B Lab, 195
    board size and, 142
    business case for increased female
        membership of, 115, 117–121,
        123–124
    and corporate culture, 122

326